Transfer of Immovables in European Private Law

The transfer of immovables in Europe creates a series of challenges and questions in practice. The increase in cross-border transactions of immovable property within the European Union has created a demand for knowledge of the system of land registration across a range of jurisdictions. This volume compares and contrasts the different legal processes of seventeen countries and includes a comprehensive analysis of the transfer of immovables and the Land Register in Europe. With fifteen case studies, it provides both theoretical and practical information on the applicable contract and land law. This volume encourages the reader to evaluate legal issues by using the wider European legal sources available. For this purpose, it is an important research tool for comparative study in the field.

LUZ M. MARTÍNEZ VELENCOSO is Professor of Civil Law at the University of Valencia. She is doctor of the University of Valencia and Magister Legum of the Humboldt University of Berlin. She is also a member of the Humboldt Foundation Network. Her research and teaching interests are in comparative law, property law, contract law, land law, and law and economics. She has been a participant in The Common Core of European Private Law project since 2003.

SAKI BAILEY is a doctoral candidate in the Department of Business, Economics and Law at the University of Gothenburg, Sweden, and a Faculty Member and Lecturer at the International University College of Turin. She received her Juris Doctor from University of California, Hastings, with an emphasis in international and comparative law. Her research and teaching interests are in legal theory, comparative law, property law, management of common resources and social and economic rights.

ANDREA PRADI is Professor of Law at the University of Trento. He obtained a PhD in Private Comparative Law from University of Trento in 1999 and a LLM from University of California Berkeley Law School in 2002. He has been a visiting scholar at Berkeley Law School and at the University Pompeu Fabra in Barcelona, where he conducted research on the comparative law and economics perspectives of property law.

The Common Core of European Private Law

For the transnational lawyer the present European situation is equivalent to that of a traveller compelled to cross legal Europe using a number of different local maps. To assist lawyers in the journey beyond their own locality *The Common Core of European Private Law Project* was launched in 1993 at the University of Trento under the auspices of the late Professor Rudolf B. Schlesinger.

The aim of this collective scholarly enterprise is to unearth what is already common to the legal systems of EU member states. Case studies widely circulated and discussed between lawyers of different traditions are employed to draw at least the main lines of a reliable map of the law of Europe.

A list of books in the series can be found at the end of this volume.

Transfer of Immovables in European Private Law

Edited by

Luz M. Martínez Velencoso, Saki Bailey and Andrea Pradi

CAMBRIDGE
UNIVERSITY PRESS

CAMBRIDGE
UNIVERSITY PRESS

University Printing House, Cambridge CB2 8BS, United Kingdom

One Liberty Plaza, 20th Floor, New York, NY 10006, USA

477 Williamstown Road, Port Melbourne, VIC 3207, Australia

4843/24, 2nd Floor, Ansari Road, Daryaganj, Delhi – 110002, India

79 Anson Road, #06–04/06, Singapore 079906

Cambridge University Press is part of the University of Cambridge.

It furthers the University's mission by disseminating knowledge in the pursuit of education, learning, and research at the highest international levels of excellence.

www.cambridge.org
Information on this title: www.cambridge.org/9781107187092
DOI: 10.1017/9781316941034

First published 2017

A catalogue record for this publication is available from the British Library.

Library of Congress Cataloging-in-Publication Data
Names: Martínez Velencoso, Luz M., author. | Bailey, Saki, author. | Pradi, Andrea, author.
Title: Transfer of immovables in European private law / Luz M. Martínez Velencoso, University of Valencia, Spain, Saki Bailey, Göteborgs Universitet, Sweden, Andrea Pradi, Università degli Studi di Trento, Italy.
Description: New York : Cambridge University Press, 2017. | Series: The common core of European private law
Identifiers: LCCN 2016052778 | ISBN 9781107187092 (Hardback)
Subjects: LCSH: Transfer (Law)–Europe. | Real property–Europe.
Classification: LCC KJC1265 .M37 2017 | DDC 346.404/36–dc23
LC record available at https://lccn.loc.gov/2016052778

ISBN 978-1-107-18709-2 Hardback

Contents

Contributors

Editors

LUZ M. MARTÍNEZ VELENCOSO, LLM Humboldt-Universität Berlin; Law Professor, University of Valencia

SAKI BAILEY, Law Professor, University of Gothenburg

ANDREA PRADI, Law Professor, University of Trento

Respondents

Austria

DAGMAR HINGHOFER-SZALKAY, Researcher, Center of Tort and Insurance Law (ECTIL), Vienna

GEORG AICHINGER, PhD Universität Graz, Attorney

ANASTASIOS MORAITIS, Research Assistant, Institute of Civil Law, Foreign and International Private Law, Karl-Franzens-Universität Graz

Belgium

VINCENT SAGAERT, Law Professor, University of Leuven

Denmark

KRISTINA SIIG, Law Professor, University of Southern Denmark Juridisk Institut

LONE HANSEN, Law Professor, University of Southern Denmark Juridisk Institut

England and Wales

MATTHEW CONAGLEN, Professor of Equity and Trusts, University of Sydney Law School

Finland

MATTI ILMARI NIEMI, Law Professor, University of Eastern Finland Law School

France

FREDERIC PLANKEEL, Law Professor, University of Lille

Germany

EGMONT NEUBAUER, PhD, Albert-Ludwigs-Universität Freiburg, Attorney

Greece

GEORGE GEORGIADES, Attorney

Holland

LARS VAN VLIET, Lecturer, Maastricht University

Irish Republic

UNA WOODS, Lecturer at the Law School, University of Limerick

Italy

ANDREA PRADI, Law Professor, University of Trento (editor)

Norway

KÅRE LILLEHOLT, Law Professor, University of Oslo

Portugal

SANDRA PASSINHAS, Law Professor, University of Coimbra

Scotland

KENNETH REID, Law Professor, University of Edinburgh, Edinburgh Law School

Spain

SONIA MARTIN SANTISTEBAN, Law Professor, University of Cantabria

Sweden

JORI MUNUKKA, Law Professor, University of Stockholm

General Editors' Preface

This is the sixteenth book in the series The Common Core of European Private Law published within Cambridge Studies in International and Comparative Law. The Project was launched in 1993 at the University of Trento under the auspices of the late Professor Rudolf B. Schlesinger.

The methodology used in the Trento project is novel. By making use of case studies it goes beyond mere description to detailed inquiry into how most EU legal systems resolve specific legal questions in practice, and to thorough comparison between those systems. It is our hope that these volumes will provide scholars with a valuable tool for research in comparative law and in their own national legal systems. The collection of materials that the Common Core Project is offering to the scholarly community is already quite extensive and will become even more so when more volumes are published. The availability of materials attempting a genuine analysis of how things are is, in our opinion, a prerequisite for an intelligent and critical discussion on how they should be. Perhaps in the future European private law will be authoritatively restated or even codified. The analytical work carried on today by the almost 200 scholars involved in the Common Core Project is also a precious asset of knowledge and legitimisation for any such normative enterprise.

We must thank the editors and contributors to these first published results. With a sense of deep gratitude we also wish to recall our late Honorary Editor, Professor Rudolf B. Schlesinger. We are sad that we have not been able to present him with the results of a project in which he believed so firmly.

No scholarly project can survive without committed sponsors. The Italian Ministry of Scientific Research is funding the project, having recognised it as a 'research of national interest'. The International University College of Turin with the Compagnia di San Paolo and the

Consiglio Nazionale del Notariato allow us to organize the General Meetings. The European Commission has partially sponsored some of our past general meetings, having included them in their High Level Conferences Program. The University of Torino, the University of Trieste, the Fromm Chair in International and Comparative Law at the University of California and the Hastings College of Law, the Centro Studi di Diritto Comparato of Trieste, have all contributed to the funding of this project. Last but not least, we must thank all those involved in our ongoing Trento projects in contract law, property, tort and other areas whose results will be the subject of future published volumes.

Our home page on the internet is at www.common-core.org. There you can follow our progress in mapping the common core of European private law.

General Editors
Mauro Bussani, University of Trieste and University of Macao
Ugo Mattei, University of Turin and University of California, Hastings College of Law

Honorary Editor
Rudolfo Sacco, University of Turin

Late Honorary Editor
Rudolf B. Schlesinger, Cornell University, University of California, Hastings College of Law

Preface

This volume is the result of many years of work of a group of researchers coming from different European countries inside The Common Core of European Private Law project.

This project began in July 2006 at the University of Trento in the framework of the 12th General Meeting of the 'Common Core' at a separate meeting of the Property Group headed by Professor Antonio Gambaro.

Soon afterwards, the 'Transfer of Immovables Group' (ToI Group) was formed out of those discussions in Trento and it initiated its work with a draft questionnaire, which was prepared by one of the editors, Luz M. Martínez Velencoso (University of Valencia), and Elizabeth Cooke (Reading University). After numerous meetings of the ToI Group engaging in heated discussions over the questionnaire, the group finally agreed on a definitive version to proceed to the next phase of designating reporters and beginning the process of answering the questionnaire.

In 2009, after having received a majority of the reports, the ToI Group met in a two-day conference that took place in Trento organised with the sponsorship of Colegio Nacional de registradores de la Propiedad y Mercantiles de España and Collegio Nazionale del Notariado. During these days the draft responses were discussed together with Professor Ugo Mattei, who brought new ideas for the volume. Meanwhile some reports had to be adapted because important legislative modifications had taken place in several countries – for instance, in England, Ireland and Scotland.

In July 2013 Andrea Pradi and Luz M. Martínez Velencoso met at the University of Trento for several weeks to work together on the reports and to conclude the comparative remarks from the case studies. In the same year, Saki Bailey was added to the editorial board to incorporate the perspective of the common law and coordinate the project in its final stage.

We would like to thank all the contributors for making this publication possible. This volume represents a tremendous amount of research on the subject, perhaps never before achieved at this level of depth and academic rigour. We would like also to extend a warm thanks to Ugo Mattei, the General Editor of the Common Core, who was present in the whole process, to Elizabeth Cooke, for her initial help, and to Abigael Ogada-Osir for her assistance in the final editing process.

Abbreviations

ABGB	*Allgemeines bürgerliches Gesetzbuch* (Civil Code, Austria)
Abs	*Absatz*
AC	Appeal Cases
AcP	*Archiv für die civilistische Praxis*
AER	*American Economic Review*
All ER	*All England Law Reports*
AllGAG	*Allgemeines Grundsbuchsanlegungsgesetz*, Austrian Statute on the Formation of a Big Book in the Land Registry
AnfO	*Anfechtungsordnung* (Statute on Rescission, Austria)
App.	Appeal
App. Cas.	Appeal Cases
Arch. Locazioni	*Archivio Locazioni*
art.	article
ARTL	Automated Registration of Title to Land
BCC	Civil Code (Belgium)
BeurkG	*Beurkundungsgesetz*
BFD	*Boletim de Faculdade de Direito* (Coimbra)
BGB	*Bürgerliches Gesetzbuch* (Civil Code, Germany)
BGBl.	*Bundesgesetzblatt*
BGH	*Bundesgerichtshof*
BGHZ	*Entscheidungen des Bundesgerichtshofs in Zivilsachen*
Bing. NC	*Bingham's New Cases*
BTVG	*Bauträgervertragsgesetz* (Building Developer's Contracts Act, Austria)
Bull. civ.	*Bulletin civil de la Cour de cassation*
BW	*Burgerlijk Wetboek* (Civil Code, the Netherlands)

Cass.	*Cour de Cassation* (in French report)
CC	Civil Code
C. civ.	*Code civil* (Civil Code, France)
CC Proc.	Code of Civil Procedure (Greece)
CED	Electronic Documentation Centre (Supreme Court of Cassation)
Ch.	Chancery Division Reports (in English report)
Ch.	*Recueil Dalloz Chroniques* (in French report)
Ch. D.	*Chancery Division Reports* (1875–90)
Civ.	*Cour de Cassation*, French Civil Chamber (First, Second or Third)
CLJ	*Cambridge Law Journal*
CLR	*Cambridge Law Reports*
CPC	Civil Procedure Code (Portugal)
CSIH	Court of Session, Inner House (Scotland)
D.	*Diki* (in Greek report)
D.	*Recueil Dalloz* (in French report)
DR	*Diarìo da República* (*Official Gazette*, Portugal)
DRPA	Act on the Distribution of Real Property (Denmark)
DULJ (NS)	*Dublin University Law Journal* (New Series)
EEA	European Economic Area
Edin. LR	*Edinburgh Law Review*
EfSIG	*Ehe und familienrechtliche Entscheidungen* (Austrian Report)
EG	*Estates Gazette*
EGBGB	*Einführungsgesetz zum Bürgerlichen Gesetzbuch* (Introductory Act to the Civil Code, Germany)
EGLR	*Estates Gazette Law Reports*
EheG	*Ehegesatz*
ELRA	European Land Registry Association
EnEG	*Energieinsparungsgesetz* (Germany)
EnEV	*Energieeinsparverordnung* (Germany)
ER	English Reports
ERPL	*European Review of Private Law*
EU	European Union
EULIS	European Land Information Service
EvBl	*Evidenzblatt der Rechtsmittelentscheidigung*
EWCA	Court of Appeal of England and Wales
EWHC	England and Wales High Court Cases
FLA	Family Law Act

FLR	*Family Law Reports*
Foro it.	*Foro Italiano*
Fw	*Faillissementswet* (Insolvency Code, the Netherlands)
Gaz. Pal.	*La Gazette du Palais*
GBG	*Grundbuchsgesetz* (Code on Land Registry, Austria)
GBO	*Grundbuchordnung* (Land Register Code, Germany)
GBV	*Verordnung zur Durchführung der Grundbuchordnung* (Germany)
GCC	Civil Code, Greece
GCCP	Code of Civil Procedure, Germany
GIU	*Glaser-Unger Sammlung von zivilrechtlich Entscheidungen des k.k. Obersten Gerichteshofes Civilsachen* (in Austrian report)
Giur. It	*Giurisprudenza italiana*
GVB	*Gesetz- und Verordnungsblatt* (in German report)
GZ	*Gerichts-Zeitung* (in Austrian report)
HCA	*Commonwealth Law Reports*
HE	*Government Bill* (Finland)
HGB	*Handelsgesetzbuch* (Commercial Code, Germany)
HL	Judicial Committee of the House of Lords
HR	*Hoge Raad* (Supreme Court, Netherlands)
H(S)A	Housing (Scotland) Act
IA	Insolvency Act
ICC	Civil Code (Italy)
IEHC	*Irish High Court Reports*
ILRM	*Irish Law Reports Monthly*
ILTR	*Irish Law Times Reports*
IMI	*Imposto Municipal sobre Imóveis* (Municipal property tax, Portugal)
ImmZ	*Immobilien Zeitung*
IMT	*Imposto sobre Transmissões Onerosas de Imóveis* (Tax on transmission of real estate, Portugal)
InsO	*Insolvenzordnung* (Insolvency Act, Germany)
IPR	Immovable Property Register (Italy)
IR	*Irish Reports*
iVm	*International Arbitration Law Reports*
JBl	*Juristische Blätter*
JCP	*Juris-Classeur Périodique*
KB	*King's Bench Division Reports*
KKO	*Korkein oikeus* (Supreme Court, Finland)

KM	*Committee Report* (Finland)
KO	Konkursordnung
LCA	Land Charges Act
LgsD	Legislative Decree
LH	*Ley Hipotecaria* (Mortgage Act, Spain)
LJN	*Landelijk Jurisprudentie*
Lloyd's Rep.	*Lloyd's Law Reports*
LPA	Law of Property Act
LP(MP)A	Law of Property (Miscellaneous Provisions) Act
LQR	*Law Quarterly Review*
LR	Land Register
LRA	Land Registration Act
LRegC	*Código do Registo Predial* (Land Registration Code, Portugal)
LR Ir.	*Irish Law Reports*
LRR	Land Registration Rules
LR(S)A	Land Registration (Scotland) Act
LTR(S)A	Land Tenure Reform (Scotland) Act
MaBV	*Makler- und Bauverträgerverordnung* (Broker and Contractor Regulation, Germany)
MLJ	*Maastricht Law Journal*
MLR	*Modern Law Review*
MR	Master of the Rolls
MRG	*Mietrechtgesetz* (Code on Tenant Law, Austria)
mwN	*mit weiteren Nachweise* (With further proofs)
My. & K.	*Mylne & Keen's Chancery Reports*
NI	*Northern Ireland Law Reports*
NJ	*Nederlandse jurisprudentie*
NJA	*Nytt juriskt arvkiv* (Supreme Court cases, Sweden)
NJW	*Neue Juristische Wochenschrift*
NotC	*Código do Notariado*
NOU	*Official Norwegian Reports*
Nuova Giur. Civ. Comm.	*Nuova Giurisprudenza Civile Commentata*
Ob	*Oberster Gerichtshof* (in Austrian report)
obs.	observations
OGH	*Oberster Gerichtshof*
OJ	*Official Journal* (EU)
P & CR	*Planning and Compensation Reports*

Prop.	Proposition (Governmental legislative proposal, Sweden)
QB	*Queen's Bench Division Reports*
QBD	Queen's Bench Division
RAO	*Rechtsanwaltsordnung* (Lawyer's Code, Austria)
Resp. Civ. prev.	*Responsibilità civile e previdenza*
RH	*Rättsfall från hovrätterna* (Court of Appeal cases, Sweden)
RH	*Reglamento Hipotecario*
Riv. Crit. Dir. Priv.	*Rivista Critica di Diretto Privato*
Riv. Dir. Civ.	*Rivista di Diretto Civile*
Riv. Not.	*Rivista Notarile*
RJ	*Reperterio de Jurisprudencia* (Law Reports, Spain)
RTD civ.	*Revue trimestrielle de droit civil*
Rv	*Wetboek van burgerlijke rechtsvordering* (Code of Civil Procedure, the Netherlands)
RvdW	*Rechtspraak van de Week*
SC	Session Cases (Reports of the Court of Sessions, Scotland)
SC	Supreme Court (in Irish report)
Sch.	Schedule
Sh. Ct.	Sheriff Court (Scotland)
SI	Statutory Instrument
Sim. & St.	*Simon & Stuart's Vice Chancellor Reports*
SLT	*Scots Law Times*
SR	*Systematische Sammlung des Bundesrechts* (in Swiss report)
SS.	*Sentencia Supremo* (resolution, Supreme Court, Spain)
SSI	Scottish Statutory Instrument
SZ	*Entscheidungen des österreichischen Obersten Gerichtshofes in Zivil- (und Justizverwaltungs-) sachen* (Supreme Court decisions, Austria)
SZ	*Süddeutsche Zeitung*
TCC	Turkish Civil Code
TCO	Turkish Code of Obligations
TLATA	Trusts of Land and Appointment of Trustees Act
TUPAS	Bank identification service (Finland)
U	*Ugeskrift for Retsvaesen*

UKHL	United Kingdom House of Lords
UKSC	United Kingdom Supreme Court
UNECE	United Nations Economic Commission for Europe
Ves.	*Vesey's English Chancery Reports*
Vita Not.	*Vita Notarile*
WLR	*Weekly Law Reports*
WR	*Woonrecht* (Living rights, the Netherlands)
WVK	*Wetboek van Koophandel* (Commercial Code, Belgium)
Zeup	*Zeitschrift für Europäisches Privatrecht* (Journal, Germany)
ZGB	*Schweitzerisches Zivil Gesetzbuch* (Civil Code, Switzerland)
ZPO	*Zivilprozessordnung* (Code of Civil Procedure, Switzerland)
ZVG	*Zwangsversteigerungsgesetz* (Statute for the Compulsory Auction and Compulsory Administration, Germany)

PART I
Introductory Matters

1 The Land Register in European Law: A Comparative and Economic Analysis

LUZ M. MARTÍNEZ VELENCOSO

1 The Land Register in European Law

1.1 *The Land Register as a Way of Publishing the Transfer*

In different European legal systems there are several models of Land Register. One of the functions of the legal system is to regulate the institutions by which rights are exchanged so that these transactions are secure and foreseeable. One of these institutions is the Land Register, which collects information on the ownership, content, reliability and expected revenue associated with rights over immovable property.[1] The Land Register therefore operates over a fundamental element of the economic system, the delimitation, attribution and protection of property rights.

By offering information on property rights, the Land Register reduces the costs associated with exchanges and facilitates the circulation of goods, and it can therefore be described as an instrument in the creation of wealth. This view is endorsed in a report published by the World Bank, the *World Development Report*.[2]

This contribution has been prepared within the Framework of the Research Project DER2013-42526-R, 'New Challenges of the Digital Society: Ownership, Contracts and Electronic Registers', funded by the Spanish Ministry of Science and Innovation.

[1] *See* Fernando Pomar Gomez, p. 1067, cited in Luz M. Martínez Velencoso, 'Transfer of Immovables and Systems of Publicity in the Western World: An Economical Approach', *Journal of Civil Law*, 6 (Summer 2013); P. Fernando Méndez González, 'La función económica de los sistemas registrales', 671 *RCDI*, 857, 881 (2002).

[2] World Bank, *World Development Report* (World Bank: Washington, DC, 2005), pp. 79–84. *See also* World Bank, *Plan to Market* (Oxford University Press, 1996), p. 89: 'For pledging to work, lenders need a cheap and easy way to determine whether a prior security interest exists against the property. Some advanced legal systems do this by maintaining a publicly accessible registry.'

This same argument was put forward many years earlier, in the explanatory preamble to the Spanish Mortgage Act of 1861:

> Our laws on Mortgages stand condemned both by science and by reason as they neither guarantee property sufficiently nor exercise a healthy influence on public property. Furthermore, they do not establish firm bases for credit secured by real estate, they do not encourage the circulation of wealth, they do not moderate interest on money, they do not facilitate the acquisition of immovable property and they do not provide sufficient assurance to those who lend money on the basis of this guarantee. Given this situation the need for reform is pressing and indispensable for the creation of mortgage banks, to create certainty regarding ownership and other property rights, to combat the effects of bad faith and to free proprietors from the yoke of merciless usurers.[3]

The Land Register publishes information on the chain of transmission of a particular property and reduces the risk of transfers being carried out without the compliance of the title-holder. It also offers security to potential acquirers of a property by providing them with information concerning the temporal validity and the legitimacy of the transmitter's title to property.

To sum up, the Land Register lowers the risk that the buyer will obtain an invalid title without increasing the threat to the seller that he may lose his title to the property without his consent.

As we shall see a little later in this chapter, there are several different types of Land Registers (i.e. register of deeds, title register ...). Some of them attest to the ownership of a property whilst others offer mechanisms to protect property rights while leaving the question of establishing ownership to the rules governing possession. In some legal systems, the Land Register is the exclusive source of information about the title-holders of immovable goods, while in others it functions alongside a system of publicity based on possession.

From the perspective of an economic analysis, the publicity afforded by the Land Registry is of greater functional value than the publicity given by the mere possession of goods when these goods are costly. For other types of goods, the maintenance costs of this system of publicity exceed the benefits obtained from the reduction of the types of risk we have mentioned. Property registers are also understood to be more efficient when: the registered properties are not subject to frequent transmissions; the properties in question have a long economic life;

[3] Spanish Mortgage Act (8 February 1861), published in *Leyes hipotecarias y registrales de Espagña: Fuentes y evolución. I. Leyes de 1861 y 1869* (1974), pp. 223–395.

and when the registered properties are susceptible to economic exploitation by several subjects at the same time (for example, when it may be possible to constitute limited real rights over the properties – such as a mortgage).

A property register can also be understood to be efficient when the descriptions of the registered property it provides, give more information about it than mere possession could.

1.2 *The Rules for the Transfer of Property as an Instrument for Sharing Risk between the Transmitter and the Acquirer of a Property*

There are currently several different types of systems in use for the transmission of immovable goods in Europe that have developed as a result of the different legal traditions throughout the continent.

The rules that govern the transmission of property are important as they provide an answer to a series of fundamental questions that arise from the circulation of property rights. Five of the most important of these questions are: (a) Who has the effective power of disposition over the property sold? (b) Who is responsible for any damages caused to third parties by the property? (c) Does the property constitute a guarantee for the creditors of the transmitter or the acquirer of the property? (d) Who supports the risk in case the property is damaged or perishes? (e) Who has the right to obtain the benefits produced by the property sold?

Broadly speaking, the main systems of ownership transmission in Europe can be divided into the following four categories:

(A) Legal systems such as the French legal system and those which developed under its influence (e.g. the Italian, the Portuguese and the Belgian legal systems), which recognise the transmission of ownership by contract, an agreement between the parties, which produces the effective transmission of property.

(B) Legal systems such as the German legal system and those over which it has exerted an influence (for example the Austrian, the Swiss and the Greek legal systems), in which the conclusion of a contract must be accompanied by a contract on the actual transfer of the property and the inscription of the transmission in the Land Registry. In most of these systems, the contract on the actual transfer of the property has been substituted by the inscription.

A characteristic of German law is that the contract on the actual transfer of ownership is disconnected causally from the contract that details the obligations of the parties, in such a way that a nullification or modification of the contract detailing the contractual obligations has no effect over the contract on the actual transfer and thus no effect on the validity of the transmission of property.

(C) The Spanish legal system shares some of the characteristics of both legal systems previously discussed. The Spanish system requires the conclusion of a contract (a title) and the *traditio* (the delivery of possession with the intention of passing ownership, which is the *modo* or correct form). These requirements are an example of how some aspects of the Spanish legal tradition have asserted themselves over the strong influence of the French tradition.

A distinctive characteristic of the Spanish system is the causal relation between the contract and the transmission of property. If the contract is invalid then the transmission of ownership cannot be said to have taken place.

(D) The common law system uses a complicated process known as 'conveyance' to transfer property. This process consists of various stages, and in some countries (such as the United Kingdom) the consummation of the process of acquisition is only achieved with the inscription of the title in the Land Registry.

From the perspective of an economic analysis,[4] an optimal system of property transfer would be one in which a single subject could be said to have: (1) an interest in safeguarding and conserving the physical condition of the property; (2) the legal means to protect the property; (3) physical contact with the property, so that a title holder would be in a position to see whichever steps might be necessary to take in order to safeguard and conserve the property. However, it is not within the power of the legislator to condition the transmission of the property and the actions associated with the transfer in such a way as to ensure that these three conditions always coincide. The legislator is forced to choose between conflicting interests and to distribute risk between the parties in one way or another.

The three conditions stated are not met in the solution provided by the French legal system. Sacco describes the French solution as 'pseudo consensual'[5] and attributes it to an intense dislike on the part of its

[4] *See* Roberto Sacco, *Conclusión: Congresso Internazionale Pisa–Viareggio–Lucca, 17–12 aprile 1990*, in Letizia Vacca (ed.), *Vendita e Trasferimento della proprietà nella prospettiva storico-comparatistica atti del congresso internazionale Pisa–Viareggio–Lucca*, 1, 17–21 April 1990 (Milan: Giuffrè, 1991).

[5] Sacco, *Conclusíon*, p. 900.

creators of the obligation to give.[6] This obligation is substituted by the automatic effect of the transmission of the property. The obligation to give is characterised by the fact that the creditor, who has an effective interest in the condition of the property, does not have any legal action at his disposal to protect it. The authority to do so is held by the proprietor, who has a number of legal actions available to him to protect the property (such as the action to recover the property from the possession of third parties and the *actio negativa*).

As a consequence, the French legislator considered it advantageous to convert the buyer automatically into the owner rather than the creditor of an obligation to give. However, this consensual system has a weakness. While it transfers authority to protect the property in the hands of the buyer, who is naturally the subject interested in preserving the property in good condition, it means that the ability to protect the property is conceded to a subject that does not have it at his disposal. This subject, who does not have the possession of the property in question, is therefore not in a position to detect potential threats to it.[7]

A part of German legal doctrine has criticised the German model of property transfer. These authors feel that in the sale of immovable property, ownership should be transmitted on the payment of the price stipulated and the handover of the property.[8] This is the thesis held by members of the school of Carl Schmitt, who do not favour the

[6] Sacco, *Conclusíon*, p. 901.

[7] Spanish legal doctrine has come to the same conclusion; see, for example, Mariano Pérez Alonso, *El riesgo en el contrato de compraventa* (Madrid: Montecorvo, 1972), p. 254. This author considers the rule *res perit domino* to be a deviation from the original *periculum est emptoris* applied in Roman law and claims it was a creation of the natural law school of rationalists. This school of thought maintained that it was against the laws of nature and therefore wrong for the buyer to have to assume all the risk of a transaction, as it had traditionally been believed was the case in Roman law, and that in fact Roman law had not actually imposed this burden on the buyer. Hugo Grotius drew attention to several passages from the Roman period that he felt clearly showed that ownership was able to be transmitted, even without the act of placing the property in the possession of the buyer (the *traditio*), by the mere consent of the parties. However, even the consecration of the maxim *res perit domino* does not eliminate the injustice of the rule *periculum est emptoris*, because making the buyer the owner of a property without handing over to him the possession and the use of it is effectively the same as making him a creditor of the right to the property. In both cases the contractual risks are assigned to the detriment of the subject who has to pay the price.

[8] This is the opinion of Hans Brandt, 'Eigentumserwerb und Austauschgeschäft, der abstrakte dingliche Vertrag und das System des deutschen Umsatzrechts im Licht der Rechtswirklichkeit', 120 *Leipziger Rechtswissenschaftliche Studien*, 322 (1940), which has been criticised by Heinrich Lange, 'Rechtswirklichkeit und Abstraktion', 148 *AcP*, 188 (1943).

current model of property transfer in the German Civil Code (*Bürgerliches Gesetzbuch*, BGB). They dispute the necessity to distinguish between obligational contracts and contracts on the actual transfer of property.

The critics of this model draw on a wide range of historical sources to support their critique, including Roman law, ancient Germanic law, natural law philosophy and nineteenth-century Prussian law.

Another controversial issue in the German system of property transfer is the principle of abstraction. This principle states that contracts on the transfer of property are independent from their cause, which means that they produce effects even if the accompanying obligational contract proves to be invalid. The decision to incorporate the principle of abstraction in the legal system is a political decision taken by the legislator in an attempt to balance the conflict of interests generated between the transmitter of the property, the acquirer and his creditors, the successors of both parties and the interests of commerce.[9]

The principle of causality and the principle of abstraction are techniques used to distribute risk between the parties to a contract. The principle of causality better protects the interests of the creditors of both parties, because only the patrimony of their debtor is placed at their disposition and it does not protect the good faith of the acquirer's creditor based on the appearance of the situation created. In this way, a subject that has goods at his disposal is able to retrieve them from the patrimony of a third party, without his interests being secondary to those of the acquirer's creditors.

The principle of abstraction guarantees equality between the parties, because both the subject that transmits the property and the subject that acquires it only have legal actions based on their contractual obligations. According to the principle of causality this would not be the case, as it presents a danger that the seller might stake a claim to the property by means of the revindicatory action (*reivindicativo*) (which is used to defend a property right), while the purchaser of the property would only have legal actions based on the other party's contractual obligations.

In the opinion of Lange, the best property transfer system would be that which combined the principle of causality with a system of acquisition of property *a non domino*.[10] This would afford the parties protection

[9] This principle was included in the BGB due to the influence of Savigny. The celebrated German jurist considered just cause to be the agreement that the parties reach over the transmission of property whilst the property agreement itself (*Einigung*) is a separate legal act that does not depend on a contract outlining the obligations of the parties.

[10] Lange, 'Rechtswirklichkeit', n. 8, p. 188.

against any possible defects in the underlying legal agreement and would also protect the interests of secure transactions and more generally of commerce.[11] This is the solution that Spanish legislators have opted for. While the Spanish system of property transfer is causal it also protects those that acquired their right from a subject that appeared in the Land Register as the title-holder of the property by maintaining the validity of their acquisition, even when the transmitter was not really the legitimate owner. It also protects the acquirer from any other resolution or revocation of rights that did not figure in the Land Registry at the time of transfer (art. 34 Spanish Mortgage Act).

2 The Economic Functions of the Land Register: A Comparative Analysis of the Different Land Registration Systems

2.1 *Systems of Land Register in Europe*

The legal systems of Europe differ not only in the rules they employ to regulate property transfer but also in the organisation and efficiency of their respective Land Registries.

In Germanic systems, the Land Registry is designed as a register of title. The Land Register has a fundamental role to play in transactions over immovable goods, as inscription in the Registry has replaced the 'traditio' or the act of handing over the physical possession of the property. In Germany itself, inscription in the Land Registry has to be preceded by an agreement over the act of transferring the property (abstracted from the separate agreement over the obligations of the parties). In Switzerland, however, the law (Swiss Civil Code, ZGB) requires a causal contract that has the specific aim of transferring ownership.[12] In both systems inscription is necessary, as without inscription neither the agreement to transfer property nor the causal contract produce the effect of transmission.

In other European countries the Land Register is organised as a register of deeds. There are several types of register of deeds, some of them are simple, rudimentary collections of unorganised deeds like the ones

[11] In the words of Lange, 'Rechtswirklichkeit', n. 8, p. 226: 'Ich habe deshalb stets gegen das Abstraktionsprinzip gekämpft und halte diesen Kampf auch heute noch aufrecht, obwohl ich die Begründung aus der Unvollstümlichkeit dieses gebildes heraus nicht mehr für zuttreffend halte.' ('That is why I have always fought against the abstraction principle and I maintain this fight even today, although I do not longer consider right the justification of the elimination of this institution').

[12] ZGB, 10 December 1907, SR 210, RS 210, arts. 657 (1) and 665 (1) (Switz.).

that exist in many parts of the United States. Nevertheless others are well organised, improved like the French, the Scottish or the Dutch Registers.[13]

2.2 *The Demand for Title Registration: An Economic Approach*

According to the way in which Registers are organised and the degree of effectiveness attributed to them, it is possible to divide them into two main categories:

(A) *The registration of deeds system.* This type of system is also termed the 'opposability system' and is currently used in France, Belgium, Portugal and Italy. The defining characteristic of this system is that documents are registered without the identification of the latest genuine title-holder, that is to say the documents are not examined beforehand as part of a process to establish the identity of the title-holder, but merely have to comply with certain formal requirements. The content of the Register, therefore, only defines a group of possible title-holders, and holds a complete set of all the documents pertaining to a property, which may be inspected on request.

Given the resulting lack of certainty of this system in some countries, as in the United States, it is quite common that subjects contract 'title insurance' to provide them with an indemnity should they be dispossessed of their title. The negative aspect of this measure is that while the indemnity provides economic security, an insurance contract obviously does not provide any degree of legal security, as the acquirer of the property may lose his title to it. Even the measure of economic security provided is limited, as the title security does not cover the full value of the property, but only the purchase price (or a percentage of the purchase price) and not any other related costs of the purchase. The payment of any indemnity is also subject to the exceptions and conditions stipulated in the insurance policy.

(B) *The registration of titles system.* This is also referred to as 'the presumption of correctness system'. This system is currently in place in Germany, Austria, Switzerland, Spain and England. In this system, rights are inscribed in the Registry, and it does not consist of a collection of original documentation pertaining to the property, as does the registration of deeds system. The Registrar is responsible for carrying

[13] Rowton Simpson would also consider them as 'title registration'. Stanhope Rowton Simpson, *Land Law and Registration* (Cambridge University Press, 1976), p. 22.

out a check on the legality of the claims presented and will not permit any inscription that contradicts a right already inscribed in the Registry without the prior authorisation of its title-holder. In this system the principles of exactness (the content of the Registrar is presumed to be a true reflection of the legal situation) and priority (by which a posterior but registered act prevails over a previous but unregistered act) both apply.

Under the registration of deeds system, courts resolve disputes by adjudicating property rights according to the moment in which the deeds were inscribed in the Register. This creates a strong incentive for subjects to inscribe the deeds to a property as soon as possible and for the parties or their intermediaries to gain the consent of the title-holders of the rights affected in order to do so. In this way, the parties can voluntarily avoid possible future conflicts over the ownership of titles.

In the registration of titles system, private contracts are also accorded priority when inscribed. However, the Registrar is accorded authority that is almost akin to that of a judge and will not inscribe a right if it negatively affects one previously inscribed, unless the title-holder gives his permission for the Registrar to do so. This eliminates a potential weakness of the Registry and means that those legal systems that have this type of Registry treat inscription as conclusive proof of the existence of the right, and establish a system of responsibility for those exceptional cases in which there is an error in the Register. As a consequence, those who acquire a property in good faith, trusting in the accuracy of the Registry, will not be stripped of their rights over the property even if the genuine title-holder subsequently appears.

The two Registry systems incur different types of expenses and provide different kinds of benefits in terms of reducing the costs derived from the uncertainty and the risk of losing property rights.

The registration of deeds system is certainly cheaper than the registration of titles system, but it is generally considered less effective. The lower cost of the registration of deeds system is due to the fact that the examination of the deeds to establish the legality of the rights contained in them is purely voluntary, and under these systems services to assess and insure the parties are provided by private companies. This has sometimes been cited as a benefit, because, as this system facilitates the intervention of the private sector, the resulting competition to provide services tends to minimise the cost of the services they provide.

However, in the opinion of Arruñada,[14] these advantages are more illusory then real. The cost of voluntarily insuring a right can be as much as and sometimes even higher than the cost occasioned by the inscription of the right in the public Registry. The organisation of this type of service by the private sector may also be inefficient in economic terms as they are often provided by monopolies and are normally tightly controlled by state regulations. Both the fees of a French notary and the prices that can be charged by an insurance company in the United States are fixed by the state, and both the notary and the insurance company are subject to legislation that limits entrance to their profession and specifies the 'products' they can offer and the procedures they must follow. As a consequence, this duplication of institutions (private companies and the Deeds Registry) to provide guarantees to the parties in a property transfer is not economically efficient.

The registration of titles system requires a prior examination of the legality of the rights to be inscribed and to be carried out by a public official. This requisite obviously increases the costs of the transaction. However, by organising the property Registry in a professional manner along the same lines as the organisation of the judiciary, a high level of productivity can be achieved. This level of productivity is even higher when the Registrar earns the benefits produced by the Registry office (as is the case in Spain).

The costs of the registration of titles system are offset by the greater security it provides,[15] as it protects those who acquire property in good faith through rules that govern the responsibility for errors in the Registrar (by which subjects are compensated for losses caused by errors).[16]

3 Harmonisation of Private Law in Europe and the Land Register

Legal harmonisation in Europe is a fact; it is a reality that is inexorably in continuous development whatever the nuances and reservations we want to contemplate.[17] In the field of patrimonial law, it is perceived as

[14] Benito Arruñada and Nuno Garoupa, *The Choice of Titling System in Land*, www.econ.upf.edu/docs/papers/downloads/607.pdf (last visited 12 April 2013).

[15] According to Harold Demsetz, 'Toward a Theory of Property Rights', 57 *AER*, 347 (1967): 'this improvement in the definition of the rights in question is only efficient when the benefits associated with it are greater than the costs it generates'.

[16] Arruñada and Garoupa, *The Choice of Titling System in Land*.

[17] L. M. Martínez Velencoso, 'CESL in Court. National Courts: How Can They Keep Track?', in M. Lehmann (ed.), *Common European Sales Law Meets Reality* (Berlin: Sellier, 2015).

a different level of evolution so that it is not possible to describe the phenomenon in a uniform way.

On one hand, in contract law there has been broader legislative work by the European institutions that have based their competence inside the Treaty, on the internal market, consumer protection and competition. There are many European norms affecting contract law that have produced some uniform regulation in the different European legal systems. In this field, a high degree of success has been achieved, and the intention is to go much further.

As daily practice has shown, it is difficult if not impossible to create a unique internal market without the existence of common regulations. The debate is open and its evolution will determine whether there will be a unique regulation for the whole of Europe or there will be only a common frame of reference.[18]

As is already known, various academic initiatives have been working on developing a European contract code or a common frame of reference. Some of these are purely private initiatives and others have responded to the initiative of the European Commission or the European Parliament.[19]

The issue is much more complex when we consider property rights, as art. 345 of the Treaty appears to be an impenetrable barrier to providing competence to the Union in this field, preventing any uniform regulation.[20] The truth is that European regulation until now has avoided the question and regulations concerning contract law carefully respect this limit.

It supposes a serious problem in relation to property law: where some subjects, especially the transfer of ownership, are regulated differently in different European states. Thus although a high uniformity should be reached in the field of contract law, the execution of a contract has in many cases consequences in the field of property law.[21]

18 Cf. 'Communication from the Commission to the Council and the European Parliament on European Contract Law', (COM(2001) 398 final – *OJ* C 255 of 13 September 2001), http://europa.eu/legislation_summaries/justice_freedom_security/judicial_cooperation_in_civil_matters/l33158 en.htm.

19 Joint Network on European Private Law – EU Sixth Framework Programme 'Network of Excellence', www.copecl.org, inside this Network is the 'Common Core of European Contract Law'.

20 For the text of the Treaty, see www.consilium.europa.eu/uedocs/cmsUpload/st06655-re01.es08.pdf.

21 Peter Sparkes, *European Contract Law: How to Exclude Land?*, http://ec.europa.eu/justice/news/consulting_public/0052/contributions/298_en.pdf.

Some academics believe that the dependence that exists between contract law and property law would justify the extension of the competence of the European Union to regulate such subject.[22] On the other hand, other authors consider the difficulty of justifying such an extension and doubt that they can undertake the task without modifying the primary law of the Union.[23]

Nevertheless, for the moment, it is clear that from the official viewpoint, the harmonisation of property law is not scheduled.

In this transition from contract law to property law we must also take into consideration the role that a uniform Register of Property in Europe should play.

3.1 *Harmonising Principles on the Land Register in Europe?*

While it is true that the study of the different systems of registration has been relegated to the comparative analysis of the law, legal scholars eager to propose solutions in case of conflict have overall failed to consider thoroughly the great variety of approaches studied by comparative law.

This perception began to change after 1990 with the collapse of the Soviet Union and the decision of the new republics to adopt a market economy. Soon, it became clear that the establishment of a registration system was a necessary condition for the circulation of wealth and thus began to increase the interest and the organisation of international conferences under the auspices of international organisations such as the United Nations, the World Bank and the European Union.

The existence of a Land Register was not a requirement for joining the European Union, but soon it became clear that without it the requirements of the unique market would not be achieved. While these new states had previously had some kind of Land Register, nevertheless this did not necessarily dictate which system should be chosen for the future.

This need or desire to 'choose' between the existing systems of register of property already functioning in other countries effected the way to approach the question. In this context, the most important thing was not

[22] Cf. António P. Pedrón, *La convergencia de los sistemas registrales en Europa, Cuadernos de derecho registral* (Zaragoza: Colegio de Registradores, 2004).

[23] About this discussion, cf. F. de la Puente Alfaro, 'Hacia una armonización del derecho registral en Europa', www.registradoresdemadrid.org/revista/32/Comentarios/HACIA-UNA-ARMONIZACION-DEL-DERECHO-REGISTRAL-EN-EUROPA.aspx. See also, W. Faber and B. Lurger, *Rules for the Transfer of Movables: A Candidate for European Harmonisation or National Reforms?* (Munich: Sellier, 2008).

to search for common features, but to provide new regulation. The question was simply to identify 'best practices' at the European level that could enable the creation and development of a new Land Register rather than to find common elements in diverse legal systems to recombine in a harmonisation process that involved a new legal institutional design of the Land Register.

Nevertheless there has been another approach to harmonising the registration system in an indirect way by the European Union represented by the 'White Paper on the Integration of EU Mortgage Credit Markets' (18 December 2007).[24] One of the most important objectives of this paper is to facilitate the cross-border supply and funding of mortgage credit. Similarly important is the Green Paper about Mortgage Credit in the EU (Brussels, 17 June 2005).[25] This paper introduces the concept of the 'Eurohypothec' ('Euromortgage') as a 'common mortgage for Europe' – that is, a common mortgage instrument to secure loans transnationally and European-wide. It is currently a Europe-wide research project being undertaken by several researchers.[26] These two documents constitute evidence that the Commission has become aware of the need to undertake some measures in the field of land registration in order to improve the functioning of the internal market.

From the above discussion, we can conclude that, more than the European institutions, it has been the academics and practitioners who have identified the rules and objectives that should be followed for a Land Register to achieve excellence. These common objectives have been incorporated more or less by the new states within their respective legislation, and European institutions have incorporated some of these goals as recommendations to be followed by the member states, fixing the bases for what, in the future, could constitute a genuine process of harmonisation.

Comparing the process of harmonisation of contract law in Europe with the achievements in the field of property law, we can say that this late process has been restricted and has only achieved the regulation of some common principles. Nevertheless some academics consider that due to the highly technical nature of the Land Register, a harmonisation process would be much easier.[27] The new technologies could also play an

24 http://ec.europa.eu/internal_market/finservices-retail/home-loans/integration_en.htm#greenpaper.

25 http://eur-lex.europa.eu/LexUriServ/site/en/com/2005/com2005_0327en01.pdf.

26 Cf. G. Watt, 'The Eurohypothec and the English Mortgage', *MLJ*, 13(2), 173–193 (2006).

27 Pedrón, *La convergencia*, pp. 42–3.

important role so that they could produce a common approach among the different systems of land registration that coexist in Europe or even also an indirect harmonisation could be achieved by creating a new pan-European Land Register.[28]

3.2 Basis for Future Harmonisation of the Registration Systems in Europe

In search of the common core of the different European systems dealing with the Register of Property there has been some work done in the last twenty years under the auspices of the European institutions and also by institutions that, without being properly European, mostly have worked within European states, especially the Human Settlements Committee of the Economic Commission for Europe of the United Nations and the World Bank. These last two are interesting because they have done work in the area of Eastern Europe where previously there was little information and coordination. These institutions have no competence problem at all so they have pointed out the precise requirements for a Land Register to acquire maximum efficiency.

In determining these rules these institutions took into account several principles coming from the European tradition such as rationality, legal certainty, and efficiency. Protection of individual rights is not only a requirement of the modern conception of protection of consumers, but it also represents a structural requirement of the system to achieve efficiency.

Based on these, as well as, our own research, we suggest that the eight principles that should be taken into consideration in the process of harmonisation of the Land Registration systems would be the following:

(1) *The Structural Organisation of the Land Register, Real Folio or Personal Folio*. Inside the European Union the majority of states follow the so-called 'real folio' that subject to registration immovables and not persons. None of the new states that emerged after the disintegration of the Soviet Union has adopted the 'personal folio', in fact, nor has any Land Register created in the last fifty years. This confirms that from a scientific point of view, the 'personal folio' is absolutely dominant. While it is only an organisational principle of the Land Register, however, its importance is such that it directly reflects the effectiveness

[28] Cf. Sergio Cámara Lapuente, 'Registration of Interest as a Formality of Contracts: Comparative Remarks on Land Registers within the Frame of European Private Law', *ERPL*, 6, 797–839 (2005).

of the system, which greatly facilitates an eventual harmonisation. It is also true that the new technologies applied to the functioning of the Land Register blur the traditional distinction between the personal folio and the real folio to the extent that it is possible to search according to different criteria; nevertheless the fact remains that the direct object of a modern Land Register is precisely the immovable.

The United Nations Economic Commission for Europe (UNECE), in its guide of good practices for 'Land Administration in the UNECE Region', indicates, as the first requirement in order to build a good system of Land Register, the need to contain a definition of the requirements for an immovable to be registered (the immovable as the basis for the registration).[29]

(2) *Accessibility*. As the goal of any Land Register is to provide legal certainty through publicity, universal accessibility should be guaranteed to everyone. A democratic society requires that information be available for everybody. According to the principle of equality, every citizen must have guaranteed open access to Land Register information. This access, in the context of Europe, to be universal, must be available to any citizen, not only for the national Land Register, but also for others.

Access to information should be carried out, if appropriate, with full respect for any possible constraints due to data protection legislation. The 'White Paper on the Integration of EU Mortgage Credit Markets' recommended member states to make information accessible via the Internet and to incorporate this information to the European Land Information Service (EULIS) information system. This initiative involves the interconnection of various electronic Land Registers in Europe. The system includes an application to translate the information and to obtain a report on the main characters of the Registry system.

As stated, the Commission assumes that the information published in the Land Register needs to be accessible electronically, although nowadays in Europe not every Land Register is capable of providing information over the network.

(3) *Publicity*. The possibility to access information is not enough; further, the information should be intelligible because otherwise it has no value. In this sense, only relevant, comprehensive and understandable information should be distributed. This supposes the treatment and management of the information for the benefit of the user of the Land Register. The UNECE guide (p. 27) points out that

[29] www.unece.org/env/documents/2005/wpla/ECE-HBP-140-e.pdf.

the system should necessarily be transparent and updated constantly. It also emphasises the need to make the system simple in its operability. All these requirements are impossible to meet if the Land Register simply collects information and publishes it directly on the web. Similarly, the 'White Paper on the Integration of EU Mortgage Credit Markets' recommends the need for transparency in the Land Register.

(4) *Non-opposability of the Information* not *Published in the Land Register.* It is the basic legal effect of the Land Registry to define the content and the scope of the information to be taken into account. This is an element so basic that without it one can hardly speak of a Land Register at all and it should not be confused with the obligatory inscription. The UNECE guide (p. 26) points out how only registered rights must be enforceable in what it calls the principle of the 'curtain effect': what lies beyond is not opposable.

(5) *Completeness of Information.* Closely linked to the above-mentioned principle is this one, which takes as a reference the existence of public law limitations that could affect third-party acquirers, and not being related directly to the immovable, but within the territory, they have not been published in the Land Register. Both the UNECE guide (p. 26) and the Commission White Paper put significant emphasis on this issue; The White Paper specifically refers to this principle as a major concern for credit institutions.

The solution to this problem would be possible through land graphic bases that include this information. In Europe, the Inspire Directive may provide the right tool for achieving this objective.[30]

(6) *Priority.* In order to achieve the maximum efficacy it is not enough that property rights are published, but also that they are hierarchically organised. A market cannot function properly if there are rights that are binding on third parties but have not been published. This issue is complex because in several circumstances there are hidden charges that have their ground in government privileges (which they are not willing to give up), social privileges, or other exceptions that conflict with desired transparency.

Both the UNECE guide and the Commission White Paper stress the need to improve transparency in the Land Register to prevent distortion of the principle of priority.

[30] Directive 2007/2/EC of the European Parliament and of the Council of 14 March 2007 establishing an Infrastructure for Spatial Information in the European Community (INSPIRE), http://inspire.jrc.ec.europa.eu/.

(7) *Positive Publicity (Acquisition in Good Faith).* The third-party acquirer who trusts in the accuracy of the Land Register should be protected. This is the maximum legal effect of the Land Register and supposes a high level of development. The UNECE guide (pp. 20, 26) also reflects this requirement as being necessary in a Land Register because this should ensure legal certainty and should also avoid the need of investigating the chain of title. The study for the European Commission (DG Competition), led by the Centre of European Law and Politics (ZERP) at Bremen University, is emphatic in stating that EU Registry systems that do not have public faith should carry out the necessary reforms.[31]

(8) *'Clarification' of the Information Published.* The system cannot provide maximum protection if any claim to modify the contents of the rights published according to the legal system have not been reviewed. This implies full control of the documentation inscribed in the Land Register. The person responsible for the Registrar should evaluate independently both legally and economically (UNECE guide, p. 9).

[31] http://ec.europa.eu/comm/competition/sectors/professional_services/studies/studies.html

2 Electronic Conveyancing of Real Property in Europe: Two Models, The English and the Finnish One

MATTI ILMARI NIEMI

1 Introduction

Electronic, that is, digital practices and networks characterise the era in which we live. They have been adopted everywhere in contemporary societies and therefore, unavoidably, they are and will be employed in the conveyancing of real property as well.

The closest standards of comparison are the electronic trading systems of shares and bonds adopted in the western world and the extensive employment of online shopping of movables. Online banking is worth special attention. It is in many ways connected with the systems of electronic conveyancing of real property. The authentication of a document or a commitment and its certification provided by a system of online banking can be combined with an electronic transaction. In addition, the payment of a purchase price as well as registration fees and taxes can be connected with an electronic conveyancing system.

As far as real property is concerned, the adoption of electronic conveyancing signifies a revolution in transactions. It is not merely a technical matter. First, electronic conveyancing technology has to be adapted to the complicated conceptual framework of land law and the system of land registration. Second, the adoption of electronic conveyancing presupposes and produces amendments to statutory laws. This is not only a matter of the valid form of a sale or another conveyance of a piece of real estate. Third, there are security problems associated with the conveyancing systems.

Systems of electronic conveyancing of real property have been developed or are being planned in many European countries. Here, I compare the systems of electronic conveyancing planned in England and adopted in Finland, the first one connected with the common law world and the second one with the continental systems.

I restrict my approach to a transfer of a piece of real estate or a leasehold. Following the continental legal concepts, I call this a transfer of ownership or a lease right.[1] From the viewpoint of registration, I focus my attention on title registration. Accordingly, I will pay no attention to mortgages or other charges or interests in land even if they are registered in the frameworks of the electronic conveyancing system. For instance, there is a distinct electronic mortgage system beside the trading system in Finland.[2] After the transition period of a few years, it will be the only valid way to use immovable property as pledge security.[3]

I employ the terms 'land registration' and 'Land Register', even though the first one does not fit the Finnish or many other continental legal systems and the second one is not very frequently used in England. Accordingly, I employ the term 'cadastre', although it is known as the 'Real Estate Register' in Finland.

2 Starting Point of the Comparison

The English plan and the Finnish system have goals similar to other European projects. They even share the same main outlines. As far as the content is concerned, there are, nevertheless, significant and interesting differences between them. They represent two different ways of putting electronic conveyancing into practice. Some differences are founded on the different conceptual and legal frameworks, some are the outcomes of different technical solutions. In addition, there are other important differences, and the short histories of these systems are different.

The planning of the English system was started early, before the twenty-first century.[4] It led to a developed proposal and draft and, without a delay, to final legislation in the form of the Land Registration

[1] According to English law, they both are, basically, possession interests in land creating an estate. They are freehold, that is, free simple estate absolute in possession and leasehold, that is, an estate with a term of years absolute in possession. Section 1 (1), Law of Property Act 1925 (hereafter, 'LPA 1925'). A registered leasehold estate has to be granted for a term of which more than seven years are unexpired, Section 3 (3), Land Registration Act 2002 (hereafter, 'LRA 2002'). For more details about the concepts of tenure and ownership in English law and its feudal roots, see Elizabeth Cooke, *Land Law*, 2nd edn. (Oxford University Press, 2012), p. 15 and Peter Sparkes, *A New Land Law*, 2nd edn. (Oxford and Portland, OR: Hart Publishing, 2003), p. 33.

[2] *See* 9a:15.1 Finnish Code of Real Estate (Chapter 9a, Section 15 (1)).

[3] The Finnish Act 3.6.2016/418.

[4] *See* Law Commission and HM Land Registry, *Land Registration for the Twenty-First Century: A Consultative Document*, Law Commission No. 254 (London: The Stationery Office, 1998) and Charles Harpum, '*Property in an Electronic Age*', in Elizabeth Cooke (ed.), *Modern Studies in Property Law, 1: Property 2000* (Oxford and Portland, OR: Hart Publishing, 2001). The

Act (LRA) 2002. The Act contains sections describing the main features of the new system and empowering its adoption.[5] However, this power has not been exercised. More precise rules creating the electronic system have not been issued and the needful technology has not been adopted. In other words, the system is not yet in use.

The English project of electronic conveyancing has been postponed: HM Land Registry decided to delay the development of the system.[6] However, the project has not been abandoned. Instead, it is treated as an object for reconsideration.

Accordingly, the English object of comparison does not bear applicable legal rules or a functioning system but is an unrealised plan. Moreover, it seems to be unlikely that the plan will be realised as such in the following years. The project has confronted various difficulties. It is, nevertheless, a detailed plan issued as a part of a legislative draft and as such a serious effort to create a system of electronic conveyancing of real property.[7] As it stands, it is an important as well as an interesting project and stage as far as development of electronic conveyancing is concerned in the field of land law.

In other words, the English project is worth attention and an eligible object of comparison, regardless of the comparison being unconventional. In addition, it is possible to learn from it in order to develop an executable system of electronic conveyancing.

In Finland, the planning started later, but the new system of electronic conveyancing of real property is already activated and it is in use.[8] The

English system was modelled after certain older systems. See Elizabeth Cooke, *The New Law of Land Registration* (Oxford and Portland, OR: Hart Publishing, 2003), p. 157.

[5] Sections 91–95, Electronic Conveyancing, Part 8.

[6] HM Land Registry, *Report on Responses to E-conveyancing*, 5.2 (London: The Stationery Office, 2011).

[7] The English legislative draft is the Law Commission and HM Land Registry, *Land Registration for the Twenty-First Century. A Conveyancing Revolution*, Law Commission, No. 271 (London: The Stationery Office, 2001).

The introduction of electronic conveyancing was the most important single function of the adoption of the English Land Registration Act 2002. There are many other significant and interesting reforms included in the Act, but nevertheless, the entire Act can be seen as a mechanism to enable the introduction of electronic conveyancing. Among the other reforms, the most important are the reform of adverse possession and strengthening of the effects of registration. In addition, the substantive changes would most probably not have been enacted without the attraction of the introduction of electronic conveyancing, Law Commission No. 271, 13.1, p. 268 and Cooke, *The New Law of Land Registration*, p. 155.

[8] See the legislative drafts KM 2006:1, the proposal for the electronic conveyancing of real property (in Finnish) and HE 2010:146, the Government Bill concerning electronic trade, liens and registration procedure (in Finnish).

new system appears as amendments of the Finnish Code of Real Estate, especially in the form of a new chapter of the code (Chapter 9a).[9] The amendments were enacted in 2011,[10] and the statute carrying them into effect was enacted in 2013.[11] Electronic conveyancing began on 1 November 2013. It is functioning, however, alongside the traditional system founded on paper documents.

On the other hand, the early stages of the use of the Finnish system have been cautious and modest. There has been no rush to adopt the new electronic system. Even after the beginning of November 2013, most transfers of real property have been made traditionally with paper documents. So far, the number of electronic transactions is very small.[12]

In the case of English law, I focus on the original plan of the electronic conveyancing introduced in the Land Registration Bill and Commentary given by the Law Commission and HM Land Registry in 2001.[13] In Finland, it is a matter of a conveyancing system regulated by the Code of Real Estate. Both systems are, naturally, subject to constant development and progress.

3 From Pre-Modern to Late Modern Law

Digital practices founded on developed computer technology and digital networks were adopted at the end of the twentieth century. They revolutionised information management and communication connections. On the other hand, this process, no doubt a rapid one, can be seen as one of the main features of contemporary societies.

Here, I employ the concept of modernity borrowed from general social theory. As far as the development of European legal systems is concerned, the highlight of the modern time can be dated to the second half of the nineteenth century and the first half of the twentieth century. As a simplification, it is the embodiment of the ideals of the French Revolution and the ideologies united with it in the field of law. The German concept of '*Rechtsstaat*' and, perhaps, the English concept of 'the rule of law' emphasising legal certainty and predictability and founded on the

9 The English translation of the Finnish Code of Real Estate (12.4. 1995/540; amendments up to 964/1998 included) introduced by the Finnish Ministry of Justice is available at www.finlex.fi/fi/laki/kaannokset/1995/en19950540.pdf. Unfortunately, the new sections of electronic conveyancing or real property enacted in 2011 are not included.

10 Statutes 4.2.2011/96–99. 11 Statutes 23.8.2013/622–624.

12 For instance, during the year 2015 1.3 per cent of all sales were made electronically.

13 Law Commission No. 271.

ideal of equal liberty are the crucial points. Accordingly, the pre-modern time precedes the modern period, and the late modern time follows the modern period. The late modern society is seen here as a modification of the modern one and as the contemporary society. The late modern society has often been defined as the 'welfare state', in German, '*Wohlfahrtsstaat*'.

In this connection, merely certain visible and superficial features of legal proceedings are relevant and worth attention.

Emphasis on traditions and oral proceedings and transactions is characteristic of pre-modern law. Forms are required and formalism is supported, for instance, as far as conveyancing of real property is concerned. The pre-modern forms are, however, not certain kinds of documents but rather certain kinds of statements as parts of oral proceedings.[14] In contrast, the employment of written documents is characteristic of modern law. A strong trust in paper documents equipped with written signatures is an essential feature of modern law. It is not a coincidence that the abandonment of written signatures is the critical point of the

[14] In England, medieval conveyancing after the Norman invasion, that is, after the Norman conquest of England commanded by William the Conqueror (William of Normandy) in 1066, took place in the form of actual physical delivery, 'feoffment with livery of seisin'. This act appeared as a delivery of possession. In addition, delivery of a charter or deed was employed showing the details of the conveyance. At the same time, according to the original feudal principles applied, the conveyance was a change of a vassal and subject to restrictions. Originally, there were family restrictions, as well. Later, evolution of the fine, in the form of a compromised fictitious personal action under the superintendence of a court, took place. The terms of the compromise were recorded by the court. Feet of fines were recorded from the year 1195 to the year 1833. See A.W.B. Simpson, *An Introduction to the History of the Land Law* (Oxford University Press, 1961), pp. 48 and 112.

In Sweden, conveyancing of real property was possible only to a restricted extent before the adoption of modern law. For instance, farms rather belonged to families than individual owners. In addition, the strong interest of the state (the crown) was involved in land law. Until the eighteenth century, conveyancing of real property was, first of all, part of a court procedure. Later, the procedure of *lagfart/lainhuudatus* (in a sense, 'land registration') as a court decision evolved from this. For a long time, it was a way to put into effect and secure the redemption right of relatives. A written conveyance document was not recognised by statutory law until the Swedish General Code of the year 1734 (Act 1734). The written form of a conveyance of a piece of real estate as a necessary condition of its validity was adopted in case law and as a new interpretation of the Act 1734 during the nineteenth century in Finland.

Finland and Sweden shared the same legal history until the year 1809. The old Swedish law was valid and applied in Finland even after that – first, under the Russian Empire, and second, after gaining independence in 1917. Accordingly, Finnish law is a successor and an heir of Swedish law. On conveyancing as a part of the Swedish pre-modern history of land law, *see* Gerhard Hafström, *Den Svenska fastighetsrättens historia* (Lund: Juridiska föreningen i Lund, 1970), pp. 20–36.

adoption of electronic conveyancing. How can we identify a party of a conveyance and authenticate an electronic document or a commitment in a reliable way?

In short, the oral form is seen here as a distinctive mark of pre-modern law, written documents as a distinctive mark of modern law, and electronic communications as a distinctive mark of late modern law.

The connection between electronic conveyance and late modern law outlined here can be disputed with the following argument: the employment of electronic networks and conveyance is merely a coincidental outcome of the development of information technology (IT) and has nothing to do with the ideology or justifications creating the foundation of the new institutions of late modern law, such as the protection of consumers.

No doubt, the new interpretation of justice adopted during the second half of the twentieth century explain contemporary consumer protection. On the other hand, there is an undisputed connection between consumer protection and the development of technology, as well. The breakthrough of the mass production of technically advanced devices and other items as well as the development of their large-scale trade were followed, firstly, by the abandonment of the *caveat emptor* rule and, secondly, by the adoption of the peremptory rules of vendors' defect responsibility as one of the essential features of consumer protection. The public at large as consumers could no longer master these new objects of trade. Responsibility for the safety, functionality and quality of these objects had to be imposed on the professional vendors as well as on the producers.

Accordingly, there is a clear connection between new technology and consumer protection. Industrialisation and new technology can be seen as an explanation for consumer protection alongside the new late modern interpretation of justice. In the same way, the adoption of electronic conveyancing can be seen as a part of contemporary late modern law founded on advanced IT. The law always reflects the entire society – technology included.

4 The European Union as the Contributor to Electronic Conveyancing

Taking full advantage of the possibilities and benefits provided by the development of IT can be seen as a general aspiration of European countries as well as the European Union. In the case of the Union, the development of electronic commerce is treated as a means to contribute to the proper functioning of the internal market development and functionality of information society services within the community without internal frontiers. In addition, it is presumed that the development of electronic commerce offers significant employment opportunities and stimulates economic growth and investments in innovation.

These aspirations had already been acknowledged by the Union in 1977 when the European Commission introduced the European Initiative in Electronic Commerce.[15] The aim of the initiative was to encourage the vigorous growth of electronic commerce in Europe.

At the legal level, the initiative brought forth, first, two directives of the Union, the directive on electronic commerce (2000/31/EC) and the directive on electronic signatures (1999/93/EC), and later, a regulation, the Regulation on electronic identification and trust services for electronic transactions in the internal market (910/2014).

According to the EU legislation, member states shall ensure that their legal system allows contracts to be concluded by electronic means without any obstacles and the validity of such a contract.[16] Member states are, however, allowed to exclude from these regulations contracts creating or transferring rights in real estate, except for rental rights, and contracts requiring by law the involvement of courts, public authorities, or professions exercising public authority.[17]

The Regulation does not apply to the provision of trust services that are used exclusively within closed systems resulting from national law or from agreements between a defined set of participants.[18] The Finnish system is a closed system.

In addition, in the area of property law, the traditional restrictions of the power of the European Union are met. Despite article 345 of the Treaty on the Functioning of the European Union (TFEU), there is no obstacle in giving EU legislation in the area of property law in general or especially in land law or developing common European property law. Most often, however, EU legislation has been withdrawn. Its legislation has contained merely minor or indirect influence in the area of property law.

These directives have been implemented in both the English and Finnish legislation.[19]

[15] Com 97 (157). [16] Art. 9 (1). [17] Art. 9 (2).

[18] Art. 2.2 of the Regulation (EU) No 910/2014.

[19] In England, with the help of the Electronic Commerce (EC Directive) Regulations 2002 and the Electronic Communications Act 2000, and in Finland, with the help of the

The European Union does not obligate member states to establish a system of electronic conveyancing of real property and does not provide any specific model or procedure for it. Furthermore, there are no plans to harmonise the systems put into practice so far. Notwithstanding, many member states, the United Kingdom and Finland included, have started to develop such systems shortly after the implementation of the directives. These projects, no doubt, realised the spirit and ambitions of the directives.

Unlike the electronic trade of movables, which is international on a large scale, the electronic conveyance of real property is not a primary concern of the Union. On the other hand, the development of information services is uniform with the goals of the Union. In addition, national registers and networks can be connected to each other at the European level, and a European-wide information network, as far as real property is concerned, is possible. The Union supports these projects. From this point of view, the development of registers and a common network uniting them is a European enterprise. EULIS and the work of ELRA (European Land Registry Association) have to be mentioned here.[20]

5 Conveyancing and Title Registration

As far as real property is concerned, the development of electronic conveyancing is closely related to title registration. According to the basic ideas on title registration, there is a direct connection between conveyancing and registration.

This is most obvious in the cases of dispositive registration: the validity or existence of property rights presumes registration. That is, in the case of a conveyance of a piece of real estate, a conveyance is not valid until it is registered. In other words, the legal title will not transfer until registration. English title registration, similarly to German, is dispositive as far as compulsory registration is concerned.[21]

Code of Information Society (7.11.2014/917) and the Act on Strong Electronic Identification and Electronic Signatures (7.8.2009/617).

[20] EULIS already provides direct access to many official national land registers in Europe. Cross-border electronic conveyancing of real property has been planned in the frames of ELRA. In addition, the so-called interoperability model for Land Registers (IMOLA) project maintained together by EULIS and ELRA has been started. See the official web sites of EULIS, http://eulis.org/, and ELRA, www.elra.eu/.

[21] See sections 7 (1) and 27 (1), LRA 2002. According to the English law, in the case of unregistered land, if the requirement of registration is not complied with, the transfer, grant or creation becomes void as regards the transfer, grant or creation of a legal estate

Finnish title registration, like the systems adopted in other Nordic countries, is protective. Protective registration merely affects the priority of property rights and strengthens the position of a transferee in certain relations with third persons. The validity of a conveyance between a transferor and a transferee does not depend on registration, and the legal title transfers to the transferee through the conveyance.

The adoption of electronic conveyancing makes the connection between conveyancing and title registration even stronger. Automatic and immediate registration is one essential feature of electronic conveyancing.[22] It can, however, be implemented in different ways. There are interested differences between the English plan and the Finnish system even in this respect, as explained in detail below.

One can consider the connection between a conveyance and registration from the viewpoint of either conveyancing or registration. The former is the conventional one. In this respect, the conveyance as a transaction of a piece of real estate in civil law is the main issue, and registration is merely a separate and secondary act and legal fact for the purposes of acknowledging and making public the transaction. This is the viewpoint of the parties of transactions. Registration renders services to the parties as well as to third persons having interests in the piece of real estate. This approach fits the protective nature of title registration in the Nordic countries.

On the other hand, from the viewpoint of registration and a Register authority, the conveyance can appear merely as a reason or a way to change the title-holder of a certain registered piece of real estate. Electronic conveyance, because of the inseparability of the transaction and registration, can be seen as a legal way and means to change the title-holder and the content of the Register. Electronic conveyance may merely be considered as a way to use a Register and enter new information into it. Dispositive registration connecting the validity of a transfer with its registration has common features with this view. A registered title-holder appears as the legal owner, that is, in the common law system, owner in law. Dispositive registration is a necessary step in creating a valid title, and not merely a confirmation of a valid title already acquired.

and, in the case of registered land, if a disposition of a registered estate or registered charge is required to be completed by registration, it does not operate at law until the relevant registration requirements are met.

22 In the case of English land registration, see sections 93 and 94, LRA 2002, and in the case of Finnish title registration, *see* 9a:12.1 Code of Real Estate. The power to require simultaneous registration is seen as an essential part of the introduction of the English electronic conveyancing. See section 93, LRA 2002.

One specific feature of the English plan is the authority to change the information content of the Land Registry provided to solicitors or licensed conveyancers. The Finnish system does not contain such an authority, but the automatic initiation of registration proceedings is an essential feature of the Finnish electronic conveyancing system, as well.

6 Electrification in the Field of Land Law

Electronic means have been adopted in the area of land law in the same way as elsewhere in western societies. The possibilities provided by new information technology were apparent long before the end of the twentieth century. In practice, the electrification of Land Registers as well as cadastres has paved the way to electronic conveyancing. Electronic registers have been the first stage of electrification in the field of land law.

All European countries currently have national Land Registers containing recorded ownerships.[23] European Land Registers were mainly adopted and developed during the last decades of the nineteenth century and the first decades of the twentieth century. The first plans to automatise and electrify registers were introduced during the 1960s and 1970s. Developed computers and digital technology were not available before the 1980s. In most European countries, manual catalogues, card registers, or books were employed until the electrification of the records. Today, nearly all European countries have electronic registers. Both in England and in Finland, the computerisation of Land Register records began in the 1980s. Electronic conveyancing, in the way it is understood today, presupposes both digital registers and the Internet brought into use during the 1990s.

European Land Registers are constructed according to either deed or title registration. Most European countries have adopted a Title Register. In many countries, Deed Registers have given way to it.[24] With good reasons, a Title Register can be seen as the more developed model, especially from the point of view of developing a system of electronic conveyancing.

A Deed Register is founded on the idea of collecting and depositing conveyance documents, that is, deeds. In practice, a Deed Register has to be equipped with indices assisting in searching for ownership information.

23 HM Land Registry, *Inventory of Land Administration Systems in Europe and North America*, 4th edn. (London: The Stationery Office, July 2005), pp. 10 and 69.
24 HM Land Registry, *Inventory of Land Administration Systems*, p. 69.

A Title Register provides independent information of ownerships of certain registered pieces of real estate, founded on their recorded acquisitions. The Register data does not appear merely as references to recorded documents, but as independent legal facts. A system of electronic conveyancing is easier to unite with a Title Register. The idea of changing the recorded ownership information with the help of electronic conveyancing is much easier to carry out with the help of an independent Register.

There is another important difference between registers affecting the possibility of implementing a functioning system of electronic conveyancing. A Land Register can be either local or national. A local registration system is decentralised, whereas a national system is centralised. There may be many independent local registers or only one national register in a country. For instance, in Germany the Land Register is maintained by the local Land Registry Authorities (*Grundbuchamt*) located at the local courts (*Amtsgerichte*).

Both in England and in Finland, the Land Registers are currently centralised, that is, there is one national electronic register that is maintained and administered in a centralised way.[25] In England, the Land

[25] It is a different matter if the administration of the registration system is centralised. Decentralised registers can be administered in a centralised or decentralised way. Local registers can be administered by local offices or officers of a national register authority, or they can be administered by independent local authorities. It is even possible to administer a centralised and national register by independent local authorities.

In England, the national administration of land registration had already been created in 1862, when the office of HM Land Registry was opened on the grounds of the Land Transfer Act 1875. However, the modern English centralised and national title register was founded later with the help of the six property statutes in 1925. In this respect, the LRA Act 1925, the LPA 1925 and the Land Charges Act 1925 are worth mentioning. For details, see Cooke, *The New Law of Land Registration*, p. 20, and Sparkes, *A New Land Law*, p. 1.

In Finland, the administration of the system of land registration was decentralised until the beginning of 2014. Registers were decentralised until the 1990s. On the grounds of the acts of the years 1985 and 1987, centralised, electronic and national registers, both the Finnish cadastre (the Real Estate Register, that is, the property register, *Kiinteistörekisteri*) and the real estate title records (*Lainhuuto- ja kiinnitysrekisteri*) were created. This work was completed in 1995. However, these registers were maintained by local authorities, the cadastre by the local land survey offices and the land register by local courts. Until 2014, the administration of these registers was divided between the local authorities and national authorities. The maintenance of the land register was transferred to the local land survey offices at the beginning of 2010. It is noteworthy that the cadastre and the Land Register are independent registers. On the other hand, together they establish a uniform information system (*kiinteistötietojärjestelm*), maintained by the National Land Survey.

Registry is maintained by HM Land Registry, and in Finland by the National Land Survey. A national system of electronic conveyancing is easier to develop together with a centralised and national Land Register maintained and administered in a centralised way.

Electronic conveyancing is a natural step in developing an online register system for real property. First, the development of computer technology has led to the everyday use of personal computers. Contracts and conveyance documents are written on computers. Second, electronic land registers are products of computer technology, as well. Third, the Internet provides the possibility to transfer information between personal computers, that is, terminals and a Register.[26]

With regard to the transfer of information between personal computers and Registers, the first, modest step has been to provide people and corporations with access to Register information through the Internet. The second step is the possibility to send information and applications to the Registrar through the Internet. The third step is electronic conveyancing.

The English Land Registry provides Register information to both private persons and professionals online. More recently, it has introduced an enhancement of the electronic document registration service (e-DRS), which enables electronic applications to be submitted to the Registry on a large scale.[27] Moreover, professionals can discharge mortgages online.

So far, the English 'electronic conveyancing' appears merely in the form of these modest entries in the Land Register. As a matter of fact, HM Land Registry seems to have concentrated on the development of these services at this stage of the process instead of on the postponed development of the system of proper electronic conveyancing.[28]

In Finland, direct access to Register information through the Internet is provided only to professionals. In addition, it means merely a possibility to see and copy Register information. There is no separate system of sending Register applications or modifying Register information of private persons, and private persons cannot make official extracts from the

[26] Here, the concept of the Internet is employed irrespective of whether the use of the network is founded on the open Internet or a restricted and closed part of it (a closed system). The crucial matter is a contemporary universal and electronic network as the medium of information. Even restricted use with the help of encryption, an access key or password or a closed part of the network means exploiting the Internet.

[27] For details, see the web site of HM Land Registry: www.landregistry.gov.uk/.

[28] See HM Land Registry, *Report on Responses to E-conveyancing Secondary Legislation, Part 3* (London: The Stationery Office, 2003), 3.2.

Register. On the other hand, the system of electronic conveyance is already available and functioning.[29]

However, it is not sufficient that people are able to obtain Register information, write contracts and conveyance documents and send registration applications to the Registrar online. If registers and conveyance documents are electronic and Internet connections are available, there should be no hindrance to treat an electronic text of a conveyance document, accepted by the parties, as a valid conveyance and have it immediately recognised by the Registrar and as a part of Register information. It makes no sense that the electronic text has to be printed and signed in the old-fashioned way by the parties and the paper document sent to the Registrar either in an envelope or as a scanned document in order to have the Registrar register the conveyance in the electronic system.

7 The English and the Finnish Ways of Carrying out Electronic Conveyancing

The English plan and the Finnish system share the same ideas and basic principles. Based on the electronic Land Registers established earlier and on computer and network technology, the main ideas of the systems are the validation of electronic conveyance documents instead of or alongside traditional written and signed paper documents and the automatic and immediate online registration of conveyances.[30] In addition, the parties have to be able to perform all stages of the binding transaction electronically. Naturally, a secure electronic communication network is required for that.

In both countries, the Registrar is given the power to provide and arrange the electronic communication network.[31] The legislation is

[29] In Finland, private persons as well as professionals can order extracts as traditional paper documents from the offices of the National Land Survey. In addition, everybody has the right to inspect the Register information at the offices of the National Land Survey.

Both in England and in Finland, access to the information is granted based on the principle of publicity of Register information.

[30] Regarding the rules of form, see section 91, English Land Registration Act 2002, and 2:1.2 Finnish Code of Real Estate. According to the English law, substitution by the electronic form is applied in relation to both statutory and common law. Law Commission No. 271, 13.18, p. 276.

[31] In England, section 92 (1), Land Registration Act 2002, and in Finland, 9a:1.2 Code of Real Estate.

intended to contain only the governing principles and crucial rules, leaving the technical details for rules and applications to be enacted and adopted by the registrar.

There are, nevertheless, many significant differences between these models at both the conceptual and practical levels.

7.1 *Certain Institutional and Conceptual Differences*

In Finland, as well as in the other Nordic countries, the distinction between personal obligations (*pactum in personam*) and rights about property (*pactum in rem*) has not been adopted in a strong sense and is not decisive at the level of jurisdiction. Hence, the difference from most other European countries and especially from Germany is apparent and worth attention.

The prevailing European way to transfer pieces of real estate is the three-stage process.[32] The first step is a contract between the parties, creating obligations to both. In England, it most often takes place through the exchange of contracts.[33] The second step is the conveyance of title or ownership, and the third step is registration.

The point of departure are the property law effects, that is, the proprietary effects united with a conventional conveyance in the form of a special kind of document, which in England is the deed. However, as in the English and German law, the proprietary effects are often connected with registration, as well. There are other deviations, as well. For instance, in England, it is an established rule in case law that an equitable title passes under a contract giving a proprietary interest founded on constructive trust.[34]

In Finland, and as far as conveyances of real property are concerned, there is normally no difference between the contract of the sale of a piece of real estate as a personal obligation and the transference of the title (ownership) of the piece of real estate. The English concept of deed has often been translated as referring to a conveyance of a

[32] *See* Sparkes, *European Land Law*, p. 300.

[33] The procedure of exchange of contracts is popular. Parties make two identical copies of the contract. One is signed by the conveyor and the other by the conveyee. When the time comes to create a binding contract, the parties exchange the copies, that is, send or give them to each other. As a result of the exchange, each party holds a copy signed by the other party. Judith-Anne MacKenzie and Mary Phillips, *Textbook on Land Law* (Oxford University Press, 2012), p. 49.

[34] For instance, *Lysaght* v. *Edwards* (1876) 2 Ch. D. 499 Jessel MR.

piece of real estate.[35] As a matter of fact, the terms 'contract' or 'bill of sale' would be better in the Nordic context.

In the Nordic countries, a conveyance document is seen as a written contract important for both of its parties and creating rights for both of them. A sale contract entitles the vendor to the purchase money and the purchaser to the ownership. As a main rule, a conveyance in the Nordic countries has normally been made by one document. Moreover, a conveyance is treated as an entity. The conveyance includes both the personal obligations (contract) and the transference of the title (conveyance of ownership) as an unseparated unity. In Finland, this entity is called and understood as a contract notwithstanding the fact that it contains a disposition of ownership, as well. In short, in the Nordic countries, a conveyance of a piece of real estate contains only two stages: the contract and registration.

In Finland, the unity of a contract and a conveyance has been granted with rules of form.[36] According to their established interpretation, a contract made without complying with the rules cannot create any conveyance of ownership of a piece of real estate or any liability to convey it.[37] The form rules are applied even to a precontract.[38] All other contracts or agreements purporting to transfer ownership or preceding a valid conveyance are neither valid nor binding.

It is obviously easier to adopt electronic conveyancing, and the conveyancing system can be a simple one if the process has only two stages. In short: a simple conveyance can be transformed into a simple electronic process.

In Finland, an electronic conveyance in the form of a contract will take place on an official Internet platform and on an official site provided by the register authority. A conveyance takes place in a closed electronic system, that is, electronic trading system, and on the platform

[35] The term 'deed' is adopted in the English translation of the Finnish Code of Real Estate, for instance, in the section regulating the legal form of the sale of a piece of real estate (2:1.1). However, the direct translation of the Finnish term '*kauppakirja*' is rather 'sale document'.

[36] According to the rules of form applied to a conveyance made with a paper document, a sale of real estate shall be concluded in writing, the seller and the buyer or their attorneys shall sign the deed of sale and a notary shall attest the sale in the presence of all the signatories of the deed of sale (2:1.1 Finnish Code of Real Estate).

[37] The prevailing interpretation has been very strict. Even a minor defect has induced invalidity. For instance, see the precedents of the Finnish Supreme Court, KKO 1954 I 98, KKO 1981 II 162, KKO 1988:106 and KKO 1992:153.

[38] 2:7.2 Finnish Code of Real Estate. A cancellation or a suspension clause of the final conveyance can be adopted as an optional solution if the parties want to reserve a possibility to waive the conveyance. See 2:2 Finnish Code of Real Estate.

maintained by an officer, not in the open Internet. Parties when logging into the platform and site are identified with the help of strong identification. The contract will be concluded and the registration procedure will begin when the parties accept the text and the terms of the contract. It is presupposed that the parties make all of the needful preparations for the conveyance before accepting the contract. In addition, they can make a separate precontract either as a paper document or in the electronic system.

In England, the plan of electronic conveyancing is founded on the three stages of a conveyance. First, a contract is made and signed by the parties. Second, the disposition itself (replacing the deed) is made and signed and, third, registration takes place simultaneously with the acceptance of the disposition. The completion of the disposition will include both the acceptance of the conveyance and registration. Both the contract and the disposition are planned to be signed with the help of a digital signature, in practice, the dual key method. All stages are intended to take place in the open Internet.

In a noteworthy way, the reliability of the English plan is founded on a digital signature while the Finnish system is founded on electronic identification. Their logic and functions are different. A digital signature contains identification but in the Finnish system identification and signature are separated from each other.

As a matter of fact, the Finnish process is also simpler in another significant respect. Only one copy of the conveyance contract is written by the parties and accepted by them on the related web site. No drafts of final documents are sent between the parties or to the Registrar. Instead, the platform connected with the official registers controls the text and its details in all stages of writing. It is presumed that the writing of the documents is overseen by the Registrar. In fact, the text on the official platform is already in the Registrar's possession. In other words, the text is made at the Registrar's office and, accordingly, no documents need to be sent. Naturally, registration begins automatically and immediately when the parties have accepted the final text of the transaction on the web site. The different practices will be explained more closely later.

The German idea of registration creating the ownership of a transferee of a piece of real estate, which is applied in the English law as well, has not been adopted in the Nordic countries.[39] Instead, a special kind of

[39] In German law, see § 873 and 891 BGB. In England, both the deed and registration are needed in order to make a conveyance of a piece of real estate. LRA 2002 significantly strengthened the effect of registration. Elizabeth Cooke has described the change as follows: a system of title by registration is adopted instead of the system of registration

analytical conception has been created. It can be described as a process conception of a transfer of ownership. Electronic conveyancing will not contain titles established by the mere fact of registration. Furthermore, no such concept as absolute title has been adopted in the Nordic countries.

According to the Nordic understanding, a transfer of ownership (title) takes place mainly by and at the moment of making a contract between the parties. Hence, a conveyee is treated as the owner immediately after finishing a contract between a vendor and a purchaser. The significance and influence of registration is weaker. Registration strengthens the position of a conveyee as an owner in relation to certain third persons, but it is not considered to create his or her right. Accordingly, the Nordic title registration bears protective registration but not dispositive.

On the other hand, there are many stages of a transfer of ownership according to this conception. A purchase or another transaction between parties is the most important. The registration, either of a conveyor or a conveyee, is a complementary stage in this process. This is the case even in electronic conveyancing. In other words, the German ideal of the transfer of ownership at a certain precise moment in all respects is not applied. Instead, the idea of a relative transfer has been adopted. The ownership transfers at a certain moment in relation to a person and at another moment in relation to another person. No problems of legal uncertainty have been recognised because of this conception.

Finland, as well as the other Nordic countries, belongs to the family of continental legal systems. Therefore, the division between law and equity (rights/claims in law or in equity) is unknown. Accordingly, questions about the interests in land founded on trusts or other equitable institutions or norms do not exist.

In addition, the distinction between statutory law and case law is understood differently. A continental lawyer sees the field of law covered, as a rule, by statutes. Therefore, the sections of statutes, especially the sections of codes with large application scopes, appear in a different way compared with English statutes. Continental sections are general and have large application fields. More detailed case law is normally manifested as interpretations of statutes or as filling the gaps of statutory law.

of title, and, a deed must be executed in order to transfer a legal estate or create a legal interest, but the registration system has taken away the power of the deed. *See* Cooke, *The New Law of Land Registration*, p. 1, and Cooke, *Land Law*, p. 48. *See also* Sparkes, *A New Land Law*, p. 117.

7.2 *Compulsory or Optional Procedure?*

According to the original plan, the English model is intended to be compulsory.[40] That is, electronic conveyancing will, after a transition period, be the only valid way to make conveyances of real property. In other words, after the transition period, only electronic conveyances will be valid. Contracts or dispositions not made electronically will be ineffective both in law and equity.[41] It is, nevertheless, possible to avoid this strict conclusion with the help of the principles of equity in case law.[42]

Compulsion is an understandable solution. After the transition period, there will be only one system in use instead of many collateral and competing systems operating simultaneously. In addition, implementation of the reform and the new system is granted through compulsion.

Compulsion is justified by the aspiration to keep the transition period as short as possible. In addition, two distinct and co-existing systems functioning at the same time for the time being or for a long time is repudiated because the benefits of electronic conveyancing and savings are achieved only by compulsion.

The most important reason is, nevertheless, the aspiration to ensure the immediate registration of conveyances. This is treated as the single most important technical objective of the Bill.[43]

One obvious reason for the difference between the English plan and the Finnish system is that in England the registration gap is considered as a significant problem in land registration.[44] Basically, the difference traces back to the difference between the dispositive registration adopted in England and protective registration adopted in Finland. The time gap between the conveyance and its registration is an obvious problem when the validity of the conveyance depends on the registration taking place later, during the registration term.

According to the English original plan, one additional benefit of compulsion is the management of transaction chains. Transaction chains are seen as one of the major problems of the contemporary English system,

[40] Law Commission No. 271, 13.74, p. 294. [41] Law Commission No. 271, 13.84, p. 297.

[42] According to section 93 (2), LRA 2002, a disposition to which this section applies, or a contract to make such a disposition, only has effect if it is made by means of a document in electronic form and if, when the document purports to take effect, (a) it is electronically communicated to the Registrar, and (b) the relevant registration requirements are met. This is called the double effect: electronic transactions are not only valid, but they are the only valid transactions. Law Commission No. 271, 13.75, p. 295. *See also* MacKenzie and Phillips, *Textbook on Land Law*, p. 132.

[43] Law Commission No. 271, 2.52, 2.59, 2.61 and 13.63, pp. 24, 26 and 291.

[44] See Law Commission No 271, 13.77, p. 295.

and chain management is treated as one of the most important features of the conveyancing reform. With the help of a chain manager and electronic conveyance, it is possible to master the problem involving chains. The Registrar will be able to use monitoring information to manage network transactions, and the power can also be delegated.[45]

In practice, however, it seems obvious that the transition period in England cannot be short, for instance, only a few years. According to recent plans, a system of electronic conveyancing will be introduced on a voluntary basis even in England.[46] In addition, the realisation of chain management seems to be unlikely.

In this respect, there is a significant difference between the English original plan and the Finnish system. Finnish electronic conveyancing is an alternative to the traditional way of making conveyances of real property. It is an optional procedure and an alternative way to make and complete a transaction.[47] The two systems will function side by side for the time being. No plans have been made to terminate the use of traditional paper documents for the transfer of real property.

In Finland, title registration is largely compulsory, applying to all types of acquisitions of real property, inheritance and wills included. However, the non-compliance of registration does not affect the validity of an acquisition between the parties. It is possible, nevertheless, that an acquisition is not effective in a certain relation with a third person, for instance, in relation to a competing conveyee (a double sale situation)

[45] See Sch. 5, section 9, LRA 2002.

A conventional chain of conveyances appears when several conveyances connected to each other take place. Conveyances presuppose each other and are financed by each other. For instance, a purchaser of a family house has to sell his or her house in order to finance the purchase. At the same time, the vendor wants to buy a new house, as well. In addition, they both often need mortgage loans. There might be even more conveyances in the chain. There is an obvious need to make the conveyances and other transactions connected to each other at the same time, or at least coordinated with each other.

According to the legislative draft, transaction chains will be managed by a chain manager and with the help of electronic conveyancing. The Land Registry or another authority will be the manager. A solicitor or another conveyancer will notify the manager when an obvious chain will take place. The manager is responsible for managing the conveyances in the chain in order to facilitate them. In fact, the manager will identify the parties of the conveyances and relevant facts and details involving them. Subsequently, the chain manager will encourage the parties to complete the steps of the process in a coordinated way.

[46] MacKenzie and Phillips, *Textbook on Land Law*, p. 132.

[47] 2:1 Finnish Code of Real Estate (as amended by the statute 4.2.2011/96). The section is applied to all types of conveyances of pieces of real estate.

if the registration or even if the non-delayed registration is neglected.[48] The official control is efficient and the benefits provided to a transferee through registration create incentives for rapid registration. For these reasons, the registration gap is not treated as a problem in Finland. Accordingly, there is no reason to expedite the elimination of the registration gap. The conveyance chain is not treated as a problem, either. As a matter of fact, the chain has not been under debate in Finland. The benefits of electronic conveyancing are, naturally, acknowledged, but taking advantage of them depends on the popularity of the electronic conveyance in the future.

Compulsion makes the reform and adoption of electronic conveyancing much more ambitious and, on the other hand, vulnerable compared with the optional solution. The system has to be planned and prepared very carefully and the adopted system must be well tested and ready for all conveyancing situations. It is no wonder that the power to use the electronic conveyance system vested in HM Land Registry in England has been described as a power that will not be exercised lightly.[49] This, obviously, is one reason for the postponement of the introduction and reconsideration of the English system. The development of a secure and comprehensive system calls for extensive resources that the English Registrar does not seem to have.

The intended short transition period provides the only possibility to test the compulsory system in actual practice and to acquire experience for the development of the system. After the transition period, the electronic system has to function in all cases. At this stage, the 'all at once' principle must be applied. In practice, no defects or deficiencies can be afforded. People and corporations must be able to make valid conveyances of real property without any delays.

An optional system of electronic conveyancing is a modest, safe and cheap choice. As a matter of fact, the new Finnish system is not even intended to function and be available in all cases. Most probably, it operates without any disruptions or delays in simple conveyance cases, for instance, in a sale of a whole registered piece of real estate between two persons. Moreover, the requirements of the electronic system restrict the application scope of the system. For instance, a person can open the system and log into it as a vendor only if he or she is registered as the contemporary owner (title-holder) of a piece of real estate. In addition, the system requires the correct facts and details of

[48] 13:3.1 Finnish Code of Real Estate. [49] Law Commission No. 271, 2.60, p. 27.

a conveyance as well as of its object and parties. In all cases in which the electronic system does not open or function or ceases to function, traditional conveyance paper documents can still be written.

Optional adoption of the electronic conveyancing can take place faster. In Finland, the system is adopted in parts. Applying to most and conventional cases, the Finnish system was brought into use on 1 November 2013, and applicable to certain more complicated situations on 1 March 2015.

It is obvious that the optional system is easier to introduce and adopt. Viewed in this light, it is no wonder that the Finnish system is already functioning but the adoption of the English system is postponed.

7.3 *Electronic Signature*

7.3.1 About Authentication

An electronic signature is a crucial matter in all electronic trading.[50] It is often treated as the main problem of electronic contracts. How can we abandon the traditional manual signature written on a paper document and replace it with another technique in a safe way? The manual signature is vulnerable to forgery, but nevertheless, we have a strong trust in it and we demand a high level of security from the electronic signature. As a matter of fact, in practice, the manual signature has carried out the numerous functions of it very well.[51] Accordingly, the level of security demanded in the case of the electronic signature is at least the same as that of the manual signature.

The requirements of an advanced electronic signature, that is, a proper digital signature, given in the directive on electronic signatures of the European Union, are embodiments of this level.[52] It is no wonder that this level is adopted as the standard of security in the case of the electronic conveyance of real property in both England and Finland. There are, nevertheless, many different ways and techniques to meet the standard. In fact, in the English plan and the Finnish law, two

[50] In the United States, even before the American Civil War a morse code was used to send messages electrically by telegraphy. Some of these messages were agreements to terms that were intended as enforceable contracts. An early acceptance of the enforceability of telegraphic messages as electronic signatures came from the New Hampshire Supreme Court in 1869.

[51] A signature has many, more than ten, functions. Only undertaking a legal commitment is taken into consideration here.

[52] See art. 26 Regulation 910/2014.

different solutions are adopted. A digital signature is presumed in the English plan and strong identification is mentioned in the Finnish legislation.[53]

An electronic signature is expected and demanded to perform the same functions as the manual signature. As far as a commitment is concerned, the fundamental questions are identification of a person as an author of the commitment and origin authentication of a commitment document. How can we be sure that an electronic commitment is given or accepted by the person mentioned?[54] In addition, we must be convinced about the non-repudiation and integrity of the text signed. The two latter concerns are addressed by the high quality of the signature and the entire conveyancing system together.

As a matter of fact, we can never be sure who has given an electronic commitment or signature. At most, we can have sufficient guarantees that the means of signing are in the possession of the person in whose name the commitment is given.

In this connection, electronic signature is an expression of acceptance of a text united with the signature and commitment expressed with the help of the text. The electronic signature as such, however, does not yield sufficient security with regard to valuable and legally binding transactions. Not even an advanced electronic signature created by a secure creation device is sufficient. In addition, a qualified certification provided by a certification-service-provider, that is, a certifier, is needed. In addition to the parties of the transaction, a qualified and trustworthy third person is needed to confirm and validate, that is, certify the signature. As a point of departure, a signature unites a commitment with a certain person as an author of the commitment. A certifier verifies this connection. The certifier is, naturally, liable for damage caused for the certification service provided.[55] An advanced signature technique together with trustworthy certification provides a sufficient guarantee for secure proof of identity and authentication.

[53] In England, section 91 (3), LRA 2002 and Law Commission No. 271, 13.15–17, p. 274, and in Finland, 9a:1.1 Code of Real Estate.

According to a general principle, strong identification is founded on two of the following three identification methods: possession of an item or a secret or recognizing a biological feature. Both the English plan and the Finnish system are founded on the first two methods: possession of an item and a secret.

[54] Here, I presume that a signature is given by a natural person. She or he can represent a corporation. Electronic labels given by corporation are not considered here.

[55] See art. 13 Regulation 910/2014.

7.3.2 England

According to the English law, as far as a sales contract is concerned, the signatures of both parties are needed, or in the exchange of the contracts, one identical copy signed by the vendor and another by the purchaser.[56] A deed must be signed by the person executing it, for instance, the vendor, and witnessed.[57]

According to the original English plan of electronic conveyancing, parties can prepare both the contract and disposition or the disposition alone in electronic form. At the stage of the contract, several offers and counter-offers can be sent between the parties. Subsequently, the final contract can be signed and sent by a party and accepted and signed by the other party, or both parties can send and sign a contract each and exchange contracts. The electronic disposition will replace the deed and its delivery.[58]

All stages of a transfer are supposed to be carried out electronically according to this plan. The crucial stage is, nevertheless, the disposition, that is, the conveyance in the strict sense and its simultaneous registration. Moreover, a conveyance can be made without any contract. The contract can be seen as a preparatory stage of the conveyance. Accordingly, here, it is sufficient to describe merely the signing of a sale disposition by a vendor. All the texts and commitments included in the conveyance system are supposed to be signed and sent in the same way.

Following the standard description of the plan, a vendor will send a disposition text to a purchaser. The well-known method of dual key cryptography is presumed to be employed.[59] In other words, an advanced electronic signature is employed.

According to the dual key method, a disposition text as a message is encrypted by using a private key. The vendor sends the encrypted text to the purchaser with the help of the open Internet. The vendor obtains his or her private key from a certification authority. The encrypted message can be decoded by the purchaser as a recipient only with the help of the public key of the holder of the private key. The public key is available to everyone.

The private key is supposed to be stored in a smart card. Certification presumes the registration of the vendor. The vendor is identified with the help of registration and the investigation process included in the registration. In other words, the correct use of the private key, and

[56] Section 2 (3), LPA 1989. [57] Section 1 (3), LPA 1989. [58] Section 91 (5), LRA 2002.
[59] This method of signing is known also as public key encryption.

authentication of the text, is confirmed by the certification authority. In addition, the non-repudiation and integrity of a text can be protected by the dual key method. Besides the smart card as the signature-creation device, a card reader is needed. Alternative electronic signature techniques can be applied, as well.[60]

The stipulated practice of an electronic sale of a piece of real estate contains sending drafts, contracts and dispositions, that is, sending documents many times and in many stages with the help of the Internet. In addition to the correspondence between the parties, copies of drafts as well as final contracts and dispositions are sent to the Registrar in electronic form, equipped with advanced signatures and qualified certification to be safe.

In practice, employment of the dual key method presupposes existing large-scale employment of this method in a society and a widely spread technical application of it irrespective of the introduction of the system of electronic conveyancing of real property. Unfortunately, this is not the case in England or in most other European countries.[61] Even worse, no other similar encryption method is commonly used. It is hardly possible to create a new method or application for electronic signatures together with the introduction of the new system.

7.3.3 Finland

In Finland, the problems of identification and authentication as well as non-repudiation and integrity have been solved otherwise. Identification of a party of a conveyance and origin authentication of a commitment are secured with the help of access to the official platform. Certification takes place at this place. Only a person identified by a certifier can log into the platform and conveyance site. Moreover, only a person who is registered as the title-holder can act as a vendor, and only a person named by the vendor can act as a purchaser on the site. Problems of non-repudiation and integrity of a commitment text have been solved with the help of the closed system, that is, the closed platform maintained and controlled by the register authority.

In the Finnish system, the electronic signatures of both parties can appear merely as acceptances of the contract text on the site. That is, a

[60] *See* Law Commission No. 271, 13.14 and 13.16, pp. 274 and 275 and Sparkes, *A New Land Law*, p. 104.

[61] This is not surprising because an advanced and qualified dual key system is, in practice, a complicated and expensive system. In addition, there are open liability problems involved in it. A dual key system is, nevertheless, treated as a safe and functional system.

signature as such can appear in a minimal form. This is possible because identification and authentication has already been secured by the certification and the closed trading system.

The Finnish solution is a simple solution. Basically, the simplicity of this practice is founded on the simplicity of the Finnish conveyance of a piece of real estate. As told above, transfer of ownership takes place with the help of one contract and appears in the form of one text.

No documents are sent between the parties or to the Registrar in the Finnish system. Consequently, messages do not require encrypting or keys. Instead, the conveyance of ownership takes place on the official platform and on the official site provided and maintained by the register authority. Everyone can access the platform on the Internet. However, logging in as a party of a conveyance and starting the conveyance of a certain piece of real estate presupposes, first, controlled identification and its certification and, second, substantive competence according to the Title and Mortgage Register. Controlling information is provided by, and conveyances are even entered into the register through, the uniform information system maintained by the Registrar.

In practice, a party can identify himself or herself with the help of the TUPAS identification service of Finnish banks.[62] Finnish banks use TUPAS to identify their own customers in online banking and act as certifiers confirming the identification of parties of trades and other transactions, in this case, parties of electronic conveyances of pieces of real estate. It is presumed that normally TUPAS identification is employed, although other means of identification and certification are possible, as well.[63]

[62] In the TUPAS service, banks identify their customers with strong identification by using their own registers. Strong identification is required both by the Finnish Act on Strong Electronic Identification and Electronic Signatures (617/2009) and 9A:1.1 Finnish Code of Real Estate.

A bank as a certifier verifies only the identity of a person. Authentication of a text and commitment is created together with the help of a signature and its certification. In practice, the whole system of the platform supports authentication. In addition, TUPAS is used as a signing device in the bank services between a bank and its customer.

For further details about the TUPAS identification service, *see* TUPAS Identification Service, Identification Principles, Version 2.0b, 20 January 2011, at www.fkl.fi/en/themes/e-services/dokumentit/tupas_identification_principles_v20b.pdf, and TUPAS Identification Service for Service Providers, Service Description and Service Provider's Guidelines, Version 2.3c, 20 January 2011, at www.fkl.fi/en/themes/e-services/Dokumentit/Tupas_Identification_Service_v23c.pdf.

[63] A party can also use the so-called HST smart card, that is, an identification card provided by the Finnish state. Even smartphone certification is available.

TUPAS is a practical solution because online banking has been adopted in Finland on a very large scale, and most people have personal online banking access codes. The codes and certification provided by TUPAS are also widely employed in the electronic trade of movables and services and often even in many non-commercial operations.[64]

In addition, payment services can be attached to the conveyance system. For instance, purchase money can be paid to the vendor with the help of his or her online bank connection united with the conveyance. However, these additional services are not yet available or functioning. So far, only appliance payments can be made in the frameworks of the conveyance system. On the other hand, a purchaser can log into an online banking system with the same codes and pay the purchase money at the same time.[65]

TUPAS identification and certification is a closed system. It is founded on the contracts between banks and their customers. Banks identify only their own customers. In addition, certification is founded on the contracts between banks and the register authority. In other words, all parties involved in electronic conveyances are in contractual relations with each other. As a matter of fact, there are two closed systems connected to each other, the platform maintained by the register authority and a certification service provided by a bank.

According to the current TUPAS practice, a party of a conveyance who is a customer of a Finnish bank has received a user ID from the bank when the customer contract with the bank has been made. Identification of all customers takes place with the help of personal appointment and identification documents. The customer has received a number card, as well. The number card contains one-time identifiers, which are changed periodically and are sent to the postal address of the customer. In addition, the customer has to create a password which must be changed regularly and supplemental identification by telephone is used. Logging into a conveyance site as a party of a conveyance presupposes each time the use of the following codes and devices: the user ID, the password and the number card and, regularly, telephone certification.

In addition to natural persons who act as conveyors or conveyees themselves, private persons as well as corporations can enter a letter of attorney in the conveyance system and certain corporations such as

[64] In practice, nearly all qualified certifications take place in the form of TUPAS in Finland.

[65] In the future, taxes and registration fees connected to a conveyance can be paid through the conveyancing system.

banks can notify that certain persons represent them. In the future, it will be possible to use corporation identifiers.

7.4 *Electronic Conveyancing Practices*

7.4.1 England

The English plan and Finnish system of electronic conveyance of real property provide two different ways of conveyancing.

The English plan is based on distributed processing with the help of the open Internet. Commitment texts are prepared as electronic documents on personal computers or workstations. Texts are encrypted and sent between the parties as well as to the Registrar.

In England, it is an established practice that both parties hire their own professional solicitors or conveyancers who prepare the conveyance and the documents and take care of registration. Less than 1 per cent of all registered transactions have been carried out without professional assistance. Even in electronic conveyancing, it is presumed that these professionals will make the transactions as representatives of the parties. Accordingly, a solicitor or a conveyancer normally acts as a 'party' of a conveyance.

A significant feature of the original English plan is the changes that will be made directly to the Land Register as the automatic result of electronic dispositions. Changes here refer to registration and not merely, for instance, entering a notice or a registration application or issuing official register extracts or copies. The power to change register information by making a disposition is founded on the presupposition that professionals who are representatives of the parties and who are licensed to use the system are capable and trustworthy operators of the system. A license will be given in the form of a network access agreement. In short, solicitors and licensed conveyancers will have access to the electronic communication network and carry out the functions of the Registrar.[66] This is an ambitious feature in the English plan and it is not easy to put into effect.

Moreover, a person authorised under the network access agreement will have implied authority to sign electronic documents, contracts and

[66] In addition, estate agents and mortgage lenders can have access to the Registry. On the other hand, the level of access may vary. If the assigned preconditions are met, an applicant will have the right to enter a network access agreement. Sch. 5, section 1, LRA 2002. Law Commission No. 271, 2.57, 13.2 and 13.36–13.40, pp. 26, 268 and 282.

dispositions on behalf of his or her clients, that is, implied authority to act as an agent.[67]

Do-it-yourself conveyancers are not, however, excluded from the electronic conveyancing system. District land Registrars will be obliged to assist the parties. In these cases, the Registrar will carry out the electronic transaction on the directions of the parties.[68]

According to the plan, the first formal stage of the English practice is the contract.[69] When parties have agreed on the terms of a contract, they can send a copy of the draft to the Registrar to be checked electronically. In other words, the facts and details of the transaction will be inspected.

In electronic conveyancing, parties can execute the contract by exchanging identical copies of it. Parties can send identical, electronic and signed copies to each other and to the Registrar.

Once the final contract is made, each party is legally obliged to give effect to the transaction. Notwithstanding the written form required in the LPA 1989, the valid contract can be in electronic form and signed electronically.[70] According to the plan, the final contract will be sent to the Registrar. The system will automatically make a notice of the contract in the Register. It is worth mentioning that the contract will be published and protected by the notice (priority protection). In other words, the electronic contract will be a stronger and more effective stage of the transaction than the paper contract.[71]

[67] Sch. 5, section 8, LRA 2002.

[68] Sch. 5, section 7, LRA 2002 and Law Commission No. 271, 2.68 and 13.72, pp. 27 and 294.

[69] There are, naturally, informal activities preceding the contract. Parties gather market information, and an estate agent is often employed. In addition, parties can make an oral agreement about the conveyance or a draft of the contract.

As of 27 September 1989, the contract must be made in writing in order to be valid. Even the application of equitable concepts, such as estoppel or constructive trust, cannot give an oral agreement the force of a valid contract. Parties often hire solicitors or conveyancers at this stage, and inquiries may be made. A surveyor can be hired and an investigation of the vendor's title might be needful. On electronic conveyance, *see* MacKenzie and Phillips, *Textbook on Land Law*, pp. 40 and 44.

[70] The power to modify legislation is given in section 8, Electronic Communication Act 2000.

[71] Law Commission No. 271, 2.53 and 2.54, p. 25.

In addition, the position of a conveyee will be stronger in relation to all equitable interests. The creation of estate contracts by electronic means only will ensure that equitable interests arising from them are automatically entered into the register. This will gradually reduce the number of interests which can be created off the Register and which either take effect as overriding interests or are protected by registration. MacKenzie and Phillips, *Textbook on Land Law*, p. 133.

A similar process will take place when the disposition is made. A draft of the disposition document and of any charges will be prepared in electronic form and agreed between the parties. The draft will be submitted to the Registry. The facts and details of the transfer will be checked electronically against the contract to ensure that there are no discrepancies. A notional Register will be prepared by the Registry in consultation with the parties to indicate the form that the Register will take when the transaction is completed.[72]

In the planned electronic conveyancing, the electronic disposition document will replace the traditional deed. The concept of delivery is not applicable in this system. Accordingly, the disposition is not treated as a deed, but it has a similar function. Because of the completing function, the date of the disposition, confirmed with an electronic signature, is an important matter.[73]

A deed has to be signed by the conveyor or on behalf of him or her, and witnessed.[74] As a rule, the plan applies the same requirement of form to an electronic disposition. An electronic signature will, however, be needed from each person by whom the disposition purports to be authenticated.[75] A conveyee is sometimes a party of the document, such as in the case of several conveyees as joint proprietors and when the conveyance sets out a trust.[76]

Each electronic signature has to be certified.[77] The presupposed dual key cryptography employing private and public keys is described above.

The completion of the conveyance will entail the simultaneous occurrence of the execution of the transfer and any charges in electronic form, their transmission to the Registry and the registration of the disposition so that the register conforms to the notional register previously agreed.

In addition, the payment of the purchase money, stamp duty and registration fees may be simultaneous with the conveyance. However, they presuppose a connection with online banking.[78] Money transfers

72 Law Commission No. 271, 2.55, p. 25.

73 Law Commission No. 271, 13.13, p. 273. Unlike executing the deed according to common law (*see Steiglitz* v. *Eggington*, 1815, Holt 141; 171 ER 193), an agent can sign a disposition on behalf of his or her principal. This is important to solicitors and licensed conveyancers taking care of the conveyance. Law Commission No. 271, 13.20, p. 276.

74 Section 1 (3) (a), LPA 1989.

75 Section 91 (3) (b), LRA 2002.

76 Law Commission No. 271, 13.15, p. 274.

A declaration of trust respecting any land or any interest therein must be manifested and proved by some writing signed by some person who is able to declare such trust or by his will (section 83 (1) (b), LPA 1925).

77 Section 91 (3) (c) LRA 2002.

78 See Law Commission No. 271, 2.62 and 2.63, p. 28.

alongside and united with the conveyance have unexpectedly proved to be a complicated matter. This problem seems to be one hindrance in realising the English plan, and it is not surprising that it is, so far, mostly excluded from the Finnish system.

7.4.2 Finland

In Finland, as we have already noticed, electronic conveyancing is not based on sending signed and encrypted documents but on making conveyances on the official platform and site provided and maintained by the Registrar. As far as a sale or another conveyance of ownership of a piece of real estate or leasehold is concerned, the system is called an electronic trading system.[79] The trading system is a public service maintained by the state.

Services provided by an estate agent or a surveyor, marketing of a piece of property, acquiring register information and negotiations most often precede formal trading. Even an informal, that is, legally non-binding agreement on a sale or a legal precontract can be made before formal trading. On the other hand, a precontract can be made with the help of the electronic trading system.[80]

Parties have to log into a certain official conveyancing platform and web site in order to make an electronic conveyance. Identification and its certification are presuppositions of logging in. The site contains electronic forms' open spaces for the parties, the piece of real estate as the object of the conveyance and, for a possible trade, the purchase price. In addition, there is a space for the terms of the conveyance agreed by the parties.[81] Here, it is important to remember that the trade contract and the conveyance of ownership are united as a one-stage transaction in Finland.

In Finland, it is presumed that the parties themselves make electronic transactions. In other words, do-it-yourself conveyancing is the normal case. As a rule, it is the title-holder, that is, the registered owner, who can log into the trading site as a possible vendor. On the other hand, a general letter of attorney as well as individual authorisation providing power to act on behalf of a certain corporation or person generally or as far as an individual transaction is concerned can be included on the trading system.[82] In practice and in most cases, an estate agent – sometimes a solicitor – can give legal aid in trading, and a party can log

[79] 9a:7.1 Code of Real Estate.
[80] 9a:14.1 Code of Real Estate.
[81] 9a:4.1 Code of Real Estate.
[82] 9a:1.3 Code of Real Estate.

into the trading site on the solicitor's or agent's computer but with the help of the party's own personal codes.

The platform and electronic trading system is connected to the Title and Mortgage Register as well as the cadastre and many other registers. The facts and details written on the trading form by the parties are controlled with the help of register information.[83]

Outside the electronic trading system, a notary shall attest the sale of a piece of real estate in the presence of all the signatories of the sale document.[84] A notary is not, however, needed in electronic trading. Instead of the notary, the facts and details of the conveyance are controlled with the help of the register connections, and the identity of each party and authentication of the sale document are certified in the way described above.

One important fact is the registered title of a conveyor. Only a person who has registered his or her title can act as a vendor of a certain piece of real estate in the trading system. The registration of title in the Title and Mortgage Register signifies the registration of a piece of real estate as the object of a conveyance in the cadastre, as well.

In the electronic trading system, a registered title-holder can start, that is, open trading by logging into the appropriate site.[85] The title-holder must identify himself or herself, and the identification is certified. The title-holder can write the first draft of the sale on the form and accept it.[86] This text is the vendor's offer. He or she has to name, that is, appoint the purchaser. There can be several vendors, for instance in the cases of co-ownership or a death estate, or several purchasers.[87]

The vendor can inform the purchaser of the opening of the trading through the trading system or by other means. An appointed purchaser can open the same trading site and form. Login by the purchaser presupposes identification and its certification in the same way as in the case of the vendor. After that, the purchaser can change the text or its details and accept the changes.[88] This is the counter-offer of the purchaser. The parties can take turns in changing the text. When both parties have accepted the same, that is, the final text, a conveyance takes place. Mutual acceptance closes the site and trading.[89]

A party can close the trading without mutual acceptance of the text at any point of the trading. Before mutual acceptance of the same text, the

83 9a:4.2 Code of Real Estate.
84 2:1.1 Code of Real Estate.
85 9a:8.1 Code of Real Estate.
86 9a:9.1 Code of Real Estate.
87 So far, several pieces of real estate cannot be sold with the help of one conveyance.
88 9a:9.1 Code of Real Estate.
89 9a:9.2 Code of Real Estate.

offers or counter-offers are not treated as legally binding. Offers and counter-offers are treated as cancelled and the trading will be closed if neither party changes the text or accepts it in thirty days.[90] Only one case of trading at a time can be open for a given piece of real estate.[91]

Automatic and immediate title registration is a cornerstone of the Finnish electronic conveyancing system in the same way as according to the English plan. There is, nevertheless, an important difference. In Finland, the Registrar immediately receives the mutual acceptance of the same conveyance text, that is, the binding conveyance as an online registration application.[92] This, however, means that the parties or their agents do not have the power to change the register information; contrary to the English plan, they do not have access to the Title and Mortgage Register or other registers, and they do not carry out any functions of the Registrar. Only the officials of the Finnish National Land Survey have the power to make entries in the title and mortgage register or change its information content.

As the point of departure, a registration application provided by the electronic trading system is treated and the registration decision is made in the same way as in the case of a traditional application with the help of paper documents. The communication network provides most of the information needed in the investigation of the applications. Accordingly, in most cases, there is no need to call for more information or documents from the applicant, that is, the purchaser or another conveyee. In addition, the investigation and decision proceedings can be automatised.

8 Conclusions

The English plan and the Finnish system of electronic conveyancing of real property appear similar in outline but differ in details. They both have their own conceptual frameworks related to the national legal institutions and systematics. They both presuppose and put forth changes in land law.

There seems to be a greater demand for electronic conveyancing in the frameworks of the English law. The elimination of the registration gap is an important reason for planning the electronic system. It is no coincidence that the English system was originally intended to be compulsory.

90 9a:11.3 Code of Real Estate.

91 9a:11.3 Code of Real Estate.

92 9a:12.1 Code of Real Estate.

The English plan is more ambitious, burdensome and complicated than the Finnish system. The practical outcome is the difference in introducing the systems. The modest, light, simple and optional Finnish system was prepared rapidly and is already functioning, whereas the implementation of the English plan has been postponed without any specific schedule. An optional system does not have to be comprehensive, it can be introduced in stages and it can be developed alongside its use. The originally planned English system seems to have a high introduction threshold.

There are significant differences in the technical solutions. The English plan is founded on electronic and encrypted documents written by the parties and sent between them as well as to the Registrar at many stages with the help of the open Internet. The three-step procedure of conveyance contains a contract, disposition and registration. Even the drafts are intended to be sent. The electronic signature is supposed to be created with smart cards and their certification.

Here, the English plan has met a crucial problem. So far, there seems to be no serviceable and widely spread electronic signature method or applications available. This is one obvious obstacle in realising the English plan. In Finland, the problem has been solved with the popular TUPAS identification and certification method provided by banks. TUPAS is a closed system founded on contracts between the participants in the system.

The Finnish electronic trading system is founded on a closed system, official platform and web sites maintained by the register authority. It is a public service. Identification and its certification take place when a party of a transaction logs into the conveyancing site. Both parties log into the same page and they can both contribute to the preparation of the same contract text. In these frameworks, the electronic signature can be a simple acceptance of the agreed text written on the site. The conveyance contains merely two steps: the contract appearing simultaneously as the disposition, and registration. Both the contract and its registration take place in the same technical system maintained by the Registrar. In addition, the conveyancing site is connected to the official registers.

The Finnish system is centralised. The entire closed system of electronic trading is maintained by the Registrar. On the other hand, certifiers certifying the identification of parties and authentication of their commitments – in practice, in the form of the TUPAS service – are private partners. On the other hand, as a closed system the Finnish electronic conveyancing may prove to be safe enough.

The English plan involves a distributed process. It is founded on the extensive employment of the open Internet. Parties are supposed to access the system on their personal computers, identify themselves and authenticate texts and commitments with the help of smart cards, use independent certifiers and send encrypted electronic texts and documents back and forth as well as to the Registrar at many stages. Moreover, professionals acting as agents of the parties are planned to be responsible for carrying out the functions of the Registrar. The planned English system seems to be more vulnerable to hacking and other abuse.

General Bibliography

Adal, E., *Fundamentals of Turkish Private Law*, 8th edn. (İstanbul, 2005)

Agell, A. and Brattström, M., *Äktenskap. Samboende. Partnerskap*, 5th edn. (Uppsala, 2011)

Ahrens, C., *Dingliche Nutzungsrechte, Nießbrauch – Dienstbarkeiten – Wohnungsrechte*, 2nd edn. (Berlin, 2007)

Albaladejo, M., *Derecho Civil*, t. III, vol. I and II. *Derecho De Bienes*, 11th edn. (Madrid, 2010)

Albuquerque, P., *Direitos Reais – Relatório sobre o Programa, Conteúdo e Métodos de Ensino* (Coimbra, 2009)

Amadio G., *I diritti edificatori: la prospettiva del civilista, in urbanistica e attività notarile. nuovi strumenti di pianificazione del territorio e sicurezza delle contrattazioni. atti del convegno* (Milan, 2012)

Andersen, L. L. and Madsen, P. B., *Aftaler og mellemmænd*, 6th edn. (Copenhagen, 2012)

Ansay, T. and Wallace, D., Jr (eds.), *Introduction to Turkish Law* (The Hague, 1996)

Antonmattéi, P. H. and Raynard, J., *Droit civil – Contrats spéciaux*, 6th edn. (Paris, 2008)

Antunes, V. and Mesquita, H., 'Anotação ao Acórdão do STJ de 3 de Junho de 1992', 126 *RLJ* (1994), pp. 19ff. and 127 *RLJ* (1997), pp. 31ff.

Aydoğdu, M. and Kahveci, N., *Türk Borçlar Hukuku Özel Borç İlişkileri* (İzmir, 2013)

Balensiefen, G., Bönker, C., Geiger, N. and Schaller, W. (eds.), *Rechtshandbuch für die Immobilienpraxis: Erwerb, Entwicklung, Bestandshaltung, Vermarktung*, 1st edn. (Munich, 2009)

Baralis, G., 'Riflessioni sull'atto di opposizione alla donazione a seguito della modifica dell'art. 563 CC', *Riv. Not.* (2006), pp. 277ff.

Bartels, S. E. and van Mierlo, A. I. M., *Asser 3–IV Algemeen goederenrecht* (Deventer, 2013)

Bassi, M., *Compendio di diritto tavolare* (Mariano del friuli, 2010)

Basty, G., *Der Bauträgervertrag*, 8th edn. (Cologne 2014)

Bauer, H. J. and Oefele, H. F. (eds.), *Grundbuchordnung: GBO*, 3rd edn. (Munich, 2013)

Baur, J. F. and Stürner, R., *Sachenrecht*, 18th edn. (Munich, 2009)

Bechini, U., 'La trascrizione del contratto preliminare', *Riv. Not.* (1999), pp. 241ff.
Bengtsson, B., *Sakrättsliga frågor i fastighetsrätten*, 6th edn. (Uppsala, 1991)
Bengtsson, B., Hager, R. and Victorin, A., *Hyra och annan nyttjanderätt till fast egendom*, 8th edn. (Stockholm, 2013)
Bercovitz, Rodríguez-Cano *et al.*, *Manual De Derecho Civil, Derechos Reales*, 3rd edn. (Madrid, 2012)
Bergel, J. L., Bruschi, M. and Cimamonti, S., *Traité de droit civil – Les biens*, 2nd edn. (Paris, 2010)
Biehler, H., *Equity and the Law of Trusts in Ireland*, 6th edn. (Dublin, 2015)
Black, R.,'Practice and Precept in Scots Law', 31 *Juridical Review* (1982), pp. 31ff.
Blanluet, G., 'Le moment du transfert de la propriété', in *1804–2004, Le Code civil, un passé, un présent, un avenir* (Paris, 2004), pp. 409ff.
Bloch, P., 'L'obligation de transférer la propriété dans la vente', *RTD civ.* (1988), pp. 694ff.
Blokland, P., *Teksten en toelichting op de Wet op het notarisambt*, 2nd edn. (Lelystad, 2001)
Borgar, H. B. and Bråthen-Otterbech, S., *Tinglysing. Lov om tinglysing 7. juni 1935 nr. 2 med kommentarer* (Oslo, 2009)
Böttcher, R. and Keller, U., *ZVG – Gesetz über die Zwangsversteigerung und Zwangsverwaltung – Kommentar*, 6th edn. (Munich, 2016)
Brand, D. A., Steven, A. J. M. and Wortley, S., *Professor McDonald's Conveyancing Manual*, 7th edn. (Edinburgh, 2004)
Braun, E. (ed.), *Insolvenzordnung: (InsO)*, 7th edn. (Munich, 2017)
Carbonnier, J., *Droit civil – Les biens*, 19th edn., PUF coll., 2002
Carlsen, B. K. *et. al.*, *Juridisk formularbog*, 16th edn. (Copenhagen, 2004)
Carlson, L., *An Introduction to Swedish Real Property Law* (Stockholm, 2008)
Carvalho Fernandes, L., 'Terceiros para Efeitos de Registo Predial', 57 *ROA* (1997), pp. 1283–1320
Lições de Direitos Reais, 6th edn. (Lisbon, 2009)
Carvalho, O., *Direito das Coisas* (Coimbra, 1977)
'Terceiros para Efeitos de Registo' *BFD* (1994), pp. 97–106
Castán Tobeñas, J., *Derecho Civil Español Común Y Foral*, t. II, vols. I and II (Madrid, 1992–4)
Castronovo, C., 'Acquisto "a non domino" e pubblica fede in tema di regolarizzazione del titolo di proprietà', *Riv. trim. dir. proc. civ.* (1971), pp. 1136ff.
Chazal, J. P. and Vicente, S., 'Le transfert de propriété par l'effet des obligations dans le code civil', *RTD civ.* (2000), pp. 477ff.
Cian, G., 'La trascrivibilità del preliminare (Ex Art. 3 D.L. 31 Dicembre 1996 N. 669)', 137 *Studium Iuris* (1997), pp. 215ff.
Conaglen, M., 'Mortgagee Powers Rhetoric', 69 *MLR* (2006), pp. 583ff.
Conway, H., *Co-Ownership of Land – Partition Actions and Remedies*, 2nd edn. (Dublin, 2012)
Courdier-Cuisinier, A. S., 'Nouvel éclairage sur l'énigme de l'obligation de donner', *RTD civ.* (2005), pp. 521ff.

Coutant, C., 'La réitération des promesses synallagmatiques de vente', *AJPI* (2009), pp. 127ff.

Cusine, D. J. and Paisley, R. R. M., *Servitudes and Rights of Way* (Edinburgh, 1998)

Daprà , S., *Il libro fondiario nelle nuove provincie e la sua popolarità nel Trentino, Riv. Dir. Agr.* (1934), pp. 585ff.

De Londras, F., *Principles of Irish Property Law*, 2nd edn. (Dublin, 2011)

De Page, H. and Meinertzhagen-Limpens, A., *Traité Élémentaire De Droit Civil Belge* (Brussels, 2013)

Del Corral, J., *De Leveringsplicht Bij De Overdracht Van Roerende Lichamelijke Goederen* (Antwerp, 2012)

Demharter, J., *Grundbuchordnung*, 30th edn. (Munich, 2016)

Di Simone, M. R., 'L'introduzione del codice civile austriaco in italia. Aspetti e momenti', *Scintillae Iuris – Studi In Memoria Di Gino Gorla* (Milan, 1994)

Díez-Picazo, L. and Ponce De León, L., *Fundamentos De Derecho Civil Patrimonial*, t. IV, *Derechos Reales* (Madrid, 2012)

Dross, W., *Droit civil – Les choses* (Paris, 2012)

Duarte Soares, Q., 'O Conceito de Terceiros para Efeitos de Registo Predial', 9 *Cadernos Direito Privado* (2005), pp. 3ff.

Eickmann, D. and Böttcher, R., *Zwangsversteigerungs-und Zwangsverwaltungsrecht*, 3rd edn. (Munich, 2013)

Erman, W. (ed. Westermann, H. P., Grunewald, B. and Maier-Reimer, G.), *Bürgerliches Gesetzbuch – BGB: Handkommentar*, 14th edn. (Cologne, 2014)

Ertaş Ş., *Yeni Türk Medeni Kanunu Hükümlerine Göre Eşya Hukuku, Gözden Geçirilmiş ve Genişletilmiş, 4. Baskı* (Ankara, 2002)

Fabre-Magnan, F., 'Le mythe de l'obligation de donner', *RTD civ.* (1996), pp. 85ff.

Falkanger, T. and Falkanger, A. T., *Tingsrett* (Oslo, 2016)

Ferrante, E., *Consesualismo e Trascrizione* (Padua, 2008)

Ferreira de Almeida, C., *Publicidade e Teoria dos Registos* (Coimbra, 1966)

Ferri, L., 'Doppia alienazione immobiliare e buona fede nel sistema dei Libri Fondiari', *Riv. Trim. Dir. Proc. Civ.* (1951), pp. 1136ff.

Fitzgerald, B., *Land Registry Practice*, 2nd edn. (Dublin, 1995)

Fournier, A., *Le malaise actuel dans le droit de la publicité foncière* (Paris, 1980)

Fox, D., 'Forgery and Alteration of the Register under the Land Registration Act 2002', in Cooke, E. (ed.), *Modern Studies in Property Law – Vol III Property 2004* (Oxford, 2005)

Gabrielli, G., *La pubblicità legale nel sistema del codice civile, Riv. Dir. Civ.* (1992), pp. 455ff.

La pubblicità immobiliare del contratto preliminare, Riv. Dir. Civ. (1997), pp. 529ff.

Garcia, M. O., *Arrendamento Urbano Anotado* (Coimbra, 2012)

Gautier, P.-Y., 'Bien aimée responsabilité civile – exercice de controverse doctrinale sur le thème de la publicité foncière', in *Rupture, mouvements et continuité du droit* (Paris, 2004), pp. 361ff.

Gazzoni, F., 'Trascrizione del preliminare di vendita e obbligo di dare', *Riv. Not.* (1997), pp. 19ff.

Georgiadis, S., *Apostolos, Property Law, vol. II*, 2nd edn. (Athens, 2010)
Ghestin, J. and Desché, B., *Traité des Contrats La vente* (Paris: LGDJ, 1990)
González, J. A., *Direitos Reais e Direito Registal Imobiliário*, 4th edn. (Lisbon, 2009)
Gordon, W. M., *Scottish Land Law*, 2nd edn. (Edinburgh, 1999)
Roman Law, Scots Law and Legal History (Edinburgh, 2007)
Gordon, W. M. and Wortley, S., *Scottish Land Law*, 3rd edn., 2 vols. (Edinburgh, 2009)
Grauers, F., *Fastighetsköp*, 21st edn. (Lund, 2016)
'Köp, byte och gåva. Jordabalk', (1970:994), in the Karnov database, 1 July 2016
Gray, K. and Gray, S. F., *Elements of Land Law*, 4th edn, (Oxford, 2005)
Gregow, T., *Samägd egendom* (Stockholm, 2016)
Gretton, G. L. and Reid, K. G. C., *Conveyancing*, 4th edn. (Edinburgh, 2011)
Gretton G. L. and Steven, A. J. M., *Property, Trusts and Succession*, 2nd edn. (Haywards Heath, 2013)
Gümüş M. A., *Türk Medeni Kanununun Getirdiği Yeni Şerhler, 1. Baskı* (Ankara, 2003)
'Yeni' 6098 Sayılı Türk Borçlar Kanunu'na Göre Kira Sözleşmesi (TBK. m. 299–356) (İstanbul, 2011)
Hellner, J., Hager, R. and Persson, A., *Speciell avtalsrätt II – Kontraktsrätt. Första häftet. Särskilda avtalstyper*, 7th edn. (Stockholm, 2015)
Hellner, J. and Radetzki, M., *Skadeståndsrätt*, 9th edn. (Stockholm, 2014)
Henrique Mesquita, M., *Direitos Reais* (Coimbra, 1967)
Obrigações Reais e Ónus Reais (Coimbra, 1990)
Hessler, H., *Nya jordabalken. Kap 16 och 18. Hävd och godtrosförvärv*, 4th edn. (Stockholm, 1983)
Hillert, S., *Servitut*, 2nd edn. (Uppsala, 1984)
Hinteregger, M., in Van Erp, S. and Akkermans, B. (eds.), *Cases, Materials and Text on Property Law*, Chapter 8, II and IV (Oxford, 2012)
Hoffmann, B. von, *Das Recht des Grundstückskaufs. Eine rechtsvergleichende Untersuchung* (Tübingen, 1982)
Huet, J., 'Des différentes sortes d'obligations et, plus particulièrement, de l'obligation de donner, la mal nommée, la mail aimée', *Études Jacques Ghestin* (Paris, 2001), pp. 425ff.
Huet, J., Decocq, G., Grimaldi, C. and Lécuyer, H., *Traité de droit civil – Les principaux contrats spéciaux*, 3rd edn. (Paris, 2012)
Huijgen, W. G. and Pleysier, A. J. H., *De wetgeving op het notarisambt*, 2nd edn. (Deventer, 2001)
Jansen, R., *Beschikkingsonbevoegdheid* (Antwerp, 2008)
Jardim, M., 'Efeitos do Registo da Penhora Convertido em Definitivo nos Termos do Artigo 119 do Código do Registo Predial', *9 Cadernos de Direito Privado* (2005), pp. 23–42
Jensen, C. H. *et al.*, *Dansk Privatret*, 18th edn. (Copenhagen, 2014)
Jensen, U., *Panträtt i fast egendom*, 10th edn. (Uppsala, 2016)
'16 kap. Hävd till fast egendom, Jordabalk' (1970:994), in the Karnov database, 1 July 2016
Johnston, D., *Prescription and Limitation*, 2nd edn. (Edinburgh, 2012)

Jokela, M., Kartio, L. and Ojanen, I., *Maakaari: The Code of Real Estate* (Helsinki, 2010)
Julstad, B., 'Sverige', in *Dannelse og transaktioner vedrørende fast ejendom i de nordiske lande* (Copenhagen, 2006)
Kılıçoğlu, A., *Türk Medenî Kanunu'nda Diğer Eşin Rızasına Bağlı Hukuksal İşlemler ve Yasal Alım Hakkı* (Ankara, 2002)
Krauß, H. F., *Immobilienkaufverträge in der Praxis – Gestaltung, Besteuerung*, 6th edn. (Münster and Cologne, 2012)
Krüger, W. and Hertel, C., *Der Grundstückskauf: höchstrichterliche Rechtsprechung und notarielle Gestaltungshinweise*, 10th edn. (Cologne, 2012)
Kuru, B., *İcra ve İflâs Hukuku İkinci Tıpkı Baskı* (İstanbul, 2006)
Kuru, B., Arslan. R., Yılmaz, E. and Medenî, *Usul Hukuku Değiştirilmiş, 18. Baskı* (Ankara, 2004)
Lacruz Berdejo, J. L., *Derecho Inmobiliario Registral* (Madrid, 2011)
Elementos De Derecho Civil, III, Derechos Reales, vol. 1 and 2 (Madrid, 2008 and 2009)
Lasarte, C., *Principios De Derecho Civil*, t. IV and V, 10th and 8th edn. (Madrid, 2010)
Lecocq, P., *Manuel De Droit Des Biens* (Brussels, 2013)
Lilleholt, K., *Allmenn formuerett* (Oslo, 2012)
Lødrup, P. and Sverdrup, T., *Familieretten*, 8th edn. (Oslo, 2016)
López, Á., Montés, V. and Roca, E. (coord. Clemente, M.), *Derecho Civil – Derechos Reales y Derecho Inmobiliario Registral*, 2nd edn. (Valencia, 2001)
Lyall, A., *Land Law in Ireland*, 3rd edn. (Dublin, 2010)
Madsen, P. B. *et al.*, *Formueretlige Emner*, 7th edn. (Copenhagen, 2013)
Malaurie, Ph., Aynès, L. and Crocq, P., *Les sûretés, la publicité foncière*, 5th edn. (Paris, 2015)
Martínez Velencoso, L. M., 'Conflicts of Interest and New Prospectives for the Spanish Land Register: a Comparative View', in Wudarski, A., *Land Register Functions in a European Perspective* (Berlin, 2016)
Marty, G., Raynaud P. and Jourdain, P., *Les biens* (Paris, 1995)
McAllister, A., *Scottish Law of Leases*, 4th edn. (Haywards Heath, 2013)
McCarthy, F., Chalmers J. and Bogle, S. (eds.), *Essays in Conveyancing and Property Law in Honour of Professor Robert Rennie* (Cambridge, 2015)
Meagher, R. P., Heydon, J. D. and Leeming, M. J., *Meagher, Gummow & Lehane's Equity: Doctrines and Remedies*, 4th edn. (Sydney, 2002)
Menezes Cordeiro, A., *Tratado de Direito Civil Português, II*, 3rd edn. (Coimbra, 2005)
Menezes Leitão, L., *Direitos Reais* (Coimbra, 2009)
Direito da Insolvência, 2nd edn. (Coimbra, 2015)
Direito das Obrigações, vol. I, 13th edn. (Coimbra, 2016)
Mengoni, L., 'La pubblicità del contratto preliminare e dei contratti condizionati nei libri fondiari', *Riv. Trim. Dir. Proc. Civ.* (1998), pp. 993ff.
Mortensen, P., *Digital tinglysning – rettigheder over fast ejendom*, 8th edn. (Copenhagen, 2007)
Indledning til tingsretten, 2nd edn. (Copenhagen, 2009)
Neubauer, E., *Easements und Servitudes – Eine rechtsvergleichende Untersuchung zu Grunddienstbarkeiten im englischen und schottischen Recht* (Berlin, 2012)

Nial, H., *Om handelsbolag och enkla bolag*, 3rd edn. (Stockholm, 1992)
Nial, H. and Hemström, C., *Om handelsbolag och enkla bolag*, 4th edn. (Stockholm, 2008)
Nicolussi, A., *Lesione del potere di disposizione e arricchimento. Un'indagine sul danno non aquiliano* (Milan, 1998)
Niemi, M. I., *Maakaaren järjestelmä III (The System of the Code of Real Estate III)* (Helsinki, 2010)
Maakaaren järjestelmä II (The System of the Code of Real Estate II) (Helsinki, 2012)
Maakaaren järjestelmä I (The System of the Code of Real Estate I) (Helsinki, 2016)
Oakley, A. J., 'Pecuniary Compensation for Failure to Complete a Contract for the Sale of Land', 39 *CLJ* (1980), pp. 58ff.
Oğuzman, K., *Turkey, trans. Toker Dereli* (The Hague, London and Boston, 1996)
Oğuzman, M. K. and Barlas, N., *Medeni Hukuk: Giriş-Kaynaklar-Temel Kavramlar 13. Bası* (İstanbul, 2006)
Oğuzman, M. K. and Öz, M. T., *Borçlar Hukuku: Genel Hükümler Gözden Geçirilmiş ve Genişletilmiş Dördüncü Bası* (İstanbul, 2005)
Oğuzman, M. K., Seliçi, Ö. and Oktay-Özdemir, S., *E°ya Hukuku Gözden Geçirilmiş 11. Bası* (İstanbul, 2006)
Oliveira Ascensão, J. A., *Tipicidade dos Direitos Reais* (Lisbon, 1968)
Direito Civil, Reais, 5th edn. (Coimbra, 1993)
Paisley, R. R. M., *Land Law* (Edinburgh, 2000)
Palandt, O., *Bürgerliches Gesetzbuch*, 76th edn. (Munich, 2017)
Passinhas, S., *Assembleia de Condóminos e o Administrador na Propriedade Horizontal*, 2nd edn. (Coimbra, 2002)
Property and Trust Law in Portugal (Deventer, 2012)
Pause, H. E., *Bauträgerkauf und Baumodelle*, 5th edn. (Munich, 2011)
Pearce, R. and Mee, J., *Land Law*, 3rd edn. (Dublin, 2011)
Pedersen, A. G. and Pedersen, H. V. G., *Familie-og arveret*, 8th edn. (Copenhagen, 2013)
Peña Bernaldo De Quirós, M., *Derechos Reales. Derecho Hipotecario*, 4th edn. (Madrid, 2011)
Pereira Mendes, I., *Código do Registo Predial – Anotado e Comentado*, 17th edn. (Coimbra, 2009)
Piedelièvre, S., *Traité de droit civil – La publicité foncière* (Paris, 2000)
Pinto Duarte, R., *Tipicidade e Atipicidade dos Contratos* (Coimbra, 2000)
Curso de Direitos Reais (Lisbon, 2007)
Puig Brutau, J., *Fundamentos De Derecho Civil*, t. III, 4th edn. (Barcelona, 1994)
Puig Peña, F., *Tratado De Derecho Civil Español*, t. III, vol. 1 (Madrid, 1958)
Reid, K. G. C., *The Law of Property in Scotland* (Edinburgh, 1996)
Reid, K. G. C. and Gretton, G. L., *Land Registration* (Edinburgh, 2017)
Rennie, R., *Conveyancing in the Electronic Age* (Edinburgh, 2008)
Leases (Edinburgh, 2015)
Riedel, E., Volmer, M., Wilsch, H., Schöner, H. and Stöber, K., *Grundbuchrecht*, 16th edn. (Munich, 2017)

Roca Sastre, R. M. and Roca Sastre Muncunill, L., *Derecho Hipotecario*, t. 9, 9th edn. (Barcelona, 2008 and 2009)
Rogers, W. V. H., *Winfield & Jolowicz on Tort*, 17th edn. (London, 2006)
Rosenmeier, H. P., *Mangler ved fast ejendom*, 6th edn. (Copenhagen, 2013)
Sacco, R., *Autonomia contrattuale e tipi, Riv. Trim. Dir. Proc. Civ.* (1966), pp. 785ff.
Sagaert, V., 'Het rechtmatig vertrouwen van de schuldeisers in de hypothecaire gegisters', in *Feestbundel Achilles Cuypers* (Brussels, 2009), pp. 221ff.
'Goederenrecht', in *Beginselen Van Belgisch Privaatrecht* (Mechelen, 2014), pp. 785ff.
Saint-Alary-Houin, C., *Réflexions sur le transfert différé de la propriété immobilière* (Paris, 1985)
Santos Justo, A., *Direitos Reais*, 4th edn. (Coimbra, 2012)
Schmidt-Szalewski, J., 'Le rôle de l'acte authentique dans la vente immobilière', *RD imm.* (1989), pp. 147ff.
Schütz, R. N., *L'exécution des promesses de vente* (Paris, 1999)
Scottish Law Commission, Report No 222 on Land Registration, 2 vols. (Edinburgh, 2010)
Simler, P. and Delebecque, Ph., *Les sûretés, la publicité foncière*, 6th edn. (Paris, 2002)
Şıp, Ş., *Aile Konutu ile İlgili İşlemlerde Diğer Eşin Rızası (TMK. m. 194)* (İstanbul, 2004)
Sirmen, L., *Eşya Hukuku Dersleri* (Ankara, 1995)
Steiner, A. and Eickmann, D., *Zwangsversteigerung und Zwangsverwaltung – Kommentar*, vol. 1, 9th edn. (Munich, 1984)
Stewart, A. and Sinclair, E., *Conveyancing Practice in Scotland*, 7th edn. (Haywards Heath, 2016)
Stöber, K., *Zwangsversteigerungsgesetz*, 21st edn. (Munich, 2016)
Strang, C., 'Sverige', in *Ejendomsregistrering i de nordiske lande* (Copenhagen, 2006)
Swiss–American Chamber of Commerce, *Swiss Code of Obligations: English Translation of Official Text*, vol. I (Zürich, 2002)
Tegnander, H., *Fastighetsskatt och fastighetsavgift*, 2nd edn. (Stockholm, 2008)
Teixeira de Sousa, M., 'Sobre o Conceito de Terceiros para Efeitos de Registo', 59 *ROA* (1999), pp. 29ff.
Tepora, J., Kartio, L., Koulu, R. and Lindfors, H., *Kiinteistön kauppa, muu luovutus ja kirjaus ('Sale of Real Estate, Other Conveyances and Registration')* (Helsinki, 2010)
Terré, F. and Simler, P., *Droit civil – Les biens*, 9th edn. (Paris, 2014)
Tilleman, B., 'De Totstandkoming en de Kwalificatie van de Koop', in *Beginselen Van Belgisch Privaatrecht* (Mechelen, 2001), pp. 681ff.
Trabucchi, A., 'La pubblicità immobiliare un sistema in evoluzione', *Riv. Dir. Hipotecario* (1982), pp. 106ff.
Turner, P. G., 'Understanding the Constructive Trust between Vendor and Purchaser', 128 *LQR* (2012), pp. 582ff.
Van der Merwe, C. and Verbeke A. L. (eds.), *Time-Limited Interests in Land* (Cambridge, 2012)
Van Vliet, L., *Transfer of Movables in German, French, English and Dutch Law* (Nijmegen, 2000)

Van Zeben, C. J. and Du Pon, J. W. (eds.), *Parlementaire Geschiedenis van het Nieuwe Burgerlijk Wetboek, Boek 3, Vermogensrecht in het algemeen* (Deventer, 1981)
Vettori, G., *Consenso traslativo e circolazione dei beni. Analisi di un principio* (Milan, 1995)
'Circolazione dei beni e ordinamento comunitario', *Riv. Dir. Priv.* (2008), pp. 285ff.
Victorin, A. and Flodin, J., *Bostadsrätt med en översikt över kooperativ hyresrätt*, 4th edn. (Uppsala, 2016)
Victorin, A. and Hager, R., *Allmän fastighetsrätt*, 7th edn. (Uppsala, 2015)
Videira Henriques, P., 'Terceiros para efeitos do artigo 5.º do Código do Registo Predial', *BFD* (2003), pp. 389ff.
Vieira, J. A., *Direitos reais: perspectiva histórica do seu ensino em Portugal* (Lisbon, 2008)
Vitucci, G., 'Proprietà e obbligazioni: il catalogo delle fonti dall'europa al diritto privato regionale', *Eur. Dir. Priv.* (2002), pp. 747ff.
Von Esben, B. and Isager, H., *Lærebog i erstatningsret*, 8th edn. (Copenhagen, 2015)
Wagemann, S. K., *Funktion und Bedeutung von Grundstücksregistern – Eine rechtsvergleichende Studie zum Liegenschaftsrecht von Deutschland, England und Frankreich* (Heidelberg, 2002)
Waldner, W., *Immobilienkaufverträge*, 2nd edn. (Munich, 2011)
Walin, G., *Samäganderätt* (Stockholm, 2000)
Walin, G., Gregow, T., Löfmarck, P., Millqvist, G. and Persson, A. H., *Utsokningsbalken*, 4th edn. (Stockholm, 2009)
Westermann, H. P., Eickmann, D. and Gursky, K. H., *Sachenrecht*, 8th edn. (Heidelberg, 2011)
Wettstein, G., *The Swiss Federal Code Of Obligations* (Zürich, 1928)
Wilhelm, J., *Sachenrecht*, 5th edn. (Berlin, 2016)
Williams, I., Wyle, S. and Wyler, B., *The Swiss Civil Code English Version, I–II* (Zürich, 1987)
Willumsen, H., *Tinglysningsloven med kommentarer*, 2nd edn. (Copenhagen, 1997)
Wylie, J. C. W., *Landlord and Tenant Law*, 3rd edn. (Dublin, 2014)
The Land and Conveyancing Law Reform Act 2009: Annotations and Commentary (Dublin, 2009)
Irish Land Law, 5th edn. (Dublin, 2013)
Wylie, J. C. W. and Woods, U., *Irish Conveyancing Law*, 3rd edn. (Haywards Heath, 2005).
Yavuz, C., *Borçlar Hukuku Dersleri (Özel Hükümler) 6098 Sayılı Türk Borçlar Kanunu'na Göre Güncellenmiş ve Yenilenmiş 11. Baskı* (İstanbul, 2012)
Zenati-Castaing, F. and Revet, T., *Droit des biens*, 3rd edn., PUF coll. Droit fondamental, 2008
Zweigert, K. and Kötz, H., *An introduction to Comparative Law* (Amsterdam, New York and Oxford, 1977)

PART II
Case Studies

(1)

The Questionnaire

Case 1

James was walking down a street in your town and saw a beautiful house. A man was working in the garden – Paul; James asked if the house was his, and he said it was. How can James check that this is true?

Case 2

Andrew wants to buy Barbara's house, and she is willing to sell it to him. What professionals might Andrew engage in order to complete his purchase?

(a) What professionals *must* he engage in order to complete this purchase?
(b) What will the professionals do?
(c) Please indicate the source of payment for each of the professionals you have mentioned under (a) and (b) above (e.g. Andrew pays, or the state pays).

Case 3

Andrew has offered to buy Barbara's house; she has agreed to sell to him, and they have agreed a price.

(a) What is the effect, if any, of this unwritten agreement? If either party changes their mind now, does the other have a remedy?
(b) Andrew and Barbara write down their agreement and sign it. What is the legal effect of this, if any? If either party changes their mind now, does the other have a remedy?

Case 4

Barbara and Andrew, from case 3 above, have now made a valid contract for sale of Barbara's house to Andrew.

(a) If either party now has a change of mind and does not want to perform the obligations under the contract, does the other have a remedy?
(b) If Andrew becomes insolvent after he has entered into the contract with Barbara, does the house form part of his property so as to be available to his creditors?

Case 5

Peter is the registered owner of a flat. He sells the flat to Elizabeth who moves in but does not register her title. Peter then sells the flat to Margaret who pays the price and registers her purchase. Margaret sues Elizabeth to recover possession of the flat. Will she succeed?

Case 6

Albert owns a house. Albert has an identical twin brother called George. Unknown to Albert, George pretends to be Albert and produces false documents to prove it. He concludes a sale of Albert's house to Bolesław, and disappears. Bolesław's purchase is registered. Bolesław does not know about the deception.

(a) Can Albert get the house back?
(b) If not, will he get any compensation?
(c) Does it make any difference if Bolesław knows about the deception?

Bolesław sells the house to Mieszko before Albert discovers what has happened.

(d) Can Albert get the house back?

Case 7

Henry wants to buy a new house. He finds a new development, in an area he likes; X Ltd owns the site and had planning permission to build thirty houses. Henry likes their plans so much that he wants to buy one now, even though the houses have not yet been built. What should he do?

Case 8

Michele and Joanna want to live together and buy a house. They contact an estate agency, and are shown a beautiful house near the city centre.

They decide to buy the house. Seven days after the completion of their purchase, they discover some cracks in the bedroom wall. An architect explains to them that the construction of the building is seriously defective. Do Michele and Joanna have any remedy and, if so, what is it?

Case 9

Oliver has agreed to buy a house in a residential area from Polly, but has not yet paid the price. Polly has not yet moved out and Oliver has not yet moved in. A week after the agreement a young mother was walking past the house, pushing her baby in a pram. A plant fell off the balcony and injured the child.

(a) Who would be responsible for the damages?
(b) Would your answer differ if what fell was not a plant but part of the roof?

Case 10

Charles has a ten-year lease of a flat owned by David for ten years. Five years after the commencement of the lease, David sells the flat to Edward, who wants to move in immediately.

(a) Can Edward move into the flat?
(b) Would your answer differ if this was a business lease?

Case 11

Philip bought a field from Quentin. The field has direct access on to the main road through a gate; but it was a term of the agreement that Philip would also be allowed to use a road that passes through Quentin's adjoining farm in order to get to another road. Quentin sells the farm to Richard. Richard has put up a gate to prevent Philip from using the road.

(a) Is Philip still entitled to pass through the field?
(b) Would it make any difference if Richard knew about Philip's right before he bought the land?
(c) Would it make any difference if Richard was a close friend of Quentin; Quentin wanted to stop Philip using the road. Quentin and Richard agreed that Richard would buy the farm in order to prevent Philip from using the road, and that Richard would later sell the farm back to Quentin.

Case 12

Dodgy Dealings Ltd owns a large piece of land, Blackacre. Blackacre is its only asset. It has failed to pay a substantial debt to Z Ltd. Z Ltd sues the company in order to recover the debt. On September 1 Dodgy Dealings Ltd agrees to sell Blackacre to Victoria. On October 1 an order is made, charging Blackacre with the debt. On November 1 Victoria registers her purchase of the land. Can Z Ltd enforce its debt against the land?

(a) Would it make any difference if Victoria knew about the proceedings?
(b) Does Z Ltd have any other rights against the land?

Case 13

Hans bought a house. Helda has made a significant contribution to the purchase price.

(a) Hans is selling the house to Chris. Helda finds out and wants to prevent the sale. Will she succeed?
(b) Hans has mortgaged the house to the Bank and has failed to pay. The Bank seeks possession of the property. Can the Bank remove Helda?
(c) Would your answer to (a) or (b) differ if Hans and Helda were married?

Case 14

Roberto and Susane are married. During the marriage Roberto inherits a house and the couple now lives there. Roberto wants to sell the house to Andrea.

(a) Susane wants to prevent the sale. Will she succeed?
(b) How would your answer differ if Roberto and Susane were living together but not married?

Case 15

Joseph owns a farm but lives in town and has not visited it for many years. Jacob has been living and working there for many years without Joseph's consent.

(a) Joseph sues to recover possession of the farm. Will he succeed?
(b) If Joseph sells the farm to Steven who then sues Jacob to recover possession, will Steven succeed?

The study of the cases proposed in this volume has been made according to the 'Common Core of International Private Law' methodology. Concretely, the aim of the questionnaire was to analyse the process of transfer in each jurisdiction and also the role and structure of the Land Register, searching for hidden analogies and differences among the different European jurisdictions.

In this field, the distinction between common law and civil law was an important issue in the redaction of the questionnaire, because all of the circumstances that affect the law in any one of the systems needed to be addressed also in all the other systems, in which such circumstances may have no practical impact or to the contrary produce a particularly important distinction from the perspective of the Common Core project, that is between legal and equitable rights, which do not exist in civil law countries.

Of course, each question was aimed at obtaining data, but without assuming anything in advance. For instance, in case 1 the aim of this question was to express the value and functions of the Land Register in each jurisdiction, nevertheless it did not directly query what kind of Land Register is present in the reporter's country, but rather how the reporter knows that the person that is willing to sell an immovable is its true owner.

Similarly, in case 2 the objective was to obtain data about which professionals are involved in the process of transfer (whether the legal system is a notarial system or not).

And cases 3 and 4 ask the reporter to explore the form of the agreement to pass property.

Case 5 explores the problem of the double sale and the issue of a good faith acquisition recorded in the Land Register. In this case, it is stated that the one who bought the flat moved into the flat. This was an important detail because in some jurisdictions, especially in common law jurisdictions, to use the immovable for residential purposes could be a signal of the existence of an equitable interest that could bind the third purchaser of the immovable. While in other jurisdictions it would not have any effect to actually reside in the immovable property.

Case 6 involves the question of an invalid contract that could produce an effect on the transfer, even if the system is a causal one or an abstract one.[1]

[1] As per the classification of the different systems of transferring property in Europe, 'causal' means that if the sale is void the transfer is also void (as in Spain), 'abstract' means the contrary (as in Germany).

Case 7 takes into account the frequently arising situation of an acquisition of a house that is yet to be constructed. In the draft questionnaire it was written ‘flat’. Finally, there was a consensus among the reporters, that the reference to flats is somewhat controversial given that there are different rules that apply to flats as distinct from other forms of immovable property, and for that reason the specific reference to flats was removed. Since we are in general not specifically addressing apartment ownership in a given jurisdiction we opted for the term ‘house’.

Another point of discussion in case 7 was the position of the seller in relation to the immovable. For that reason, we indicated that the seller ‘owns’ the development site in order to keep it simple, and to exclude the possibility of Henry having to deal with an unknown third party to buy the plot of land on which the house would be built. Nevertheless, if the word ‘own’ presented a problem to reporters due to its vague and essentialised nature, they were free to suggest alternative ways to express this in a way more suited to how such ‘ownership’ actually operated in their jurisdiction.

Case 8 is aimed at obtaining information about the defects of the immovable transferred, especially if the defects of the immovable appear after the sale was complete.

Case 9 deals with the treatment of responsibility for the damages caused by the immovable or pieces of it to third parties. This case was intended to deal with some of the complexities regarding the possession of the flat. The point about possession is important here; and we have added an alternative that will make a difference in some systems regarding the duty of care, which is implicit in the first subquestion.

In Case 10 the immovable sold was leased to someone else. The question here is if the new acquirer is bound to this lease. In this case, the reporters from England, Ireland and Scotland added details relevant to the importance of the lessee’s possession in some cases.

Case 11 deals with the ‘right to pass’, which required some terminological discussion that resulted in an agreement to use the terms ‘easement’ and ‘servitude’ as equivalents in this context. We also agreed that the question was not related to an easement of necessity.

Case 12 applies to those jurisdictions in which the transfer of property is conceived of as a process and not taking place precisely at any one unique stage.

Case 13 explores the unique case for ‘common law’ jurisdictions where it is possible for an individual to gain an equitable proprietary interest in another's property, either by contributing to its purchase or by detrimental reliance on the promise of shared ownership.

Case 14 is about marital property regimes. In civil law jurisdictions this question is solved in several Civil Codes.

Finally Case 15 deals with the issue of adverse possession. The law relating to adverse possession operates predominantly in the common law world, with the extent of its application varying where title is registered. While the doctrine is less dominant in civil law jurisdictions, we note a similar relationship between the doctrine and registration of title.

(II)

Synthesis of Comparative Case Studies by Jurisdiction

Case 1

James was walking down a street in your town and saw a beautiful house. A man was working in the garden – Paul; James asked if the house was his, and he said it was. How can James check that this is true?

(A) Foundational Concepts for Understanding Case 1

European states each have one or more competent national authority for registering ownership of and charges on land. This institution has an identical name in three of the groups of legal systems studied. In Germany and the Central European legal systems most influenced by it, we find the name '*Grundbuch*' (Land Book). This is particularly the case in Austria and Germany. Countries most influenced by the Napoleonic Code use the '*conservation des hypothèques*' (mortgage register). There are also some similarities in the Nordic system. On the other hand, in the British Isles, such as Ireland and Scotland, there are two different registers – the 'Land Register' and the 'Register of Deeds'.

For historical reasons, it is possible to find several types of Land Registers within one legal system, as the case of France, Greece, or Italy or while a system is being changed, as in Ireland and Scotland. France and Italy have different registers in the territories that were annexed after the First World War, namely Haut-Rhin, Bas-Rhin and Moselle in France, as well as the former Austrian provinces in north-eastern Italy. These newer territories have kept their pre-existing Land Book system (*livre foncier, Grundbuch*), whereas the 'mortgage register' system applies in older territories.

In Ireland and Scotland, an old system of deeds registration (known as the 'Registry of Deeds' in Ireland,[1] 'Register of Sasins' in Scotland) co-exists with a new system of title registration ('Land Registry' in Ireland, 'Land Register' in Scotland). England uses two different registration methods – the old registration of deeds and the new registration of titles.

1 *The Relationship between the Land Register and the Cadastre in the Different European Legal Systems*

Generally, in European legal systems there are two different authorities involved in questions relating to land ownership. Technical mapping and land surveying is usually done by the cadastre, while the Land Register is responsible for registering ownership and charges on the land.

Even in jurisdictions where only one institution has responsibility for both functions, the two functions are usually clearly distinguished by the law. A separate cadastre authority exists in most countries within the Napoleonic Code and German legal families (e.g. Austria, Belgium, Denmark, France, Germany, Poland, Slovenia and Spain). Greece has started to build up a Land Register, but in the absence of such a register the interested party would execute a title search in the Transcription Registry of immovable property in the district.

In another group of legal systems, the cadastre and Land Register are in one institution but operate as two distinctly separate divisions with different staff. These multifunctional institutions have names like the 'Land Agency' (Italy, Sweden) or 'Land Information System' (Finland), the latter consisting of two different agencies with a unique database.

On the other hand, in the Netherlands, the cadastre and the Land Register have different functions, but the same official complies with both of these functions.

The common law systems are the only ones where the functions of land surveying and title registration seem to be more or less combined. England, Ireland and Scotland adopt the approach of having one agency exercise both functions in a single register.

The cadastre can also serve for tax purposes, particularly in the countries most influenced by the Napoleonic Code, such as Spain.

[1] In Ireland, the Registry of Deeds currently operates under the provisions of part 3 of the Registration of Deeds and Title Act 2006 and the Registration of Deeds Rules 2008, which came into effect on 1 May 2008.

2 *Systems of Land Registration in Europe: The Registration of Rights or of Titles and the Constitutive or Declaratory Effect of Registration*

The legal systems of Europe differ not only in the rules they employ to regulate property transfer but also in the organisation and efficiency of their respective land registries.

In Germanic systems, the Land Registry is designed as a register of titles. The Land Register has a fundamental role to play in transactions over immovable goods, as inscription in the Land Registry has replaced the '*traditio*' or the act of handing over the physical possession of the property. In Germany itself, inscription in the Land Registry has to be preceded by an agreement over the act of transferring the property, which is abstracted from the separate agreement over the obligations of the parties. However, in Switzerland, the law requires a causal contract that has the specific aim of transferring ownership. In both systems inscription is necessary, as without inscription neither the agreement to transfer property nor the causal contract produce the effect of transmission.

In other European countries the Land Register is organised as a register of deeds. There are several types of registers of deeds; some are simple, rudimentary collections of unorganised deeds like those that exist in many parts of the United States, while others are well organised and sophisticated like the French, Scottish, or Dutch ones.

In the Nordic legal systems, as a rule, registration of title only has declaratory, not constitutive, effect. Ownership passes at the moment the contract is concluded, and is not dependent on subsequent registration. Registration may, however, give protection for a buyer who trusts the contents of the register. Also, in cases of double sales, i.e. when the owner has sold the property twice, the buyer that registers its title first may get priority. And, with the exception of Norway, registration is needed for an unlawful possessor to ultimately become owner of a property held for a long period of time.

3 *The Format of Registration*

There are two basic formats for registration: (a) '*realfolium*' (real folio), where the register is structured on the basis of the land; and (b) '*personalfolium*' (personal folio), where it is scheduled by the name of the respective owner. These are necessary in order to achieve certainty about the registration.

In many countries, including Spain, the *realfolium* has a similar structure with three or four separate parts that contain: (a) a description of the land; (b) ownership; (c) charges that are sometimes divided in rights to use; and (d) security rights or mortgages. Usually each registration gets a consecutive number. Frequently, there is a special annotation file where changes are registered, for example in Germany or Spain.

(B) The Jurisdictions (Presented by Related Jurisdictions)

1 *Germany and related jurisdictions*

(a) Germany

James can check whether Paul is the owner of the house by inspecting the Land Register (*Grundbuch*), which is a register of title. As the ownership of land normally includes the ownership of buildings erected on that land, it is sufficient to check who owns the plot of land that the house stands on.[2]

The Land Register shows the owner of a plot of land and real rights burdening or benefiting it. It is run by the Land Registry (*Grundbuchamt*) at the local courts (*Amtsgerichte*)[3] and it includes almost every piece of land in Germany.[4] The Land Register is not open for inspection by the general public. James would only be permitted to inspect and take copies of the Land Register if he showed a legitimate interest,[5] or if Paul consented to the inspection.[6] A legitimate interest in inspecting the Land Register would normally not be recognised until a prospective buyer started negotiations about a purchase of the house.[7] The authorised representatives of

[2] § 94 of the German Civil Code (*Bürgerliches Gesetzbuch*, hereafter 'BGB'). There are exceptions which will not be dealt with here.

[3] In the federal state of Baden-Württemberg the Land Register is at present principally not administered by the local courts but by notary's offices or in some areas by the municipal administrations. But a reform is already initiated. In April 2012 a centralisation of the land registries at the local courts (*Amtsgerichte*) has already begun. This reform shall be completed on 1 January 2018.

[4] Properties owned by the state, by local authorities, by churches, by cloisters or by schools as well as rivers, public ways and railways are not necessarily found on the Land Register. These are registered on the application of the owner only (§ 3 para. 2 of the German Land Register Act [*Grundbuchordnung*, hereafter 'GBO']).

[5] § 12 para. 1 GBO.

[6] § 43 para. 2 sentence 2 of the statutory instrument for the execution of the German Land Register Act (*Verordnung zur Durchführung der Grundbuchordnung*, hereafter 'GBV').

[7] See Johann Demharter, *Grundbuchordnung: GBO*, 30th edn. (Munich: C.H. Beck Verlag, 2016), § 12 note 12; Eckart Maaß in Hans-Joachim Bauer / Helmut Freiherr von Oefele, *Grundbuchordnung: GBO*, 3rd edn. (Munich: Vahlen Verlag, 2013), § 12 note 40.

public authorities, notaries, officially appointed surveyors and people with a real right in the property do not have to show a legitimate interest.[8]

On checking the Land Register, James would find that the reference list (*Bestandsverzeichnis*) contains a description of the plot of land (location, size, type of use) with referral to the cadastre (*Liegenschaftskataster*).[9] In particular, section I (*Abteilung I*) contains the name of the current registered owner.[10] The cadastre is held separately from the Land Register. It contains a map and factual details about a piece of land. The cadastre divides the land into cadastral parcels (*Flurstücke*), which are not necessarily identical to a plot of land in the same sense as in the Land Register (*Grundstück*). Only the latter can be the subject-matter of a real right. It obtains its legal quality by being registered with an individual number in the reference list of the land register and may be formed by one or more cadastral parcels.

If Paul is registered in the Land Register as the owner of the land the house stands on, it does not necessarily mean that he really is the owner. In addition to the registration of the change of rights in the Land Register, the transfer of the ownership of a plot of land also requires an agreement between the alienor and the acquirer.[11] However, there is a rebuttable presumption that the registered owner is entitled to ownership of the described land.[12] This assumption can be rebutted by proving that the registered owner is not the true owner – for example, if the acquisition of ownership were void.

However, if James takes a transfer from Paul, the registered owner, in good faith and registers it, James will become the owner. This is due to § 892, para. 1 BGB, which states that in favour of the person who acquires a right in a plot of land or a right in such a right by legal transaction, the contents of the Land Register are presumed to be correct, unless an objection to the accuracy is registered or the inaccuracy is known to the acquirer.

(b) Austria

All real estate is required to be registered and therefore it can be found in the Big Book on Land Registry for real estate.[13] Nevertheless, there

[8] See § 43 GBV. [9] § 6 para. 3a GBV, § 2 para. 2 GBO.

[10] § 9 GBV. Usually section 1 also shows the previous owner(s) of the plot of land. If an entry has to be amended or deleted, it will not be removed from the register. The entry, which is no longer valid, remains on the register but it will be underlined or crossed through.

[11] § 873 para. 1 BGB. [12] § 891 BGB.

[13] Comp § 1 AllGAG (*Allgemeines Grundsbuchsanlegungsgesetz*, Statute on the formation of a Big Book on Land Registry); Gert M. Iro, *Sachenrecht*, 3rd edn. (Vienna: Österreich Verlag, 2008), No. 3/5.

are some special regulations for public property[14] and certain real estate that has to be registered in special books, such as real estate owned by railroad companies.[15]

The Big Book is conclusive, meaning that a person checking it is guaranteed that all entries registered in it are true and complete (*Vetrauensgrundsatz*). The Big Book is also conclusive in another sense: a person purchasing real estate from the person registered in the Big Book can achieve ownership and the associated legal protection regardless whether the transferor should not have been registered (*Eintragungsgrundsatz*).[16]

The Austrian Big Book on Land Registry is accessible by the public,[17] meaning that entries in the Land Registry (*Grundbuchseintragungen*), the document collections (*Urkundensammlung*) and other Registers (*Hilfsverzeichnisse*) can be inspected without giving a reason, which does not apply for the Register of Persons[18] (*Personenverzeichnis*).[19] Seeking information about a property right over a piece of real estate is the first step to finding out which cadastral community (*Katastralgemeinde*) the real estate forms part of, and what the unit number (*Einlagezahl des Grundbuchskörpers*) of the property is.[20] The unit number can be found by looking at the Register of Owners (*Eigentümerverzeichnis*) or the register of roads (*Straßenverzeichnis, Anschriftenverzeichnis*). So, if James knows the name or the address of the owner and he offers a reason for the inquiry he can find out about the unit number (*Einlagezahl*) and check whether the man who purports to be the owner is actually the legal owner.

14 See for the consequences § 434 ABGB (*Allgemeines bürgerliches Gesetzbuch*, Austrian Civil Code). See further Iro, *Sachenrecht*, No. 3/62.

15 Also Helmut Koziol and Rudolf Welser, *Bürgerliches Recht, I*, 13th edn. (Vienna: Manz Verlag, 2006), p. 353; Iro, *Sachenrecht*, No. 3/5.

16 Iro, *Sachenrecht*, No. 3/40f.

17 § 7 Abs 1 GBG (*Grundbuchsgesetz*, Austrian Code on Land Registry). Koziol and Welser, *Bürgerliches Recht, I*, p. 361; Iro, *Sachenrecht*, No. 3/39.

18 Which lists the owners of real estate in alphabetical order, see Koziol and Welser, *Bürgerliches Recht, I*, p. 356.

19 § 6 GUG (*Grundbuchsumstellungsgesetz*, Austrian Code on changing the Land Registry to electronic direct access). See also Koziol and Welser, *Bürgerliches Recht, I*, p. 361; Iro, *Sachenrecht*, No. 3/39. According to § 5 GUG – when using electronic direct access – the right to public inspection (*Einsicht*) is granted by providing an extract (*Auszug*) from the Land Register, see further Koziol and Welser, *Bürgerliches Recht, I*, p. 361; Iro, *Sachenrecht*, No. 3/39.

20 Koziol and Welser, *Bürgerliches Recht, I*, p. 356.

If even James does not know the address, he only needs to know the location to look at the cadastre. The cadastral system, which was used mainly to provide a basis for assessing tax contributions, is an official register that verifies property lines (*Grundstücksgrenzen*) and displays how the property is used and the measurements of the real estate. The Cadastral Register also contains the cadastral map (*Grundbuchsmappe*), which is sent within reasonable time intervals to the responsible district court (*Grundbuchsgericht*).[21] This map shows the location and property lines of the real estate, as well as where the number for the real estate can be found. This number leads to the Register of Real Estate (*Grundstücksverzeichnis*) where the unit number (*Einlagezahl, Grundbuchskörper dem das Grundstück zugehört*) can be located.[22]

James, knowing the unit number (*Einlagezahl des Grundbuchskörpers*) or the address can therefore order an office copy of the Register (*Grundbuchsauszug*), the document collections (*Urkundensammlung*) and other indexes (*Hilfsverzeichnisse*) for the real estate. In order to do so, one used to have to go to the responsible title registration office (*Grundbuchsabteilung*) at the district court where the real estate was located.[23] Nowadays, the electronic direct access line can also be used,[24] which can be accessed from other courts, notaries and lawyers' offices and banks.[25]

(c) The Netherlands

The Dutch law has two closely connected and complementary registers for the administration of land; the cadastre (*kadaster*) and the Deeds Register (*openbare registers*). The cadastre is a public law instrument that was originally set up for taxation purposes (levy of land taxes). It resembles a title register in that it contains records for each plot of land. The cadastre is based on the registration of separate plots of land, which all

[21] Iro, *Sachenrecht*, No. 3/7. [22] Koziol and Welser, *Bürgerliches Recht, I*, p. 356.

[23] Short information can be provided orally if requested, nevertheless public access can be granted by handing out copies or providing access via technical utilities (telescreens), Koziol and Welser, *Bürgerliches Recht, I*, pp. 356, 361.

[24] See § 6 GUG.

[25] § 7 GUG for notaries, who are obliged by law to supply technical resources for such access and to grant access to the Big Book to the public. See also Koziol and Welser, *Bürgerliches Recht, I*, pp. 356, 361. § 5 Abs 5 GUG holds that the right to public inspection (*Einsicht*) and to be provided with an extract (*Auszug*) from the Land Register can be claimed at a title registration office at any district court (*bei jedem Grundbuchsgericht*) even on land registries (*Grundbücher*) which are monitored by another responsible district court, Koziol and Welser, *Bürgerliches Recht, I*, pp. 356, 361.

have a unique number. Such a plot of land is called 'perceel' (cf. 'parcel'). The entry of every parcel shows its owner and any limited real rights burdening the land, such as a mortgage or a servitude.

It should be noted, however, that the cadastre is meant only to give easy access to the Deeds Register. The Deeds Register should be regarded as the genuine Register. For example, a transfer of land ownership is valid only if the deed of transfer is registered in the Deeds Register (arts. 3:84 and 3:89 BW[26]). Ownership passes at the moment of registration in the Deeds Register. Similarly, a mortgage or other limited real right becomes valid only if the deed of creation is registered in the Deeds Register (art. 3:98 read with art. 3:84 and 3:89 BW). Some time soon after this registration, the civil servants at the Registry will update the cadastre to the last registered deed. The cadastre will not only mention the name of the new owner, but it will also mention the number of the deed transferring ownership to the current owner.

In order to check whether someone owns a piece of land one has to check the Deeds Register and look for a document which shows that the person claiming ownership is the owner of the land. This may be a deed of transfer, but it may also be a notarial declaration of succession if the current owner inherited the property. In order to find the relevant deed one first needs to check the cadastre in order to find the relevant deed number. As the cadastre and the Deeds Register are public no permission is required from the registered owner in order to check the Register. Nor is permission required to show any interest in obtaining the information.

It should be stressed that the fact that a certain person has been registered as owner does not give them ownership. Registration does not create ownership. If a deed of transfer turns out to be void, or if it is subsequently voided, the registration in favour of the buyer does not give the buyer ownership. In such a case, the seller remains the owner despite the registration. If the civil servants at the Registry make a mistake and enter the name of a wrong person as owner, this will not give the wrong person ownership. As a result, there is no way to ascertain ownership with certainty.

However, in certain cases third parties will be protected against a false appearance in the Register, despite the fact that the Register does not guarantee that all rights and facts that appear in the Register are valid or true. In principle the Register cannot be trusted. Before 1992 it was called a negative registration system for that reason. However, third-

[26] BW stands for *Burgerlijk Wetboek* (Civil Code, the Netherlands).

party protection has increased considerably since 1992. To a large extent innocent third parties are now protected against incorrectness and incompleteness of the Register, and the registration system can no longer be called negative. The level of protection could be compared to the German system, which is often called positive. However, all these terms are quite misleading. Neither Dutch law nor German law has a system in which registration creates title. What is more, even those registration systems that do recognise title by registration have a mechanism to rectify incorrect registrations, which also works against third parties in the German system. The provisions giving this protection in Dutch law are very technical.

Example (A): Defects in a Previous Transaction

Let us take the following example: A sells and transfers his land to B. Subsequently, B sells and transfers the same land to C. A entered into the contract A–B under the influence of a mistake, rendering the contract voidable[27] (rather than void from the outset).[28] The mistake gives A the power to avoid the contract. The voidable contract is valid until A exercises his power to annul the contract. After avoidance, which has retroactive effect, it is deemed that the contract had never been valid. As a valid underlying contract is a requirement for a valid transfer of ownership, the transfer becomes void with retroactive effect.[29] That is to say, the legal act of transferring ownership, embodied in the notarial deed, becomes void, despite the registration in the Deeds Register. It is deemed that A has always remained the owner of the land. As a result, B has never been the owner of the land and has therefore never been able to give a good title to C under the *nemo dat* rule. The transfer B–C is void because B is not the owner of the land. In English law the same idea is often expressed by saying that if the transfer A–B is voidable C's title is voidable as well. The same problem occurs either where the contract A–B is *void from the outset*, or where there is a defect in the *transfer* between A and B (formal requirements have not been fulfilled).

27 Unlike in the English law, mistake renders the contract voidable rather than void.

28 The same reasoning applies to contracts entered into under the influence of other defects of will, such as fraud, duress and undue influence. The sanction in all these instances is voidability rather than voidness.

29 Dutch law has a so-called causal transfer system in which every transfer of property should be based on a valid legal ground, commonly a valid contract preceding the transfer. If the contract is void, the transfer is void as well. If the contract is voidable, avoidance of it will also avoid the transfer of property. See in general Lars van Vliet, *Transfer of Movables in German, French, English and Dutch Law* (Nijmegen: Ars Aequi Libri, 2000), pp. 24–5.

Example (A): *(cont.)*

C may nevertheless be protected under art. 3:88 BW and acquire ownership if two conditions are met: C must have acquired the property in good faith, and the voidness of the earlier transfer A–B must not be the result of A having been unauthorised to dispose of the land. Dutch law does not want to protect C where A, starting the sequence of transactions, was not the owner of the land or was unauthorised to dispose for another reason, such as insolvency. If A is not the owner, the transfer to B is void from the outset. C will not be protected, even though he acted in good faith.

If the protection of art. 3:88 BW applies to C, the defect of the transfer A–B will commonly be caused by voidness or avoiding of the contract between A and B (as in the above instance) or a formal defect in the notarial deed embodying the transfer A–B. If C is protected he will become[30] or remain[31] the owner of the land. In the above example, C will become and remain the owner of the land if he did not know, nor should have known, of the mistake made by A. A will not be compensated by the Registry, but A may sue B for damages.

Art. 3:24 BW offers broad protection against incompleteness of the Deeds Register. If at the moment an acquisition of a right in land (e.g. the transfer of ownership) is registered a certain fact or right which can be registered has not yet been registered, this fact or right cannot be set up against the acquirer under the transaction, unless he knew the fact or right. One such example would be if A transferred land ownership to B under a resolutive condition and by mistake the condition was not laid down in the notarial conveyance deed and thus not entered into the Register. Afterwards if B transferred the same land to C, who was unaware of the resolutive condition between A and B, then A would not be able to require C to fulfil the condition.

Arts. 3:24 (2) and (3) BW provide some exceptions to this rule, such as where the acquisition of land is a result of adverse possession. Although acquisition by adverse possession has not been registered, it works against everyone, even against third parties acting in good faith. In the English terminology this amounts to an overriding interest. When there is adverse possession of part of the neighbour's land it means that the legal boundary between the two pieces of land no longer corresponds with the cadastral boundary as laid down in the cadastral chart. For this reason the cadastral boundary as shown in the cadastral chart is not decisive and may become outdated as a result of adverse possession.

Art. 3:25 BW gives protection against certain mistakes in notarial deeds. An example of this can be found in the answer to case 6.

Another article giving protection against errors is art. 3:26 BW. If at the moment the acquisition of a right in land is registered an incorrect fact has been registered, the person who could reasonably have asked for rectification

[30] Where the earlier transaction is void. [31] Where the earlier transaction is voidable.

Example (A): *(cont.)*

of the register cannot use this mistake against a third party, unless the latter knew of the mistake or could have known the mistake when consulting the register.

Let us take the following example: A sells and transfers his land to B under a suspensive condition. At a later stage, an entry is made in the Land Register noting that the condition has been fulfilled, and thereby vesting ownership to B. Now B transfers ownership to C. In reality, the condition had not yet been fully fulfilled. A knew this but did not bother to have the Register rectified. If C is an innocent third party within the definition of art. 3:26 BW, he will become owner of the land.

The protection given in arts. 3:24, 25, 26 and 88 BW does not depend on the question of whether the innocent third party acquired his right for valuable consideration nor on the question of whether the third party or the owner is in actual possession of the land. Nor is actual possession relevant for rectification of the Register.

Under certain conditions, art. 117 *Kadasterwet* (Cadastre Act) offers compensation if civil servants of the cadastre and Deeds Registry make a mistake. Moreover, the state will give compensation in rare instances, such as destruction of deeds due to a fire at the Land Registry (art. 3:30 BW).

(d) Turkey

As a fundamental rule, every immovable property has its own page and number in the Land Register (in the Big Book).[32] The Land Register consists of the Big Book, supplementary plans, the title deeds and the Day Book.[33] The Land Register is public and indicates the name of the current registered owner of the land. Thus, any person who can give *prima facie* proof of being an interested party can demand either to inspect specific pages of the Register together with the deeds and documents belonging to them in the presence of a Registry official, or to have the relevant extracts prepared for them.[34]

[32] See art. 1000 TCC; Ivy Williams, Siegfried Wyler and Barbara Wyler, *The Swiss Civil Code English Version, II*, art. 945, para.1 (Zürich: ReMAK Verlag, 1987); M. Kemal Oğuzman, Özer Seliçi and Saibe Oktay-Özdemir, *Eşya Hukuku, Gözden Geçirilmiş 11. Bası* (İstanbul: Filiz Kitabevi, 2006), p. 122; Lale Sirmen, *Eşya Hukuku Dersleri*, (Ankara: Savaş Yayınları, 1995), p. 113; Şeref Ertaş, *Yeni Türk Medeni Kanunu Hükümlerine Göre Eşya Hukuku, Gözden Geçirilmiş ve Genişletilmiş 4. Baskı* (Ankara: Seçkin 2002), p. 93.

[33] See art. 997, para. 2 TCC; Williams, Wyler and Wyler, *The Swiss Civil Code, II*, art. 942, para. 2; Oğuzman, Seliçi and Oktay-Özdemir, *Eşya*, p. 122; Sirmen, *Eşya*, p. 114; Ertaş, *Eşya*, p. 94.

[34] See art. 1020, paras. 1–2 TCC; Williams, Wyler and Wyler, *The Swiss Civil Code, II*, art. 970, paras. 1–2; Oğuzman, Seliçi and Oktay-Özdemir, *Eşya*, p. 134; Sirmen, *Eşya*, p. 122; Ertaş, *Eşya*, p. 97, No. 436.

Where this man is registered as the owner, art. 7 of the Turkish Civil Code (TCC) will be applied, according to which entries made in public registers and duly authenticated documents are sufficient evidence of the facts they state, provided that they have not been proved to be inaccurate.[35] If this registration is true, James can acquire property rights for the immovable.

Where this registration is not true, art. 1023 TCC states, 'Where any person has acquired the ownership or other real right by *bona fide* relying on an entry in the Register, his rights are protected'.[36] Even if the registration is wrong, a third party can trust the accuracy of the entry in the Land Register with good faith and can acquire property rights to the land or a real right on it. Therefore, if James acquires the ownership by *bona fide* relying on this entry in the Register, his right is protected under art. 1023 TCC.[37]

2 *Scandinavian jurisdictions*

(a) Finland

In order to gain trustworthy and official information on ownership (titles) and other rights over pieces of real estate or certain other land units, James has to inspect the Finnish Title and Mortgage Register (*lainhuuto-ja kiinnitysrekisteri*), which is the Finnish Register of rights in immovable property (Land Register in the English sense). James can either monitor the Register in the offices of certain local authorities or he can order a certificate. It is also possible to use the electronic direct access line. The Register is subject to public access and its trustworthiness is assured by the Finnish state. Almost all pieces of real estate are included in the register. Today, the local offices of the National Land Survey of Finland administer the Register.[38]

[35] See Williams, Wyler and Wyler, *The Swiss Civil Code, I*, art. 9.

[36] See Williams, Wyler and Wyler, *The Swiss Civil Code, II*, art. 973.

[37] See Williams, Wyler and Wyler, *The Swiss Civil Code, II*, art. 973; Oğuzman, Seliçi and Oktay-Özdemir, *Eşya*, pp. 196ff.

[38] Chapter 5, section 2 (5:2) and chapter 7, section 2 (7:2) Finnish Code of Real Estate (1995). English translations of many Finnish statutes are provided by the data bank Finlex. For instance, the Code of Real Estate is at www.finlex.fi/en/laki/kaannokset/1995/en19950540.pdf.

There is Finnish literature about the Finnish land law: Matti Ilmari Niemi, *Maakaaren järjestelmä, I, II* and *III* (*The System of the Code of Real Estate I, II* and *III*, Helsinki: WSOY, 2016, 2012 and 2010); Marjut Jokela, Leena Kartio and Ilmari Ojanen, *Maakaari* (*The Code of Real Estate*, Helsinki: Talentum, 2010); Jarno Tepora, Leena Kartio, Risto Koulu and Heidi Lindfors, *Kiinteistön kauppa, muu luovutus ja kirjaus* (*Sale of Real Estate, Other Conveyances and Registration*, Helsinki: Talentum, 2010).

Firstly, James has to inspect the separate Real Estate Register (*Kiinteistörekisteri*), which is the Finnish cadastre (a unit or a property register), in order to gain trustworthy information about the objects of ownership and other rights. For instance, the Real Estate Register contains information about the areas and borders of pieces of real estate. With the unit number and the Register map, James can individuate the piece of real estate he is looking at.[39] The unit number is also necessary when inspecting the Title and Mortgage Register. In practice, James can check the unit number by consulting the available documents or maps. A new unit of land is only entered into the Real Estate Register when it is established by an official land survey. Nevertheless, information about conveyed but unseparated parcels is included in the Register.

The Finnish registration system relating to land and water areas has traditionally been divided into two parts; registration has been divided even at the organisational level. Since the system was reformed in 2010, the National Land Survey now maintains both the Title and Mortgage Register and the Real Estate Register. Moreover, a unified information system covering both of these Registers has been adopted.

Trust in the registered titles and other rights are founded on the trustworthiness of the Title and Mortgage Register and on the good faith of a transferee.[40] For instance, the sale of a piece of real estate will be permanent even if the vendor was not the rightful title-holder due to a defect in his acquisition or that of a previous title-holder, if the title of the vendor was registered at the time of acquisition and the purchaser, at that time, did not know nor should have known that the vendor was not the rightful title-holder (the legitimation effect of the Title and Mortgage Register).[41] This is the main rule applying to all kinds of conveyances (but not to all kinds of acquisitions). However, there are certain important exceptions that will be discussed later in case 6. Registration of the transferee's title has no significance in this situation. The Finnish legal system does not provide any stronger legal protection *in rem* to a transferee.

In Finland, the registration of a title does not create an absolute title. Title registration does not preclude a legal dispute over the title of a piece of real estate or ensure the validity of an acquisition in a trial.[42]

39 Section 1, Real Estate Register Act 1985, at www.finlex.fi/en/laki/kaannokset/1985/en19850392.pdf.

40 The good faith of a person is presumed. The fact that a person knew or should have known something has to be proved.

41 13:4 Code of Real Estate.

42 13:2 Code of Real Estate.

Registration is not itself or alone a decision or degree of material ownership. Moreover, registration does not create ownership by a purchaser or another conveyee, and it is not a necessary condition of his or her ownership. The same applies to other kinds of acquisitions, such as inheritance. According to the Finnish regulation, a conveyance of ownership takes place mainly by and at the moment of a transaction between parties.[43] On the other hand, registration does strengthen the position of a conveyee as an owner, especially in relation to certain third persons. In practice, a registered acquisition is very seldom contested and therefore the Title and Mortgage Register is considered to be very trustworthy. Moreover, there is state assurance that acts as a secondary form of protection for a transferee or rightful title-holder because a transferee or a rightful title-holder who loses their right to a piece of real estate on the account of the abovementioned rules is entitled to due compensation from state funds.[44]

In order to register a title or another right in the Title and Mortgage Register, one has to present either a formally valid deed of conveyance or another acquisition document. A written sale contract witnessed by a notary is treated as a deed. Even a precontract has to be made in the same way.[45] In contrast, no other documents showing the preceding stages of the chain of acquisitions before last registration are needed in a new registration.

In addition to the traditional system of paper documents, Finland has adopted an electronic system of real property exchanges.[46] According to it, the conveyance of a piece of real estate can take place in the electronic system, with the help of the Internet. Official forms can be found on web sites maintained by the National Land Survey.[47] An application for title registration will occur automatically and immediately when a conveyance has taken place with the help of the online form.[48] The sections of the Code of Real Estate that regulate the electronic system became

[43] Strictly speaking, the terms 'contract or bill of purchase or another conveyance' or 'another acquisition document' are better than 'deed', in the Nordic context. In these countries, a purchase contract or another conveyance is seen as a contract important for both of its parties and creating rights for both of them. A purchase contract entitles the vendor to the purchase money and the purchaser to the ownership. In Finland, a conveyance is made with one document, a purchase contract or a corresponding document. No separate deed of conveyance transferring ownership or a difference between this kind of document and the purchase contract is known.

[44] 13:6 Code of Real Estate. [45] 2:7.2 Code of Real Estate. [46] Statute 4.2.2011/96.

[47] 2: 1.2 Code of Real Estate. [48] 9a:12.1 and 9a:14.2 Code of Real Estate.

effective in 2013 and the system has been used since the beginning of November 2013.[49]

Pieces of real estate are normally registered both in the Title and Mortgage Register and the Real Estate Register. It is possible, nevertheless, that a piece of real estate or the title of its contemporary owner is not registered. In that case, James has to trust deeds of earlier conveyances or other documents or information. However, the information that is gained from these alternative sources is not as trustworthy as the Registers. As a rule, it is the responsibility of a new owner of a piece of real estate to register his or her acquisition within six months of drawing up of the deed of conveyance or another acquisition document.[50] However, preliminary acquisition information about conveyances will be included *ex officio* in the Title and Mortgage Register within a few days after conveyances by the notices of notaries.[51]

Generally, houses are parts of registered pieces of real estate, or parcels of them. Only pieces of real estate and certain other land and water areas are treated as real property in Finland. Houses as such or their parts (flats) are included in the movables. Nevertheless, it is common for a house to be a part of a lease in Finland (a lease house, a leasehold). A lease is also included in the movable property. Paul can be a lease holder. The Title and Mortgage Register normally contains information about leases and their holders. A lease and a house together establish a property similar to a piece of real estate, and most often the same rules are applied.

In addition, James has to check Paul's identity by asking to see his identification card or another similar document.

(b) Sweden

If James intends to buy the property, he ought to apply for information from the official Real Property Register.[52] Before 1 July 2000, the register was freely accessible, based on the constitutional principle of public access to official documents.[53] Since then, access to the Register has been

[49] Statute 622/2013. See the comparison between the Finnish system and the English plan of electronic conveyancing of real property in Chapter 2.

[50] 11:1 Code of Real Estate. [51] 7:5 Code of Real Estate.

[52] Accessibility of real estate information is regulated in the Real Property Register Act: *lagen (2000:224) om fastighetsregister*. See the introduction for further information on the nature of the Register.

[53] *See* the governmental proposal *prop. 1999/2000:39, Registrering av fastighetsrättsliga förhållanden m.m.*, pp. 10ff. Cf. also Cecilia Strang, 'Sverige', in *Ejendomsregistrering i de nordiske lande* (Copenhagen: Kort & Matrikelstyrelsen, 2006), p. 296f.

restricted in order to comply with the EC Personal Data Directive on privacy and electronic communications.[54] The Swedish Cadastral Authority (*Lantmäteriet*) is responsible for the personal data in the Real Property Register and decides whether and how property information should be supplied.[55] Decisions are based on how the applicants plan to use the information. One of the permitted grounds for access to information in the Register is the transfer of real property.[56] The information is supplied without cost.[57]

The Register consists of five parts.[58] The general part includes information about the geographical location of property units, maps and municipal land plans. The inscription part contains information regarding rights to the property units, such as ownership and mortgages.[59]

If James engages in a sales process and eventually buys the property, he would be granted protection even if the seller (Paul) was not the rightful owner, provided that Paul was registered as owner in the Real Property Register and that at the time of the contract was concluded James was acting in good faith as to who the rightful owner was.[60] In this case the good faith threshold is an objective one. James will be in good faith if he does not know, and ought not to know, about the legal deficiency. In most cases, an acquisition in good faith will extinguish the ownership of the registered owner. The registered owner may claim compensation from the state, based on the fact there was incorrect information on the title. The rightful owner's right to compensation may be reduced to a reasonable amount, or be precluded altogether, due to contributory negligence or insufficient mitigation of loss.[61] This may be the case when the rightful owner has failed to protect his or her

[54] Directive 95/46/EC of the European Parliament and of the Council of 24 October 1995 on the protection of individuals with regard to the processing of personal data and on the free movement of such data, *OJ* L 281, 23.11.1995, pp. 31–50. *See* also the Directive on privacy and electronic communications, Directive 2002/58/EC of the European Parliament and of the Council of 12 July 2002 concerning the processing of personal data and the protection of privacy in the electronic communications sector, *OJ* L 201, 31.7.2002, pp. 37–47.

[55] § 6 Real Property Register Act. [56] § 2 (2) Real Property Register Act.

[57] The applicant must pay for excerpt prints only if the number of pages exceeds ten pages in accordance with the Fee Ordinance, § 15, *avgiftsförordningen (1992:191)*. In addition, one may obtain a restricted online access to the Register through a fee-based subscription, §§ 7 and 7a Real Property Register Act.

[58] § 3 Real Property Register Act.

[59] *See* the Real Property Register Ordinance; *förordningen (2000:308) om fastighetsregister*.

[60] 18:1 (1) Land Code. [61] 18:4 (1) Land Code.

rights by acting passively, for instance by refraining from claiming the property in court.[62]

The rightful owner may vindicate the property in qualified cases of invalidity, but James would be entitled to monetary compensation from the state in these cases, unless he had already successfully sought compensation from Paul (the seller).[63] This right to compensation operates regardless of fault on the part of the state. The content of the Register's inscription section is, as an exception to the general rule,[64] said to have substantive legal effect in order to protect the general interest of exchange.[65] The instances of qualified invalidity are: forged documents of title, false representation of the rightful owner, inducement of the sale by force or under the threat of violence, want of the rightful owner's legal capacity (such as minority or bankruptcy at the time of conclusion of the contract) and deficiencies as to statutory requirements.[66]

(c) Denmark

The question of who owns a property may be checked in two registers. The Land Registry will keep a record of the ownership of the house. The Land Registry is intended to primarily take care of the private law effects of rights in real property. Alternatively, James may consult the Cadastral Register, known as the BBR Register. The BBR Register lists ownership, as well as type of property and taxable value for public law purposes. Both registers may be consulted online and the BBR is free while the Land Registry charges a fee.[67] It is necessary to note that both Registers are only *prima facie* proof of ownership.

At the Land Registry, the Buildings and Dwellings Register contains a separate gazette for all real estate, ordered according to the title number. The gazette lists information such as ownerships, mortgages, pledges and easements. The Registry is available to the general public and anyone

[62] Folke Grauers, *Fastighetsköp*, 21st edn. (Lund: Juristförlaget i Lund, 2016), pp. 325 and 332.
[63] 18:4 (2) Land Code.
[64] 19:40 Land Code. Cf. also Supreme Court judgment, *NJA* (1997), 660 and Bertil Bengtsson, *Sakrättsliga frågor i fastighetsrätten*, 6th edn. (Uppsala: Iustus Förlag, 1991), p. 8.
[65] Henrik Hessler, *Nya jordabalken. Kap 16 och 18. Hävd och godtrosförvärv*, 4th edn. (Stockholm: Juristförlaget, 1983), p. 9f.
[66] 18:3 Land Code.
[67] The Danish Enterprise and Construction Authority maintains the web-site at https://www.ois.dk/.

may request information from the gazette. The Buildings and Dwellings Register has been digitalised since 2009, but this has not led to major changes in the substantive law.

All real rights in land should be registered in the Land Registry[68] and the effects of registration are plural. Firstly, registration creates perfection. From the time of the registration, a registered right has priority over rights that are subsequently registered and a registered right cannot be extinguished by rights that are subsequently registered. Secondly, registration effects validity. The application of the LRA[69] means that if a transferee in good faith has a document regarding registered rights in real property, objections regarding the validity of this document cannot be made, except where an objection is based on certain grounds relating to lack of consent, for example where the document is forged, issued because of physical coercion or immediate threat thereof, or where the transferor lacked capacity to issue the document. Any transferee may therefore assume that a right that has been registered in the Land Registry is valid. Please note that the transferor's creditors are not protected by this provision and thus they may only rely on the Register for priority (but not validity). Finally, registration has the effect of justification. A document concerning a right over real property can only be registered if the document appears to be issued by a person who according to the Land Registry has the property at his disposal. Thus, the Land Registry only shows who is the formal owner. The fact that a person is also the real owner of the property is not itself a condition for registration, and consequently it cannot be deduced from the registration.[70]

As mentioned, the purpose of the Cadastral Register is mainly for public law issues, such as tax, building permits, or the levy of duties for waste disposal. As a starting point, the BBR Register has no private law effects and it is searched simply based on the address. James may find the full cadastral report on any property registered as belonging to him online, and an updated version will be sent to him every year. A limited cadastral report, containing the name of the owner(s), the title number, the area in square metres and the tax value of any property is publicly available to any interested party.

[68] Section 1, Land Registration Act. [69] Section 27, Land Registration Act.
[70] Peter Mortensen, *Indledning til tingsretten* (Copenhagen: Karnov Group, 2009), p. 173.

(d) Norway

The answer depends on the purpose of James' query. We will suppose that he wants to buy the house or to enter into some other transaction with the owner, like renting the house or obtaining a security right in it. However, the answer might be different if James were the man's creditor looking for assets out of which he could satisfy his claims, or a neighbour wishing to complain about emissions or noise from the property, or a tax officer wondering where to send the tax bill.

James can check who has a *bona fide* claim or 'ownership' of the house by inspecting the Land Register (*grunnboka*). The Land Register is a register of rights in immovable property that also includes rights in shares in housing cooperatives. For all practical purposes, the Land Register contains every piece of land in Norway (excluding Svalbard) and it is open for inspection by everybody either via telephone, post, or in person attendance. The Land Register should not be confused with the cadastre (*matrikkelen*), which was originally a register for taxation purposes. Nevertheless, there are close links between the Land Register and the cadastre. The Land Register is a register of rights, while the cadastre contains information of a factual nature. For instance, a new unit of land is only entered into the cadastre when it is established as a unit in the Land Register.[71]

Suppose James finds that Paul is registered as the owner, and therefore buys the land from him; can he be sure that he will obtain a right that is protected against other persons who pretend to have a right to the property? The short answer is that, as a buyer of the property, James will generally be protected against claims from persons with a better right to the property than his, so long as James registers his right in the Land Register in good faith. James is in good faith if he does not know, and has no reason to know, of the better right at the time of registration. However, there are some exceptions to this principle, which will be explained below.[72]

[71] The rules on registration in the Land Register are found in the Judicial registration act (*lov om tinglysing*, 7 June 1935 No. 2). A new system for and a new legal regime of the cadastre was launched successively through 2008 and 2009, see the Cadastre Act (*lov om eigedomsregistrering (matrikkellova)*, 17 June 2005 No. 101). As for literature, see in general Thor Falkanger and Aage Thor Falkanger, *Tingsrett*, 8th edn. (Oslo: Universitetsforlaget, 2016), pp. 683–5; Borgar Høgetveit Berg and Stein Bråthen-Otterbech, *Tinglysing. Lov om tinglysing 7. juni 1935 nr. 2 med kommentarer* (Oslo: Universitetsforlaget, 2009), Kåre Lilleholt, *Allmenn formuerett* (Oslo: Universitetsforlaget, 2012).

[72] Double sale will be discussed in case 5.

In order to register a right in the Land Register, one must present a document signed by the holder of the registered title of a relevant right. For example, a buyer must present a document signed by the registered owner, a transferee of a lease must present a document signed by a registered lessee and an acquirer of a new lease must present a document signed by the registered owner. In a sale transaction, the buyer usually receives a deed (*skøyte*), which confirms the character of the transaction and the payment of the purchase money. This document only serves for registration purposes and it does not have other legal effects (contrary to popular belief, the document may perfectly well be discarded after registration).

As the seller, Paul may have obtained a registered title on the basis of a document issued by the true owner – let us call him Henry – and resulting from a sale contract which is voidable, for example due to fraud. If the buyer (James) has registered his right in good faith and according to his (valid) sale contract with Paul, then James is protected against Henry's objections (there will be no 'vindication'). If, however, Paul's title is based on a forged document or a document that is voidable because of threats of violence or because Henry was under age, then James must respect Henry's right to the property. These rules come from § 27 Judicial Registration Act. In the latter cases, where the buyer is not protected in spite of registration in good faith, the buyer may be entitled to damages from the state if they suffer a loss by relying on the register.[73] Under Norwegian law, registration has no effect on the relationship between parties to the contract. If the contract of sale between James and the holder of the registered title is voidable, for whatever reason, registration will not change that.

Furthermore, registration will not be of any use to James should the man in the garden turn out to be a swindler who falsely purports to be the person registered as an owner and has forged the owner's and necessary witnesses' signatures on a deed. James may lose the money he paid to the swindler against registration of the document, but he cannot claim damages against the state. On registration, there is only a formal checking of the document and no verification of the signatures of the title-holder or the witnesses. So, James should check this himself.

[73] Section 35, Judicial Registration Act (*lov om tinglysing*), 7 June 1935 No. 2.

3 *Romanic–Mediterranean jurisdictions*

(a) Italy

In order to check if Paul is the owner of the house, James could directly examine and take copies of the title registration (transcription) regarding the property held at the Immovable Property Register (IPR).[74] In practice, since the Italian IPR is organised on a personal basis, rather than on the basis of the property, James should look under the name of the person asserting ownership (Paul) so as to confirm whether there is an entry in the IPR for Paul – that is, if the contract under which he has purchased the house has been registered in his name (*a suo favore* or 'in his favour'). However, even if James found a registration 'in favour' of Paul regarding the house that he wants to buy, James still cannot be sure about ownership. Indeed, in Italy the registration merely has a declaratory function and it serves to disclose to third parties all contracts that relate to the transfer of immovable property, but it does not transfer property itself.[75] In order to be sure, once James has found the registration of the title of acquisition in Paul's name, he should look back and check if it is a continuous sequence of registrations covering a sufficient period of time for acquisition by adverse possession. Moreover, James should also check that there is no entry against Paul (*contro Paul*) in relation to the house, in order to be sure that Paul has not sold it.

It is necessary to bear in mind that James will not be able to identify the immovable property from the IPR, nor can he detect the exact nature of it or other information regarding it. In order to verify this information, James (or the notary in charge of drafting the contract of sale) should take a look at the Cadastral System. The Cadastral System is the general inventory of immovable property based on a land survey (*rilevamento topografico*). While the Cadastral System's function is to allow for the identification of immovable property in order to assess what it consists of and its value primarily for tax purposes, in practice the cadastral data is used to identify premises that are subject to a sales agreement. However, information from the Cadastral System does not constitute evidence of ownership, nor does it function as a declaration of transfer. However, in a boundary dispute courts may, in the absence of other evidence, take into account the Cadastral System to ascertain the exact extent of the premises.[76]

[74] See art. 2673 Italian Civil Code (hereafter, ICC).

[75] See in conjunction with arts. 1376 and 2643 ICC.

[76] See art. 950 c 3 ICC.

(b) Spain

James can apply to the Land Register (*Registro de la Propiedad*), which provides information to interested parties and the community at large on ownership rights and other rights *in rem* in previously unregistered immovable property. Any person who, in the view of the Land Registrar (the *registrador*), has a legitimate interest in knowing the state of an immovable property and the rights *in rem* registered in connection with it is granted access to the content of the *Registro de la Propiedad*. Direct access is not available. James would have to apply, by any medium, to the relevant *Registro de la Propiedad*.[77] Applicants can also obtain a certified abstract of entries in the *Registro de la Propiedad* and a certified abstract serves as official proof of the contents for the purposes of dealings beyond the *Registro*.

However, the *Catastro* (cadastre) is an administrative register containing descriptions of urban, rustic and special immovable properties. The purpose of the *Catastro* is not to provide details about the ownership of an estate, but rather details of its physical features, such as surface area, location and boundaries and the year of construction. The *Catastro* also contains economic specifics, including the value of the underlying land, the value of the building and cadastral value. The owner of a property has a duty to register it with the *Catastro* because the cadastral value ascribed to a property by the *Dirección General del Catastro* (a division of the Finance Ministry) is used for the purpose of calculating several taxes. If the ownership of an urban property is transferred under a notarial act, or registration of the property with the *Registro de la Propiedad* is applied for within two months following transfer, the civil law notary and the Land Registrar are in charge of reporting the change of ownership to the *Catastro*.

As a general rule, under Spanish law registration with the *Registro de la Propiedad* does not have constitutive effect. Ownership can be acquired and rights *in rem* can emerge and exist to full effect outside the *Registro*, and sometimes even in contradiction with it. So, even if Paul is named in an entry on the register as the owner of the house, he might not actually be the owner. Paul might have transferred ownership of the house to a

[77] The instruments by which the information is released are the Registrar's disclosure, within the offices of the *Registro* itself, of the contents of the Register books, and *notas simples*, certified abstracts of the entries relating to a given property (under art. 222 of the *Ley Hipotecaria*, the Spanish statute on mortgages, in its consolidated text introduced by the *Decreto* of 8 February 1946, referred to in the remainder of this chapter as 'Mortgage Act 1946').

third party who has not yet registered the deed of sale or gift with the *Registro de la Propiedad*, and this would not prevent the third party from being the present owner. Alternatively, the registered act that names Paul as owner might be void, for example if it contravenes a statutory prohibition. All else being equal, a void act should not attain registration. But, if it does, the fact of registration does not make valid an act that is invalid under the law.[78] A court could declare the sale void and this would affect the registered ownership of the man in the garden and his successors and assigns.

However, the law applies a rebuttable presumption of the accuracy of the *Registro de la Propiedad* in favour of the registered owner.[79] That presumption is non-rebuttable when it operates in favour of a third-party buyer who satisfies the requirements under art. 34 Mortgage Act 1946. Art. 34 Mortgage Act 1946 relates to acquisition in good faith, for value, from a person named in the *Registro de la Propiedad* as entitled to transfer ownership and registration of the acquired right. This means that if Paul is the registered owner, James' acquisition will be protected if he decides to buy the house and acts in good faith and registers the deed of sale with the *Registro de la Propiedad*. If James fails any of these requirements (i.e. he does not register the sale), he nonetheless enjoys the benefit of the presumption that the *Registro de la Propiedad* is accurate. Anyone claiming that the *Registro* is inaccurate must prove that:

(i) the Register entry or the title giving rise to it is void, false or mistaken;
(ii) an unregistered title that modifies the facts as registered exists; or
(iii) the registered right is extinct.

(c) Portugal

The Portuguese statutory basis for land registration is the Land Registration Code (*Código do Registo Predial*), approved by Decree Law 224/84 of 6 July[80] (LRegC). The Land Registry is in charge of the legal registration

[78] Art. 33 Mortgage Act 1946. [79] Art. 38 Mortgage Act 1946.

[80] As amended by Decree Laws 355/85, of 2 September; 60/90, of 14 February; 80/92, of 7 May; 30/93, of 12 February; 255/93, of 15 July; 227/94, of 8 September; 267/94, of 25 October; 67/96, of 31 May; 375-A/9, of 20 September; 533/99, of 11 December; 273/2001, of 13 October; 322-A/2001, of 14 February; 323/2001, of 17 December; 38/2003, of 8 March; 194/2003, of 23 August; 6/2006, of 27 February; 263-A/2007, of 23 July; 34/2008, of 26 February; 116/2008, of 4 July; 47/2008, of 25 August; 122/2009, of 21 May; 185/2009, of 12 August; 209/2012, of 19 September; and by Laws 29/2009, of 12 August and 1/2010, of 15 January.

of land and property,[81] and it contains information about the rights acquired and transferred on distinct pieces of real estate. Registrars are legally certified government officials that work on the basis of functional autonomy; they depend on the Ministry of Justice, through the General Directorate of Registries and Notaries (*Direcção Geral dos Registos e Notariado*).

The Land Registry operates a system of title registration where each property is described in a separate file, which contains the physical description of the land, the name of the owner and other real rights to which the property is subject, such as usufruct, superficies and mortgages. Arts. 2 and 3 LRegC enunciate the facts (e.g. constitution, recognition, acquisition or modification of rights *in rem*) and the judicial proceedings subject to registration. In this sense, judicial proceedings include: cases brought before a court aiming at the recognition, constitution, or modification of facts subject to registration; cases aiming at the reformulation, declaration of nullity, or avoidance of a registration or its cancellation; and the final decisions of any such proceedings.

Land registration aims to give publicity to the legal rights pertaining to each property, in order to improve security on real estate transmissions.[82] According to art. 104 LRegC, data on the Land Registry can be freely accessed by everyone.[83] James could ask for an abstract of the title (*certidão do registo predial*) that certifies who owns the house and the inscriptions of proprietary rights in force.[84] Since the Land Registry is held in electronic form, and Decree Law 116/2008 of 4 July abolished the territorial jurisdiction of Land Registry offices, since 1 January 2009, James has been able to ask for an abstract of the title at any Land Registration office, regardless of where the property is located. Where an abstract of the title is required as an official sample,

[81] There is no cadastre in Portugal. There is a descriptive database of the physical configuration of properties; its goal is mainly fiscal, in order to set real estate evaluations and calculate the adequate taxes.

[82] Art. 1 LRegC.

[83] Only the staff has direct access to the books, folders and documents; only in special circumstances are judicial authorities and other entities also granted direct access.

[84] If the house were not yet described in the Land Registry, James should ask for a negative certificate (*certidão negative*). In that case, the submitter might identify the building through its precise location; indicate the urban or agricultural nature of the building; and the name, civil status and residence of the actual owner (art. 111 (5) LRegC). In order to get the precise location of the building, the submitter might ask further information in the City Hall. See Isabel Pereira Mendes, *Código do Registo Predial – Anotado he Comentado* (Coimbra: Almedina, 2009), p. 450.

it can be handed over in the Land Registry Office, sent by post or fax, or obtained via an internet-based inquiry service (arts. 41-B *ex vi* art. 111 (3) LRegC). The requisition of a certificate must contain the identification of the submitter, the number of the description of the building in the Land Registry and the parish and the city where the building is located.

It should also be emphasised that James could not acquire the house from Paul unless it was registered as Paul's property. Art. 9 LRegC requires that the notary or public official in charge of the conveyance of the transfer ask for a certification from the Land Registry (or check it online), so as to ensure that Paul is actually the registered owner of the house.

The fact that Paul is registered as the owner of the house does not mean that he really is the owner. However, registration produces very important effects because it offers a rebuttable presumption (*juris tantum*) that the registered owner is entitled to property, that is to say the registered proprietary right exists and is vested in the person inscribed in the Register (art. 7 LRegC). Conversely, it also allows the assumption that a right, such as a mortgage or a usufruct that has been cancelled, no longer exists. Accordingly, if Paul is registered as the owner of the house, he is presumably its owner and the burden of proof supports this presumption.

Lastly, if James buys the house from Paul and registers his acquisition, his right becomes enforceable against third parties.[85] The question about whether good faith is required remains controversial in the doctrine. The debate is set among those who consider good faith as a general principle in the Portuguese legal system,[86] and those who consider that good faith is not relevant with respect to protection from registration.[87] Further, if James pays a consideration for the house to Paul, the registered owner, in

[85] Art. 5 (1) LRegC.

[86] António Menezes Cordeiro, *Tratado de Direito Civil Portugês, II*, 3rd edn. (Coimbra: Almedina, 2005), p. 276; Luis Carvalho Fernandes, 'Terceiros para efeitos de Registrao Predial', 57 *ROA* (1997), pp. 1283–1320; António Santos Justo, *Direitos Reais*, 4th edn. (Coimbra: Coimbra Editora, 2012), pp. 73–4; Isabel Pereira Mendes, *Código*, p. 143; José A. Vieira, *Direitos Reais: perspectiva histórica do seu ensino em Portugal* (Lisbon: Coimbra Editora, 2008), p. 297.

[87] See Carvalho Fernandes, 'Terceiros para efeito de Registo Predial', pp. 1283–1320; Rui Pinto Duarte, *Curso do Direitos Reais* (Lisbon: Principia, 2007), p. 150; Paulo Videira Henriques, 'Terceiros para efeitos do artigo 5.º do Código do Registo Predial', *BFD* (2003), pp. 443–5.

good faith and registers his acquisition, he will be protected according to art. 17 LRegC (see case 6).

(d) Greece

In Greece, the ownership of a piece of a land includes the ownership of buildings erected on that land as well, since they are considered components of the land (*superficies solo cedit*).[88] Recently, there has been some change in this principle, but this solely concerns public property.[89] Ownership is fully passed at the moment of registration in a specific registry.[90] This also applies for any limited real right burdening or benefiting the immovable property.

The verification of the ownership of the house depends upon the specific area in which the property lies. Until recently, Greece had no Land Registry. In the absence of a Land Registry, the interested party would execute a title search in the Transcription Registry in the district of the immovable property. This search would start with the name of the alleged owner. By looking in an alphabetical index, James will find the 'share number' of the alleged owner. With this number, James will find the so-called 'share' where all actions relating to the immovable property within the specific district are registered in chronological order. Focusing on the specific property for which he is interested, James must be able to trace the title for at least twenty years into the past, in order to ensure that any adverse claims are prescripted[91] and Paul enjoys at least the benefits of acquisition by possession.[92] The fact that Paul appears in the Transcription Register as the lawful owner of the house bears no significance.[93] If the person who sold the house to Paul was not the lawful owner, the latter would not acquire ownership despite that which is registered in the Transcription Registry.

Even though the Greek Civil Code (GCC) foresees that the Transcription Registry will be accessible to the public,[94] it is not open for inspection by the general public in order to protect the books from being ruined. Only lawyers, notaries and authorised representatives of public authorities are allowed to conduct a search in the books and documents.[95] However, no legitimate interest is required in order to do so.

[88] Arts. 948, 953 and 954 GCC.
[89] Arts. 18–26 Law 3986/2011 (the state remains the owner of the land but an investor may acquire the ownership of the building).
[90] Arts. 1033, 1192 and 1198 GCC. [91] Art. 249 GCC. [92] Art. 1045 GCC.
[93] Arts. 1203 and 1204 GCC introduce an exception for third-party protection.
[94] Arts. 1200, 1201 and 1339 GCC.
[95] See art. 41 law 3026/1954 and art. 22 § 2 law 2318/1995.

In recent years, Greece has gradually introduced a Land Registry. If a Land Registry is already established in the district of the house in question, then James would search under either Paul's name or the address of the house. This search would bring up a code number that corresponds to a unique piece of immovable property. This number leads to the print-out of the so-called 'Land Registry Sheet', which is supposed to provide an accurate picture of all rights *in rem* at the given time. From when the Greek Land Registry enters into full operational mode (sometime in the future), it is foreseen that it will provide a presumption of accuracy for all details contained therein.

4 *France and related jurisdictions*

(a) France

James can inquire about the property or Paul with the Land Registry. The French system for transferring immovable property is especially complex. It is widely based only on the will of the parties, and there is no register that can guarantee in an infallible way whether the transferred right really exists.

The method of transfer is entirely under the principle of consensualism, which allows for exceptions to be applied to all the methods of transfer (sale, barter transaction, contribution to a company) and to all properties (immovable and movable). The French law requires neither delivery, conclusion of an additional contract, nor inscription in an official register. Conclusion of the initial contract is enough in principle to effectuate the transfer of property;[96] this is called 'transfer *solo consensu*'. Consequently, despite the fact that the existence of the obligation to transfer (*dare* in Latin) is recognised by the C. civ.,[97] many experts consider that the transfer is a statutory effect of the contract.[98] However, some experts acknowledge this obligation to transfer,[99] and add that at the same time as the parties conclude the contract they proceed to the

[96] Art. 1138 C. civ. [97] Arts. 1136–1141 C. civ.

[98] Muriel Fabre-Magnan, 'Le mythe de l'obligation de donner', *RTD civ.* (1996), p. 85; Corinne Saint-Alary-Houin, 'Réflexions sur le transfert différé de la propriété immobilière', *Mélanges Pierre Raynaud* (Paris: Dalloz, 1985), p. 747; Denis Tallon, 'Le surprenant réveil de l'obligation de donner', D. 1992, chron. 3, p. 68. See for a summary and an analysis of the controversy A.-S. Courdier-Cuisinier, 'Nouvel éclairage sur l'énigme de l'obligation de donner', *RTD civ.* (2005), p. 521.

[99] Pascale Bloch, 'L'obligation de transférer la propriété dans la vente', *RTD civ.* (1988), p. 694; Jérôme Huet, 'Des différentes sortes d'obligations et, plus particulièrement, de l'obligation de donner, la mal nommée, la mal aimée', *Études Jacques Ghestin* (Paris: LGDJ, 2001), p. 425.

'civil delivery' of the immovable property, and this delivery only takes place with the consent of the parties.[100] Regardless, there is no doubt about the principle. Unless otherwise agreed, the transfer takes place immediately. In practice, the transfer and the payment of the price are usually postponed until the reiteration of the contract in front of the notary (a necessary formality to set the transfer against certain third parties), but this is just a short suspensive term on the performance of the contract. The principle of the *solo consensu* transfer is only qualified in its application by the necessity of protecting certain third parties, for which the 'Land Publicity' was conceived.[101]

France possesses both a system of Land Publicity and a cadastre, which for historic and fiscal reasons are connected with the Ministry of Finance. Control of the formalities is thus restricted, which limits the legal reach of the land publicity and the cadastre.

The Land Publicity is organised by the decree of 4 January 1955,[102] which aims to publicise the diverse acts and facts that modify the legal status of a piece of immovable property, in order to improve information regarding third parties. The essence of this system consists of the obligation to publish acts, sentences and legal facts (i.e. a death) that create or transfer an immovable real right. The act must be deposited at a local office called the Land Registry and placed under the responsibility of a civil servant of the Ministry of Finance called a Land Registrar, who also collects expenses and fiscal taxes. This Land Registrar registers the deposit of acts on a register held from day to day, which allows parties to establish the order in which acts were published. Since 1955, the Land Registrar must establish a real estate file that lists extracts of the published acts by owners using personal index cards, and by properties using real index cards. This mixed system makes it possible to obtain information either about a particular person's real estate or the rights and charges on a particular property. To allow the establishment of the real index cards, the decree of 4 January 1955 created a correlation between the land publicity and the cadastre, even if they are managed by two different services. Originally, the cadastre had essentially a fiscal

[100] Jean Pascal Chazal and Serge Vicente, 'Le transfert de propriété par l'effet des obligations dans le code civil', *RTD civ.* (2000), p. 477; Frédéric Zenati-Castaing and Thierry Revet, *Droit des biens*, 3rd édn., PUF coll. Droit fondamental, No. 178 (2008). This civil tradition would be presumed by the C. civ. and was systematically practised before the French Revolution.

[101] '*Publicité foncière*' in French.

[102] And by the decree of 14 October 1955 for details.

function of establishing land tax. Nowadays, it also serves to identify the properties for which the Land Registrar receives acts.

The cadastre does not guarantee the owner of the property in question. Indications on the cadastre can be disputed and only amount to an element that needs to be considered when determining a case. In the French law, with the exception of acquisitive prescription, there is no perfect evidence of ownership. It can be established by any means, including title, possession and the configuration of place, and decided by courts according to their hierarchy of authority. Contrary to the German Land Book, land publicity is not attributive of real right and is not considered to be convincing. The Land Registrar does not control the reality about the right of the assignor. Rather, the land publicity only serves as evidence that can be used against third parties to prove that B acquired his right of A. However, it does not prove that A was actually the owner. The Land Registrar does not verify the intrinsic regularity of the translative contract – those who want to deal with B must know that his title is exposed to an action in nullity or in avoidance, which would override the disposal concluded with B.[103]

Compulsory land publicity has affected the manner in which the contracts transferring immovable property are concluded. On the one hand, the contract must be certified by an authentic act for its publication and this makes a notary's involvement necessary, mostly to reiterate a transfer already agreed by simple contract. On the other hand, the publication conditions the possibility of the transfer being against certain interested third parties, such as where the particular assignees of the same assignor, or of a common assignor, would claim a competing right over the property.[104] For example, this could occur if A sells the property to B, then A sells the property again to C. B can only set his acquisition against C if B is the first to publish it. C will prevail over B if C is the first to publish it, at a moment when A still appeared in the real estate file as being the owner.

However, this rule of conflict has a limited domain. In particular, the land publicity does not protect the purchaser against a competitor who claims to have acquired his third-party right without having sought registration on the real estate file. It only protects him against the existence of non-public acts coming from his assignor. The Court of

103 Art. 28 of the decree of 4 January 1955 moderates this inconvenience by imposing the publication of the request of nullity or avoidance of the contract.

104 The heirs are not considered as third parties and are considered in the same position as the assignor.

Cassation had developed a very important doctrine based initially on fraud, then on civil liability[105]: if C is the first to publish a right that he has acquired from A while knowing that A had already transferred it to B, then C is at fault and this means that C cannot profit from the land publicity. However, if C resells to D and D publishes before B does, then D will only lose the profit of his land publicity if he bought the property with full knowledge of the facts.[106] This application of civil liability restrains the extent to which land publicity is automatic. However, recent sentences of 10 February 2010 and 12 January 2011 clearly give up this jurisprudence[107] because despite the fact that a second buyer had knowledge of an agreement that the seller had with a third party, the Court of Cassation declared this preceding sale non-invocable to the second buyer, only due to the fact that it was not published.

Although the legal consequences of land publicity are limited, land publicity gives real estate transactions a sufficient security because it is common practice for conflicts to be settled by the Decree of 4 January 1955. Actions by a third party for property recovery who is totally absent from the real index card generally only concern the ground that is on the verge of two properties, rather than a whole property.

(b) Belgium

The Belgian law has two real estate registers that can help to assess the proprietary status of the house: the Hypothec Register (mortgage register) and the Cadastral Register.

The proprietary status of the house will emerge from an inspection of the Hypothec Register because it will determine who the owner of the house is and whether a third person has a proprietary right on the house. However, Belgian law follows a 'negative' system of registries.[108] The registration of rights does not ensure the validity of the registered rights. In other words, the rights that are registered are merely rights that have

[105] Cass. 3ème civ., 30 January 1974, No. 72-14197: D. 1974, p. 427, note J. Penneau; *JCP* 1975, ed. G, II, 18001, note M. Dagot.

[106] Cass. 3ème civ., 11 June 1992, No. 90-10687: D. 1993, p. 528, note A. Fournier.

[107] Cass. 3ème civ., 10 February 2010, No. 08–21656: *Droit civile: les sûretés, la publicité foncière*, 5th edn., Laurent Aynès, Pierre Crocq (Paris: Defrénois, 2011), p. 1073, note S. Piédelièvre; *Rev. contrats* 2010, p. 895, obs. S. Pimont – Cass. 3ème civ., 12 January 2011, No. 10–10667: D. 2011, p. 851, note L. Aynès; *Defrénois* 2011, p. 479, note C. Grimaldi; *RTD civ.* 2011, p. 158, obs. P. Crocq, and p. 369, obs. T. Revet.

[108] See on this point, Vincent Sagaert, 'Het rechtmatig vertrouwen van de schuldeisers in de hypothecaire registers', in *Feestbundel Achilles Cuypers* (Brussels: Larcier, 2009), pp. 221–236.

been vested or transferred, but James must still assess their validity. It is possible that the title of the person who is registered as the owner could subsequently be disputed, in which case this subsequent action should be mentioned in the margin of the Hypothec Register. If a person is registered as the owner on the basis of an invalid title and James buys the house and registers the sales agreement, James will not become the owner until the period for acquisitive prescription has expired. Registration by James, in the same way as the registration by his predecessor does not cover invalid transfers.

It is only possible to search the Hypothec Register on the basis of the family names because the Hypothec Register is structured alongside the name of the person who holds a property right. If the man working in the garden has disclosed his family name, it will be possible for James (or most frequently his public notary) to search the Hypothec Register.

James cannot search the Hypothec Register on the basis of the cadastral number or the address of the house. Moreover, some parcels of land, such as most public domain grounds, do not have a cadastral identification number. Therefore, James (or his public notary) will have to undertake a prior search in the Cadastral Register. The Cadastral Register does not have any proprietary impact and as with many other European countries it originates from the taxation system. James can search the Cadastral Register on the basis of the address of the premise or the name (s) of the person(s) holding property rights on the premise. The information that emerges from the Cadastral Register does not give James any certainty about the proprietary status of the house, although it will enable him to make a search in the Hypothec Register on the basis of these names.

5 *England and related jurisdictions*

(a) England

Since 1989, James has been entitled to inspect and take copies of the Register of title held at HM Land Registry regarding the property.[109] The Register can also be searched online. In particular, the Proprietorship Register will indicate the name of the current registered owner of the land[110] and it is conclusive evidence of title.[111]

[109] See now section 66, LRA 2002.
[110] Rule 8 (1) (b) Land Registration Rules 2003 (hereafter, 'LRR 2003').
[111] Section 58, LRA 2002.

If the land is not registered, which is increasingly unlikely but nonetheless possible,[112] James should ask Paul to produce the title deeds which detail successive transactions involving the land. These deeds are normally provided in the form of photocopies of the documents or of an epitome and describe each transaction involving the land. James would check that the deeds prove title for at least the last fifteen years,[113] in order to form his judgment as to whether Paul has title to the land, 'for no person in his senses would take an offer of a purchase from a man, merely because he stood upon the ground'.[114]

(b) Scotland

Registration has been mandatory in Scotland since 1617, in the sense that it is the final and essential step for transferring landownership.[115] As a result, virtually all land is registered and the Register is (and always has been) open to the public, without restriction. The original register of 1617, known as the Register of Sasines, was a register of deeds. This is being phased out and replaced by a new register, the Land Register of Scotland, which operates a system of title registration.[116] Today, where land is transferred, the transaction must be registered in the new Register. As a result, the title to some 55 per cent of properties is held in the Land Register, and the numbers are rising gradually. This, however, represents only 21 per cent of Scotland's land mass, and many large rural estates remain on the Register of Sasines. Both registers are administered by Registers of Scotland, a government agency.[117]

The Land Register is held in electronic form. For each property there is a separate title sheet that describes the property, names the owner, and lists any limited real rights which affect the property, such as rights in security ('mortgages').[118] The boundaries are shown on a cadastral map.[119]

[112] According to the Land Registry's estimates, over 87 per cent of titles to land in England and Wales are registered: see Land Registry, *Annual Report and Accounts 2005/6* (London: The Stationery Office, 2006) indicating that over 20 million titles are registered (p. 19) out of an estimated total of 23 million titles (p. 117).

[113] Section 44 (1), LPA 1925 and section 23, LPA 1969.

[114] *Hiern* v. *Mill* (1806) 13 Ves. 114 at p. 122.

[115] Registration Act 1617.

[116] The relevant legislation is the Land Registration etc. (Scotland) Act 2012, replacing an earlier Land Registration (Scotland) Act (LR(S)A) 1979. UK legislation is available at www.legislation.gov.uk. For an explanation of the many changes introduced by the 2012 Act, see Scottish Law Commission, *Report on Land Registration* (Scot Law Com No 222, 2010), available at www.scotlawcom.gov.uk.

[117] See www.ros.gov.uk.

[118] Sections 5–10, Land Registration etc. (Scotland) Act 2012.

[119] Sections 11–13, Land Registration etc. (Scotland) Act 2012.

James can consult the title sheet in person, use an internet-based inquiry service,[120] or employ a law firm or a firm of professional searchers.

James' task is harder if the property is still held on the Register of Sasines. The Register of Sasines is indexed by property as well as by person, so a search of the Register will reveal all the deeds that affect the house in question. Copies of the deeds can also be obtained. Almost certainly, the owner of the house will be the person in whose favour the most recent deed of conveyance (known as a 'disposition') was granted. But the evaluation of deeds is beyond the layman, and if James wants a definitive answer he will need to employ a solicitor to examine the deeds on his behalf.

Suppose that James decides to buy the house from Paul. Assuming that the title is registered in Paul's name on the Land Register, James can go ahead without anxiety. For, even if the registration was in error – even if, in other words, Paul was *not* the owner despite being registered as such – Paul can nonetheless confer ownership on James provided James was acting in good faith.[121] If, however, the house is still on the Register of Sasines, the normal rules of property law apply by which a good title can only be conferred by an owner or a person acting with the owner's authority.[122] If, therefore, it turned out that Paul was not the owner, Paul would be unable to confer ownership on James. It would make no difference that James *thought* that Paul was the owner: no title is conferred merely by good faith.

(c) Ireland

Presumably, James wishes to purchase the house and is anxious to verify Paul's title. If the house is registered in the Land Registry[123] James may visit a public office of the Property Registry Authority to inspect the register and ascertain the registered owner. If this is not convenient, James' solicitor will be able to conduct an online search of the register and identify the registered owner of the property at that address. The register provides a conclusive state guaranteed record of the ownership

[120] Known as 'Registers Direct'.

[121] Section 86, Land Registration etc. (Scotland) Act 2012. There are some qualifications, as can be seen from the answer to case 6 below.

[122] This is the familiar rule in *Digest* 50.17.54: *nemo plus iuris ad alium transferre potest, quam ipse haberet*.

[123] Approximately 93 per cent of the land mass in Ireland is registered in the Land Registry, although much valuable land located in urban centres such as Dublin and Cork remains unregistered.

and certain burdens affecting the property.[124] When James purchases the house he will receive a deed of transfer but he does not become the owner until he registers his deed of transfer in the Land Registry. Once his transfer has been registered, if he purchased in good faith and it subsequently transpires that Paul was wrongfully registered as the owner, James' title will not be disturbed. However, if James is guilty of fraud in relation to the transaction, the register may be rectified to represent the true position.[125]

If the property is not registered in the Land Registry Paul's title must be investigated to establish if he is the owner. Paul must be able to produce the deed transferring ownership from the previous owner to Paul, and he must also be able to trace his ownership through previous transactions for a sufficient period of time. The current practice is to insist on proof of twenty years of title,[126] although proof of fifteen years of title may become acceptable in the future.[127] In contrast to the position in relation to registered land, once the deed has been executed (i.e. the signatures have been witnessed)[128] and delivered to James or his solicitor, ownership of unregistered land will pass to him. However, James has the option of registering his deed in the Registry of Deeds, a separate registration system applying to land that is not registered in the Land Registry. Registration of the deed does not guarantee its validity and it is not compulsory; its sole purpose is to secure priority for James over other unregistered transactions that Paul may have entered into in relation to the same piece of land.[129]

[124] Section 31, Registration of Title Act 1964. See Brendan Fitzgerald, *Land Registry Practice*, 2nd edn. (Dublin: Sweet & Maxwell, 1995).

[125] The circumstances in which the Register may be rectified are discussed in more detail in the response to case 6.

[126] Note that if the contract for sale does not specify any proof of title requirements (i.e. in an 'open' contract), section 56, Land and Conveyancing Law Reform Act 2009 provides that the purchaser may insist on proof of fifteen years of title. Previously, section 1, Vendor and Purchaser Act 1874 applied, which provided that a purchaser could insist on proof of forty years of title in such circumstances.

[127] It is anticipated that the reduction in the period of title required in an open contract implemented by section 56, Land and Conveyancing Law Reform Act 2009 will influence future conveyancing practice in this respect.

[128] See section 64 (2) (b), Land and Conveyancing Law Reform Act 2009.

[129] Section 38, Registration of Deeds and Title Act 2006.

Case 2

Andrew wants to buy Barbara's house, and she is willing to sell it to him. What professionals might Andrew engage in order to complete his purchase?

(a) What professionals *must* he engage in order to complete this purchase?
(b) What will the professionals do?
(c) Please indicate the source of payment for each of the professionals you have mentioned under (a) and (b) above (e.g. Andrew pays, or the state pays).

(A) Foundational Concepts for Understanding Case 2

It is very common for parties to require professional advice when seeking to transfer property, even where professional advice is not mandated by law. This is without doubt due to the economic importance of immovable property and the potentially high economic risk involved.

Nevertheless there are some countries inside a Latin notarial system that require the authentication of a notary either for the juridical transaction that is governing the transfer or for the registration of the transfer in the Land Register. The Latin notary public plays an important role in the procedures, being the private professional person appointed by the state to draw up authentic deeds of transfer. Usually this formal requirement also makes it possible for the parties to receive professional advice by the notary. This professional will draw up a notarial deed of transfer, after verifying the seller's right to dispose and consensus by the parties.

On the other hand, although statutes do not necessarily require the assistance of a legal professional, usually the parties are willing to get advice from a specialist. The aim of this participation would be primarily to ensure that the parties are following the correct process so that the transfer is valid, and secondly to assist with the execution of the transfer. This latest function can be stated especially in the English system, where solicitors act as intermediaries who hold the sales deed and the payment in escrow.

In addition, there are third parties who are interested in the professionals' participation so that security is reached. For instance, banks usually participate in the process of transfer by conferring credit to the acquirer.

There are several types of professionals, including Latin civil law notaries, British solicitors and Nordic licensed real estate agents. Generally, in many European countries, advice is provided by notaries. On the other hand, in the Nordic countries, the Nordic licensed real estate agent is the professional responsible for drafting the contract and execution. Nevertheless in Finland apart from this licensed real estate agent, the notary witnesses the conveyance. For that reason, the requirements to become real estate agents are strictly regulated in the Nordic countries.[1] In the United Kingdom and Ireland, the real estate agent's role is more limited.

The civil law notary taking into account his statutory professional duties has to act as a neutral intermediary. For that reason, in many countries it is sufficient for one notary to participate.

In the United Kingdom and Ireland, normally two solicitors are participating in the transfer, with one representing the seller and another representing the buyer. The seller's solicitor drafts the contract and the buyer's solicitor reviews it.

In relation to payment, the general rule is that there are statutory provisions establishing that the buyer should pay (Germany, Austria, Finland, Italy, Spain, Greece, France, Belgium, England, Scotland or Ireland). In some countries, such as Sweden, Denmark or Norway, the person who contracted the service is required to pay.

(B) The Jurisdictions (Presented by Related Jurisdictions)

1 *Germany and related jurisdictions*

(a) Germany

Andrew will engage a notary. He might also seek legal advice by a lawyer and appoint a property valuer and a surveyor.

[1] Illustrative in this sense is the Danish report on the requirements for becoming a real estate agent.

(a) Due to formal requirements (see case 3), Andrew must engage a notary.

Andrew can demand an energy performance certificate (*Energieausweis*) from Barbara. Any seller of a building that is not a heritage-listed building is obliged to present an energy performance certificate to the buyer.[2] The energy performance certificate can only be issued by qualified or accredited experts. It can be based on the energy needs of the building (*Bedarfsausweis*) or on the consumption of energy (*Verbrauchsausweis*).

(b) The notary and sometimes also the solicitor will inspect the Land Register for the title and encumbrances,[3] make enquiries about land charges noted in other registers (e.g. public easements or *Baulasten*),[4] advise Andrew about legal matters concerning the purchase, procure the official certificates necessary for the completion of the transfer and formulate a draft contract of sale and a declaration of conveyance (*Auflassung*). Only the notary can authenticate the final contract of sale and the declaration of conveyance. The latter has to be declared orally in the presence of both Andrew and Barbara before the notary.[5]

In most cases, the notary will also make the applications for registration of a priority notice (*Vormerkung*) and (after the payment of the purchase price is assured) of the transfer of ownership to Andrew.[6] The registration of the priority notice has the effect that an encumbrance of the property (e.g. mortgaging the house) or an acquisition of the property by someone other than Andrew is void

2 See § 16 para. 2 Energy Regulation (*Energieeinsparverordnung* [EnEV]). The EnEV is based on the Energy Saving Act (*Energieeinsparungsgesetz* [EnEG]). Both serve to implement the EU Directives 2002/91/EC and 2010/31/EU into national law.

3 The notary (a solicitor only if mandated by the notary) does not need to show a legitimate interest in inspecting the Land Register (§ 43 GBV). The notary is legally obligated to check the Land Register (§ 21, para. 1 *Beurkundungsgesetz*, BeurkG).

4 In practice, notaries usually do not inspect the *Baulastenverzeichnis* (register of public easements). Therefore the buyer should examine it by himself. It is also advisable for the buyer to inspect the *Altlastenkataster* (register of contaminated sites).

5 § 925, para. 1 BGB (A declaration of conveyance may also be made in an in-court settlement or in an insolvency plan that has been finally and non-appealably confirmed.). The additional recording of the declaration of conveyance by the notary is not a formal requirement for the effectiveness of the transfer but necessary for the application to register Andrew as new proprietor in the land register (see §§ 20, 29, para. 1 GBO). Moreover the recording has the effect, that the declaration of conveyance becomes binding for the parties (§ 873, para. 2 BGB).

6 § 15 GBO authorises the notary who authenticated the declarations for the purchase to make the relevant applications on behalf of the purchaser and the seller.

against him.[7] It provides security to Andrew and allows him to pay the purchase price without any risk. In order to secure the seller (Barbara), the parties can advise the notary to act as an escrow agent. In that case, the notary is obliged not to make the application for registration of the transfer until Andrew has paid the purchase price into a notarial escrow account. The property valuer will value the house and the surveyor will report on its physical condition.

(c) Following the statutory provisions, Andrew (the buyer) bears the costs of the notarial recording of the sales contract and the declaration of conveyance.[8] But Andrew and Barbara can agree on a different distribution of costs. The notarial charges which are not covered by these costs, the solicitor's fees and the costs for the property valuer or the surveyor will be paid by Andrew, as he is the person who engaged the relevant professionals.

(b) Austria

When contracting parties have agreed on buying or selling an immovable they almost always appoint a trustee (usually a notary or a lawyer) to settle the property transaction. The reason for that is to ensure a concurrent performance which otherwise cannot be achieved.

According to Austrian law (§ 431 ABGB), Andrew does not acquire property before completion of the registration in the Land Register. But therefore several legal and contractual (quite time-consuming) preconditions have to be fulfilled. For example, the land transfer tax has to be paid, official permits have to be obtained (e.g. the separation of property approval, or *Grundtrennungsbewilligung*) or the affirmation of release of land charges (*Lastenfreistellung*) has to be effected. Furthermore, the tax clearance certificate (*steuerliche Unbedenklichkeitsbescheinigung*) has to be submitted.

(a) Andrew is not obliged to engage a professional to complete his purchase after the sales contract has been signed and notarially certified or legalised (cf. § 31 GBG), but it would be unwise to continue without the help of a fiduciary. The seller will assuredly demand payment before signing other relevant documents. That will force Andrew to bear the advance risk. If the registration (*Intabulation* – § 8 No. 1 GBG) eventually fails because a permission (e.g. the

[7] See §§ 883, para. 2 and 888, para. 1 BGB. The priority notice does not affect the validity of the dispositions between Barbara and other persons than Andrew.

[8] § 448 para. 2 BGB.

grundverkehrsbehördliche Genehmigung) is not granted, he would have difficulties retrieving his money. Especially in the case of insolvency Andrew will suffer losses.

(b) Usually it is the professional who prepared the sales contract who will also look after the registration and take the purchase money into safekeeping. The amount will temporarily be transferred to a special trust account (*Treuhandkonto* or *Anderkonto*). When the buyer's ownership is finally registered the commissioned notary or lawyer is obliged to remit the given money to the vendor, but certainly not before that point of time.

(c) Andrew will have to pay for the legal advice and help of the professional he consulted unless something particular (e.g. free of charge or cost division) has been agreed upon. A certain professional fee is normally taken for granted (cf. § 1004 ABGB; § 16, para. 1 RAO).

(c) The Netherlands

(a) In the Dutch system the seller and buyer must engage a notary in order to transfer ownership. On a voluntary basis, the seller and buyer may use an estate agent, and the buyer may also use an architect, engineer, or other expert to inspect the house.

(b) Under the Dutch law, a sales contract does not pass ownership. In order to transfer ownership a separate legal act is needed on the basis of a valid legal ground (in our case, the sales contract) (art. 3:84 BW). This also applies to land. Below I shall discuss these two legal acts separately.

In order to make a valid sales contract no professional is needed. However, many estate agents offer to draft a contract for their clients as part of their service. They normally use a contract model that was jointly produced by the consumers' association and the association of home owners (one of the largest associations of estate agents). Notaries also offer this service and make use of a different contract model, which was set up by the Royal Notarial Society. The contract models contain a list of goods that may be included in the contract of sale, such as a garden house, lamps, alarm, curtains, parquet floor and sun blinds. The list may be extended by writing on dotted lines or attaching extra pages.

A notarial deed of conveyance is needed in order to transfer ownership of land. In addition, the deed should be entered into the Deeds Register. Ownership only passes to the buyer after the deed is registered and provided all other transfer requirements have been fulfilled (art. 3:89 BW). By definition, only a public notary can make a notarial deed. Art. 3:89 BW states that either the transferor or the transferee can have the deed registered. In practice the notary will take care of this and will offer the deed to the civil servants of the Deeds Register. The buyer himself is responsible for the physical inspection of the property. The buyer may contract a professional architect or engineer, although this is not done very often.

(c) The costs of the notary will not be paid by the state, but rather by the parties to the contract. A very common contract term in the sale of land is: 'costs buyer', meaning that the buyer will bear these costs. However, this formula is confined to the costs of the notarial transfer deed, registration of the deed and the transfer tax of 2 per cent for houses and 6 per cent for other immovables. Often the buyer also needs financing with a mortgage deed, the costs of which also fall on the buyer. The notarial tariffs are not fixed by the state or the legal profession. Every notary is free to charge the amount he or she thinks fit. If the seller wishes to sell the land via an estate agent, the seller will in principle pay the estate agent's costs. Of course, the parties can provide otherwise in their contract.

(d) Turkey

(a) Andrew might engage an attorney at law or a broker who is involved in real estate contracts.

(b) Andrew is not legally obliged to engage any professionals. The Turkish legal system allows every person who wants to sell, buy, or mortgage an immovable to realise the related contracts without engaging any professionals.

(c) As stated above, it is not mandatory to engage any professionals. If Andrew engages an attorney at law or a broker (estate agency) who is involved in real estate contracts, then he will pay the professional's fees.

2 *Scandinavian jurisdictions*

(a) Finland

(a) It is popular to use a real estate agent's services in Finland. In addition, testers who inspect the physical condition of houses are often used. It is conventional for a solicitor or a bank clerk to write a conveyance contract (a deed of a transferee). There is, nevertheless, no legal obligation to use these services. Parties to transactions often inspect the houses themselves and sometimes prepare the documents themselves.

(b) A special kind of public notary is required to attest the conveyance of a piece of real estate, a share of it, or a parcel. The participation of a notary is a part of the mandatory form rules applying to real estate conveyancing.[9] There is no such obligation in relation to rental property agreements. After the conveyance, Andrew must contact the Title and Mortgage Register. In Finland, there is a general obligation to register all real estate acquisitions, including interests in real estate, parcels and leases.[10]

A notary does not, however, participate in a conveyance when the conveyance is made via the new electronic system for real property exchange. The controls that exist within the electronic system can substitute the notary's work. The electronic conveyancing system is connected with official registers and a proposed conveyance is excluded if it is not uniform with the information on official registers.[11]

In addition, after the conveyance of an unseparated parcel of a registered piece of real estate the transferee shall, as a main rule, contact the local surveying office.[12] The parcel will form a new registered piece of real estate, or be transferred into an existing one as a part of an official land survey (i.e. a subdivision procedure).[13] However, the subdivision will be *ex officio* and contingent on the arrival of the notice from the legal registration authority to confirm the acquisition of title.

While it is possible to transfer ownership of an unseparated parcel, the register system merely records unseparated parcels as parts of register units. In order to update the registers, new units or the new official border lines have to be established via an official land survey procedure. On the other hand, and as a rule, the owner of an unseparated parcel is treated equally to an owner of a registered piece of real estate.

(c) A notary witnesses the conveyance, signs the deed, examines the general validity of the conveyance and reports the conveyance to a number of authorities, such as the register authority. Notaries also

9 2:1.1 and 4:3 Code of Real Estate.

10 11:1 and 14:2 Code of Real Estate.

11 9a:7.2 Code of Real Estate.

12 An unseparated parcel is an area with border lines prescribed in a conveyance and a part of a registered piece of real estate.

13 Real Estate Formation Act 1995 22 at www.finlex.fi/en/laki/kaannokset/1995/en19950554.pdf.

perform many more minor duties that are connected with the conveyance.

The local surveying office will arrange for official executors to perform the subdivision procedure. New pieces of real estate and border lines become official (that is, registered in the Real Estate Register) after they have been decided by an official land survey procedure performed by an executor. As a rule, these executors are professional land surveyors and two layman trustees. Minor procedures can be executed by a land surveyor without the trustees, if the use of trustees is not necessary, and not demanded by an interested party.[14]

As a purchaser, Andrew will pay the notary's fee as well as the registration fees and the cost of the land survey. Other professionals can be engaged by either of the parties, and the party that engages the professional will be required to pay. Parties often opt for the inspection of the physical condition of the house.

(b) Sweden

(a) The buyer has a duty to investigate. Any detectable defect falling within this duty would be precluded from a buyer's claim that the property does not conform with the contract. There are some narrow exceptions to this rule.[15] The seller is liable for defects that are not reasonably detectable.

Consequently, Andrew might want to have the house inspected by a building engineer, or some other technician who specialises in house inspections. House inspectors have a contractual obligation to use their skills and reasonable care when investigating a property.[16] If an inspector fails to take note of detectable defects, this fault on the part of the inspector does not relieve a buyer from their obligation to discover detectable defects.

If the inspector fails to detect defects that are reasonably detectable, the inspector would normally be in breach of contract and therefore liable for damages. If the inspector does take note of a defect, the inspector has quite a far-reaching obligation, which includes not only informing the buyer in writing, but also explaining the nature, severity and possible consequences of the defect or symptom and recommending a technical measure to deal with it.[17] The inspector

[14] See § 4 Real Estate Formation Act. [15] 4:19 (2) Land Code; see case 8 below.
[16] Cf. § 4 Consumer Services Act; *konsumenttjänstlagen* 716: 1985.
[17] Supreme Court judgments *NJA* 1997, 65 and *NJA* 2001, 269.

may make a disclaimer about the duty to recommend future measures, which could relieve the inspector from this duty if the disclaimer is sufficiently clear.

Such inspections are increasingly frequently supplied by the seller, in order to facilitate prospective purchases and speed up the sale process. The buyer may rely on the seller's expert's opinion and use it as evidence that any unrealised defect was reasonably undetectable. If a subsequently discovered defect is deemed 'detectable', the buyer may claim damages from the external expert based on a quasi-contractual relationship, assuming the buyer could be said to have reasonably relied on the expert opinion.[18]

Andrew may wish to obtain an estimation of the market price from a real estate agent or a specialised real estate evaluator. The seller might also supply such an evaluation from an external expert.

Buyers often want to engage an inspector or evaluator of their own, regardless of whether such information has been supplied by the seller, and sellers generally will not object to this.

Even though a vast majority of sales are made with the assistance of real estate agents, parties can conclude a purchase by themselves. The formal statutory requirements are quite easy to comply with and the parties can use standard form contracts available at bookshops, or use a model contract as their own contract. The buyer may subsequently apply to register the title based on the contract. In order to register a title, the seller's written assignment of the property must be confirmed by two witnesses' signatures.[19] The witness requirement is not a formal requirement of the sale itself, it is only a requirement for registration.

Real estate agents are obliged to observe good practice, act with due care, act impartially towards the seller and the buyer and inform the parties about everything of any material importance that the agent has knowledge of,[20] whether it be positive or negative.[21] Real estate agents need to be authorised as real estate agents, after completing two years of education.[22] Only practising lawyers (i.e. members of the national bar association) are exempted from this requirement.[23]

The sale is sometimes concluded at a bank, and bank officials may assist the parties if they have a mortgage or are intending to get a

18 Cf. Supreme Court judgments *NJA* 1987, 692 and *NJA* 2001, 878.
19 20:7 (1) Land Code. 20 §§ 8 and 16 Estate Agents Act; *fastighetsmäklarlagen* (2011:666).
21 *See* Supreme Administrative Court's decision RÅ 2003 ref. 51.
22 § 6 Estate Agents Act. 23 § 5 (1) (2) Estate Agents Act.

mortgage upon the property. Even if the system is simple enough to allow owners to handle the registration of mortgages by themselves, owners usually leave such tasks to their lenders (banks or other credit institutions). Only the registered owner may apply to register a mortgage,[24] but in practice lenders, or the buyers' lenders in cases of a conveyance, fill out the application form, which is then signed by the owner. In these cases, the standard form signed by the owner instructs the Cadastral Authority to send the mortgage deed directly to the registered holder of the mortgage deed, generally the lender.

The Cadastral Authority controls whether an application to register a title or a mortgage is in formal compliance with the legal requirements.

(b) Sweden does not have a notarial system. There is no requirement to engage professionals, apart from the civil servants in the Registry offices, although these civil servants are not 'engaged' by anyone.

(c) Real estate agents will assist the parties with most of the usual tasks involved in the purchase and sale of a property. The agent will produce the contract in accordance with the wishes of the parties and supply official information relating to it. The agent is forbidden from representing any of the parties, however the agent may perform tasks of lesser importance on behalf of one of the parties, such as receiving the payment on behalf of the seller. The real estate agent must try to convince the seller that the buyer would need a termination clause, for example subject to a bank loan.

Real estate agents are almost without exception engaged by the seller, who therefore pays the agent. The fee is usually in the form of a commission based on a percentage of the sales price (generally 2–6 per cent). Property evaluations made by real estate agents in the course of a selling process are free of charge unless the seller has agreed to the contrary.[25] Inspections and evaluations by other professionals normally cost about €500. The fee is paid by the person who engages the professional. Professional lenders will usually have minor handling fees of about €50 for the mortgaging process. For the lending process, some lenders would have a fee of about €100, but today many lenders refrain charging a fee.

The state demands a fee of 1.5 per cent of the sales price through the Cadastral Authority. If new mortgages are registered, the fee is 2 per cent of the new mortgage registration sum.[26]

[24] 6:1 (1) and 22:2 (1) Land Code. [25] § 23 Estate Agents Act.

[26] §§ 8 (1) and 24 (1) Act on Stamp Duties at Registry Authorities, *lagen (1984:404) om stämpelskatt vid inskrivningsmyndigheter.*

(c) Denmark

(a) In most cases Andrew would engage a solicitor to overlook the formalities of the purchase. In addition, he might engage a realtor or surveyor for a second opinion on the condition and value of the property.

(b) There are no statutory requirements to engage *any* professional. Thus, Andrew and Barbara can take care of all the formalities themselves. For example, Danish law does not require lawyers or notaries to take part in any contract negotiations.

(c) Different professionals have different obligations and tasks in connection with the purchase of a property. Only real estate agents and solicitors are considered below.

1 *Real Estate Agents/Realtors, etc.*

Professional advisors dealing with the purchase and sale of real estate are subject to the regulation in the Transfer of Real Estate Act (hereafter, DRPA).[27] Only real estate agents who are registered with the Danish Business Authority and solicitors may engage in the business of purchase and sale of real estate.

The primary task for the agent/realtor is to procure the sale of a property. Thus, the agent shall procure the sale of the property under the conditions agreed with the principal. As with other agents, the agent may only bind the principal directly towards a third party if specifically authorised to do so. However, the main duty of the real estate agent is towards the seller. Thus, the agent has a duty to advise the seller but only a duty of information towards the buyer.[28]

The core obligations of the agents include a duty of information, a duty of examination, a duty to provide consumer-oriented advice and a duty to perform (at least) a minimum sales job. Further, the agent is under a duty only to represent one of the parties, and to suggest to the buyer that he or she takes independent advice in case the buyer is not represented by a real estate agent or other adviser.[29]

2 *Solicitors, etc.*

Until a few years ago, only lawyers could draft the deed. However, this monopoly has been broken, and anyone may draft a deed concerning the transfer of property of real estate. Thus, a solicitor working in connection with the sale of a property will have the same duties as a

[27] Act of 28 May 2014, No. 526, on the Distribution of Real Property (DRPA).

[28] Sections 24 and 25, DRPA. [29] Chapter 5, DRPA.

real estate agent under the DRPA. The solicitor will have to be listed in the Danish Business Authority's list of real estate agents.[30] Under the trade rules regarding lawyers' liability towards their clients, not taking care of the registry of the deed in the Buildings and Dwellings Register will lead to a penalty payable to the Bar Association and damages to the client. However, taking care of the registry of the deed is not specifically mentioned as a duty for real estate agents under the DRPA. Thus, on this particular point a lawyer's duty of care is more extensive.

3 The Importance of the Certificate of Condition

Under the Purchase of Real Estate Act (Consolidation Act No. 265 of 21 March 2014), a seller may protect him or herself against claims from the buyer if they provide the buyer with a Certificate of Condition issued by an authorised building inspector, as well as information that the buyer may take out a transfer of ownership insurance. There is no strict requirement that a Certificate of Condition be made, but it is now the norm due to the beneficial legal position it provides the seller.

Generally, the party who undertakes the services of one of the above-mentioned professionals pays for the services (meaning that Andrew pays). This is also the case in regard to real estate agents and solicitors acting as real estate agents.[31] Please note that the price of the Certificate of Condition is paid by the seller.

(d) Norway

(a) Norway does not have a notarial system[32] and Andrew is not obliged to engage any professionals in order to complete his purchase. Andrew and Barbara can take care of the transaction themselves, including submitting documents to the Land Register for to transfer the registered title.[33] Andrew and Barbara will need witnesses to sign the registration document, but any adult can serve as a witness.

(b) Even in a case like this, where the seller and the buyer have already established contact and agree to enter into a contract of sale, the parties

30 § 5 DRPA, cf. § 14.2. 31 Section 32, DRPA.

32 The judges of the courts of the first instance have the function of *notarius publicus* (Notarius Publicus Act, *lov om notarius publicus*, 26 April 2002 No. 12). Apart from registering marriages, the *notarius* may confirm signatures, etc., mostly for documents that will be used abroad. The *notarius* has no function related to the domestic transfer of property.

33 See case 1.

will normally wish to engage professionals to write a contract and, more importantly, settle the payment. This entails *inter alia* transfer of the registered title to the buyer, or more often the registering of new security rights to the buyer's lenders as the mortgagees. Similarly, it entails *inter alia* transfer of payment to the seller and the holders of security rights in the property, namely the seller's lenders. These actions should be performed more or less simultaneously in order to avoid the risk of loss to either party. As a rule, only practising lawyers and authorised real estate agents are allowed to render such services professionally.[34] The more basic services of a real estate agent, like marketing the property and negotiating with prospective buyers, are not needed here.

(c) In a case like this, a lawyer or real estate agent may be engaged by either of the parties, or by both of them together, and that engagement will decide who is responsible for paying the professional's fees.
Such services are normally paid by the person who has commissioned the service.[35]

There is no requirement to survey the property (inspect its physical condition). Energy performance certificates are mandatory,[36] while studies concerning general survey reports in connection with transferring dwellings have not led to legislation so far.[37] In practice, the seller will often present at least a valuation of the property, sometimes also a more comprehensive survey. The valuation or the survey must be paid for by the person who ordered it.

3 *Romanic–Mediterranean jurisdictions*

(a) Italy

(a) Since a property transfer can only take place with the parties' consent (art. 1376 ICC), Andrew should not engage any professional. While the purchase by Andrew is valid and effective if done in writing

[34] Section 2-1, Act Relating to Real Estate Agency (*lov om eiendomsmegling*, 29 June 2007 No. 73). In addition, banks may assist in settling the purchase price.

[35] Section 7-2 (4), Act Relating to Real Estate Agency Act. The purpose of this rule is to counteract what was a widespread practice, where the seller engaged the real estate agent and the property was sold on the condition that the buyer covered all costs; the reasoning being that the person who negotiates the service contract should also be the one who pays for the service.

[36] This is a consequence of the implementation under the EEA Agreement of Directive 2002/91 EC.

[37] Official Norwegian Reports (NOU) 2009: 6 *Tilstandsrapport ved salg av bolig* ('survey reports in connection with transfer of dwellings')

(art. 1350 ICC), it cannot be enforced against third parties if it is not registered. In order to register the contract, the ICC only requires acts whose authenticity is certain. It means that the document must comply with specific formal requirements: it must be a judicial decision, a notarial deed (*atto pubblico*), or a private agreement with signatures authenticated by a notary or judicially certified (*scrittura privata autenticata*).[38] The notarial formality is required as a practical matter, in order to register the contract in the Land Register.

(b) In order to complete the transfer, Andrew and Barbara have to instruct a notary to notarise the deed of purchase, or authenticate the signing of the contract between them. In the first case, the deed is written by the notary. In the second case, the notary only takes responsibility for certifying that they witnessed Barbara and Andrew, at the time and place specified, sign at the bottom of the private deed and on the margins of each intermediate page.

The notarised public deed constitutes full proof of the fact that the seller and the buyer entered into the transaction and reached agreement as specified in the contract for the transfer of the immovable property in question at the nominated price. The public deed itself should be capable of transferring ownership to the buyer.

The notary is not only required to verify the parties' intentions to transfer the immovable property and change the title in the Land Register (art. 2671 ICC) – the notary must also perform any act necessary for the identification, verification of ownership and the legal status of the immovable property. The notary will be required to verify in the Land Register that the seller is the owner of the immovable property she is selling and that she is legally able to do so. Other than this, the notary has the duty to verify the absence of registrations that may affect the rights of the purchaser, that the immovable property is free from mortgages and other legal constraints and that the house has not been constructed in violation of town planning regulations. The notary is liable for damages if the contract is made in the absence of these conditions of validity or effectiveness.

(c) Since the the buyer chooses which notary will be in charge of drafting the deed, the buyer must bear the costs, unless otherwise agreed between the parties. Such costs include also the notary's fee excluding the registration fees.[39]

[38] See art. 2657 ICC. [39] Art. 2670 ICC.

(b) Spain

(a) and (c) If, before entering into the transaction, Andrew wants to check that Barbara owns the house and that no third parties hold rights *in rem* in the property, he must apply to the *Registro de la Propiedad* for a certified abstract, known as a *nota simple*. In the *nota simple*, the Registrar will disclose the registered owner, and any other details requested by Andrew that the Registrar thinks fit to disclose. This information does not give Andrew certainty that Barbara is the true owner (see case 1), but provided that Andrew registers the deed with the *Registro de la Propiedad* after completing the transaction, he will enjoy the protection afforded by the *Registro de la Propiedad* to persons acquiring perperty in good faith and for value from the registered owner. To do so, Andrew and Barbara will have to engage a civil law notary to attest the private contract of sale as a notarial act, because only notarial acts are eligible for entry in the *Registro de la Propiedad*. The notary is chosen and paid for by Andrew, as buyer.

The notary authenticates the content of the deed of sale, which sets out the parties' identities, a description of the property, the price, the terms of payment, any charges or encumbrances on the house, the date the property will be handed over and any penalty clauses that would apply in the event of a breach. The parties could in fact go straight to the notary, without first signing a private contract, but this would be unwise if there were more than a negligible lapse of time between the agreement and the parties' appointment with the notary, or if Andrew needed to apply for a mortgage. It is in Andrew's interest to make sure that he can prove the existence of a contract in case Barbara has a change of heart. Proving that a contract exists is far easier to do if there is a written document to rely on.

It is particularly common for parties to use a firm known as a *gestoría* when a property is under a mortgage that is now paid off or passed on to the new owner, or where a property is clear of charges but the buyer is establishing a new mortgage in order to buy it. A *gestoría* handles the steps required to complete the sale and, if applicable, pay off any existing mortgage or create a new one. Such steps include paying taxes and filing documents with the *Registro de la Propiedad*. If the buyer is using a mortgage, the *gestoría* firm that is attached to the mortgage lender handles the loan application. The buyer is generally asked for a down payment to cover the expenses associated with the sale, the mortgage loan and the *gestoría*'s own fees. Any surplus is returned to the seller at the end of the process.

Spanish law does not require a physical inspection of the property prior to sale. However, if the buyer wishes to use a mortgage, the mortgage lender retains a surveyor to value the property, at the buyer's expense. As a rule, this surveyed value is higher than the cadastral value (ascribed by a government body, and composed of the value of the land and the value of the building), yet it is slightly lower than the market value. The surveyed value is the bank's reference figure for the purposes of considering the buyer's loan application.

Given that Andrew and Barbara (buyer and seller) are already in touch with each other, there is no need to use an estate agent.

(b) Andrew and Barbara could complete the transaction without engaging any professional assistance, but this would be unwise. For ownership to be conveyed, it would suffice for Andrew and Barbara to enter into a contract of sale, and for Barbara to put Andrew in possession of the house, for instance by handing over the keys. The contract may be written or oral, and it need not conform to any formal requirement. The transfer of possession must be made on the basis of the parties' respective intentions to acquire and to transfer ownership, which means Barbara must possess the house as owner.

The buyer normally pays both the notary's fees and the Registrar's fees (for attending pre-sale scrutiny and subsequent registration). These fees amount to about 2–3 per cent of the total value of the sale. In addition, the law determines that Andrew must pay stamp duty (*Impuesto de Transmisiones Patrimoniales*) at a rate of 7 per cent, while Barbara must pay a tax on the difference between the value of the underlying land when she bought the house and when she sold it (*Impuesto sobre el Incremento de Valor de los Terrenos*). The parties are free to agree to distribute these burdens differently.

(c) Portugal

(a) Normally, if Barbara seeks to sell her house she would engage a real estate agency.[40] On the other hand, Andrew might engage a bank and a solicitor.

[40] The real estate activity consists of achieving someone interested in acquiring, selling, renting or developing a real estate. In Portugal, estate agents act as intermediaries between a seller and an acquirer. Their activity is ruled by Decree Law 211/2004, of 20 August, and it is limited to companies or business persons legally qualified by the

Generally, Andrew will engage a bank if he asks for a bank loan. However, the role of banks is not limited to financing. Decree Law 255/93 of 15 July, as amended by Decree Law 38/2003 of 8 March, established that authorised credit institutions could certify the sale and acquisition of a dwelling for residential purposes when they finance the purchase. The contract of sale should be concluded in a private document, according to a sample approved by law. More recently, the government is extending the One Stop House Scheme (*Casa Pronta*) to bank services by establishing One Stop House counters in bank branches in order to provide assistance to individuals when the transaction requires a bank loan.[41]

If Andrew engages a legal professional, they will be responsible for drawing up the various agreements and contracts for the property transfer, as well as providing Andrew with tax advice.

In Portugal, no one is responsible for obtaining a survey of the property. It should be emphasised, however, that Decree Law 68/2004 of 25 March regulates the advertising and information made available to consumers regarding the acquisition of real estate for residential purposes. Information made available to consumers must be inscribed in a technical description of the dwelling (*ficha técnica da habitação*) and signed by the developer and the technician in charge of the work (art. 4). The technical description of the building is a document that describes the technical and functional characteristics of the dwelling. One copy of the description must be kept by the developer, and another must be deposited in the Town Hall. The description encompasses information about the people involved in the project, construction, reconstruction, making improvements, modification and acquisition of the dwelling. It also contains information about subdivision, the building and the individual unit, in case of apartment ownership.

(b) Andrew and Barbara can make use of the *Casa Pronta*, a recently introduced fast-track home-buying system. The scheme aims to

Instituto dos Mercados de Obras Públicas e Particulares e do Imobiliário (IMOPPI, created by Decree Law 60/99 of 2 March). The contract of intermediation must be in writing (art. 19), and must contain a long list of elements and descriptions. Before the conclusion of the contract of intermediation, real estates agencies have the duty to check if the parties have legal capacity, the description of the immovable, and if it is burdened with any charge or mortgage. After the conclusion of the contract of intermediation, real estate agencies shall provide clear, objective, and adequate information about the legal and material situation of the building. If Barbara engages a real estate agency in the sale, it would be in charge of the necessary proceedings for completion of the sales contract.

41 See question (b) above.

make the process of buying or selling a property simpler and faster by eliminating formalities and allowing everything to be done at a single contact point. The *Casa Pronta* is implemented by Land Registry Offices and can be found in Registrars located in Citizens' Shops (*Lojas do Cidadão*).

In January 2007, the European Commission launched the foundations for an 'Action Programme to Reduce the Administrative Burden of Existing Regulation in the EU'. The 2007 Spring European Council ratified this programme and set a goal of reducing 25 per cent of the administrative burden on enterprises by 2012, via a joint effort by the European Union and individual member states. The European Council invited member states to set comparable goals of their own at the national level. Portugal responded by committing itself to actively take steps to pursue a programme called Simplex, aimed at reducing the administrative burden on enterprises at both EU and national level. One of the measures adopted within the Simplex Program is the One Stop House Scheme (*Processo Especial de Aquisição, Oneração e Registo de Imóveis em Atendimento Presencial Único*), implemented by Decree Law 263-A/2007 of 23 July.[42]

At the One Stop House users can pay property transfer taxes;[43] conclude the contract of sale, bank loan and mortgage; register their assets as required; request changes to their fiscal address; obtain drawings of the newly acquired property from the municipal authorities; request exemption from the municipal property tax, where relevant;[44] and submit the data required to register the property or update the Property Register.

Although the One Stop House scheme was only foreseen for the sale of urban immovables, it was extended by Implementing Order 1126/2009 of 1 October to contracts over agricultural immovables, and to the *datio in solutio* (besides the sale, bank loan and mortgage). Since the

[42] As amended by Decree Law 122/2009, of 21 May; 99/2010, of 2 September; 209/2012, of 19 September. For a general overview, see José Mouteira Guerreiro, *Tema de Registos e de Notariado* (Coimbra: Almedina, 2010), pp. 547ff.

[43] The *Imposto sobre Transmissões Onerosas de Imóveis* (IMT) is a tax over the transmission of real estates with consideration. A document certifying payment or exemption of payment of the tax must be issued by the respective Tax Office. James would also have to pay the Duty Stamp (*Imposto de Selo*) at the rate of 0.8 per cent which is calculated on the same terms as IMT.

[44] Owners must pay Property Municipal Tax (*Imposto Municipal sobre Imóveis, IMI*), with the amount due depending on the rate approved by the Town Hall.

Implementing Order 67/2010 of 3 February, the One Stop House Scheme can also be used for contracts of gift and exchange of immovables.[45]

But Andrew and Barbara could still follow the traditional way of conveying property. In that case, the title deed would normally be drawn up at the Notary Office.[46] The sales contract would be concluded in an oral hearing, usually at the notary's office[47] and in the presence of both parties.[48] At that time, the buyer would pay the purchase price to the seller because the purchase price is paid immediately, unless the parties agree otherwise. At the same meeting, the seller would give the buyer possession and the mortgage title would be signed, where relevant. When payment is financed through a mortgage loan, both notarial acts (deed of sale and of mortgage) are usually signed in the same act and the bank provides the loan in that moment, even if the mortgage is not yet registered.

The documents necessary for the public deed are: the identification documents and Portuguese tax numbers of the parties (the tax number of a foreign purchaser is obtained prior to the act); the Property Tax Document (*Caderneta Predial*), issued by the Tax Office of the area in which the property is located; the abstract of title (*Certidão do Registo Predial*) issued by the Land Registry; the use license (*Licença de Utilização*) issued by the local Town Hall; certification of the payment of the tax over the transmission of real estates with consideration (*IMT*) issued by the respective Tax Office. If there is an exemption for the tax, it must also be certified by a document. If the acquirer is a consumer, the technical description of the building (*Ficha Técnica de Habitação*) shall also be presented to the notary.

45 The Implementing Order 1167/2010 of 10 November extended the One Stop House Scheme to the division of a building in apartment ownership.

46 Decree Law 116/2008, of 4 July (with effect from 1 January 2009), has eliminated the requirement to execute public deeds for acts relating to real property. The sale and purchase of real estate can now be executed either by public deed or by privately executed contract, which must be certified by some authorised entities: lawyers, Chambers of Commerce and Industry; and paralegals (*solicitadores*). Those entities must ensure registration of the acts they have certified. Although intervention of notaries is no longer mandatory, contracts are still executed in a public deed, namely when banks are involved providing financing secured by mortgages. For criticism on the dematerialisation and informality implemented by Decree Law 116/2008, see Mouteira Guerreiro, *Tema de Registos e de Notariado*, pp. 569ff.

47 Parties may agree to conclude the contract somewhere else (for instance, in the Bank). The Notary can provide for this external service under an extra payment.

48 And a Bank's representative, if a mortgage is to be concluded.

The original deed document is then held by the Public Notary, and a copy is registered with the Central Registration Office. According to art. 8-B LRegC, the notary must ensure registration of the purchase in the Land Register, which usually entails the conversion of a provisional inscription into a definitive one, and keeping the same rank.[49]

(c) In the One Stop House Scheme, the public official must firstly check the identity and legal capacity of the parties and the legal status of the immovable. Then, the public official must inscribe the legal transaction in the agenda; draw up the document for the property transfer; control the payment of required taxes; receive the transaction fees; monitor the signature of the contract by both parties; ensure that the seller delivers the technical description of the building to the acquirer; immediately inscribe the transaction in the Land Registry; and complete the description of the building with the number and the date of the use permit issued by the municipality. Upon request, the public official might also ask for the parties' updated fiscal address, for exemption of payment of the *IMI* and to update of the legal status of the building with the Tax Office.

Traditionally, the Notary is responsible for checking and certifying the legal exactness of the entire transaction and ensuring that all documents are in perfect order, that any applicable purchase taxes have been paid and that all parties agree upon the terms of the transaction. The Notary must also promote registration of the legal act.

According to art. 878 CC, the transfer costs are the purchaser's responsibility, unless the parties agree otherwise.[50] Therefore, by default, Andrew would have to pay the *IMT*, fees due at the conclusion and registration of the contract, and the stamp duty.

(d) Greece

(a) Due to formal requirements, Andrew is obliged to engage a public notary[51] to proceed with the contract of sale. He will most probably

[49] The owner shall apply for registration in the respective Tax Office (*Repartição de Finanças*). The registration in the Tax Office will serve to establish the annual property tax (*IMI*), which is based on the property's taxable value.

[50] The real estate agencies can only receive remuneration from the party that first contacts them, usually the seller; it is forbidden to be paid by the two parties to the same contract (art. 16 (2) (a), Decree Law 211/2004, of 20 August). The duty to pay the remuneration arises only after the conclusion of the contract (art. 18 (1)) and it is forbidden to receive any amount in advance (art. 18 (3)).

[51] Art. 1033 GCC.

also engage a topographer or a civil engineer, and a lawyer to conduct a title search in the Registry due to the limitation of public access to the books.

(b) Andrew must engage only a notary public and possibly a lawyer.[52]

(c) From a property law perspective, for the valid acquisition of immovable property it is necessary to have an agreement between the seller and the buyer and to register this agreement in a notarial deed. In theory, the only person necessary would be the public notary. However, in practice a variety of special provisions make the engagement of additional professionals necessary. Most importantly, if the value of the property exceeds approximately €10,000,[53] both seller and buyer are obliged by law to consult a lawyer. The buyer's lawyer will conduct the relevant title search, and prepare the conveyance agreement with the seller's lawyer.

Due to the uncertainty stemming from the absence of a Land Register, it is common for the buyer to engage a topographer to survey the plot of land and provide a blueprint of the property that can be attached to the contract. Moreover, due to the absence of a Register of Forests, if the property is outside a city, village or other known residential area it is necessary to provide a certificate from the Forest Authority stating that the property is not situated in a forest area. The parties' lawyers will prepare a draft of the conveyance agreement. This draft will be signed by both the seller and the buyer before the public notary.

With the exception of the seller's lawyer, the expenses of all other professionals are usually borne by the buyer.

4 *France and related jurisdictions*

(a) France

Andrew can use a notary, a real estate agent or possibly a lawyer.

(a) Due to the principle of consensualism French law does not oblige parties to use a professional when drafting the contract of sale. However, a notary is required to draft an authentic act that can be published in the real estate file, which is necessary in order to confirm the transfer against any potential third parties.

In order to ensure that buyers have information about the state of the building, the law mandates multiple inspections by registered

52 If the value of the property exceeds €10,000.

53 Or €29,347 for immovable property lying in the district of Athens and Piraeus.

professionals to confirm whether there is asbestos, lead, or termites, as well as to confirm energy performance and that the electric installation conforms with the relevant standards.

(b) The real estate agent is appointed to look for a buyer, advise the seller and possibly draft the simple contract of sale (*compromis de vente*). A lawyer can also draft the contract and advise the parties about the possible legal consequences of the sale. A notary will draft the authentic act. The notary must ensure that the act is correct, inform the parties about its effects and the status of the real estate (town planning, easements and real rights and rents), then ensure that the act is published in the Land Registry.

(c) It results both from art. 1593 C. civ. and from the practice that the buyer is responsible for all of the expenses incurred during the sale, in particular the real estate agent's commission and the notary's fees.

(b) Belgium

(a) In Belgian law, the sales agreement can be binding upon parties without any professional intervening (art. 1583 BCC). However, a public notary will have to intervene in order to formalise this agreement and register it in the Hypothec Register. Only notarial deeds can be registered in the Hypothec Register, and this registration is necessary in order to make the sales agreement enforceable against third parties. If the seller is a public authority, the public notary can be replaced by the public officer of the Sales Committee. However, public authorities can also use a public notary.

The Public Office on Soil Pollution also frequently intervenes. Without going into extensive detail on the rules relating to soil pollution, it is worth noting that it plays an important role because compliance with public law obligations is required in order to validly transfer ownership. Therefore, a private deed of sale is concluded after having complied with the soil pollution provisions and the notarial deed is concluded once these obligations have been complied with.[54] This issue is highly complex in the Belgian law and has become increasingly complex due to the fact that this area of law falls under regional jurisdiction.

[54] According to the case law of the Supreme Court, it would even be possible to attack the validity of a consensual sales agreement which has been agreed upon subject to the condition precedent of complying with the soil pollution provisions (Belgian Supreme Court, 24 June 2010, *Notarieel Fiscaal Maandblad* 2011, 51, note A. Lemmerling, Pasicrisie 2010, 2017, *Rechtskundig Weekblad* 2010-11, 1520, note J. Del Corral).

The applicable laws are the Flemish Region Decree of 27 October 2006[55] for the Brussels Region by the Ordonnance of 5 March 2009,[56] and for the Walloon (French-speaking) Region the Decree of 5 December 2008.[57]

The private or notarial deed has to be deposited at the office for transfer taxes within four months of the realisation of all conditions precedent. Transfers of ownership are, according to Belgian law subject to transfer taxes that vary from region to region and generally amount up to between 10 per cent and 12.5 per cent of the property price. The parties tend not to hire a solicitor for regular transactions.

(b) Firstly, the public notary will search through the Hypothec Register using the methods described under question 1 in order to assess whether the transferor is registered as owner of the property right that he is purporting to transfer and whether there are other property rights burdening the premises. Furthermore, the public notary has to obtain the soil pollution permits, which is necessary in order to operate a valid transfer of property rights on the premises (see below). The soil pollution status of the premise will be described in the notarial deed. Furthermore, the public notary needs to determine whether the premise is burdened with statutory conventional and statutory purchase options. There is a huge and very diverse range of statutory options, which are most frequently in favour of public authorities. Based on this information, the public notary will draft the notarial deed, thereby formalising the sales agreement that has been entered into privately between the parties. Finally, the public notary ensures that the sales agreement is registered in the Hypothec Register.

The notarial deed is not necessary in order to complete the sales agreement, but is necessary to make the transfer enforceable against third parties with competing rights in good faith. Only a notarial deed can be registered in the Hypothec Register, and this registration is necessary in order for the sale to affect third parties.

The public notary is not obliged to inspect the physical condition of the house, and such inspections are between the seller and buyer themselves. In practice, the notarial deed includes a clause of the type 'the Buyer declares that he is fully aware of and accepts the premises in

[55] *Belgian Official Gazette*, 22 January 2007. [56] *Belgian Official Gazette*, 10 March 2009.
[57] *Belgian Official Gazette*, 18 February 2009.

its current state'. This clause exonerates the seller from his contractual liability, except in the case of hidden defects.

(c) The expenses for the public notary and the transfer taxes will have to be paid by the transferee, as he is the most interested party. However, in legal practice, all notarial deeds provide for an express arrangement with regard to those expenses.

In principle, expenses associated with soil decontamination are the transferor's responsibility. However, the parties can agree that the transferor will fully or partly recover these expenses to the transferee.

5 *England and related jurisdictions*

(a) England

Andrew would most likely engage a solicitor. He might also engage a surveyor or valuer, although for the reasons explained in response to case 2, question (b), this is less likely.

(a) Andrew is not legally obliged to engage any professionals. However, as a practical matter he may be forced to engage a solicitor. For example, most building societies will not release mortgage funds other than to a qualified solicitor and so Andrew may need to engage a solicitor, even if only to hold the mortgage monies pending completion. That consideration does not arise if Andrew has sufficient cash in hand to buy Barbara's property without mortgage finance.

(b) Andrew's solicitor may arrange for a survey of Barbara's land to be acquired, although this might be arranged instead by any prospective mortgagee (possibly at Andrew's expense). Andrew's solicitor might also search the Land Register or, if the land is unregistered, the Land Charges Register to determine whether any interests are registered against Barbara's title. Andrew's solicitor will also organise a 'local authority search', which will elicit information about local land charges, developments, conservation, structure plans and other amenity issues.

A surveyor would check that the property is reasonably sound, advising on any defects, and may indicate his or her view of the current market value of the property.

Barbara will also be obliged to provide Andrew with an energy performance certificate for the property.[58]

[58] Reg. 6, Energy Performance of Buildings (England and Wales) Regulations 2012 (SI 2012/3118).

Andrew's solicitor would complete the paperwork necessary to finalise the sale and transfer of title from Barbara to Andrew (Barbara is also likely to instruct a solicitor).

(c) Andrew will pay the fees of any professionals he chooses to engage.

(b) Scotland

(a) Andrew is likely to engage a solicitor and may also engage a surveyor.

(b) The only requirement to engage professionals falls on Barbara, as the seller. All houses that are put on the market must have an official 'home report', which is made available to potential buyers.[59] The home report comprises (i) a survey report, (ii) an energy report (implementing in part EU Directives 2002/91/EC and 2010/31/EU)[60] and (iii) a property questionnaire. The first two documents must be prepared by a qualified surveyor. The third, which provides information on a whole range of topics such as council tax, alterations to the building, the heating system, services, the extent of responsibility for shared maintenance, access rights and boundaries, and specialist treatments for dry rot, can be prepared by the seller but in practice will usually involve the seller's solicitor or estate agent.

By contrast, there is no requirement on Andrew, the buyer, to engage professionals. Scotland does not have a notarial system in the sense found in many countries of continental Europe. Thus, in theory Andrew could complete the legal formalities on his own, without the help of a solicitor, but this is almost unknown in practice. If Andrew is financing the purchase by a loan that is to be secured on the house, the lender will instruct a solicitor to check Barbara's title on its behalf and to prepare the security documentation.

(c) Andrew's solicitor will negotiate the contract of sale, verify Barbara's title to the house, examine the home report, check various local authority permissions relating to matters such as planning and building control, and draw up a deed of conveyance (known as a 'disposition'). In practice, Barbara will be represented by a different solicitor. On the date agreed in the contract, Andrew's solicitor will

59 Part 3, Housing (Scotland) Act 2006; Housing (Scotland) Act 2006 (Prescribed Documents) Regulations 2008, SSI 2008/76.

60 See Energy Performance of Buildings (Scotland) Regulations 2008, SSI 2008/309, as amended by SSI 2012/190, SSI 2012/208 and SSI 2012/315.

arrange for payment of the purchase price against delivery, by Barbara's solicitor, of the title deeds, the disposition and the keys to the house. Andrew's solicitor will then register the disposition in the Land Register. Traditionally, the entire transaction was carried out on paper, but electronic documents with an electronic signature may now be used in place of paper documents.[61] Indeed, by entering the Land Register computer system, solicitors can even register the disposition themselves although, so far at least, few have troubled to do so.[62]

Although the home report contains a survey, instructed by Barbara, Andrew may want to instruct a survey of his own. Indeed if the purchase is being financed by a bank loan, the lender will sometimes insist on an additional survey. Surveyors value the property and report on its physical condition.

Andrew will pay for any professionals whom he engages. In addition, where a loan is being taken out he will have to meet the lender's legal expenses, as well as the cost of any survey required by the lender.

(c) Ireland

Andrew may hire an architect or engineer and a solicitor.

(a) Theoretically, Andrew does not need to engage any professionals but, as Barbara has no duty to disclose any physical defects in the condition of the property, he should inspect it or preferably engage a qualified architect or engineer to carry out a structural survey of the house before he agrees to purchase it. Ireland does not operate a notarial system and therefore Andrew is not legally required to engage a solicitor to carry out the conveyancing. However, if he is obtaining a mortgage to purchase the property, the bank will only release funds to a solicitor who certifies that the title is in order. The bank will rely on the solicitor's expertise and professional indemnity insurance in such circumstances. The bank will also insist that a valuation survey is carried out to ensure that the property value is sufficient to provide adequate security for the loan being made.[63]

[61] Sections 1 (2), 9B and 9C, Requirements of Writing (Scotland) Act 1995.

[62] This is known as automated registration of title to land ('ARTL'). See further Robert Rennie and Stewart Brymer, *Conveyancing in the Electronic Age* (Edinburgh: W. Green & Son, 2008). Registration in this way is possible only in straightforward transactions, and where the land is already on the Land Register.

[63] There are dangers in a purchaser relying on this report and not carrying out his own independent survey, see *O'Connor* v. *First National Building Society* [1991] ILRM 208.

(b) The architect or engineer will survey the property to identify any defects in its physical condition. He may also be requested to check the boundaries of the property on the ground to ensure that they correspond with the boundaries as they appear on any map furnished with the contract for sale. In addition, he may check that no unauthorised developments have taken place on the premises, that no applications for planning permission have been lodged with the local authority for a development on an adjoining property which could negatively affect the premises or that the property will not be affected by zoning proposals or proposals for road widening.

Andrew's solicitor will approve or amend the contract for sale, which is usually drafted by the vendor's solicitor. He or she will investigate Barbara's title and make certain enquiries of Barbara's solicitor in relation to the property.[64] He will draft the deed in favour of Andrew and carry out pre-completion searches to ensure that no undisclosed interests affect the property, which would bind Andrew. If the property is being financed by a mortgage Andrew's solicitor will usually also act on behalf of the bank. In that capacity, Andrew's solicitor will be required to certify that the title being acquired by Andrew is a good marketable title and to ensure that the mortgage documentation is properly executed. After the transaction has been completed, Andrew's solicitor will arrange for the deeds to be stamped and registered and if a mortgage is involved, he will forward the title documentation to the bank.[65]

(c) Andrew pays the solicitor for the legal work and the architect/engineer for the cost of the structural survey. The bank may pay for the valuation survey, or alternatively it may pass on this cost to the borrower.

[64] Known as 'Objections and Requisitions on Title'.

[65] See J.C.W. Wylie and Una Woods, *Irish Conveyancing Law*, 3rd edn. (Haywards Heath: Bloomsbury Professional, 2005).

Case 3

Andrew has offered to buy Barbara's house; she has agreed to sell to him, and they have agreed a price.

(a) What is the effect, if any, of this unwritten agreement? If either party changes their mind now, does the other have a remedy?
(b) Andrew and Barbara write down their agreement and sign it. What is the legal effect of this, if any? If either party changes their mind now, does the other have a remedy?

(A) Foundational Concepts for Understanding Case 3

The question is answered differently according to the several European legal systems (see also case 4). In Germany, parties first conclude the contract of sale by notarial act. After that, the notary orders a registration in the Land Register for this contract (*Vormerkung*, § 883 BGB). This inscription has the consequence that all subsequent transfers are invalid against the holder of the priority notice. For that reason, the buyer can pay without any additional risk.

The system is a little complicated as it also requires a separate agreement on the transfer of ownership (*Auflassung*, § 925 BGB). Although in practice this agreement is contained in the same document as contract of sale, the notary does not register it until after the payment has been produced. Finally, it is required in order to transfer property by registration in the Land Register.

In England, the documents for the contract of sale are produced between the seller's and the buyer's solicitors. Generally, at this moment there is a down payment of 10 per cent of the purchase price. The conclusion of the process is called 'completion', when the remaining amount of the price is paid. This payment is made into an escrow account of the conveyance acting for the seller and also the keys are handed over and the purchaser takes possession. After that, the transfer is registered, and the money is paid out from the escrow account.

In Napoleonic Code countries such as France, Belgium, Italy and Portugal, first a preliminary contract is signed. Usually a payment of between 5 per cent and 10 per cent is also made. After the buyer has obtained financing, the contract of sale is concluded in a notarial act. At the same time, payment must be made, as the contract of sale already transfers ownership. Registration is done afterwards, but it usually has a declaratory effect, with some particularities depending on the particular legal system.

In order to register a contract of sale for land it must be in a certain form: an authentic act is required for every real estate sale of real property in Germany (§ 311b, para. 1 BGB). In the Napoleonic Code countries, only notarial documents can be registered (Belgium, France, Italy, Luxembourg, Portugal and Spain). The sales contract is binding among the parties even without this form. Nevertheless, the transfer of ownership requires the form of an authentic act.

In the Netherlands, an authentic act is required for the (separate) agreement for the transfer of ownership. In German law the sales contract needs to be notarial (thus an authentic deed).

In the other systems, there is no formal requirement for the validity of the sales contract or the transfer.

In Austria, there are only procedural requirements for the registration (certification of signature), which do not affect the substantive validity of the obligations or the transfer of ownership.

In Finland and Sweden a sale must be made in writing. In Sweden it is very common to use two consecutive documents, the second one being a condition for the buyer to get possession. In Finland, only one sale contract with strict formal requirements is recognised by the law. In Denmark and Norway there are no formal requirements, but oral agreements of sale are rare. In Nordic law, registration mainly has a declaratory effect. Registration of the buyer as owner is not a requirement for validity; nor does registration heal invalidity.

The main effect of requiring a notarial document to transfer or to register the transfer in the Land Register is that it achieves a high degree of legal security. In some cases an authentic document is also required for the contract of sale and the participation of the notary provides the parties with authorised legal advice.

The transfer of immovable property seems to happen as part of a process, rather than at a unique moment. The reports demonstrate that in almost all countries, in practice there are at least two consecutive transactions: at the very beginning there is an agreement that gives rise to contractual obligations. Afterwards, there is a second moment when ownership passes. The price is paid either between the two transactions or at the same time as ownership is transferred.

There are some countries that require the obligational contract and agreement to transfer ownership. The relationship among them could be abstract (in Germany) or causal (in the Netherlands).

In those systems in which only the sale is necessary to transfer ownership, it is very common that in practice parties first sign a preliminary contract and in a second step the contract that produces the effect of the transfer (as in Italy or in France).

In conclusion, the requirements to transfer ownership vary according to the different European legal systems. In the countries influenced by the French C. civ. (Belgium, France, Italy, Luxembourg, Portugal), the sales contract already transfers ownership. There is a special situation in Spain more related to the 'titulus and modus' theory as in Austria, where in addition to the contract something else is necessary and this is the delivery (the transmission of possession, the so-called '*traditio*'). Registration is not compulsory but merely declaratory.

In England, the system has been reformed so that ownership is transferred by registration in the Land Register. On the other hand, in Austria the contract and registration in the Land Register are both necessary.

In Germany, the system is very complex and requires agreement on the transfer of ownership (*Auflassung*) and registration. If the sale contract is null and void it does not affect the transfer. The German legal system and the English are both abstract.

In the Netherlands, there are three requirements: the sales contract, a separate agreement on the transfer of ownership and registration.

(B) The Jurisdictions (Presented by Related Jurisdictions)

1 *Germany and related jurisdictions*

(a) Germany

(a) The oral agreement has no legal effect. It neither is a valid contract of sale nor a valid declaration of conveyance because it does not comply with the forms prescribed by law.

The contract of sale (*Kaufvertrag*), which is the contract *in personam* whereby one party obliges himself to transfer or acquire ownership of a plot of land, must be authenticated by a notary.[1] As the unwritten agreement lacks the form prescribed by law it is void.[2] But a defect in the formal requirement is cured if there is a declaration of conveyance and registration in the Land Register.[3] In very exceptional cases (e.g. where one party fraudulently prevents the other from observing the formal requirements) it might be possible to enforce a formally invalid contract of sale with reference to the general rule of good faith (§ 242 BGB).

The declaration of conveyance (*Auflassung*) is the agreement *in rem* that the plot of land should be transferred. This agreement and the corresponding registration are both indispensable for the transfer of ownership of a plot of land to take effect.[4] The declaration of conveyance must be declared in the presence of both parties (representation is possible) before a notary or another competent authority, such as a court.[5] Otherwise, the agreement is void.[6] If Andrew gets registered in the Land Register the defect can be cured by prescription if the registration existed for thirty years and he had the plot of land in proprietary possession for this period.[7]

(b) A written agreement not authenticated by a notary is void (see above). Therefore, there is no remedy if one party changes its mind.

(b) Austria

(a) A verbal contract is also binding when transferring immovable property. The legal effect is that both parties are bound to the oral agreement and the rules of the law of obligation apply.

(b) The fact that the contract has now been written down and signed by the parties is important for the registration in the Big Book, which leads the buyer to become the owner.[8] Nevertheless, this registration requires certain formal standards: a public document (*Urkunde*) on the purchase, the explicit consent of the person whose right

[1] § 311b, para. 1 sentence 1 BGB [2] See § 125 BGB. [3] § 311b, para. 1 sentence 2 BGB.
[4] § 873, para. 1 BGB. [5] § 925, para. 1 BGB. [6] § 125 BGB. [7] § 900, para. 1 BGB.
[8] § 431 ABGB. Also Helmut Koziol and Rudolf Welser, *Bürgerliches Recht, I*, 13th edn. (Vienna: Manz Verlag, 2006), p. 358; Gert M. Iro, *Sachenrecht*, 3rd edn. (Vienna: Österreich Verlag, 2008), No. 3/21.

is to be annulled, transferred, limited or burdened (*Aufsandungserklärung*) and a form stating that all taxes required were paid (*steuerliche Unbedenklichkeitsbescheinigung*).[9] All documents required for the registration have to meet certain formal standards, the most important of which is that either a public document (*Urkunde*) (for example, certified by a notary), or a private document containing signatures certified/attested by a notary or court is necessary.[10] Therefore, once the formal requirements are met, the legal effect is that the registration can be conducted (*Einverleibung*). The registration makes the buyer the official owner of the property.[11]

(c) The Netherlands

(a) The principal rule is that an oral contract of sale of immovable property is binding. There is, however, an important exception. If the buyer is a non-professional and he buys a dwelling, the contract of sale is binding only if made in writing (art. 7:2 (1) BW). This rule was introduced in 2003 in order to protect non-professional buyers of dwellings. On the basis of this article, a distinction should be made as to the object bought and who the buyer is. The requirement of writing applies only to houses or parts of houses to be used for habitation. Moreover, the requirement applies only if the buyer is a non-professional.

If a non-professional buys a plot of land or if a company or businessman buys a house in the exercise of his profession, an oral sales contract will be valid and may be evidenced by witnesses. In practice, the oral contract will be followed by a written contract, but the oral contract is already binding. The effect of a valid sales contract is to create an obligation for the seller to transfer ownership of the land and an obligation for the buyer to pay the purchase price. It does not pass ownership or any other right that works against the world.

The relatively new art. 7:2 BW created uncertainty about the following. Let us say that a non-professional buyer B has reached oral agreement with seller A to purchase a dwelling. Before the oral agreement is put into writing, A sells the same property to C for a higher price. Following a strict interpretation of art. 7:2 BW the

9 § 432f ABGB; §§ 31ff. GBG. See further Koziol and Welser, *Bürgerliches Recht, I*, p. 358; Iro, *Sachenrecht*, No. 3/23f.

10 Iro, *Sachenrecht*, No. 3/23; Koziol and Welser, *Bürgerliches Recht, I*, p. 358.

11 Iro, *Sachenrecht*, No. 3/21; Koziol and Welser, *Bürgerliches Recht, I*, p. 358.

oral agreement is void and B is therefore unable to demand specific performance or damages for breach of contract. After all, there is no contract between A and B.[12] The provision introduced to protect the non-professional buyer now backfires on him. If the buyer were able to force the seller to put the agreement in writing, the requirement of writing would be undermined.

In a 2011 judgment,[13] the Dutch Supreme Court introduced a further refinement of the requirement of writing, distinguishing between a professional and non-professional *seller*. In this case a non-professional seller reached an oral agreement about the sale of a dwelling to a non-professional buyer. The seller then refused to put the agreement in writing. The Supreme Court held that the requirement of writing is not only intended to protect the buyer but also to protect the seller and other potential buyers. The Supreme Court continues that an oral agreement is indeed not binding on the seller. It notes that this is difficult to reconcile with the intention of art. 7:2 BW to protect the buyer and therefore holds that this effect of voidness only applies where the seller is also a non-professional. A professional seller is therefore unable to set up the voidness against the buyer, as professional sellers can be forced to put the agreement in writing and perform the contract.

A non-professional seller can only be bound to an oral agreement in rare circumstances. However, in such a case specific performance is unavailable. The only remedy is payment of the damage caused by the fact that the agreement will not be performed. The Supreme Court expressly holds that the mere fact that the seller finds another buyer prepared to pay more for the property, or the fact that the buyer has second thoughts and wants to buy another house, does not qualify as an exceptional circumstance. The seller and buyer can, in these cases, refuse to sign a written contract.

(b) If after having entered into a valid contract the seller refuses to transfer ownership of the land, he is in breach of the contract and the normal remedies under Dutch law will apply. The buyer may demand specific performance. A very effective path to follow is to ask the judge to appoint a compulsory agent who will sign the transfer deed in the seller's name, which has the same legal effect as if the

12 As the requirement of writing not only serves the protection of the buyer but also the interests of the seller and third parties, the oral agreement is not merely a voidable contract but a void contract.

13 HR 9 December 2011, RvdW 2011/1541, LJN: BU7412.

seller had signed the deed himself. Another option is to ask the judge to rule that his judgment replaces the transfer deed. After entering the judgment into the deeds register ownership passes to the buyer (art. 3:300 BW).

If the contract is binding, the buyer should pay the purchase price. In practice, the non-professional buyer will normally order his bankers to credit a special bank account belonging to the notary office. The notary will not make the transfer deed and will not have it signed by the parties before the purchase price has been credited to this bank account. When he receives the money, the parties will sign the deed. After the notary has had the deed registered and received confirmation from the Registry that the deed has been registered without any intervening seizure in execution by a creditor of the seller, he will have the seller's bank account credited for the purchase price. This protects both parties against the counterparty's insolvency or unwillingness to comply with their obligations.

The 2003 amendment introducing protection for non-professional buyers also introduced a so-called 'change of mind' period for the non-professional buyer (art. 7:2 (2) BW). When a dwelling is sold to a non-professional party, the contract should be in writing and the buyer should receive the deed or a certified copy of it. From the moment the (copy of the) deed of sale is given to the buyer, the buyer has a period of three days during which he may terminate the contract of sale.

If the contract of sale is valid and it has not been terminated under art. 7:2 (2) BW, and the buyer refuses to pay, the buyer will not receive ownership of the land because the transfer deed will be made only after payment of the purchase price to the notary's office. The seller could make use of the traditional contractual remedies available in the case of non-performance of a monetary obligation. The most common contract model, which is produced by the home owners' association and the consumers' association, contains a provision that if payment is not received before the agreed time, the buyer has to pay a fixed amount of damages (a penalty clause). In most cases these are set at 10 per cent of the purchase price.

(d) Turkey

(a) This has no legal effect at all since a contract for the transfer of ownership of land is void unless made by a duly authenticated instrument.[14] According to the TCC, the contract for the transfer of an immovable property must be realised before the Land Register officer (art. 706, para. 1 TCC). Otherwise the contract will be null and void (art. 12, para. 2 Turkish Code of Obligations (TCO)).

Since the contract is null and void, if either party changes their mind, the other has no remedy.

(b) As stated above, this kind of contract is null and void since where a contract is subject to an official form, the parties have to obey this type of form, they cannot realise the contract in an ordinary written form.[15]

If either party changes their mind, *as a rule*, the other does not have a remedy: the judge has to take the nullity of the contract into consideration *ex officio*. However, if Andrew were to pay for the land and Barbara transferred possession of the land to him, Barbara could not claim that the contract is null and void since this kind of a defence would be contrary to art. 2 TCC, which states that every person is bound to exercise his rights and fulfil his obligations according to the principles of good faith. The law does not sanction the evident abuse of a person's rights. If this is the case, the contract can be accepted as valid by the judge and Andrew can succeed.[16]

2 *Scandinavian jurisdictions*

(a) Finland

(a) It is not possible to transfer the ownership of a house by an unwritten agreement if the transference contains both the house and

[14] See art. 706, para. 1 TCC; Ivy Williams, Siegfried Wyler and Barbara Wyler, *The Swiss Civil Code, Version II* (Zürich: ReMAK Verlag, 1987), art. 657, para. 1; Erhan Adal, *Fundamentals of Turkish Private Law*, rev. 8th edn. (İstanbul: Legal Yayıncılık, 2005), p. 148; Ertaş, S., *Eşya Yeni Türk Medeni Kanunu Hükümlerine Göre Eşya Hukuku, Gözden Geçirilmiş ve Genişletilmiş, 4. Baskı*, No. 1254, p. 258; M. Kemal Oğuzman, Özer Seliçi and Saibe Oktay-Özdemir, *Eşya Hukuku, Gözden Geçirilmiş 11. Bası* (İstanbul: Filiz Kitabevi, 2006), pp. 289ff.

[15] See art. 12, para. 2 TCO; Georg Wettstein, trans. and ed., *The Swiss Code of Obligations with Turkish Alterations* (Zürich, 1928), art. 11, para. 2; Kemal Oğuzman, *Turkey*, trans. Toker Dereli (The Hague, London and Boston, MA: Kluwer Law International, 1996), p. 44; Tuğrul Ansay and Don Wallace, Jr (eds.), *Introduction to Turkish Law* (The Hague: Kluwer Law International, 1996), p. 157.

[16] See art. 2 TCC; Williams, Wyler, and Wyler, *The Swiss Civil Code, I*, art. 2; Kemal Oğuzman and Nami Barlas, *Medeni Hukuk, Giriş – Kaynaklar – Temel Kavramlar, 13. Bası* (İstanbul: Arıkan Basım Yayım Dağıtım, 2006), p. 199.

the land. There is no valid agreement. The same rule applies to all kinds of pieces of real estate and parcels. In this respect, an oral agreement has no legal effect.[17] Andrew cannot have any right *in rem* to the land and the house.

The same holds true with an electronic conveyance. There is no valid agreement before the transfer has taken place with the help of the electronic form.

Nevertheless, a party liable for the non-conclusion of the agreement can be responsible for damages to the other party on account of negligence (*culpa in contrahendo*). The invalid contract is treated as a non-binding pre-contract. Principles of tort are applied in this case.[18]

However, if the house were subject to a lease, the sale via an oral contract would still be valid and legal. Regulation applies to this kind of conveyance, but the rules are not mandatory.[19] As a purchaser, Andrew can enforce a claim for specific performance, and all the other normal remedies connected with a breach of contract remain available for both parties. In practice, leased houses are sold by concluding a written contract. Normally, a purchaser has to register his or her acquisition, and registration presupposes a written acquisition document or a judgment by a court.

(b) The same rules outlined above as answers to case 3 are applied in this case. If the house is a part of a conveyanced piece of real estate, a written agreement is necessary but it is not sufficient to fulfil the demands of the form regulation. The crucial matter is the participation and signature of a notary.[20] Another option is to use the electronic exchange system for real property.

However, it is possible for a minor mistake in the formal register to be corrected if the title is registered in Andrew's name but the register authority did not recognise the mistake.[21] The correction means that Andrew's acquisition and the contract (the deed) are treated valid in relation to both the parties and third persons. The absence of a notary's signature prevents registration.

[17] See 2:1.1 Code of Real Estate, containing the mandatory form rules of conveyances of pieces of real estate.

[18] 2:8 Code of Real Estate.

[19] 4:4.2 Code of Real Estate.

[20] See 2:1.1 and 4:3 Code of Real Estate.

[21] See 13:1 Code of Real Estate.

(b) Sweden

(a) There are formal requirements governing the conveyance of real property, one of which is that the agreement must be made in writing.[22] One reason for the written requirement is the notion that parties should only make a decision on the conveyance of real property after having given serious consideration to the matter. The seller and the buyer are therefore free to change their minds. Before signing a written contract, as a rule, the other party does not have any remedy.[23] However, it is possible to recover expenses incurred as a consequence of the non-completion of the contract (i.e. the reliance interest). If the withdrawing party has acted wilfully or negligently, he or she might be liable under the rules of *dolus* or *culpa in contrahendo*.[24]

The binding nature of the agreement depends on its contents. For agreements in general (i.e. consensual agreements), both the binding nature and the contents are governed first and foremost by the parties' mutual intent. Since the conveyance of real property is a formal type of agreement, the agreement must meet the statutory requirements. One requirement is that the contract must contain an unequivocal declaration of assignment by the owner of the property. The agreement is invalid if it does not contain such a declaration.[25] Even if there is a declaration of assignment, but the contract also states that the completion of the conveyance is conditional upon the parties issuing another contract of conveyance, the payment of the price is construed as a condition of the completion.[26]

The usage of double sales documents is very widespread. The first document, called the 'contract of sale' (*köpekontraktet*), is normally 5–15 pages long, plus any attachments relating to the property. In addition to the statutory requirements, it contains both the relevant information on the property and all the terms of the sale. The second document, the 'sales deed' (*köpebrevet*), only contains the statutory

[22] A contract of conveyance must be in writing, be signed by both parties, identify the property unit, specify the price (if any) and contain the owner's unequivocal declaration of assignment, 4:1 (1) Land Code.

[23] See Supreme Court judgment *NJA* 1973, 175, where an owner of a property made substantial adjustments of his house to conform with the wishes of the expected buyer (alterations of the entrance floor into a surgery). The owner was not entitled to recover the costs.

[24] *See* Supreme Court judgment *NJA* 2012, 1095, and the Appeal Court decision RH 1996:154.

[25] 4:1 (3) Land Code. [26] 4:5 Land Code.

requirements, any possible remaining conditions of the sale,[27] and a declaration by the seller that payment is complete. The sales deed normally consists of only one page. It is not obligatory to use double sale documents and the parties may choose to use just one document, which becomes the definitive sales document.[28]

The seller may not hold the buyer to the contract and demand performance until a formally correct sales document (normally a sales deed) is issued by the parties. Instead, the seller must void the contract and seek compensation if the buyer wants to withdraw from the contract.

Generally, the parties agree that the buyer must pay a deposit after the conclusion of the sales contract (10 per cent of the purchase price is common), which is to be deducted upon payment of the full price. The deposit is forfeited if the buyer does not pursue the purchase and the seller declares the contract voided. The forfeiture is limited to losses incurred, unless the sales contract gives reason to interpret that the parties intended otherwise.[29]

The sales contract often contains some conditions to the advantage of the buyer, making it possible for the buyer to withdraw without sanctions. The usual conditions are that: an inspection made by an impartial construction inspector does not reveal defects of fundamental importance; the estimated costs of curing revealed defects does not exceed a fixed sum; the buyer can sell his or her own dwelling within a specified time; or that the purchase is subject to finance. Today, it is not uncommon to have a term in the contract that allows the buyer to terminate the contract after the house inspection without even having to invoke any kind of defect, which in practice means the contract is not binding on the buyer. If the sale is interrupted by the buyer for some reason, other than that which is stated in the conditions of the contract, the seller has a right to damages if the contract has been breached. The seller's right to compensation is normally not limited to the deposit,[30] but ambiguity in the deposit clause may lead to the opposite conclusion.[31]

(b) The contract is binding once the sale is concluded in writing and signed by both parties. If either of the parties wishes to withdraw

[27] See 4:6 Land Code. If a sales deed is issued by the parties after the sales contract containing conditions of the sale, the sales deed must also state the conditions to have effect.

[28] Cf. Supreme Court judgment *NJA* 1987, 211 with references.

[29] Supreme Court judgments *NJA* 1974, 526, *NJA* 1982, 613 and *NJA* 1985, 573.

[30] 4:25 (2) Land Code.

[31] See the Appeal Court decision RH 62:83.

from the contract, it will not be possible without sanctions. The other party may resort to the remedies for breach of contract (see case 4, question (a) below).

If the parties did not sign the contract simultaneously, the contract is mutually binding when the mutually signed contract is received by the first signer, or by someone competent to receive the document on behalf of the first signer. Real estate agents are considered competent to receive sales documents on behalf of both parties.[32]

(c) Denmark

(a) The starting point under the Danish law is that there are no formal requirements governing how a contract must be entered into.[33] Thus, when Andrew gives an offer and Barbara accepts it, there is a binding agreement (a contract) according to the rules of the Contracts Act. However, strictly oral agreements may be difficult to prove and it is only possible to register written deeds and documents in the Buildings and Dwellings Register. While registration is not a prerequisite for validity, rights (including ownership rights) that are not registered may be extinguished by a third party in good faith and by creditors (even if these are not in good faith). Furthermore, the purchase of real property is a complicated legal construction that involves many documents and consequently the courts require firm proof of such agreements. As a consequence, even if there is no statutory provision requiring a written agreement, it is nevertheless probably correct to say that a strictly oral agreement will not suffice to transfer ownership to Andrew. However, from a theoretical point of view this is not due to a technical lack of formal validity, but rather it is due to the court's standard of proof.[34] If the courts were to find the existence of the agreement to be proven, then Andrew would have the same remedies as described below in case 4.

On a final note: since the acceptance of digital registration in the Land Register, digital documents confirmed with digital signatures are the basis for the registration. Thus, no written and signed agreement in the traditional – analogue – sense is required.[35]

32 Supreme Court judgments *NJA* 2000, 747 I and II, and *NJA* 2012, 1095.
33 Chapter 1, Consolidation of Acts of 26 August 1996, No. 781 on agreements.
34 Lennart L. Andersen and Palle B. Madsen, *Aftaler og mellemmæn*, 6th edn. (Copenhagen: Karnov Group, 2012), p. 85f.; Camilla H. Jensen *et al.*, *Dansk Privatret*, 17th edn. (Copenhagen: Djøf/Jurist- og Økomomforbiunder, 2012), p. 334.
35 Section 7, LRA.

(b) As stated above, as a starting point the unwritten agreement is valid. However, since the contents of the agreement must be proven, the courts are more likely to find that the existence and contents of the agreement is proven. Regarding remedies, see case 4.

(d) Norway

(a) Immovable property may be sold without any formalities, however a document is still needed for registration purposes. An oral agreement is valid and enforceable. If the seller changes her mind the buyer can in principle enforce a claim for specific performance,[36] meaning that the buyer can have the registered title transferred to him by court order, against payment of the price. A more complicated way is to get a judgment imposing coercive fines on the seller until she signs a document to transfer the registered title (the 'deed'). More often, the buyer will terminate the contract for non-performance and claim damages for the loss caused by the non-performance.[37] If the buyer changes his mind the seller may enforce the claim for the purchase money,[38] or take the more practical approach of terminating the contract and claiming damages.[39]

(b) Strictly speaking, there is no difference between an oral agreement and a signed document. In practice, however, the document is regarded as much stronger evidence that sufficient agreement was reached. In some cases the courts have been reluctant to find that the parties were in sufficient agreement unless a written contract was signed.[40] In property sales through professional intermediaries (real estate agents, practising lawyers), the parties are regularly contractually bound by oral agreement before the contract document is signed.

3 *Romanic–Mediterranean jurisdictions*

(a) Italy

(a) According to Italian law the contract that transfers ownership or other proprietary rights over immovable property must be made in

[36] Section 4-2, Act Relating to the Sale of Real Property (*lov om avhending av fast eigedom*, 3 July 1992, No. 53).

[37] Sections 4-3 and 405, Act Relating to the Sale of Real Property.

[38] Section 5-2, Act Relating to the Sale of Real Property.

[39] Sections 5-3 and 5-4, Act Relating to the Sale of Real Property.

[40] See, e.g., Supreme Court decisions in *Norsk Retstidende* 1985, 1265. See also *Norsk lovkommentar*, www.rettsdata.no, commentary 14 to § 1–3 Act Relating to the Sale of Real Property, by Ernst Nordtveit.

writing and therefore an unwritten agreement has no legal effect.[41] The parties can legitimately change their minds without any legal consequence, unless it amounts to a sudden and unjustified breach of pre-contractual negotiations.[42] In this case, those who breach the duty of good faith in negotiations and cause damage to the other party are required to pay damages.

(b) In Italy a written agreement of sale most commonly takes the form of a preliminary contract. With the preliminary contract of sale, the parties are bound to conclude the final sale in the future. The preliminary contract does not transfer ownership between the parties, but it constitutes a source of obligation for one party to sell and for the other to buy. Therefore, if either party refuses to perform their obligations, the other party could take legal action in order to obtain an order for specific performance of the obligation from the court, which arises under the preliminary contract. If the court finds in favour of the plaintiff, an order that will produce the same effects as the definitive contract of sale will be made.[43] In our case, the order will transfer the ownership of Barbara's house to Andrew, if it is still possible. It is possible that in the meantime Barbara already sold her house to a third party, so as to neutralise the effect of the judgment. As we will see in question 5 below, in this case Andrew would only be awarded damages, unless he had registered the preliminary contract. In 1996 the CC was amended to provide for registration of the preliminary contract of sale of immovable property.[44] The new art. 2645 *bis* provides that the preliminary contracts concerning the conclusion of a definitive contract of sale of immovable property must be registered if completed in the form of notarial deed.[45] The registration of the preliminary contract has a so-called 'booking effect': (1) the subsequent registration of the order in Andrew's favour for specific execution of the preliminary contract under art. 2932 ICC; and (2) the registration of the final contract of sale, if the two parties voluntarily perform the obligation deriving from the preliminary contract of sale, shall prevail over registrations entered by third parties to which Barbara has sold her house if they were made after the registration of the preliminary contract.

[41] Art. 1350 CC. [42] Art. 1337 CC. [43] See art. 2932 c.1 CC.
[44] See art. 3, para.1, Legislative Decree 31.12.2001, No. 669.
[45] See above under case 2.

(b) Spain

(a) As noted in case 2, in order for property rights to a house to change, it would suffice for Andrew and Barbara to enter into a contract of sale (or any other contract involving transfer of ownership), and for Barbara to put Andrew in possession of the house. The transfer of possession is normally effected by handing over keys to the house or the execution of a notarial act (unless the buyer was already living in the house as a tenant, or if the buyer and seller agree that the seller will continue to occupy the house as a tenant). There must generally be an outward signal to third parties that possession has shifted.

The contract can be set down in writing, thereby making it easier to prove its existence if one of the parties refuses to perform and denies there was an agreement. However, the contract need not be in writing. If Barbara and Andrew agreed, respectively, to sell and buy the house at a specified price, whether orally or in writing, the agreement is valid and binding on the parties. However, if the agreement was not accompanied by transfer of possession, ownership will not have passed, either.

(b) The remedies that are available if one party refuses to perform are examined in case 4.

(c) Portugal

(a) An unwritten agreement between Andrew and Barbara is not legally binding in order to legally transfer the property. Andrew and Barbara should convey their contract of sale in a notary deed or in a duly certified private document (see case 2, question (b)). Nevertheless, it should be emphasised that art. 227 CC provides that parties are subject to a duty of good faith in the bargaining process (*culpa in contrahendo*). Therefore, liability can be imposed on a party who withdraws from negotiations (against the legitimate expectations of the other party and in an unjust way) prior to the conclusion of a contract.[46]

[46] See Decision of the Supreme Court of 27 September 2012, at www.dgsi.pt (www.dgsi.pt/jstj.nsf/954f0ce6ad9dd8b980256b5f003fa814/a4018e5f26fc0fd180257a86004a7c36?OpenDocument&Highlight=0,responsabilidade,pr%C3%A9-contratual last visited 28 November 2012) and Júlio de Almeida Costa, *Direito das Obrigações* (Coimbra: Almedina, 2009), pp. 263ff.

(b) A legal agreement between Andrew and Barbara to sell and acquire a house must either be signed in a One Stop House desk or made in a public deed at a notary's office. However, the written agreement between Andrew and Barbara can be considered as a preliminary contract.

The preliminary contract (*contrato-promessa de compra e venda*) consists of a commitment to buy and sell, and it is regulated by art. 410ff. CC. The provisions that govern contracts also apply to preliminary contracts, except those that concern formalities.

The preliminary contract has to be signed by the parties to be legally binding. If the future contract is for the acquisition or constitution of a real right over a dwelling, the notary or an authorising entity must certify the signature of the parties and the existence of a permit to use the property or to construct on it. However, the party that promises to sell or create the real right may only invoke non-compliance with those requirements when the acquirer is at fault. If Andrew and Barbara had entered into a valid contract, the one who later changed their mind would be liable.

If the person who pays the down payment does not comply with the contract, the other party has the right to keep it as their own. If the party that receives the down payment does not comply, the acquirer has the right to receive it in double, or to demand specific performance. A third possibility also exists under Portuguese law. If there was a down payment and *traditio* of the property, the acquirer can ask for the difference between the objective value of the property minus the price agreed upon by parties and the value of the deposit (art. 442 (2) CC). If there was *traditio* of the property to the future acquirer, Andrew holds a lien (*direito de retenção*) over the house. He is required to give the house back but he has the right to receive double the down payment, or the difference between the objective value of the property minus the price agreed by the parties plus the value of the deposit. Andrew is entitled to retain the house until full payment of the total amount of compensation owing (art. 755 (1) (f) CC).

The situation would be different if Andrew and Barbara had conferred real effects to the preliminary contract (art. 413 CC). They have to mention their intention on the preliminary contract and they have to submit it for registration. A right to acquire the property that is enforceable against third parties arises from the contract. If the seller does not comply with her duty, the acquirer is entitled to request specific performance.[47]

[47] Almeida Costa, *Direito das Obrigações*, p. 365.

(d) Greece

(a) In accordance with art. 159 GCC, 'compliance with form for the conclusion of a transaction shall only be required where the law so provides'. Art. 369 CC states expressly that 'contracts aiming at the constitution or extinction of rights in rem on immovables must be drawn up in the presence of a notary'. Moreover, art. 1033 provides that in order to transfer the ownership of an immovable it is necessary to have an agreement incorporated in a notarial deed, subject to registration.

In the light of the above, an oral agreement does not bring about any change in the ownership of immovable property. Should either party change their mind, the other party might only be entitled to claim damages in accordance with the provisions on pre-contractual liability. In this context, art. 198 GCC provides that 'a person who in the course of negotiations for the conclusion of a contract has through its fault caused prejudice to the other party, shall be liable for compensation even if the contract has not been concluded'.

(b) A written agreement that is not drawn up in the presence of a public notary has no effect insofar as the transfer of the ownership of the house is concerned.

4 *France and related jurisdictions*

(a) France

(a) This agreement is valid and the property can be transferred, consistent with art. 1583 C. civ.[48] The completion of the sale results only from the agreement of the parties on the thing and on the price. However, written evidence of agreement is required for contracts involving a transaction above €1,500.[49] Furthermore, it is only possible to use the transfer against third parties after it has been published in the land publicity, which supposes the drafting of a notarial act.

[48] According to art. 1583 French CC: 'It is complete between the parties, and ownership is acquired as of right by the buyer with respect to the seller as soon as the thing and the price have been agreed upon, although the thing has not yet been delivered or the price paid.'

[49] Art 1341 C. civ. But the evidence is free against the storekeepers (art. L. 110–3 Code de commerce).

Where the buyer of a residential building (even ancient) is not a professional, they benefit from a cooling-off period of seven days during which they can freely retract.[50] When the parties have not drafted any papers and ask the notary to draft the bill of sale, the buyer's protection is assured by a seven-day cooling-off period that begins from the notification or the delivery of the building to the buyer. The seller cannot benefit from this cooling-off right of retraction.

Except where cooling-off rights are exercised by the buyer, and subject to the evidentiary problem underlined above, the principle that contracts are binding excludes any retraction by the seller or the buyer. If one of the parties refuses to reiterate the sale in front of a notary, according to the common law of contracts the other can request that a judge either enforce the sale, or void the contract and/or associated damages.[51] To ensure enforcement, the judge can either impose a daily penalty on the party that failed to sign the notarial act, or make a judgment that outlines the terms of the agreement between the parties. A judgment would be considered an authentic act and could be registered instead of the notarial act.

(b) This written agreement has the same value as the oral agreement, but the written nature of it brings indisputable proof. If it is a simple contract, it must be reiterated in front of a notary for land publicity. As for the remedy, it is the same answer as above.

(b) Belgium

(a) According to the Belgian law, the sale of an immovable or movable good is by consensual agreement. It is completed by an oral agreement between the parties (art. 1138 BCC). Unless Barbara and Andrew have verbally agreed otherwise, the contractual rights and obligations between the parties come into existence immediately and ownership is transferred immediately. Art. 1583 BCC provides that 'it[52] is complete between the parties, and ownership is acquired as the buyer's right with respect to the seller, as soon as the object and the price have been agreed upon, despite the fact that the

[50] Art. L. 271-1 Code de la construction et de l'habitation, arising from the act of 13 December 2000.

[51] See for example Cass. 3ème civ., 29 November 2000, No. 98-20502.

[52] Meaning: a sale.

object has not yet been delivered or the price paid'.[53] Consequently, transfer of ownership is an essential feature of a sales agreement.[54]

However, a problem of proof will emerge. Art. 1341 BCC provides that a notarial deed under private signature must be executed in all matters exceeding a sum of €375, even for voluntary deposits. Moreover, no proof by a witness is allowed against or beyond the contents of written documents, or as to what is alleged to have been said before, at the time of, or after the written document, although it is a question of a lesser sum or value. This is without prejudice to that which is prescribed in the statutory provisions on commercial law. The statutory provisions on commercial law are the rules of evidence that apply to commercial relationships, which provide that proof can be given by any legal means, including presumptions and witnesses.[55]

Therefore, despite the fact that the oral arrangement concluded the sales agreement, neither party would not be able to prove the existence of the verbal agreement if it were contested by the other party, unless the transaction was a commercial transaction, in which case the statutory provisions on commercial law would apply.

(b) As it was the case under question (a), the sales agreement existed and was binding upon Andrew and Barbara from the moment of the oral consent. However, the private deed will overcome the problem of proving a verbal sales agreement. It is possible to prove the agreement on the basis of a privately signed document. From a theoretical point of view, it can also prove Andrew's ownership. However, in legal practice the private deed usually contains a provision postponing the passing of ownership until the moment that the notarial deed is signed. In practice, the notarial deed is signed at the moment when the price for the good is paid.

In order to avoid tax penalties, the sales agreement must be given a certain date within four months of the agreement coming into existence. This date is the date at which the agreement affects third parties and it is usually determined by the signature of a notarial deed or by the registration of a private deed at the Tax Authorities Registration.

[53] The original French text provides as follows: 'Elle est parfaite entre les parties, et la propriété est acquise de droit à l'acheteur à l'égard du vendeur, dès qu'on est convenu de la chose et du prix, quoique la chose n'ait pas encore été livrée ni le prix payé.'

[54] H. de Page and A. Meinertzhagen-Limpens, *Traité élémentaire de droit civil belge*, IV, No. 21 (Brussels: Bruylant, 1997).

[55] Art. 25 Belgian Commercial Code (*Wetboek van Koophandel*, WVK).

If one party, after signing a private deed, refuses to cooperate to pass the notarial deed, the other party can introduce judicial proceedings with the aim of obtaining a judgment that obliges the refusing party to cooperate. If the other party does not cooperate within a fixed term after the judgment, then the judgment itself can be registered in the Hypothec Register. In this manner, it is possible to 'perfect' the sales agreement without further cooperation by one of the parties.

5 *England and related jurisdictions*

(a) England

(a) There is no contract for the sale of land until the contract is recorded in writing and signed by both parties.[56] Prior to that time, Andrew can only hope that Barbara will complete the sale. Barbara may withdraw from the sale if she finds another purchaser who is willing to pay more than Andrew (thereby 'gazumping' Andrew).

(b) This is now a binding contract, provided the agreement records all the terms which the parties have expressly agreed upon.[57] Thus, if either party changes his or her mind, the other has a remedy: they can choose to terminate the contract and seek damages for the breach, or they can seek an order for specific performance of the contract.

(b) Scotland

(a) There is no legal effect because a contract for the sale of immovable property must be constituted by a written document or documents signed at the end by both parties, or if the electronic equivalent is being used then the electronic contract must be completed with electronic signatures.[58] But if one of the parties (Andrew or Barbara) proceeds to rely upon the informal agreement, with the knowledge of the other party, the agreement is enforceable despite the absence of formality.[59] To qualify, the act must be sufficiently significant that the failure of the agreement would be materially prejudicial to the party who acted. An example would be where Andrew sold his existing house in reliance on the agreement to buy Barbara's.

[56] Section 2 (1), Law of Property (Miscellaneous Provisions) Act 1989 (for contracts created after 26 September 1989).
[57] Section 2 (1), Law of Property (Miscellaneous Provisions) Act 1989.
[58] Section 1 (2) (a) (i), Requirements of Writing (Scotland) Act 1995.
[59] Section 1 (3), (4), Requirements of Writing (Scotland) Act 1995.

(b) Assuming agreement as to the property, price and parties, there is a binding contract for the sale of the house. That means that Andrew must pay the price and Barbara must grant the deed necessary to transfer ownership. The consequences of a change of mind are considered in the answer to case 4, but in brief the innocent party can seek implementation of the contract or damages.

(c) Ireland

(a) Andrew and Barbara have made an oral agreement in relation to the sale of the house, which is perfectly valid and may lead to the eventual completion of the sale by the execution and delivery of a deed in Andrew's favour, followed by its registration if the land is registered in the Land Registry. However, if either party changes their mind, the other will only be able to enforce the agreement if it complies with the statutory formalities set out in section 51 (1), Land and Conveyancing Law Reform Act 2009[60] or it has been partly performed by the plaintiff. Section 51 provides that a contract for the sale of land shall not be enforceable unless the agreement, or some memorandum or note of it, is in writing and signed by the person against whom the action is brought or that person's authorised agent.[61] Alternatively, a court will enforce an oral agreement if the doctrine of part performance applies,[62] for example, if Andrew was allowed into possession of the house in reliance on the agreement.[63] Finally, Andrew may be entitled to a remedy under the doctrine of proprietary estoppel[64] if it can be proved that Barbara made a representation that he would have an interest in the land and Andrew relied to his detriment on that representation in circumstances where it would be unconscionable for Barbara to insist on the strict legal position.[65]

[60] Section 51 (1), Land and Conveyancing Law Reform Act 2009 re-enacts section 2, Statute of Frauds (Ireland) Act 1695 in more modern language.

[61] Note, however, that an oral agreement may be enforced by action if the other party fails to plead non-compliance with the statutory formalities as a defence, see *McCarron* v. *McCarron* [1997] 2 ILRM 349. Also, section 51 (2) clarifies that subsection (1) does not affect the law relating to part performance or other equitable doctrines, such as the doctrine of proprietary estoppel.

[62] See *Mackie* v. *Wilde* [1998] 2 IR 578 for a discussion of the doctrine of part performance.

[63] See *Corrigan* v. *Woods* (1883) 11 LR Ir 106.

[64] See Hilary Biehler, *Equity and the Law of Trusts in Ireland*, 6th edn. (Dublin: Round Hall, 2015), Chapter 18.

[65] See *Courtney* v. *McCarthy* [2007] IESC 58; *An Cumann Peile Boitheimach Teoranta (Bohemians Football Club)* v. *Albion Properties Ltd & Others* [2008] IEHC 447.

(b) As has already been mentioned, to enforce a contract for the sale of land, the contract, or some memorandum or note of it, must be in writing and signed by the party against whom the action is being brought. There is no requirement for a standard form agreement[66] but any memorandum or note of the agreement must contain what are known as 'the four Ps': the parties, the property, the price and any other essential provisions.[67] The courts will examine whether a provision was essential from the subjective point of view of the parties and will not, for example, insist on the inclusion of the amount of the deposit[68] or the closing date[69] in the note or memorandum if these issues were not considered by the parties to be essential or material to their agreement. Although only the essential terms must be included in the written note or memorandum, there must be express or implied agreement on all the terms of the agreement before a concluded agreement can be said to exist.[70] The courts have, however, been willing to imply certain terms where there was no discussion between the parties, for example, that the sale was to close within a reasonable time.[71] If these requirements have been met, either party may seek specific performance of the agreement or damages for breach of contract if the other party refuses to complete the transaction.

66 Such as an agreement incorporating the Law Society of Ireland, *General Conditions of Sale*, 2017 edn.

67 See J.C.W. Wylie and Una Woods, *Irish Conveyancing Law*, 3rd edn. (Haywards Heath: Bloomsbury Professional, 2005), paras. 6.17–25.

68 See *Shirley Engineering Ltd* v. *Irish Telecommunications Investment plc* [1999] IEHC 204; *Supermacs Ireland Ltd* v. *Katesan (Naas) Ltd* [2000] 4 IR 273; *Higgins* v. *Argent Developments Ltd* [2002] IEHC 171, affirmed *ex tempore* (13 May 2003) SC. See also section 51 (3), Land and Conveyancing Law Reform Act 2009.

69 *Barratt* v. *Costelloe* (1973) 107 ILTSJ 239

70 See *Supermacs Ireland Ltd* v. *Katesan (Naas) Ltd* [2000] 4 IR 273.

71 See *Supermacs Ireland Ltd* v. *Katesan (Naas) Ltd* [2000] 4 IR 273.

Case 4

Barbara and Andrew, from case 3 above, have now made a valid contract for sale of Barbara's house to Andrew.

(a) If either party now has a change of mind and does not want to perform the obligations under the contract, does the other have a remedy?
(b) If Andrew becomes insolvent after he has entered into the contract with Barbara, does the house form part of his property so as to be available to his creditors?

(A) Foundational Concepts for Understanding Case 4

This case, like the previous one, has the aim to explore the form of the agreement to pass property in the different jurisdictions analysed in this volume. For the foundational concepts of this case, see case 3 above.

(B) The Jurisdictions (Presented by Related Jurisdictions)

1 Germany and related jurisdictions

(a) Germany

(a) After Andrew and Barbara have signed the contract of sale authenticated by a notary,[1] Barbara is obliged to transfer the house to Andrew and Andrew has to pay the purchase price.[2] Either party can enforce these obligations against the other.

If Barbara does not want to sell the house to Andrew, Andrew can enforce a claim for specific performance. That usually implies that Andrew has to go to court to obtain an enforceable title. This

[1] See § 311b, para. 1 sentence 1 BGB. [2] § 433 BGB.

time-consuming process can be avoided if Barbara has explicitly declared submission to immediate enforcement (*Unterwerfung unter die sofortige Zwangsvollstreckung*)[3] in the sales contract. In that case, the contract would have been enforceable without the need for a court procedure.

Alternatively, Andrew can demand damages for non-performance.[4] Before seeking damages, Andrew normally has to set aside a reasonable period for performance. If Barbara seriously and definitively refuses to sell the house, Andrew can claim damages without setting aside a period for performance.[5]

If Andrew refuses to pay the purchase price, Barbara can enforce the payment. This can be done without court action, if Andrew has declared submission to immediate enforcement of the contract for the sale of land.[6] Such a declaration is a typical clause of a contract of sale for land.

(b) After Andrew has become insolvent, insolvency proceedings may be initiated by adjudication on the insolvency by the court.[7] When insolvency proceedings commence, Andrew's right to manage and transfer the assets involved in the insolvency proceedings are vested in the insolvency administrator.[8]

While the house does not form part of Andrew's property, the formally concluded contract of sale gives Andrew a personal right to acquire the house from Barbara. This outstanding claim is part of Andrew's insolvency estate.

If Andrew has not paid the purchase price, the insolvency administrator can demand that Barbara perform the contract of sale, i.e. to transfer the house to Andrew[9] and pay the full purchase price from the insolvency estate.[10] In that case the house will become available to Andrew's creditors who acquire an insolvency quota of the insolvency estate. If the insolvency administrator does not opt for performance, Barbara can keep the house and claim damages for non-performance of the contract as a creditor in insolvency (i.e. she would only obtain an insolvency quota).[11]

3 Compare § 794, para. 1 No. 5 of the Code of Civil Procedure (*Zivilprozessordnung*, hereafter, 'ZPO').
4 See §§ 280, 281 BGB. 5 § 281, para. 2 BGB. 6 See section 794, para. 1 No. 5 ZPO.
7 It is assumed that Andrew is an individual who does not pursue any independent economic activity. Therefore the rules on the consumer insolvency proceedings apply (§§ 304ff. German Insolvency Act (*Insolvenzordnung*, hereafter, 'InsO')).
8 § 80 InsO. 9 § 103, para. 1 InsO. 10 § 55, para. 1 No. 2 InsO.
11 § 103, para. 2 InsO with § 281 BGB ('compensation in lieu of performance').

If Andrew has already paid the purchase price, Barbara has to transfer the house to the insolvency administrator because it becomes part of the insolvency estate.

When the contract of sale is authenticated by a notary the parties usually also make the formal declaration of conveyance together with consent and the applications needed to register the property. But this does not transfer the house to Andrew unless he is registered in the Land Register. If the document has already been submitted to the Land Registry, Andrew will become the owner of the house as soon as the registration is made. The house will then be part of Andrew's insolvency estate.

(b) Austria

(a) Here, the legal situation depends mainly on whether the property was already transferred to Andrew and registered (*Einverleibung*) in the Big Book. If the property was neither transferred nor registered, Barbara is still the owner. The party who is not willing to perform according to the written agreement is in default (*Verzug*) and the other can sue for performance of the contract, or can withdraw from the contract, giving an additional grace period.[12]

If the property was transferred to Andrew but not registered, Barbara is still the owner and possessor regarding the facts in the Big Book (*Buchbesitzer*). Andrew is possessor regarding the actual facts (*Naturalbesitzer*). This means that Barbara has stronger procedural rights against third persons, as there is *rei vindicatio*, *actio negatoria* for Barbara and *actio publiciana* for Andrew. However, *inter partes* Andrew has the stronger rights because he can call upon a valid contract when sued to hand over the property by Barbara (*exceptio rei vindicatae et traditae*). According to the Law of Obligations, the consequences are the same as those described for the case in which the property was neither transferred nor registered.

(b) § 21 Abs 1 IO (Code on Insolvency) states that if at the time when bankruptcy proceedings are commenced a bilateral contract has not (yet) been fulfilled by the bankrupt or the other party then the bankruptcy administrator (*Masseverwalter*) may either fulfil the contract instead of bankruptcy and demand fulfilment from the other party or withdraw from the contract. When it comes to real estate purchase, fulfilment of the contract means that the seller has in fact transferred

[12] § 918; § 921 iVm; § 1435 ABGB.

the real estate and provided the necessary declarations and public documents (compare case 3) for the transfer of the real estate, whereas the buyer is not required to already be registered as owner in the Big Book.[13]

Nevertheless, § 21 Abs 1 IO applies only if neither the buyer nor the seller has already fulfilled their contractual obligations. The *Masseverwalter* may choose to fulfil the contract instead of bankruptcy and demand fulfilment from the other party (Barbara). He can apply to be registered in the Big Book, so that the house forms part of Andrew's property and is consequentially available to his creditors. He can also choose to withdraw from the contract, in which case the real estate will not be available to Andrew's creditors.

If both the person being bankrupted (*Gemeinschuldner*, Andrew) and the other party (Barbara) have fulfilled their obligations the *Masseverwalter* has no right to choose between the possibilities mentioned in § 21 Abs 1 KO. The *Masseverwalter* can apply for registration in the Big Book, and this would mean that the house forms part of Andrew's property and will consequentially be available to his creditors.

If the person who is subject to bankruptcy proceedings (*Gemeinschuldner*) has fulfilled their obligations and the other party (Barbara) has not, the *Masseverwalter* can demand fulfilment from the other party (Barbara). Consequently, the *Masseverwalter* can demand registration in the Big Book (*Antrag auf Eintragung*) and the house then forms part of Andrew's property and will be consequentially available to his creditors.

(c) The Netherlands

(a) The Dutch law makes a distinction between the contract of sale and the subsequent transfer deed. It does not distinguish between a contract of sale, an agreement to sell and a sales contract. For that reason, case 4 is irrelevant under Dutch law because the sale has already taken place. The sale is binding and the only relevant question is what remedy the buyer has if the contract is breached and the seller does not want to transfer ownership to the buyer (see case 3).

[13] Markus Dellinger and Paul Oberhammer, *Insolvenzrecht*, 2nd edn. (Vienna: Manz Verlag, 2004), No. 412. Consider in relation to this issue the Land on Insolvency Act enacted in 2012.

(b) As ownership of the land passes only upon registration of the transfer deed, the land is available to the seller's creditors until registration. After registration, the land is available to the buyer's creditors. This equally applies in insolvency and outside insolvency. The insolvency proceedings start from the moment that the court declares the person in question insolvent. So, the answer to case 4, question (b) is that the house Andrew bought is not available to his creditors. Under art. 37 Fw[14] the administrator in Andrew's insolvency has an option either to perform or not to perform the contract. If the administrator chooses not to perform, the seller can terminate the contract and claim damages if she can prove to have suffered damages. After all, she has not paid the purchase price yet. Any claim for damages will be an unsecured claim.

In the period between making the contract and registering the transfer deed, the buyer may protect himself against the seller's insolvency by having the contract of sale registered (art. 7:3 BW). After registration the contract of sale is protected against the seller's creditors and insolvency administrator (art. 7:3 (3) BW) for six months (art. 7:3 (4) BW). Despite the opening of the insolvency procedure, the insolvency administrator is obliged to transfer ownership of the land to the buyer. However, the buyer would normally not have paid before having become the owner, so that they did not risk their purchase money.

(d) Turkey

(a) According to art. 705 TCC, as a fundamental rule for the transfer of an immovable property, after the completion of the contract the new owner's name must be registered in the Land Register (the Big Book). Entries are made in the Land Register on a written statement by the owner of the property to which the purported transaction refers (art. 1013, para. 1 TCC). This kind of registration is constitutive for the transfer of the immovable. Both contract and transfer are needed.

In the case that Andrew (buyer) changes his mind, art. 117 TCO provides that if Andrew's obligation is due, he will be in default upon being reminded thereof by Barbara.

According to art. 123 TCO, in a bilateral contract like the sales contract, the creditor (Barbara) is entitled to fix an appropriate time

[14] Fw stands for 'Faillissementswet', the Insolvency Act.

limit for subsequent performance, or to have a time limit fixed by the court. If there is no performance by the expiration of this time limit, the creditor (Barbara) may still sue for performance plus damages (default interest) due to delay. Alternatively, if she so declares without delay, she may waive subsequent performance and ask for compensation for damages arising out of the non-performance or withdraw from the contract.

If Barbara (seller) changes her mind, the immovable property may be acquired also without any registration. According to art. 716, para. 2 TCC,[15] where a person has acquired good title to the ownership of property, they have a right *in personam* against the owner for the registration of their title. If the seller refuses, the buyer is entitled to apply to the court to establish their ownership rights. This person acquires rights to the land by the decision of the judge. Thus, the registration that is written in the Land Register is declarative.

(b) If Andrew is adjudicated as bankrupt by the court after he enters into the agreement with Barbara and his name is registered as an owner in the Land Register, Andrew becomes the owner,[16] thus the immovable forms part of his property and is available to his creditors.

2 *Scandinavian jurisdictions*

(a) Finland

(a) After making a valid contract, the change of mind described relates to fulfilment of the contract. As a rule, all the normal remedies connected with a breach of contract are available to both parties. The valid contract is treated as the deed and it contains the conveyance of ownership as well.

As the purchaser, Andrew can enforce a claim for specific performance. Andrew can demand the transfer of possession of the house according to the clauses in the agreement. Alternatively, he can demand cancellation of the agreement if the delay is essential. In addition, he has the right to due compensation.[17]

[15] See art. 716, para. 2 TCC; Williams, Wyler and Wyler, *The Swiss Civil Code, II*, art. 665, para. 2.

[16] See art. 705, para. 1 TCC; Williams, Wyler and Wyler, *The Swiss Civil Code, II*, art. 656, para. 1.

[17] 2:27.1 Code of Real Estate.

As the vendor, Barbara can demand payment from Andrew. Besides, she is entitled to demand penal interest and compensation. Barbara can only claim the sold property if it has been agreed in the contract (deed) that the payment of the price is a conditional on the retention or transfer of title to the property.[18]

There is no equity or equitable rights or differences between law and equity in the Finnish legal system and hence there is no corresponding difference between remedies. Specific performance is prior to damages or other monetary compensation.

(b) The house is immediately treated as Andrew's property when a valid contract of conveyance has been made.[19] In this respect, registration or an application for registration in the Title and Mortgage Register, payment of the purchase money, or transfer of possession of the house or keys are not decisive. Hence, after contracting the house is available to Andrew's creditors. Insolvency proceedings (bankruptcy and rehabilitation proceedings) can commence via a court order, and each of Andrew's general creditors (creditors without positions of privilege) may seek satisfaction of their claim out of the house in the normal way.

It is possible to agree that Andrew will pay the purchase money after the contracting day. Nevertheless, as the vendor and a creditor Barbara does not have a privileged position if her claim is not backed by a mortgage over the sold property, or if it is not agreed in the contract (deed) that the payment of the price is a condition on the retention or transfer of title to the property. If there is such a clause, Barbara can either cancel the agreement (in the case of Andrew's bankruptcy) or claim the purchase money with a position of specific privilege (in the case of debt execution directed to Andrew).[20]

A purchaser of a piece of real estate has the normal obligation to register his or her acquisition irrespective of a possible cancellation or suspension clause. The registration will not be granted in this case and the application will be left in abeyance until the clause is valid.[21] Irrespective of such a clause, the house is not treated as the vendor's asset. Instead, the vendor's money claim backed by the clause as its

[18] 2:28.1 Code of Real Estate.

[19] 4:13.1 Enforcement Code (2007) at www.finlex.fi/fi/laki/kaannokset/2007/en20070705.pdf.

[20] 5:26.1–3 Enforcement Code.

[21] 12:2.1/1 Code of Real Estate. A cancellation or a suspension clause as a part of a sale of a piece or real property can be valid no more than five years. 2:2.2 Code of Real Estate.

security is treated as his or her asset.[22] This situation only changes if the sale is cancelled. The restituted purchase money will be treated as the purchaser's asset instead of the house after cancellation.[23] The same rules apply to a conventional leasehold.

(b) Sweden

(a) Either party can hold the other party to the contract and demand performance. The seller can claim the price[24] and the buyer can demand possession.[25] The seller is entitled to interest, and might also have a right to damages, even if the contract is not voided by the seller.[26]

The buyer may avoid the contract if the delay amounts to a breach of substantial importance, and he or she also has a right to damages in the case of late performance.[27] The seller cannot avoid the contract unless the sale is conditional upon payment. Avoidance is not available even if the buyer admits to that remedy.[28] Completion of the sale is mostly made conditional on full payment. If this is not the case, Barbara may have lost her right of disposition.[29]

The seller's right to withhold performance (i.e. to refuse the buyer to take possession) is according to the legislative preparatory works subject to that the sale is still conditional upon payment:[30] this view has been questioned in the literature.[31]

The seller may give the buyer credit. If payment is a condition for the final transfer of property, the seller may avoid the contract in the case of the buyer's default.[32] Even if the conditions for the final property

22 4:15.2 Enforcement Code. 23 4:15.1 Enforcement Code.

24 Jan Hellner, Richard Hager and Annina Persson, *Speciell avtalsrätt II. Kontraktsrätt. Första häftet. Särskilda avtalstyper*, 6th edn. (Stockholm: Norstedts Juridik, 2015), p. 85.

25 Folke Grauers, *4 kap. Köp, byte och gåva. Jordabalk (1970:994)*, in the database Karnov, per 1 July 2016, note 174.

26 Hellner, Hager and Persson, *Speciell avtalsrätt II. Kontraktsrätt. Första häftet. Särskilda avtalstyper*, p. 85.

27 4:13 Land Code.

28 Supreme Court judgment *NJA* 1986, 205 and Hellner, Hager and Persson, *Speciell avtalsrätt II. Kontraktsrätt. Första häftet. Särskilda avtalstyper*, p. 85f.

29 Until the buyer has made an application for registration of title, it is nonetheless possible for the seller to make dispositions with the property, 22:1 Land Code, cf. Anders Victorin and Richard Hager, *Allmän fastighetsrätt*, 7th edn. (Uppsala: Iustus Förlag, 2016), p. 247.

30 Governmental proposal *prop. 1970:20 med förslag till jordabalk. Del B 1*, p. 192f.

31 Hellner, Hager and Persson, *Speciell avtalsrätt II. Kontraktsrätt. Första häftet. Särskilda avtalstyper*, p. 83 and Folke Grauers, *Fastighetsköp* (Lund: Juristförlaget, 2001), p. 128f. with nn. 143 and 144, and pp. 277ff.

32 4:25 (2) Land Code. Hellner, Hager and Persson, *Speciell avtalsrätt II. Kontraktsrätt. Första häftet. Särskilda avtalstyper*, p. 85f.

transfer generally are valid only for two years from the issuing of the definitive sales document,[33] this does not apply to payment of the price.[34] If no period is mentioned, the period is construed as being two years.[35]

(b) Parties often agree that the property does not pass over to the buyer until the buyer has possession. This postponement of the passing of property seems to be respected for taxation purposes,[36] but lacks effect in private law, not only against the creditors, but also between the parties.[37] It is enough to have a valid and unconditional contract for the transfer of real property. The house is therefore available to Andrew's creditors even if he did not have possession of the house.[38]

If Andrew is declared bankrupt when the property has already passed over to him, the property belongs to the bankruptcy estate. If Andrew is not declared bankrupt, but still insolvent, his creditors may seek execution, and the house will be part of Andrew's realisable assets. If full payment was a condition for the property transfer, Barbara can avoid the contract if Andrew became insolvent and he or his estate does not provide adequate assurance of payment without undue delay.[39] Barbara may therefore save the property from execution.

(c) Denmark

(a) Danish law on remedies for breach of contract does not distinguish between the two situations described in case 3, questions (a) and (b), nor does it distinguish between the issues dealt with in case 3 and case 4, respectively. Consequently, the question of remedies will be answered together.

The seller of a property does not have a right to unilaterally annul the contract. Therefore, if Barbara (seller) changes her mind and does not want to sell, Andrew may sue Barbara for specific performance. Andrew should initiate an action of declaration, and his plea to the Court should be that Barbara must accept the sales agreement (meaning that she should upon receiving the purchase price provide Andrew with the documents necessary for him to register his ownership of the house

[33] Supreme Court judgment *NJA* 1987, 211 with references and Victorin and Hager, *Allmän fastighetsrätt*, p. 87 with n. 6.

[34] 4:4 (2) Land Code. Victorin and Hager, *Allmän fastighetsrätt*, p. 95.

[35] 4:4 (1) Land Code. Cf. Victorin and Hager, *Allmän fastighetsrätt*, p. 97f.

[36] Supreme Administrative Court decisions RÅ 1950 ref. 5 and RÅ 1993 ref. 16. Hans Tegnander, *Fastighetsskatt och fastighetsavgift*, 2nd edn. (Stockholm: Norstedts Juridik, 2008), p. 90.

[37] Supreme Court judgment *NJA* 1995, 178. Victorin and Hager, *Allmän fastighetsrätt*, p. 88.

[38] Supreme Court judgment *NJA* 1995, 178.

[39] 4:26 Land Code.

and she should vacate the premises in accordance with the agreement). A judgment to that effect may be enforced by the bailiffs – if need be by forcibly removing Barbara and her belongings from the house. Alternatively, Andrew may cancel the contract based on Barbara's breach of contract and claim compensation in the form of the expected interest. Realistically, though, Andrew must show a written sales agreement to be successful. As mentioned, even if an oral agreement between Andrew and Barbara is binding in principle, the Courts will be reluctant to consider Barbara as having sold the property to Andrew based on an oral agreement alone, see above case 3, question (a).

As a starting point, Andrew (buyer) will have to honour his commitment to pay the purchase price and to take over the property. However, if the buyer is a *consumer* there is a narrow exception to this rule, which is outlined in Chapter 2, Consumer Protection Regarding the Purchase of Real Estate Act 1995.[40] The Act provides for a cooling-off period of six working days after the conclusion of the contract if the property is bought mainly with a view to providing housing for the buyer. However, Andrew will have to pay a fixed compensation of 1 per cent of the purchase price.[41]

Assuming that the six-day cooling-off period is exceeded without Andrew paying according to the contract, Barbara may cancel the agreement and sue for damages. Under the Danish general rules of the Law of Obligations, the threshold for cancellation is a 'substantial breach'. Generally, any refusal to pay the purchase price for an asset (and in particular for a valuable asset) will amount to a 'substantial breach'.

Finally, Barbara may opt to insist on the specific performance of the contract by suing Andrew to pay the purchase price according to the contract in return for being put in possession of the house. If Andrew, after such a judgment has been issued, still refuses to pay, Barbara may put the case before the Bailiff's Court. The bailiff may levy execution on any assets belonging to Andrew as security for Barbara's claim for the purchase price and damages.

Please note that the Consumer Protection Regarding the Purchase of Real Estate Act[42] only applies to *buyers* of real estate. Thus, it does not provide an opportunity for *Barbara* to change her mind.

40 Sections 7 and 8, Consumer Protection Regarding the Purchase of Real Estate Act 1995.
41 Section 11, Consumer Protection Regarding the Purchase of Real Estate Act 1995.
42 Sections 7 and 8, Consumer Protection Regarding the Purchase of Real Estate Act 1995.

(b) The answer to this question depends both on the Law of Obligations, the Law of Property, the Laws of Bankruptcy and the rules on registration in the Land Register.

An important distinction here in Danish law is that the Law of Obligations may give you a *claim to a property*, whereas only the Law of Property can give you *a proprietary right over a property.* In plain language, you may easily acquire a claim on a property, but that claim only becomes a right to a property when sufficient steps to protect the claim have been made.[43]

As a starting point, the Law of Obligations provides that if a final agreement to sell the house to Andrew is proven to exist, the property forms part of Andrew's patrimony and the creditors may avail themselves of it. However, the creditors have no better claim on the property than Andrew had. Thus, if the sale of the property is conditioned on the payment of the purchase price (in which case the contract/deed will have to state that it is conditional, and not outright), Barbara may retain the property until such a time as the estate in bankruptcy pays out the full purchase price. If, on the other hand, the deed has been made for an outright sale, the creditors may avail themselves of the full value of the house in exchange for paying Barbara a dividend. Needless to say most deeds are made for the conditioned sale of the property.[44]

Other claims made by Barbara may take precedence over Andrew's creditors' claims. Thus, any claim made by Barbara in case the agreement to sell the property is found to be invalid will have priority, and Andrew's right to the property may, depending on the circumstances, be extinguished by Barbara's creditors or contractual partners (e.g. in a double sale).

Under Danish bankruptcy laws, a creditor may be either an individual creditor or a creditor in bankruptcy. Individual creditors may levy a distress on the property by applying to the Bailiff's Court. Apart from stoppage *in transitu*, the term 'insolvency' has no legal meaning in itself under Danish law. However, if Andrew is found to be unable to pay his creditors,[45] the debtor or any of his creditors may request that he be declared bankrupt by the Bankruptcy Court. Bankruptcy proceedings will then take place, and all of Andrew's assets will be split between his creditors according to their share of his debt. In both

[43] Peter Mortensen, *Indledning til tingsretten* (Copenhagen: Karnov Group, 2009), p. 173.

[44] Lennart L. Andersen and Palle B. Madsen, *Aftaler og mellemmænd*, 6th edn. (Copenhagen: Karnov Group, 2012), p. 129.

[45] Section 17, Act of 6 January 2014, No. 11 on Bankruptcy (The Bankruptcy Act).

cases, the Court can only enforce orders against properties of which Andrew is the registered owner in the Buildings and Dwellings Register.[46] Thus, their claim on the property does not become a proprietary right until such a time as Andrew's claim on the property is registered as unconditional. Normally, the deed is first registered as conditional and then, when the purchase sum is transferred, as unconditional.

(d) Norway

(a) The answer to (a) follows from case 3: either party may enforce a claim for performance, or terminate the contract for non-performance and claim damages for loss caused by non-performance.

(b) Andrew's right under the contract is considered to be one of the assets available to his creditors. If Andrew is insolvent, insolvency proceedings (bankruptcy, rehabilitation) may be opened by a court order.[47] Independent of insolvency, each of Andrew's general creditors may seek satisfaction of their claim out of Andrew's right under the contract.[48]

There will be a conflict between Barbara and Andrew's creditors if the purchase money is still not paid by the time insolvency proceedings commence (or by the time a compulsory security right in favour of an individual creditor is established). Barbara either wants to obtain the agreed purchase price, or to terminate the contract of sale, thus keeping the property for herself. If the registered title has already been transferred to Andrew (which is usually *not* the case when the purchase money is not paid), Barbara will only have an unsecured claim for the remainder of the agreed purchase price, i.e. a claim for a dividend in the case of bankruptcy.[49] The rules are not altogether clear where the registered title has not yet been transferred to Andrew. From the moment Andrew takes factual control of the property, Barbara is no longer allowed to terminate the contract for non-performance of Andrew's obligation to pay, unless she has made a reservation for this.[50]

[46] See Section 10, LRA.

[47] Sections 1 and 60, Act Relating to Bankruptcy (*lov om gjeldsforhandling og konkurs*, 8. June 1984 No. 58).

[48] Section 2-2, Act Relating to Creditors' Right to Satisfaction of Claims (*lov om fordringshavernes dekningsrett*, 8. June 1984 No. 59), cf. Section 7-1 (2), Act Relating to Enforcement of Claims (*lov om tvangsfullbyrdelse*, 26 June 1992 No. 96).

[49] Section 7-7 (2), Act Relating to Creditors' Right to Satisfaction of Claims.

[50] Section 5-3 (4), Act Relating to the Sale of Real Property.

The prevailing view is, however, that Barbara is not obliged to transfer the registered title to Andrew (or his creditors) unless the purchase money is paid, meaning in practice that the creditors will either pay the money or leave the property to Barbara.[51] Barbara has lost her right to terminate for non-payment from the moment she gave Andrew a signed 'deed', even if Andrew has not yet had the document registered.[52] Arguably, the creditors can register this document so as to take the property, as no further contribution is needed from Barbara in order to transfer the property. In short, Andrew's creditors may seek to satisfy their claims out of Andrew's right under the contract without paying the outstanding purchase money if the registered title has been transferred to Andrew, and arguably also if Barbara has delivered a signed deed even if the signed deed is yet to be registered.

It should be remembered that Andrew's right under the contract may be of value to his creditors even if the creditors have to pay the outstanding purchase money because the contract may still be a 'good bargain'. Barbara must as a rule accept that the bankrupt's estate is substituted as a party to the contract.[53] On the other hand, the creditors are never obliged to take over the contract.

3 *Romanic–Mediterranean jurisdictions*

(a) Italy

(a) According to art. 1376 ICC, ownership is transferred upon legally expressed consent. A valid contract of sale made in writing and signed by both parties has the legal effect of transferring ownership.[54] Theoretically no other formality is required, neither delivery, payment of the price, nor registration. Once the contract is signed, Andrew must pay the price, which normally happens when the parties sign the contract,[55] and Barbara must deliver the thing to Andrew that gives Andrew possession of the house.[56] So, if Barbara changes her mind and does not fulfil her obligation to deliver the thing, Andrew can sue her for specific performance in order to get a court order for possession of the house, which he already owns.[57] Conversely, if Andrew changes his mind and does not

[51] Kåre Lilleholt, *Allmenn formuerett* (Oslo: Universitetsforlaget, 2012), pp. 271–3.
[52] Section 5-3 (4), Act Relating to the Sale of Real Property.
[53] Section 7-3, Act Relating to Creditors' Right to Satisfaction of Claims.
[54] See art. 1470 ICC. [55] Art. 1498 ICC. [56] Art. 1476 n.1 ICC. [57] Art. 2930 ICC.

want to pay the price, Barbara can sue Andrew for payment of the price.

Moreover, in order to register the contract, notarial formality is practically unavoidable.[58]

(b) In principle, just because a written contract signed by both parties constitutes a sufficient requirement to transfer ownership over immovable property, once Andrew and Barbara have concluded the contract of sale for the house, the house should be considered part of Andrew's property and thus contribute a generic guarantee for his creditors[59] (including Barbara, if the price has not yet been paid). However, art. 2817 No. 1 ICC assigns a legal mortgage to the unpaid seller over the property sold, as a guarantee of the obligation to pay the price. Barbara could then register her legal mortgage together with the contract of sale and this mortgage will prevail over all registrations on the house that are made 'against' Andrew.[60] In this way, Barbara's interest will prevail over both Andrew's unsecured creditors and mortgage-holders who have registered their mortgage on the house before the sale is registered. Therefore, even if ownership of the house has been formally transferred to Andrew, it will not be available for his creditors while Barbara has not been paid. Note that in the absence of the notarial formality as required by art. 2657 ICC, the mere written contract of sale cannot be registered and the mortgage cannot be constituted. Barbara should then apply to the court to validate the registration under art. 216, para. 2 Code of Civil Procedure and ask for a judgment to be entered together with the written contract of sale. At the same time the legal mortgage will be recorded and constituted in her favour.

(b) Spain

(a) If either party changes their mind after the signing of the contract and refuses to perform the agreement, the other party may apply to a court to enforce performance or rescind the contract by reason of breach, and in either case seek damages.

However, it may be the case that the parties have entered into a contract of sale involving a deposit of earnest money, known in Spanish as a *contrato de arras*. This transaction is, again, a sale, entailing obligations for both parties – the seller to deliver the thing, the buyer to

[58] As we have seen in the answer to case 2, question (b).
[59] See art. 2740 ICC.
[60] See art. 2650, para. 3 ICC.

pay the price. However, unlike a firm sale, where if one party fails to perform the non-breaching party may either enforce performance or rescind the contract, under a sale involving earnest money either party is free to abandon his or her obligation. If the buyer abandons, he or she is released merely by forfeiture of the earnest money deposited. If the seller abandons, he or she is released by refunding the buyer with double the amount of the earnest money. The earnest money, termed *arras*, is usually 5 per cent to 10 per cent of the price of the property. If the sale is completed, the earnest money counts towards the total agreed price.

(b) Whether or not Andrew is declared insolvent by a court, if any of his creditors can successfully show that Andrew is insolvent, they can take over Andrew's right to hold Barbara to perform her side of the contract, i.e. to hand over the house. In order for this to occur, Andrew must have already paid the price, which generally does not occur until the property is handed over, or he must have secured payment of the price. Otherwise, Barbara is under no obligation to perform her obligation of handover.[61] Once Barbara has transferred possession and Andrew has acquired ownership, the creditor taking action and any other creditor may satisfy his or her rights against the house. If, for whatever reason, Andrew has already paid the price, his creditors may hold Barbara to performance of her side of the contract. If Barbara has already performed her side, Andrew will have acquired ownership of the house even if he has not yet paid the price, but Barbara may seek rescission on grounds of breach if Andrew fails to pay. It could be in Andrew's creditors' interests to prevent rescission because, say, the value of the house is greater than the agreed price, and suffices to cover both the agreed price and the amount of debt that Andrew owes his creditors. If this is the case, the creditor might come to an agreement with Andrew whereby the creditor lends Andrew the price of the house, and subsequently recovers the whole amount owed to him or her against the value of the house.

If Andrew is declared insolvent by a court, and neither he nor Barbara has yet performed the obligations to pay the price or hand over the house, then a court-appointed receiver (if Andrew has been suspended from his powers of administration and disposal) or Andrew himself (if he has not been barred from managing and disposing of his property) may apply to rescind the contract. This releases Andrew from the obligation to pay the price, but also deprives him of the right to acquire

[61] Article 1467 Spanish CC, enacted under the *Real Decreto* of 24 July 1889.

the house. The court will summons Andrew, the receiver and Barbara. If the parties so agree, the court will then order rescission of the contract accordingly. If the parties do not reach agreement, the court will decide whether or not the contract should be rescinded.[62] If Andrew or his creditors oppose rescission because it is in their interest to acquire the house, the sale price is payable out of the bankrupt's (Andrew's) estate.

If at the time he was declared insolvent Andrew had already paid the sale price, his right to hold Barbara to handing over the house now falls within his insolvent estate. This means that it is the receiver who will require Barbara to transfer possession of the house. But if it is Barbara who has already performed her obligation to hand over, and Andrew has not yet paid the price, Barbara may apply for rescission of the contract instead of demanding performance against the insolvent estate. The court, however, may decide to order performance plus damages if it thinks the insolvency process is better served by performance.[63]

(c) Portugal

(a) The Portuguese system is a causal one, since it requires a valid contract for the transfer of ownership, and consensual, since that contract is enough to transfer property. *Traditio*, payment of the price or registration are not a requirement for property transfer. Therefore, if Andrew and Barbara have a legally binding sales agreement, the property transfer has occurred (arts. 408 (1) and 879 (a) CC). Parties have now to perform the obligations under the contract, namely the duty to deliver the thing (art. 878 (b) CC) and the duty to pay the price (art. 879 (c) CC).

The vendor, who has already delivered the thing, cannot rescind the contract by reason of breach, if the acquirer does not pay the price (art. 886 CC).[64] Either the vendor, to obtain payment, or the acquirer, to obtain delivery of the thing, may apply to a court to enforce performance (art. 818 CC).

Consideration is essential to the sale. However, the payment of the price is not a condition for the conclusion of the sale. Art. 885 CC provides that the payment is due at the moment and in the place of the delivery of the thing sold, unless the parties agree otherwise. Practice

62 Art. 61 (2) *Ley 22/2003, de 9 de julio, Concursal* ('Insolvency Act 2003').
63 Art. 62 (3) Insolvency Act 2003.
64 This provision is a logical consequence of the former transmission of property at the moment of the conclusion of the contract.

provides for entry into enjoyment at the same time as the transfer of the property. However, as for the payment, entry into enjoyment may also be deferred or anticipated.

(b) If Andrew has already paid the price and Barbara has delivered the house, it forms part of Andrew's property and is available to his creditors (art. 601 CC).

The Insolvency Code[65] sets the proceedings to follow when a debtor is not able to meet his commitments as they fall due. Legal persons, and autonomous groups of assets and liabilities where no individual has unlimited personal liability for the debts, are also considered to be insolvent when their liabilities clearly exceed their assets.

If Andrew had already paid the sale price, when he was declared insolvent, his right to hold Barbara to handing over the house would fall within his insolvent estate. This means that it is the administrator who will require Barbara to transfer possession of the house (art. 81 Insolvency Code).

But if Barbara has not performed her obligation to hand over, and Andrew has not yet paid the price, the situation would be different. Any bilateral agreement entered into between the insolvent and a third party, which has not been performed at the date of the declaration of the insolvency, will be suspended until the insolvency administrator decides whether or not to comply with such an agreement. However, the third party may set a time-limit for the administrator to decide. Once this term has elapsed, the agreement will be considered as annulled and Barbara would have a credit over the insolvent estate, corresponding to the difference between the value agreed upon at the moment of sale and the value of the house at the moment of the refusal (arts. 105 (1) (b), 102 (3) and 104 (5) Insolvency Code).[66]

(d) Greece

(a) Whenever a valid contract for the sale of a house is in place, the seller is under an obligation to transfer ownership of the house to the buyer and give possession thereof, and the buyer is under an obligation to pay the agreed price. If either party does not perform its obligations,

[65] As approved by Decree Law 53/2004, of 18 March, and amended by Decree Laws: 200/2004, of 18 August; 76-A/2006, of 29 March; 282/2007, of 7 August; 116/2008, of 4 July; and 185/2009, of 12 August; and by Law 16/2012, of 20 April.

[66] Luía M. T. de Menezes Leitão, *Direito da Insolvência* (Coimbra: Almedina, 2015), pp. 144–5; Luís A. Carvalho Fernandes and João Labareda, *Código da Insolvência e da Recuperacão de Empresas Anotado* (Coimbra; Almedina, 2015), pp. 398–9.

the other party has all the remedies provided by law for contractual non-performance, including the option to force the other party's performance by means of an award by a Court.

Andrew can therefore sue Barbara for specific performance in order to achieve an award by a Court in lieu of Barbara's consent to convey the property.[67] Otherwise he can rescind the agreement or seek compensation for the non-fulfilment of it. If he chooses to rescind the contract, he may also have a right to compensation for damages from the non-fulfilment.[68]

Barbara also has all of the usual remedies for contractual non-performance, for example, she can demand payment from Andrew as compensation or choose to rescind the contract.

(b) In order for the house to form part of Andrew's property, besides the need for a valid contract in the presence of a public notary, the law also requires registration in the local Transcription Registry.[69] From the moment of registration, the house becomes Andrew's asset and his creditors can claim it. However, the following possibilities exist in the period before the contract is registered.[70]

If Andrew and Barbara have both fulfilled their contractual obligations, the bankruptcy administrator can apply for registration in the Transcription Registry, and by the time of the registration the house forms part of Andrew's property and is available to his creditors.

Furthermore, if at the time when bankruptcy proceedings are commenced the bilateral contract has not yet been fulfilled, art. 28 Greek Code of Insolvency[71] provides that it remains valid. However, the bankruptcy administrator can choose either to fulfil the contract and demand fulfilment from the other party,[72] or rescind the contract.

4 *France and related jurisdictions*

(a) France

(a) The same answer as provided above in question 3(a) applies.

(b) Yes – if the transfer has already taken place between the parties, because their creditors are not third parties according to the Land

[67] Art. 949 GCCP. [68] Arts. 516, 383 and 387 GCC.

[69] For the transfer of real rights on immovables, see the answer to question 1.

[70] According to the Greek Code of Insolvency.

[71] Law 3588/2007 as amended by law 4013/2011. [72] Art. 29 Greek Code of Insolvency.

Registry. The house is a part of Andrew's property and it is available to his creditors, even if he has not paid the price yet!

(b) Belgium

(a) The answer to question 3(a) applies.

(b) If the buyer becomes insolvent after the sale, the immovable is part of Andrew's estate and will thus become part of the insolvency estate. The proceeds of the sale of the house will be distributed in the insolvency. However, if the insolvency price has not been paid yet, the insolvency administrator can decide, according to Belgian insolvency law, not to comply with the obligations under the purchase agreement, and thus to dissolve the agreement and reverse (retroactively) the transfer of property.[73]

Belgian law provides a statutory protection for the seller against a buyer's insolvency. According to art. 27 1° Belgian Hypothec Act,[74] Barbara – as seller of an immovable – has a statutory lien that allows her to be paid out of the proceeds of the immovable in priority to Andrew's other creditors. The mere requirement is that the lien is registered in the Hypothec Register. However, the Hypothec Registrar will automatically register the lien when he registers the sales agreement, except if the parties have discharged him from this obligation. The latter will generally only be the case if the buyer has made an immediate payment, which allows him or her to avoid the registration taxes.

5 *England and related jurisdictions*

(a) England

(a) If Barbara refuses to perform her obligation to sell to Andrew, Andrew can choose between suing for damages for breach of contract or seeking specific performance of the contract. The order of specific performance is an equitable remedy and therefore it may be refused on settled equitable principles governing discretionary relief (e.g. where it would cause excessive hardship[75] or where a substantial lapse of time would make it inequitable to enforce the claim). It is also limited to cases where damages would be an inadequate remedy for the relevant breach

[73] Eric Dirix, 'Faillissement en lopende overeenkomsten', *Rechtskundig Weekblad*, 2003-04, p. 207.

[74] Act of 16 December 1851, *Belgian Official Gazette* 22 December 1851. This Act has been inserted in the BCC.

[75] See, e.g., *Patel* v. *Ali* [1984] Ch. 283.

of contract. There is a high likelihood of Andrew securing an order for specific performance of the contract, as land is normally considered to be of unique value so that damages are an inadequate remedy.[76]

If Andrew refuses to perform his obligation to buy the house from Barbara, Barbara can also sue for specific performance, subject to application of the normal equitable principles governing discretionary relief.[77] Alternatively, she may choose to terminate the contract and sue for damages for its breach. Such damages will probably be measured as the difference between the price agreed with Andrew and the value of the property as it is left in her hands[78] or (if she re-sells the property) the difference between the price agreed with Andrew and the price for which she eventually sold the property, plus the expenses of that sale.[79] Barbara can elect between these alternative remedies.

(b) On its own, Andrew's insolvency does not affect his (or anyone else's) property rights – he must first be adjudicated bankrupt before the insolvency regime affects his property.

Assuming, therefore, that Andrew has been adjudicated bankrupt, if he had already paid the purchase price, Barbara will hold the property on trust for Andrew and his equitable interest in the property will pass to his trustee in bankruptcy, effectively allowing the house to be sold for the benefit of his creditors.[80]

Pending payment of the purchase price, Andrew holds an equitable interest in the land that reflects the extent to which equitable remedies (such as specific performance) are available to protect his contractual rights.[81] However, this does not give him a right to possess and use the property,[82] until the full purchase price has been paid. If bankruptcy intervenes after the contract is entered into, but before the price has been paid, the trustee in bankruptcy acquires

[76] See, e.g., *Adderley* v. *Dixon* (1824) 1 Sim. & St. 607 at p. 610.

[77] See, e.g., *Rutherford* v. *Acton-Adams* [1915] AC 866 at pp. 869–70.

[78] See A.J. Oakley, 'Pecuniary Compensation for Failure to Complete a Contract for the Sale of Land', (1980) *CLJ* 58 at p. 70.

[79] See, e.g., *Janred Properties Ltd* v. *Ente Nazionale Italiano per il Turismo* [1989] 2 All ER 444 at p. 456.

[80] Sections 283, 306 and 436, Insolvency Act 1986 (hereafter, 'IA 1986'). A bankrupt's house is not exempt from realisation for the creditors' benefit, although it will be returned to the bankrupt if it has not been realised within three years of the bankruptcy: section 283A, IA 1986.

[81] See Peter G. Turner, 'Understanding the Constructive Trust between Vendor and Purchaser', (2012) 128 *LQR* 582.

[82] See, e.g., *Jerome* v. *Kelly* [2004] UKHL 25, [2004] 1 WLR 1409 at [32].

Andrew's equitable interest, which will allow the trustee in bankruptcy to acquire the property, but only if he or she pays the purchase price.[83] The property would then be available for Andrew's creditors.

(b) Scotland

(a) Both have remedies. As Barbara is contractually bound to sell to Andrew, this obligation can, if necessary, be enforced by a court action for specific implement. Equally, Andrew can be forced to pay the price, with interest, although it would be unusual to require him to do so.[84] Alternatively, the innocent party can rescind the contract and seek damages.

(b) Insolvency has no effect on property rights without a court order sequestrating the insolvent person's estate and appointing a trustee to manage it on behalf of the creditors. The trustee becomes the owner of all the assets comprised in the insolvent person's patrimony.

The house does not form part of Andrew's patrimony and so cannot be attached by the trustee in sequestration (or by individual creditors). For ownership to pass to Andrew, it would have been necessary to register the deed of transfer (the 'disposition') in the Land Register. In the absence of registration, Barbara has ownership of the house. Andrew's right under the contract is available to the trustee (and creditors), although its value is likely to be negligible unless Andrew bought the house at a favourable price.

(c) Ireland

(a) If Andrew refuses to proceed with the transaction, Barbara may seek specific performance of the contract but the courts will not grant this remedy in certain circumstances, such as where Andrew does not have the funds to complete the purchase[85] or if Barbara's title to the property is bad.[86] Alternatively, Barbara could forfeit any deposit paid by Andrew, and sue for damages for breach of contract. She may not

[83] *Crosbie* v. *Tooke* (1833) 1 My. & K. 431 at pp. 433–4; *Morgan* v. *Rhodes* (1834) 1 My. & K. 435 at pp. 438–9; *Buckland* v. *Papillon* (1866) LR 2 Ch. App. 67. However, the contract cannot be specifically enforced *against* the trustee in bankruptcy: *Holloway* v. *York* (1877) 25 WR 627.

[84] The competency of this remedy was challenged but upheld in *AMA (New Town) Ltd* v. *Law* [2013] CSIH 61, 2013 SC 608.

[85] *Aranbel Ltd* v. *Darcy* [2010] IEHC at 272.

[86] *Larkin* v. *Lord Rosse* (1846) 10 IR Eq. R. 70 at 74 per Smith MR.

recover damages because even if the house has fallen in value so that its resale value is below the contract price, that fall may be more than offset by the deposit paid, which must be taken into account. In a rising property market, vendors usually choose to forfeit the deposit and treat the contract as rescinded, which allows them to re-sell the property to someone else and keep any profit made. If Barbara refuses to proceed with the transaction Andrew may also seek an order for specific performance or damages for breach of contract. He may seek damages for the loss of the bargain (i.e. the difference between the contract purchase price and the property market value at the date of the breach) and, in such circumstances, he will also be entitled to recover any deposit he paid to Barbara, with interest for loss of its use.[87]

(b) Once Andrew has entered into an enforceable contract he becomes the beneficial owner of Barbara's house.[88] However, this does not affect Barbara's right to rescind the contract if he fails to complete the transaction by paying the purchase price.[89] As Andrew has been adjudicated bankrupt, the Official Assignee in Bankruptcy must either complete the contract or disclaim it as unprofitable.[90] He must pay the balance of the purchase price in order to complete the contract and, if he does, the house can be sold to satisfy claims by Andrew's creditors.[91] If he disclaims the contract, Barbara can forfeit any deposit paid by Andrew and she becomes a creditor who may apply for damages in the bankruptcy proceedings for any losses she has suffered.[92]

[87] For more discussion of the remedies available for the enforcement of a contract for the sale of land, see J.C.W. Woods and Una Wylie, *Irish Conveyancing Law* (Haywards Heath: Bloomsbury Professional, 2005), Chapter 13.

[88] Section 52 (1), Land and Conveyancing Law Reform Act 2009.

[89] Section 53 (2) (c), Land and Conveyancing Law Reform Act 2009.

[90] Section 56, Bankruptcy Act 1988.

[91] Section 61 (3) (a), Bankruptcy Act 1988.

[92] See *Re Parnell* (1875) 10 Ch App 512.

Case 5

Peter is the registered owner of a flat. He sells the house to Elizabeth who moves in but does not register her title. Peter then sells the flat to Margaret who pays the price and registers her purchase. Margaret sues Elizabeth to recover possession of the flat. Will she succeed?[1]

(A) Foundational Concepts for Understanding Case 5

In systems that follow the so-called 'consensualism principle', ownership is transferred before the immovable is delivered or the transfer is made public in the Land Register. These private transfers, however, sometimes present some obstacles to the legal security, especially if there is a double sale or double acquisition, as in this case.

In the French legal system and similar systems (as in Belgium) the effect of registration is called '*opposabilité*'. By reason of the publicity, a person who obtains the '*opposabilité*' by registration is placed in a superior position to a person who has not. Outside the '*opposabilité effect*', the person first in time is given precedence.

Neither registration of transfer nor delivery is necessary to complete the sale under the contract between A and B, but they are necessary in order to enforce property rights against a third party (*opposabilité*). Without registration, B cannot assert his acquisition of the property against C, a third party unrelated to the contract of sale between A and B. In particular, in France case law has developed some rules about how to understand the good faith of the acquirer.

On the one hand, in other systems that demand delivery or registration the situation changes. Even when the seller is no longer the owner,

[1] The distinction between 'house' and 'flat' can have its importance in some jurisdictions. Nevertheless it does not affect the aim of the case.

they can still transfer the property to the second purchaser, as long as the seller still retains the registration as the owner.

In countries like Germany, where inscription is constitutive, if there is no inscription, there is no transfer of ownership. Furthermore, the non-registered acquirer should not be preferred. The situation is the same in Austria, where the ownership of an immovable is acquired by the person who applies for registration first. The one who registers his purchase first acquires ownership even though this person is not yet in possession of the flat.

In Dutch law a contract of sale does not pass ownership; it merely creates a personal duty for the seller to transfer ownership, inscription is also necessary to acquire ownership. This result would be the same in Turkey.

In Nordic law, the first acquirer has priority, unless the second acquirer in good faith registers the title first. Accordingly, the good faith must sustain from concluding the contract until the moment of seeking registration.

In Italy, a conflict between two buyers of the same immovable property is resolved in favour of the person who registers their interest first. This constitutes a broad exception to the consent principle. In Spain, although there is currently some discussion about the solution to this problem, the third acquirer who registered first and is acting in good faith would be protected. Portugal has the same approach, where if the owner sells the same property to two different acquirers, whoever registers first becomes the new owner.

In England, as a general rule the registered acquirer would prevail in a conflict with the non-registered party. However, if the party who did not register is in possession of the flat, it seems likely that his occupation would have been obvious during a reasonably careful inspection of the flat, and consequently the occupying party's interest in the property is likely to bind the third acquirer. Also this person could ask the Registrar to alter the register to reflect her title. Similarly, in Scotland the solution to this case would be that the one who registered their title would be preferred. However, if this person was acting in bad faith, knowing of the other sale, their deed of conveyance could be set aside by the court to allow the non-registered acquirer to register her own disposition. Finally, in Ireland if the non-registered acquirer is in occupation of the flat at the time of the transaction, they could have an overriding interest that could bind the registered acquirer.

(B) The Jurisdictions (Presented by Related Jurisdictions)

(1) Germany and related jurisdictions

(a) Germany

After the declaration of conveyance and the registration in the Land Register have both been made, Margaret acquires ownership of the flat.[2] Elizabeth did not become owner because she did not register her title. Margaret, being the owner of the flat, is entitled to recover possession of it from Elizabeth.[3] Elizabeth cannot claim a right of possession against Margaret because she did not enter into a contractual relationship with her. She can only sue Peter for damages for non-performance of the sales contract.[4]

In most practical cases, however, the result would be different. Normally the buyer will be secured by the registration of a priority notice (*Vormerkung*). If a priority notice had been entered in the Land Register in favour of Elizabeth, the transfer of the flat to Margaret would have been void in relation to Elizabeth (but not against other persons).[5] In this case, Margaret would not succeed with her claim.

(b) Austria

According to the registration principle (§ 431 ABGB) and the priority maxim (§ 440 ABGB) ownership of an immovable is acquired by the person who applies for registration first.[6] Since Margaret registers her purchase (first) she acquires ownership even though she is not yet in possession of the flat.

It should not go unmentioned that this legal opinion was highly controversial in the past. In former times it was held in the literature[7] that also the acquisition of possession constitutes a legal position *in rem*. Of course this was contrary to the wording of the law. Notwithstanding, the High Court[8]

[2] §§ 873, para. 1; 925, para. 1 BGB. [3] §§ 985, 986 BGB.

[4] §§ 437 No. 3, 280, 281, 283 BGB. [5] See § 883, para. 2 BGB.

[6] To be precise: the arriving of the documents at the competent court is *de facto* decisive (§ 29 GBG).

[7] In particular Klang, in Heinrich Klang (ed.), *Kommentar zum allgemeinen bürgerlichen Gesetzbuch, II*, 2nd edn. (Vienna: Staatsdruckerei, 1950), pp. 357ff; cf in detail with further references: Renate Pletzer, *Doppelveräußerung und Forderungseingriff* (Vienna: Orac, 2000), p. 33.

[8] OGH 29.5.1953, 1 Ob 441/53, JBl 1954, 68; OGH 17.10.1956, 1 Ob 485/56, JBl 1957, 290; OGH 9.11.1960, 1 Ob 222/60, JBl 1961, 416; OGH 8.2.1972, 4 Ob 635/71, JBl 1972, 429; change in jurisdiction by OGH 21.12.1972, 6 Ob 132/72, JBl 1973, 524 – confirmed in OGH 14.10.1975, 5 Ob 183/75, SZ 48/104.

also temporarily followed the doctrine of the acquisition of informal (not registered) ownership (*Lehre vom außerbücherlichen Eigentum*).

Basically, there is no general obligation to investigate whether the facts in the Land Register conform to the actual conditions[9] because that would put a question mark over the reliability of the Land Register. Margaret is nevertheless at least expected to take a look at the flat she intends to acquire.[10] Should it become apparent that the flat is being used by someone else, she is obligated to ask about that. Assuming that Peter is able to give a good reason for the occupation, Margaret is not obliged to obtain further information.[11] It depends on the single case and the circumstances if mistrust (and therefore negligence) has to be assumed. Therefore, the fact that Elizabeth already moved into the flat can absolutely be of importance.

In conclusion, the chronological order of the underlying transactions (here: sales contracts) does not play a role and is not decisive in determining a dispute over the acquisition of immovable property. If Margaret was actually justified in trusting Peter, Elizabeth would have to move out and she would only be able to sue her opponent for damages due to non-performance of the sales contract. Margaret will not succeed if she knew or must have known (see above) about the infringement.

It should be noted that Elizabeth at least ought to have made a note on the impending acquisition of ownership in the Land Register (*Vormerkung*) according to § 35 GBG. That is standard practice if a title registration cannot yet be effected, and it would have prevented a possible success of Margaret's claim, since in such a case good faith acquisition is deemed to be excluded.

(c) The Netherlands

The problem as described above could hardly happen under Dutch law. Normally, Elizabeth would only move in after the transfer deed of the right to the apartment had been signed. At the moment the notarial deed is made, the keys to the flat are handed over to the buyer. After the deed has been made and signed by both parties, the notary registers the deed. After the notary receives confirmation of the registration from the Registry, they forward the purchase price to the seller.

[9] OGH 9.7.1963, 8 Ob 185/63, EvBl 1963/419; OGH 26.5.1964, 8 Ob 155/64, EvBl 1965/64.

[10] Cf OGH 31.8.1983, 1 Ob 674/83, SZ 56/125; OGH 11.6.1987, 8 Ob 533, 534/87, NZ 1988, 98.

[11] Cf. Monika Hinteregger, in Michael Schwimann (ed), *Praxiskommentar zum ABGB*, II, 3rd edn. (Vienna: LexisNexis, 2005), § 440 mn 19.

Before the deed is made, the buyer has to credit the notary's office's bank account with the purchase price.

If in an exceptional case Elizabeth moves in after the contract of sale without any conveyance deed being made and registered, Elizabeth has a mere contractual claim against the seller (Peter). She cannot use this right against Margaret. If the flat is then sold and transferred to Margaret, Elizabeth must move out. Margaret is able to revindicate the flat.

It was previously noted that in the Dutch law a contract of sale does not pass ownership; it merely creates a personal duty for the seller to transfer ownership to Elizabeth. This duty is not binding upon Margaret, even where Margaret knows that the flat has already been sold to Elizabeth. Only in extreme cases, where Margaret misuses her personal relationship to incite Peter to sell her the same land, can Elizabeth obtain ownership of the land in an indirect way. The fact that Margaret knowingly incites Peter to breach a contract is seen as a tort and the judge can order Margaret to pay damages in kind, ordering that the land be transferred to Elizabeth.[12] A practical example of a double sale is the case in which the seller himself still occupies the flat, or the case in which the flat is empty. The first transfer is then decisive. If the transfer is made to the second buyer, they will become owner of the flat (or more precisely, the holder of the apartment right). The seller will be liable in damages for breach of contract as against the first buyer.

If Elizabeth bought the flat and is now living in it despite the fact that there was no transfer of the flat right, and afterwards the seller sells and transfers the flat right to a second buyer, the transfer to the second buyer would be valid because it is the first and only transfer. The second buyer will be able to demand that the first buyer leave the flat (revindication). However, if the first buyer were able to assert a lease on the flat, the outcome would be different. The new owner's rights are subject to the lease. Yet, in the given case a lease would not exist and cannot easily be inferred from the circumstances.

(d) Turkey

Elizabeth cannot own the house unless her name is registered in the Land Register. Margaret is the owner of the flat and she may claim her right and request redress from whoever violated it, and from Elizabeth as well. Margaret will succeed.

[12] HR 17 November 1967, *NJ* 1968/42 (Pos/Van den Bosch).

2 *Scandinavian jurisdictions*

(a) Finland

The question is treated here as the problem of a double sale of a piece of real estate. The same rules are applied to a house as a part of a leasehold.[13] According to Finnish law, a flat is treated as movable property and it is ignored here.

The point of departure is the priority in time. According to the major rule the first purchaser, Elizabeth, has priority in this case.[14] It is nevertheless possible for a later conveyance to take precedence. This exceptional solution presupposes that the later purchaser applies first for the registration of the title. Second, the later purchaser cannot have known of the previous conveyance at the time of acquisition.[15] Hence, the exception is founded on the activity of the later purchaser (and the passivity of the previous purchaser), as well as the good faith of the later purchaser. In practice, both purchasers trust in the Title and Mortgage Register to ascertain the registered title of the vendor. However, in this situation the rules are not founded on that trust. If registrations of title to several acquisitions are applied for on the same day, the earliest conveyance takes precedence. Payment of the purchase price or possession of the piece of real estate or the house (moving in) makes no difference in this situation. In the form of acquisition information, information on a conveyance of a piece of real estate is entered into the Title and Mortgage Register a few days after the conveyance by a notice of a notary.

These solutions and rules are substantial: they decide the ownership of a piece of real estate. Therefore, Margaret can claim ownership and possession of the piece of real estate if the presuppositions of the exceptional solution are at hand. On the other hand, Elizabeth's ownership can be confirmed and she can claim possession if the major rule is applied and if Margaret possesses the piece of real estate. Possible cancellation or suspension clauses of the sales do not affect the solutions.

In the double sale situation, the vendor is liable for damages to both purchasers suffering costs or losses caused by the vendor. Moreover, the vendor is liable towards the purchaser whose acquisition does not prevail. Normally, there is a defect in title at hand: the purchaser loses his or her title in favour of the rightful titleholder or the sale may be voided

[13] 4:4.1 and 14:7.1 Code of Real Estate. [14] 3:6.1 Code of Real Estate.
[15] 13:3.1 Code of Real Estate.

upon the request of a third party. The purchaser is entitled, naturally, to cancel the sale.[16]

In practice, it is very exceptional that a later purchaser can enjoy the protection described above. Regardless of the registration information on the conveyances of real estate that are entered into the Title and Mortgage Register, a few days after the conveyances as acquisition information by the notices of notaries.[17] All register entries including acquisition information are deemed public knowledge as from the first weekday after the date of entry. No one can enjoy the protection of good faith (lack of knowledge) about these entries. On the other hand, the rules of acquisition information are not applied to conveyances of leaseholds. After adopting the system of electronic conveyances containing real time registration, similar protection founded on earlier registration is no longer possible.

After adopting the system of electronic conveyances containing real time registration, similar protection founded on earlier registration is no longer possible. In the frame of the system, a double conveyance is not possible. Opening a transaction in the system excludes other rival transactions, and the transferee is immediately registered as a part of the conveyance.[18] On the other hand, a double conveyance is possible if one transaction is made using a paper document and the other is made on the electronic conveyancing system.

(b) Sweden

In the case of a double sale of real property, the first buyer has priority. However, if the second buyer is acting in good faith at the time when the sale is concluded and (in good or bad faith)[19] seeks registration of title before the first buyer, the second buyer is protected.[20]

Some flats, today about a thousand but slowly increasing, are owner apartments. Owner apartments are pieces of real property. The flats in housing cooperatives, about a million, are under a different legal construct. The 'owner' of a flat in a housing cooperative has a strong ownership-like right to the flat. An assignment is binding when the

[16] 2:19 Code of Real Estate.

[17] 7:5.1 Code of Real Estate and legislation on the public notaries.

[18] 9a:11.1 and 9a:12.1 Code of Real Estate.

[19] Bertil Bengtsson, *Sakrättsliga frågor i fastighetsrätten* (Uppsala: Iustus Förlag, 1991), p. 57. Folke Grauers, *Fastighetsköp*, 21st edn. (Lund: Juristförlaget i Lund, 2016), p. 325. Anders Victorin and Richard Hager, *Allmän fastighetsrätt*, 6th edn. (Uppsala: Iustus Förlag, 2015), p. 251.

[20] 17:2 Land Code.

formal requirements are fulfilled,[21] but in order to have an effect towards third parties it is necessary to notify the cooperative.[22] In a double sale, the first buyer has priority, but the second buyer may get priority if he or she in good faith notified the cooperative before the first buyer.[23] Unlike the rules on real property, good faith must be sustained until the notification. By analogy, these rules also apply to the relatively few flats in housing associations and joint-stock housing companies.[24]

If Peter has sold the flat twice, Margaret will be protected if she bought the flat in good faith and registered ownership. She may therefore have Elizabeth evicted. Elizabeth's possession is therefore not a guarantee for protection.

(c) Denmark

As a starting point, the one who first acquires a right has the better right. However, Elizabeth must protect her right against third parties by registering it in the Buildings and Dwellings Register at the Land Register.[25] She failed to do this. Therefore, when Margaret registers her right to the property in good faith, Margaret's registered right will prevail over Elizabeth's unregistered right. Thus, Margaret will be able to obtain possession of the flat. Please note that if Margaret knows that Elizabeth is living in the flat, depending on the circumstances she might fall short of the good faith criterion in the Land Registration Act.[26]

(d) Norway

Two types of flats can be registered in Norway[27]: (a) commonhold/condominium, where one is a co-owner of the entire property and has exclusive right to use one dwelling: and (b) flats in housing cooperatives, where one can register membership in the cooperative and therefore has the exclusive right to use the flat.[28]

[21] 6:4 Housing Cooperative Act. [22] *NJA* 1971, 66. *NJA* 1993, 560.

[23] Cf. § 31 (2) Act on Letters of Credit and § 3 (3) Act Relating to Some Promises of Gifts; *lagen (1936:81) om skuldebrev* and *lagen (1936:83) om vissa utfästelser om gåva*. Cf. also Anders Victorin and Jonny Flodin, *Bostadsrätt med en översikt över kooperativ hyresrätt*, 4th edn. (Uppsala: Iustus, 2015), p. 188f.

[24] *NJA* 1993, 560. Cf. the governmental proposal *prop. 1983/84:67 om ändrade beskattningsregler för realisationsvinster på bostadsrätter*, p. 59f.

[25] Section 1, Land Registration Act. [26] Section 5, Land Registration Act.

[27] In Norway, a 'flat' is defined as a dwelling not consisting of an entire house.

[28] The general regulation is found in the Act Relating to Owner-tenant Sections (*lov om eierseksjoner*, 23 May 1997 No. 31) and the Act Relating to Housing Cooperatives (*lov om burettslag*, 6 June 2003 No. 39).

Both types of flats are units of the Land Register (see question 1).

Peter has a good registered title, but when he sold the property to Margaret, he had already concluded a contract of sale with another person (Elizabeth). The view under Norwegian law is that Elizabeth has a better right than Margaret, as Elizabeth's right was established first, even if Elizabeth has not yet registered her right. However, if Margaret, without knowing or having reason to know of Elizabeth's right, registers her right first, she is protected against Elizabeth.[29] Margaret can rely on the registered title held by the seller. On the other hand, should Elizabeth succeed in registering her right before Margaret, Elizabeth has a better right and it is immaterial whether or not Elizabeth knew that Margaret has concluded a contract with Peter in the interim.

As Elizabeth lives in the flat, the question of Margaret's good faith may turn out to be complicated. Under normal circumstances, a buyer of a flat will inspect the flat before buying it, and if a person other than the seller lives in the flat the buyer should make further inquiries. Good faith is, however, not entirely excluded in this situation. One could for example imagine that Peter had an extra key, showed Margaret the flat while Elizabeth was not there and presented the furniture as his own.

If Margaret is protected against Elizabeth's right in the flat, Margaret may as an owner evict Elizabeth from it.[30] Under Norwegian law, the enforcement of rights in immovable property – here the right to obtain possession of the property – is based on general rules of procedure and enforcement, and there are no special 'actions' for this purpose.

If Elizabeth has lived in the flat for twenty years, her right will be protected without registration according to the rules on acquisition by continuous possession.[31]

3 *Romanic–Mediterranean jurisdictions*

(a) Italy

In the Italian legal system, the conflict between two buyers of the same immovable property is resolved in favour of the person who registered their interest first,[32] regardless of the date of the contract of purchase. Though Elizabeth concluded her contract first, thereby becoming the owner of Peter's house by virtue of art. 1376 ICC, the fact that she has not

[29] Sections 20 and 21 (1), Judicial Registration Act.
[30] Section 13-2 (3) (e), Act Relating to Enforcement of Claims.
[31] Section 21 (2), Judicial Registration Act.
[32] See art. 2644 c 2 ICC and the answer under questions 1 and 5.

proceeded to register the contract does not protect her from a subsequent sale by Peter. Indeed art. 2644 ICC, in regulating the effects of transcription,[33] provides that contracts that transfer title to immovable property have no effect on those third parties who acquired rights over the same immovable property through a contract that is registered first.[34] This measure constitutes a broad exception to the consent principle stated in art. 1376, because it limits the right to transfer to the original buyer after the sale, if the second buyer is the first to register their purchase. By virtue of her timely registration, Margaret's purchase will prevail over Elizabeth's. Margaret could recover possession of the immovable property through an executive order of the court, which obliges Elizabeth to release the house to Margaret.[35] Elizabeth is not provided with a 'real' remedy that allows her to retain the house regardless of the subjective state of Margaret's good or bad faith. If Margaret acted in bad faith, she could be held liable for monetary damages but she would not be required to release the property to Elizabeth.[36]

(b) Spain

The legal doctrine and case law on how to settle this dispute are divided. The earlier position of some authoritative books and of case law up to the 1990s, holds that there is a duplicate sale because Peter has sold his flat to two different people. Margaret's title takes precedence, because she was the first to enter it in the *Registro de la Propiedad*, provided that she acted in good faith.[37] Margaret must, despite using the diligence commonly practised in business, have excusably not known of the conclusion of the earlier sale.[38] A later view, which now enjoys the most support in case law, sees this scenario as the sale of a thing that is not the seller's own. When Peter sold the flat to Margaret, Elizabeth had already acquired ownership, having entered into a valid contract of sale and

[33] See art. 2644, para.1. [34] See art. 2644, para. 2. [35] See art. 2930 ICC.
[36] Court of Cassation 8 January 1982 No. 76 in *Foro it.*, 1982, I, 334. [37] Art. 1473 (2) CC.
[38] A decision of the *Tribunal Supremo*, the Spanish Supreme Court, dated 4 March 1988 (RJ 1988/1554), ruled on a suit in which a sale under a private contract dated 1981, coupled with actual possession of the property by the buyer, opposed a sale under a notarial act dated 1983 and registered with the *Registro de la Propiedad.* The court declared that the dispute came under art. 1473 CC: '[T]here being a registered title, and possession resting with the unregistered litigant, no value attaches to the actual element of acquisition, because precedence rests with the more important and legally beneficent functioning – for the good of society and legal certainty – of authentication by registration, always assuming, of course, the good faith of the registered buyer, which has not been challenged in this appeal.'

being in possession of the flat transferred to her.[39] But if Margaret has registered her deed of sale in good faith and made her purchase, for value from Peter, who was still the registered owner, her acquisition prevails.[40] She may contest any action of vindication brought by Elizabeth and, to demand handover of the flat, she need only bring an action as registered owner under art. 41 Mortgage Act 1946. However, Margaret must challenge Elizabeth's possession before the statutory period elapses for the acquisition of ownership of an immovable property through uninterrupted possession. In fact, Margaret must commence proceedings

[39] In its decision of 11 April 1992 (Col. Leg. No. 388) onward, the *Tribunal Supremo* ruled as follows: 'For an event to qualify as a duplicate sale, it is a requirement that upon the conclusion of the second sale – by the buyer and seller agreeing on the object of the contract and the price (art. 1450 CC) – the first sale has not yet been consummated (implying a measure of simultaneity or proximity in time between the two sales), for if the earlier sale were already wholly consummated (through full payment of the price by the buyer, and handover of the thing by the seller), there would no longer be a true instance of duplicate sale, but a sale of a thing not the seller's own, or a non-existence of the second sale through lack of object.' This view is again declared in the *Tribunal Supremo* decisions of 8 March 1993 (RJ 1993/2052), 25 March 1994 (RJ 1994/2535) and 5 March 2007 (RJ 2007/723). However, in its decisions dated 5 March 2007 (RJ 2007/723) and 7 September 2007 (RJ 2007/5303), the *Tribunal Supremo* turned back to its previous position. In the decision of 7 September 2007 the High Court stated that '... the application of art.1473 CC does not require necessarely chronological simultaneity between the two or more sales in conflict'. The Tribunal added that '. . . the article already foresees that the first buyer entered in possession of the thing before the second buyer. Therefore, the first sale was already consummated from the perspective of the seller's obligations, through the material tradition . . .'

[40] Art. 34 Mortage Act 1946. *Tribunal Supremo* decisions of 10 December 1999 (RJ 1999, 9484) and 24 July 2000 (RJ 2000/7142). The latter rules on duplicate sale of one and the same thing by the registered owner. One sale was entered into under a private contract dated 9 October 1992. The buyer received possession of the thing. The next sale was made under a notarial act dated 28 October 1993, entered in the *Registro* 18 July 1994. The court ruled as follows: 'If possession was handed over to the appellant, the seller sold a thing not his own, but the buyer is protected if he satisfies the requirements of article 34 Mortgage Act 1946', and later adds: 'If there was no handover of possession, the problem is subject to article 1473 Civil Code, in favour of a bona fide registrant, pursuant to the consistent doctrine held by this Court.' In its decision of 5 March 2007 (RJ 2007/723), the *Tribunal Supremo* looked back on the development in case law regarding the registral protection of a *bona fide* acquirer for value in the face of the transferor's lack of entitlement to dispose. The decision concerns a property acquired in enforcement proceedings; the court laid down the following doctrine on art. 34 Mortgage Act 1946: '[F]irst, this provision protects acquisitions from non-owners precisely because it makes good the defect of title or power of disposal of the transferor who, in the Land Register, is named as having authority to transfer the property, as held most consistently by this Court; and, second, the provision does not necessarily imply an intermediate conveyance that is voided or rescinded for reasons not set out in the register, because the first part of its first paragraph enjoys substantive force of its own to protect a *bona fide* acquirer for value from a registered owner who subsequently registers his own right, without need of voidance or rescission of his transferor's.'

within a year of her purchase if she is to successfully rely on the protection afforded to the registered owner by art. 41 Mortgage Act 1946.[41]

So, under any approach, if Margaret was excusably unaware of the first transfer, and assuming the rest of requirements are satisfied, she may successfully recover possession of the flat. Elizabeth will then only have a claim against Peter. If he acted in bad faith, she can sue for penal liability[42] and, in any event, for compensation for all of the damages she suffered as a result of his breach of the contract.[43]

If Peter (improbably) did not act in bad faith or negligently, Elizabeth could still claim for those damages in contract that were foreseeable at the time of conclusion of the contract.[44] Some of the views in legal doctrine and case law also allow Elizabeth to bring an action for *evicción* (damages for dispossession) against Peter for breaching his obligation to ensure that she has lawful and peaceful possession of the flat; however, this position is disputed.[45] If this approach were upheld, Elizabeth could require Peter to pay her the price of the flat at the time she was deprived of it, and if Peter acted in bad faith he would also have to pay her damages and interest.[46]

(c) Portugal

Margaret will succeed in recovering possession of the flat. The role of land registration is to solve conflicts where different assignees claim incompatible or conflicting rights to the same property. Under Portuguese law, preference is given to the first party to register their interest, and consequently the fact that Elizabeth has moved in is not important.

41 Art. 36 Mortgage Act 1946.

42 Art. 251 *Ley Orgánica 10/1995, de 23 de noviembre, del Código Penal* ('Penal Code').

43 Arts. 1106 and 1107(2) CC. The *Tribunal Supremo* decision of 19 May 1978 (division 2) examines the conduct of a duplicate seller in bad faith, and orders her to refund the downpayment on the price and, in addition, compensation for interest and currency depreciation, 'and even for the moral or affective harm arising from the loss of the property under the contract'.

44 Arts. 1106 and 1107 (1).

45 The *Tribunal Supremo* rules out this possibility in its decision of 23 May 2000 (RJ 2000/3917). Other *Tribunal Supremo* decisions, however, support the view, though mostly *obiter dicta*. The decision of 4 March 1988 (*Jurisprudencia Civil*, No. 165, pp. 899–908. Point of law 9) thus says that in an event of duplicate sale there lies an action of redress for dispossession (*saneamiento por evicción*). In its decision of 27 May 1982, the *Tribunal Supremo* holds that the seller need not be owner of the thing, but need only redress for dispossession (*Jurisprudencia Civil*, No. 254, pp. 535–53), and in its decision of 31 December 1981 it holds that the seller must either surrender the thing or pay damages (*Jurisprudencia Civil*, November–December 1981, No. 510, pp. 955–62), as if these were alternative obligations.

46 Art. 1478 CC.

Under the Portuguese legal system, registration is not necessary for the creation or transfer of a real right, except where a mortgage is concerned (art. 4 (2) LRegC). Ownership and real rights over property are validly acquired without the necessity of registering them. Facts subject to registration are still effective *inter partes* and may be invoked by their heirs (art. 4 (1) LRegC). Since the function of Land Registry in Portugal is to provide publicity to the legal status of property, registration of the legal act that impinges upon property is necessary for its enforceability (*oponobilidade*) against third parties (art. 5 (1) LRegC).

The definition of 'third parties' is the subject of strong debate in Portugal. Decree Law 533/99 of 11 December introduced art. 5 (4) LRegC, that provides that third parties are those who acquire from the same person, totally or partially incompatible rights over the same thing. Therefore, if the owner sells the same property to two different acquirers, whoever registers first becomes the new owner. Preference among the successive buyers depends on the order in which they seek to enter their respective titles in the Land Registry.

In casu, Margaret has a real right over the house enforceable against Elizabeth. Some authors consider that in this case registration has an acquisitive function.[47] In fact, registration allocates an enforceable right to Margaret, whereas she made an agreement with Peter when he was no longer the owner of the property, according to the general rules of the CC (cf. art. 408 CC). On the other hand, Peter lawfully transferred ownership over the flat to Elizabeth, but since she did not register her acquisition, her right is not enforceable against Margaret.

(d) Greece

The rules of priority (*prior tempore potior jure*) and publicity through registration govern the acquisition of real rights in the Greek legal system. Therefore, in order to become owner of the flat Elizabeth should have registered the contract in the local Transcription Registry or Land Registry. Since Margaret registered her purchase first, the property is Margaret's, regardless of the date of the contract of purchase. Elizabeth never became owner of the flat because she did not register her title.

[47] José de Oliveira Ascensão, *Direito Civil, Reais*, 5th edn. (Coimbra: Coimbra Editora, 1993), p. 366; António dos Santos Just, *Direitos Reais*, 4th edn. (Coimbra: Coimbra Editora, 2012), p. 66; Luís M. Menezes Leitão, *Direitos Reais* (Coimbra: Almedina, 2009), p. 288; José A. Vieira, *Direitos Reais: Perspectiva Histórica do Seu Ensio em Portugal* (Coimbra: Coimbra Editora, 2008), p. 289.

Margaret has all the means provided by Greek Law in order to recover possession on the flat from Elizabeth,[48] who cannot claim a right of possession against Margaret.[49]

Elizabeth can sue Peter for damages for non-performance of the contract of sale[50] and if Margaret acted in bad faith, she could be held liable for monetary damages.[51]

4 *France and related jurisdictions*

(a) France

In principle, Margaret will prevail in France due to the application of the rules of the land publicity,[52] which give preference to the party who publishes first. Before the reversal of jurisprudence of the Court of Cassation,[53] Elizabeth would have been able to try to prove that Margaret knew about the first sale when she bought the flat.[54] The inferior jurisdictions would have considered whether the fact Elizabeth moved in was effectively known to Margaret and could be interpreted as resulting from a previous sale. Simple carelessness on the part of the second buyer was not enough to deprive them from profiting from the land publicity.[55] However, the fact that Elizabeth did not publish the first sale means that she cannot set her acquisition against Margaret, except possibly in a case where Elizabeth can prove that both Peter and Margaret defrauded her.

(b) Belgium

The sales agreement is binding between parties from the moment of consent, but it is only applicable against third parties if it has been

[48] I.e.: art. 1094 (*rei vindicatio*), art. 984 and 987 GCC.

[49] The GCC provides protection even for someone who is in the possession of an object despite the fact that he may not be the legal owner. This protection is only temporary and the real owner is the one who will be protected finally. So Elizabeth would be protected against third parties (arts. 998, 984 and 987, 985 GCC) but not against Margaret. This is due to a major distinction that is made in the Greek legal system between ownership, i.e. the real situation of conquering the *object corpus* and *animus*, and possession. As a possessor, Elizabeth is protected, but only temporarily.

[50] Arts. 514, 516, 381, 380, etc. GCC. [51] Art. 914 GCC.

[52] Art. 30. of the decree of 4 January 1955.

[53] Cass. 3ème civ., 10 February 2010, No. 08–21656: *Defrénois* 2010, p. 1073, note S. Piédelièvre; *Rev. contrats* 2010, p. 895, obs. S. Pimont – Cass. 3ème civ., 12 January 2011, No. 10–10667: D. 2011, p. 851, note L. Aynès; *Defrénois* 2011, p. 479, note C. Grimaldi; *RTD civ.* 2011, p. 158, obs. P. Crocq, et p.369, obs. T. Revet.

[54] Cass. 3ème civ., 4 January 1983, No. 81-14546: *Bull. civ.*, III, No. 3 – Cass. 3ème civ., 22 May 1990, No. 88-11643: D. 1991, p. 326, note A. Fournier.

[55] Cass. 3ème civ., 28 May 1979, No. 77-14164: *Bull. civ.*, III, No. 116.

registered in the Hypothec Register. If a conflict arises between the competing rights of two parties who are both acting in good faith, the first party to have registered their title in the Hypothec Register will prevail.[56] In this case, Margaret will prevail if she is considered to be acting in good faith at the moment of the sales agreement between her and Peter. The good faith of Margaret is presumed, so it will be up to Peter or Elizabeth to prove the bad faith by Margaret, e.g. to prove that Margaret knew or ought to have known that there was a previous sales agreement. The fact that Elizabeth already moved in does not deprive Margaret from fulfilling the good faith requirement. Margaret is entitled to an ownership action against Elizabeth.

5 *England and related jurisdictions*

(a) England

Elizabeth's failure to register her title leaves Peter on the register as registered proprietor. As such, he has the powers of a full owner of the property, including the power to sell it.[57] Margaret has now been registered as proprietor of the property pursuant to a disposition for valuable consideration, with the effect that her interest in the property takes priority over any other interest in the property whose priority is not protected at the time of her registration as the new owner.[58] Elizabeth's interest in the property has not been protected by registration. However, its priority will be protected if Elizabeth was in actual occupation of the property at the time when Margaret bought it from Peter, unless either (a) Elizabeth's occupation would not have been obvious on a reasonably careful inspection of the flat and was not known to Margaret; or (b) Elizabeth was asked about her interest in the property prior to the disposition to Margaret but she did not disclose her interest in the property.[59] Given that Elizabeth moved into the flat prior to Margaret's purchase, it seems likely that her occupation would have been obvious on a reasonably careful inspection of the flat, and so her interest in the property is likely to bind Margaret. In other words, Margaret will not be able to recover possession of the flat from Elizabeth.

Therefore, Elizabeth is entitled to ask the Registrar to alter the register to reflect her title. Such an alteration is probably not the correction of a mistake by the Registrar, as Peter's powers as registered proprietor mean that the registration of Margaret as owner was not a mistake.

56 According to art. 1 Mortgage Act of 18 August 1851.
57 Sections 24 and 23, LRA 2002.
58 Section 29 (1), LRA 2002.
59 Schedule 3, para. 2 LRA 2002.

The alteration is more likely to be done pursuant to the Registrar's power to bring the register up to date (to reflect Elizabeth's title).[60] As such, the alteration does not entitle Margaret to any payment of compensation by the Registrar[61] and she is left to take action against Peter for damages for misrepresentation or breach of contract.

(b) Scotland

Registration is required for the transfer of ownership.[62] In its absence, Peter is owner and not Elizabeth. When Peter sells to Margaret he is breaching his contract with Elizabeth, but he is acting within his powers as owner. Consequently, the conveyance to Margaret is effective and Margaret becomes owner on registration. As owner, Margaret can recover possession from Elizabeth.

Yet in the end success may lie with Elizabeth and not with Margaret. For even if Elizabeth did not register her title (i.e. her 'disposition'), she probably registered an 'advance notice', conferring a protected period of thirty-five days. If Elizabeth goes on to register her disposition within this period, she will become owner even if Margaret's disposition was registered first.[63]

Alternatively, Elizabeth will also prevail if Margaret was acting in bad faith, i.e. if Margaret knew that Peter was already under a binding obligation to transfer the flat to Elizabeth.[64] In that case, Elizabeth can apply for Margaret's disposition to be set aside ('reduced') by the court, allowing Elizabeth to register her own disposition. Assuming that Margaret knew of Elizabeth's possession of the flat (as seems likely), she was almost certainly acting in bad faith. At the least, Elizabeth's possession would have indicated the need for further inquiry that would, or should, have revealed the prior contractual right.

(c) Ireland

As Elizabeth paid the purchase price for the flat she is the beneficial owner[65] and her actual occupation of the flat at the time of the transaction in favour of Margaret renders her interest an overriding interest.

[60] Schedule 4, para. (b) LRA 2002. [61] See Schedule 8, para. 1, LRA 2002.

[62] Section 50, Land Registration etc. (Scotland) Act 2012.

[63] Sections 56–59, Land Registration etc. (Scotland) Act 2012.

[64] Bad faith triggers the rule against 'offside goals': Margaret's registration is regarded as 'offside' if it was accomplished in bad faith. See Kenneth G.C. Reid, *The Law of Property in Scotland* (Edinburgh: Butterworths/Law Society of Scotland,1996), paras. 695–701.

[65] Under a purchase money resulting trust. See also the response to case 13.

It will bind Margaret, regardless of whether it is registered, unless Margaret made enquiries of Elizabeth and she failed to disclose her interest.[66] As the beneficial owner of the property, Elizabeth is entitled to continue her occupation of it and Margaret will be unable to recover possession of the flat against her. If Elizabeth had not gone into actual occupation, her interest would not constitute an overriding interest and therefore registration of the transfer in favour of Margaret would overreach Elizabeth's equitable interest in the land.[67] In such circumstances Elizabeth's interest in the flat is transformed into an interest in the sales proceeds received by Peter on the re-sale to Margaret. Margaret would succeed in recovering possession of the flat from Elizabeth, although Elizabeth could sue Peter to recover the purchase price.

[66] Section 72 (1) (j), Registration of Title Act 1964.

[67] See section 21 (1), Land and Conveyancing Law Reform Act 2009. Note that if the transfer to Margaret was made for fraudulent purposes, to which Margaret was a party or actually knew about at the time of the transaction, Margaret will be bound by Elizabeth's interest and she will be unable to recover possession, see section 21 (3) (a), Land and Conveyancing Reform Act 2009.

Case 6

Albert owns a house. Albert has an identical twin brother called George. Unknown to Albert, George pretends to be Albert and produces false documents to prove it. He concludes a sale of Albert's house to Bolesław, and disappears. Bolesław's purchase is registered. Bolesław does not know about the deception.

(a) Can Albert get the house back?
(b) If not, will he get any compensation?
(c) Does it make any difference if Bolesław knows about the deception?

Bolesław sells the house to Mieszko before Albert discovers what has happened.

(d) Can Albert get the house back?

(A) Foundational Concepts for Understanding Case 6

In Germany the mere fact of appearing in the Land Register as the owner of land does not confer ownership because a valid agreement to transfer is also necessary. In this case, the content of the Land Register would be inaccurate. But if the land was then transferred to a third person acting in good faith, the third party would be considered as owner. The situation is similar in Austria. On the other hand, under Dutch law the sales contract does not pass ownership to the buyer, it only passes when the transfer deed has been made and registered, provided that all other requirements for a valid transfer have been met. Nevertheless, art. 3:25 BW protects a *bona fide* third party against errors in the Deeds Register that are the result of a notarial deed registered before the third party's deed was registered. In Turkey, it is also possible to acquire rights in good faith according to the Register.

In the Nordic countries, a forgery invalidates any contract that is made based on the forgery, including here where there is a subsequent resale. This result is not altered in the case where the title of the transferor was registered. The third acquirer is protected by the legitimating effect of the register, in the sense that the acquirer is entitled to obtain compensation (damages) in a case where he was in good faith. To achieve this result, it is necessary in Denmark and Norway that the acquirer in good faith registers the acquisition. These solutions allow for a rather simple registration procedure and can be compared to a model with title insurance.

In Italy, the protection of the third acquirer is not automatic since the judgment declaring the nullity of the original contract would not be enforceable against the third acquirer if they had acted in good faith and registered their purchase before the real owner registered his claim against the fraudulent party. In the Spanish legal system the main consequence of recording a right with the Land Registry is that it grants protection to good faith third-party purchasers who acquire a right from its registered holder. This means that the right acquired cannot be successfully challenged by anyone holding a right that is not recorded in the Land Registry, even if the title of the registered transferor is later deemed void for reasons which do not appear in the Land Registry. This principle is subject to certain exceptions for encumbrances whose registration is not compulsory, and it is also subject to Spanish insolvency laws. The situation is similar in Portugal.

On the other hand, in France the fact that a third acquirer relied on the Register that deceived him does not protect him against the obligation to make restitution of the immovable. He could only acquire the ownership via the rules of adverse possession.

In England, according to the Land Registration Act 2002 the purchaser of real property may generally rely on the accuracy of entries in the Land Register if the purchaser is acting in good faith. It is possible to apply for rectification of the Register or also for compensation of damages. In Scotland, although the Register remains inaccurate, the third acquirer should be protected against the Register's rectification provided that they are in possession. Finally, in Ireland if the house is registered in the Land Registry, a third acquirer acting in good faith could get a good title. A rectification would not be ordered by the courts in such circumstances. However, if the original owner was in actual occupation of the house when the third acquirer purchased the house, then the original owner could have an overriding interest.

In conclusion, in countries where registration has a constitutive effect, good faith in the Register is generally also protected (e.g. Austria, England, Germany and Scotland).

In England, Ireland and Scotland, ownership is acquired even though the seller was not the owner. However, this is not exactly a case of acquisition in good faith, because for instance art. 23, para. 1 LRA 2002 grants the power to dispose of the land to whoever has been registered. Nevertheless, an equitable proprietor in possession may be protected against an alteration of the Register (section 65.4, LRA 2002).

On the other hand, in some other countries, where registration is only declaratory, good faith in the Register is still protected (e.g. Denmark, Finland, Portugal and Spain).

There are also some legal systems in which registration is merely declaratory and there is no protection of good faith in the Register (e.g. Belgium and France).

We have to take into consideration that in Europe, title insurance is almost non-existent (unlike in the United States) and it is mainly due to the possibility of acquisition in good faith. In many legal systems, the buyer's good faith is protected so long as the buyer registers in the Land Register. On the other hand, the seller will be paid from an indemnity fund for any losses occurred due to mistakes in the Register.

Another good reason for that is the existence of sufficient professional liability for the civil law notary (or solicitor) who researches the seller's title. Economically, there is a system of (or similar to) state insurance and/or satisfactory professional liability of the civil law notary or solicitor who researches the seller's title.

Another question arises from the effect that a void or voidable contract can have on the transfer of ownership. The majority of systems follow the rule that there should be a causal ground for the transfer of ownership, in other words the majority of European systems are 'causal'.

Nevertheless, in Germany and in the British Isles[1] there is an 'abstract' system, so that the transfer is also valid in the case of an invalid sales contract. The difference is that in the British system only registration matters and even a mistaken registration transfers ownership. On the other hand, German law requires an agreement for the transfer (*Auflassung*).

[1] According to the new regulation in LRA 2002, a UK Act that repealed and replaced LRA 1925.

(B) The Jurisdictions (Presented by Related Jurisdictions)

1 *Germany and related jurisdictions*

(a) Germany

(a) Albert remains owner of his house because there was no valid transfer of ownership. An agreement to transfer a plot of land is only effective if made by the person who owns the land or their representative.[2] The mere registration of Bolesław in the Land Register as owner does not confer ownership. A valid agreement to transfer is also needed (see question 1).

Therefore, the Land Register which shows Bolesław as the owner is inaccurate. Albert can apply to correct the Land Register.[3] If Bolesław is already in possession of the house, Albert can recover possession from Bolesław.[4]

(b) No, it does not make any difference.

(c) Albert cannot get the house back if Mieszko did not know that Bolesław was not the true owner. In this case Mieszko becomes the owner by acquisition in good faith.[5] Albert can claim restitution of the purchase price from Bolesław due to unjust enrichment[6] or damages from George on the ground of deception.[7]

(d) If Albert had discovered what happened, he could have prevented acquisition in good faith by entering an objection to the accuracy (*Widerspruch*)[8] in the Land Register. The registration of an objection to the accuracy is much faster than the procedure for correcting the Register.

(b) Austria

(a) Yes, Albert can get the house back because George was definitely not the owner of the house and therefore not entitled to sell it. Since George was not Albert's substitute, he was also not in the position to negotiate or transfer ownership in his name. To sum up, George had no ability to create obligations that legally bind Albert.

The registration is based on a transaction that is deemed to be void. Even so, it is valid towards everybody except the wronged party (Albert) since the formal requirements have been fulfilled. That follows from the maxim of the general reliability of the Land Register.

[2] See § 873, para. 1 BGB. [3] § 894 BGB. [4] §§ 985, 986 BGB. [5] See § 892 BGB.
[6] § 816, para. 1 BGB. [7] § 823, para. 1 BGB. [8] § 899 BGB.

The registration is subject to appeal *in rem* and there is no such thing as a correction *ex officio*.[9] Albert has to bring a suit for the cancellation (*Löschungsklage*) according to §§ 61 ff GBG. He is the former/originally registered owner whose rights have been infringed.

George's behaviour is not only subject to civil law; he has also committed a criminal offence due to the deception and falsification of documents.[10]

If Albert's brother is successfully sentenced, the criminal court can subsequently declare the cancellation (§§ 66 ff GBG), so long as Albert applies for it within sixty days of the punitive sentence obtaining legal force (§ 67 GBG). Of course there has to be a connection between the registration and the illegal act that finally led to the voidance act.[11] However, this connection is a given in our case study.

At the same time, Albert can apply to make a note of the lawsuit (*Streitanmerkung*) in the Land Register, which makes the associated judgment affect a person who acquires registered rights after that point of time (§ 61, para 2 GBG). The limitation complies here with § 62 GBG.

Such a notation takes an existing debatable registration for granted. Albert has to submit confirmation about the complaint and must (in concrete terms and conclusively)[12] affirm that the registration took place on the basis of a criminal act.[13] Given the facts of this case study, Albert would easily meet those requirements.

(c) No, it makes no difference. Furthermore, it is not necessary that the person for whose benefit the registration was effected (Bolesław) also committed or participated in the commission of a criminal act.[14]

Mieszko acquires ownership of the house in good faith since Bolesław appears in the Land Register as the registered owner. This is provided that Mieszko was not or could not have been aware of the true and actual conditions. The legal consequence arises from the principle of positive reliance on the Land Register (*Grundsatz der positiven Publizität, Publizität*

[9] Erich Feil, Karl-Heinz Marent and Gerhard Preisl (eds.), *Grundbuchsrecht Kommentar* (Vienna: Linde Verlag, 2005), § 61 mn 2.

[10] Cf. also the following cases: OGH 6.2.1969, 1 Ob 30/69, SZ 42/25 (simulated transaction); OGH 31.1.1893, No. 900, GlU 14.567 = NZ 1894/1 (falsification of signatures).

[11] OGH 22.11.1995, 5 Ob 32/94, ÖBA 1995/497 = *NZ* 1995/338 (GBSlg).

[12] OGH 28.4.1964, 5 Ob 79/64, SZ 37/65 = EvBl 1964/413.

[13] Georg E. Kodek, *Kommentar zum Grundbuchsrecht* (Vienna: MANZ'sche Wien, 2007), § 66 GBG mn 7; OGH 15.5.2001, 5 Ob 101/01s, *NZ* 2002/98.

[14] Cf. OGH 17.10.1893, No. 13.301, GlU 14.873 = GZ 1894/7.

im materiellen Sinn). A legal fact that has been published therein (i.e. ownership) is deemed to be true and complete (*Vertrauensgrundsatz*).[15]

(b) Albert cannot get back the house under these new circumstances. He can only refer to George and claim for damages (which will be difficult since his twin brother has disappeared). If Mieszko has not yet paid for the house, Albert can directly claim the purchase price according to § 1041 ABGB arising from unjust enrichment. Otherwise, he can claim restitution from Bolesław.

(d) If Albert had discovered what happened early enough, he could have prevented acquisition in good faith by entering a note in the Land Register (*Streitanmerkung*).[16] If the registration is not yet absolute, he can appeal to the court (*Rekursmöglichkeit*).

(c) The Netherlands

(a) Under Dutch law the contract of sale does not pass ownership to the buyer. Ownership only passes when the transfer deed is made and registered, provided that all the other requirements of a valid transfer are met. The problem here is that according to the *nemo dat* rule, a valid transfer requires a right to alienate the thing in question (art. 3:84 BW). As the transferor was not the owner nor otherwise entitled to alienate, the transfer is void, even if the notary and the buyer did not and could not have known.

A Dutch notary has the duty to check the identity of the persons signing any deed (a disposition or any other notarial deed). Dutch notaries have a similar duty to verify a written mandate giving a non-owner a power of agency.[17] The notary must check the identity of the seller and the buyer by verifying their passports or equivalent identification papers, and if a mandate is used, the notary has to check the principal's signature on the written mandate.[18] In the case of doubt, the notary should check the Verification Information System of the CRI (a criminal investigation department). If the notary does not thoroughly verify the identity of the relevant persons,

[15] Helmut Koziol and Rudolf Welser, *Bürgerliches Recht, I*, 13th edn. (Vienna: Manz Verlag, 2006) p. 364f.

[16] See above, question (a).

[17] Art. 39 Wet op het notarisambt. See P. Blokland, *Teksten en toelichting op de Wet op het notarisambt*, 2nd edn. (Lelystad: Vermande, 2001), pp. 88–90.

[18] In practice, if the mandator lives far away the notary will ask him to have a notarial deed of mandate made by a local notary. The local notary of course has the same duty to verify the mandator's identity.

the notary is liable for damages in tort.[19] In Hof 's-Gravenhage on 18 March 1982, the Court of Appeal in The Hague held the notary liable in tort because he had not at all checked the identity of one of three parties to a mortgage deed, namely a pretended fiancée of the borrower who had the duty to sign as surety. There is no case law, however, about a situation in which someone makes use of a professionally falsified passport.

When after the void transfer to Bolesław (who did not become owner) the latter sells and transfers the house to Mieszko, Mieszko will acquire ownership of the house, provided that he is acting in good faith and all other transfer requirements have been met. Art. 3:25 BW protects the *bona fide* third party against errors in the Deeds Register which are the result of a notarial deed registered before the third party's deed is registered. The error in the Deeds Register should be the result of an error of fact made by the notary in the official exercise of his function when making the notarial deed. The scope of this provision is very narrow, but according to the *Parliamentary History* it protects against the fact that in a transfer deed between George and Bolesław the notary has wrongly confirmed that the owner of the land (Albert) declared to sell and transfer the land to the buyer.[20]

(b) If Mieszko is protected and becomes owner of the house, Albert has an action in tort (art. 6:162 BW) against George and an action for unjustified enrichment (art. 6:212 BW) against Bolesław for the purchase price which Bolesław received from Mieszko.

(c) Article 3:25 BW, however, does not protect the first acquirer Bolesław. He is not a third party but the second party. His good faith does not help him.

(d) Turkey

(a), (b) Yes, he can get his house back since George does not have the right to dispose of the house. According to art. 1024 TCC, the entry is wrongful where it has been made without the existence of a good title or by virtue of a void transaction. Thus, Albert can commence an action against Bolesław based on the wrongfulness of the entry.

[19] Hof 's-Gravenhage 18 maart 1982, NJ 1983/273. See also Blokland, *Teksten en toelichting op de Wet op het notarisambt*, p. 89 and W.G. Huijgen and A.J.H. Pleysier, *De wetgeving op het notarisambt*, 2nd edn. (Deventer: Wolters Kluwer, 2001), p. 155

[20] Toelichting Meijers at art. 3.1.2.8, Parlementaire Geschiedenis Boek 3, p. 138.

The good faith of Bolesław, as a rule, cannot affect the wrongfulness of the entry because the Turkish legal system is causal. Where the contract is invalid then the transfer also becomes invalid and this kind of registration is wrong. Nevertheless, according to art. 712 TCC, where a person has been entered in the Land Register as owner of an immovable without having any title to it, his right to the ownership in it cannot be contested after he has been for ten years in continuous *bona fide* peaceable possession of it.[21] In this case, at the end of ten years' continuous and *bona fide* peaceable possession, the wrongful registration would become valid. Therefore, Bolesław's right to the ownership in this immovable cannot be contested after he has been in continuous *bona fide* peaceable possession of it for ten years.

(c) If Bolesław knows about the deception, the legal consequence is the same. As for the question about Albert having the possibility to recover the house, it depends on the good or bad faith of Mieszko.

> According to art. 1023 TCC: 'Where any person has acquired the ownership or other real right by "bona fide" relying on entry in the Register, his rights are protected.'[22]

Accordingly, if Mieszko does not know the real situation of the land, he can acquire ownership of it. Thus, Albert cannot get the house back.

If Mieszko knows the real situation of the land, he cannot acquire the ownership of it. Albert can contest the wrongful entry in an action against Mieszko, who acted in bad faith.

2 *Scandinavian jurisdictions*

(a) Finland

(a) It is not easy for a party to a conveyance in Finland to pretend to be another person. Notaries witness all transactions and they inspect the identities of parties or their representatives. Nevertheless, it is possible to pretend to be a person with a similar appearance or to forge an identification card, the power of attorney, a deed, or another document.

It is clear that a transaction made by false documents or without legal power is not valid. George had no authority or appointment given by

[21] See art. 712 TCC; Ivy Williams, Siegfried Wyler and Barbara Wyler, *The Swiss Civil Code, Version II*, art. 661 (Zürich, 1987); Erhan Adal, *The Fundamentals of Turkish Private Law* (Istanbul: Legal, 2004) p. 149.

[22] See Williams, Wyler and Wyler, *The Swiss Civil Code, II*, art. 973.

Albert to sell his property. A more interesting question is if there are possible exceptions. In the Finnish legal system parties need to consider whether the invalidity can be improved. In many situations this kind of resolution is justified by the good faith of the transferee. It is not, however, possible to enjoy the good faith protection in cases where there is a total lack of legal power according to the principles of Finnish law. As a rule, Albert can claim the house back.

Nevertheless, one can ask whether there are any special rules applying to real property. Would the registration of Albert's acquisition in the Title and Mortgage Register make any difference? In other words, could the rules regarding the legitimising effect of the Register provide legal protection to Bolesław?

Indeed, according to the Finnish Code of Real Estate a transferee can trust the transferor's registration.[23]

However, there is an important exception and an important restriction. First, no protection is provided if the purchase contract or other acquisition document (the deed) of the rightful title-holder or the power of attorney or other competence document of his representative has been forged.[24] In this case, the identification card as a competence document presented by George can be forged. More importantly, there is a forgery when George signs the contract as a vendor pretending to be Albert, the rightful owner.

Second, the rules of public trustworthiness of the Title and Mortgage Register do not apply to the defects of the transferee's own acquisition. Instead, they apply to the defects of the transferor's or the transferor's predecessor's acquisition. Only the latter situation is seen as a matter of trust in the Register.

The rules applied to real property are uniform with the general principles. Hence, even according to these rules, Albert can claim the piece of real estate back.[25] Albert has to bring an action against Bolesław. Albert's or George's possession of the house or registration of Bolesław's acquisition does not make any difference. Moreover, these principles and rules also apply to conventional leaseholds.[26]

There is, nevertheless, a traditional rule regarding the so-called protection of enjoyment in the Finnish Code of Real Estate.[27] In this context, 'enjoyment' means possession as an owner. A person whose title

[23] 13:4.1 Code of Real Estate. [24] 13:5.1 Code of Real Estate.
[25] 3:1.1 Code of Real Estate (as the main rule). [26] 14:7.3 Code of Real Estate.
[27] 13:10.1 Code of Real Estate.

to a piece of real estate has been registered and who thereafter has possessed the estate for ten years may keep the estate if he or she at the time of acquisition did not know nor should have known that the estate had been taken from the rightful title-holder. If no action for a better right to the piece of real estate is brought during this time, the rightful title-holder shall forfeit his right to demand the return of the real estate. In this case, it is a matter of the effect of a transferee's registration. This rule applies even in the case of forgery or other strong reasons for invalidity, and Bolesław can appeal to it even in relation to Albert (it is a question of a defect of Bolesław's acquisition). In these conditions it is possible that Albert cannot claim the house back. It is worth noting that this judgment presumes that Albert has lost his owner's possession for ten years. This rule does not apply to a leasehold.

(b) A rightful title-holder who has lost his piece of real estate to a transferee justified by the protection of good faith based on the legitimation effect of the transferor's registered title (i.e. trustworthiness of the Register) is entitled to due compensation from the Finnish state.[28] The liability of the state is justified by its position as the registration authority. In proportion, the same right belongs to a transferee who has lost a piece of real estate because of forgery or another strong reason for invalidity.[29]

However, these rules cannot be applied in this case because they are connected with the rules establishing the public trustworthiness of the Title and Mortgage Register. In addition, no compensation is provided on the grounds of the rule of protection of enjoyment.

George, naturally, is liable to pay damages to Bolesław as well as to any other person who has suffered costs or loss due to the forgery. Unfortunately, people like George are often insolvent.

(c) Good faith requires that the transferee did not know nor should have known about the defect. Good faith is one of the preconditions for legal protection of a transferee of a piece of real estate, both in the cases of enjoyment and of the legitimation effect of the Title and Mortgage Register. As noted above, the rules relating to the legitimation effect do not apply in this case. Instead, it is possible that Bolesław enjoys the protection of enjoyment. In addition to good faith, there are many other preconditions to fulfil, such as the fixed-term possession as an owner and registration of the transferee. In practice, it is not easy to meet the requirement of ten years' possession.

[28] 13:6.1 Code of Real Estate. [29] 13:6.2 Code of Real Estate.

(d) As stated above, unlike in the case of Bolesław, Mieszko as Bolesław's successor can enjoy the protection of the legitimation effect of the Title and Mortgage Register. As a major rule, a transferee can trust the transferor's registration. The preconditions of a transferee's protection are his or her good faith and registration of the transferor's acquisition.

The consequence of this rule is that the transferee can keep the property and the transferor has to settle for compensation provided by the state.

In this case, however, the exception to the major rule is applied. Mieszko's protection is prevented because forgery of an acquisition document is treated as a strong reason for invalidity. Instead, Mieszko may be entitled to the State compensation. Albert can claim the house back even in this case.

Mieszko as well as Bolesław can enjoy the protection of enjoyment. In addition, Mieszko can appeal to his own possession or to the possession of his predecessor (Bolesław), as well as to his own good faith or to the good faith of his predecessor.[30]

(b) Sweden

(a)–(c) Rightful owners may, in qualified cases of invalidity, vindicate their property from good faith acquirers (see under question 1). The assignment to Bolesław was induced by forgery. Since forgery counts as a qualified case of invalidity, Bolesław's good faith does not render him any protection, other than a right to claim damages from George. Bolesław's registration of title does not help him either.

Mieszko's acquisition is not protected even if he was acting in good faith at the time the contract was concluded.[31] But, since Bolesław was registered as the owner when he sold the property and Mieszko bought it in good faith, Mieszko will get monetary compensation from the state (see question 1).[32] Albert is entitled to compensation from the state for the costs associated with the proceedings he issued to claim the property back, including the costs that may arise in relation to Mieszko.[33]

[30] 13:10.2 Code of Real Estate.

[31] 18:3 (1) Land Code. Folke Grauers, *Fastighetsköp*, 21st edn. (Lund: Juristförlaget i Lund, 2016), p. 322f.

[32] 18:4 (2) Land Code.

[33] 18:1a (1) Land Code.

(c) Denmark

(a) Forgery makes a contract void *ab initio*.[34] Consequently, Albert may invoke the invalidity against Bolesław, despite Bolesław's good faith. Thus, Albert can retain the property. This applies even if Bolesław registers his claim on the property in the Buildings and Dwellings Register at the Land Register.[35]

(b) As Albert retains possession of the property, Bolesław may direct a claim in tort against George.

(c) A forgery can even be invoked against a third party acting in good faith and relying upon the accuracy of forged documents. Thus, Bolesław's right over the property is extinguished in both respects. Nevertheless, for Bolesław to obtain compensation under the LRA, he is required to have acted in good faith. Therefore, if he knew about the deception, he will not be compensated.

(d) A forgery invalidates any contracts made based on the forgery, including in the case of a resale. This applies even if Mieszko has his right registered in the Buildings and Dwellings Register at the Land Register.[36]

(d) Norway

(a)–(c) The answer to this question follows from the explanations under question 1: the registration of a forged document does not affect Albert's right in the house and there is nothing to 'get back' apart from the mere correction of the Register. Bolesław's good or bad faith is of no relevance in this situation. In relation to Bolesław, the registration is insignificant and he cannot claim against any person except for the swindler.

(d) Mieszko relies on Bolesław's registered title. Mieszko gains no protection against Albert's right, as the registered title is based on a forged document, but Mieszko may be entitled to damages from the state.[37]

3 *Romanic–Mediterranean jurisdictions*

(a) Italy

(a) Yes, since George lacks the power to sell – Bolesław's acquisition is considered '*a non domino*' (it originates from a non-owner), meaning

[34] Lennart L. Andersen and Palle B. Madsen, *Aftaler og mellemmænd*, 6th edn. (Copenhagen: Karnov Group, 2012), p. 138.

[35] Section 27, LRA, 2nd sentence.

[36] Section 27, LRA, 2nd sentence.

[37] §§ 27 (2) and 35 Judicial Registration Act.

that no potential effect could derive from the contract between the two. Therefore, Albert can recover possession of the house by bringing an action for a declaration of nullity of the contract.[38] Once the contract is declared void, the court could oblige Bolesław to release possession of the house to Albert under art. 2930 ICC. The registration of the contract is useless because registration in general does not confer validity or effectiveness upon an invalid contract,[39] except for the case of acquisition by adverse possession.[40] If ten years has elapsed since Bolesław registered his acquisition of the house in his favour without Albert filing an action for a declaration of nullity (better before the transcription of the claim for nullity), an order declaring the nullity of the contract will be ineffective against Bolesław. Therefore, Bolesław cannot be forced to return the immovable property to Albert because he has become the owner by adverse possession.

(b) See under (a).

(c) The fact that Bolesław was aware of the deception means that he cannot acquire the house by adverse possession in the shortened term of ten years (*usucapione abbreviata*). In addition to registration of title, art. 1159 ICC also requires the good faith of the purchaser as a necessary requirement to enjoy the benefit of abridged adverse possession. However, Bolesław could acquire ownership of the house through the course of the standard period of adverse possession, which art. 1158 ICC states to be twenty years. In this case, the ICC does not distinguish between possession in good or bad faith. However, bad faith is relevant in order to calculate the day from which the time for adverse possession runs. If in fact the possession was acquired by deception, possession for the purposes of adverse possession starts on the day on which the original owner became aware of the deception.[41] Bolesław's time for

[38] Under art. 1418 ICC a contract is void (*nullo*) if it presents structural defects: either if the contract is contrary to mandatory rules (para. 1) or if it lacks one of the requirements provided by art. 1325 ICC (parties' agreement; objective justification of the contract (*causa*); object; form, if it is required by law); if either the *causa* or the motives of the agreement are unlawful (art. 1345 ICC); if the object of the contract is unfeasible, indeterminate, or indeterminable (para. 2); or if the law expressly provides for cases of nullity (para. 3).

[39] But see the role of art. 2652 No. 6 ICC in part (b) of the answer.

[40] Art. 1159 ICC requires that the purchaser in good faith from someone who does not own the immovable property, through a contract that is capable (theoretically) of transferring ownership and which has been duly registered, will acquire the property by adverse possession after ten years from the date of the registration.

[41] See art. 1163 ICC.

acquisition by adverse possession starts from the day on which Albert first became aware of the sale by his twin George.

(d) In principle, a judgment declaring the nullity of a contract retrospectively eliminates all its effects, including all the rights acquired by third parties, even though the third party had registered his purchase before the transcription of the claim for nullity. There is, however, an exception to this principle: if the void contract has been registered and five years have passed without the claim for nullity being registered, the decision declaring the contract invalid shall not affect rights acquired by third parties in good faith under a void contract and registered before the claim for nullity.[42] So, if Albert filed and registered the action for nullity five years after the registration of the contract between George and Bolesław, the judgment declaring the nullity of the original contract is not enforceable against Mieszko if he acted in good faith and had registered his purchase from Bolesław before Albert registered his claim against Bolesław.

(b) Spain

(a), (b) The contract entered into between George and Bolesław is void. As noted in question 1, a void act should not in principle attain registration, but if it does, the fact of registration does not make it valid. Albert could apply to a court to declare the sale void and thus have the Register entry in Bolesław's name rectified.[43]

(c) Whether Bolesław acted in good faith or not is irrelevant. As he was a party to the contract, he does not qualify as a third party whose acquisition would be protected. His only action lies against George, from whom he could claim restitution of the price and payment of damages.

But Mieszko does qualify as a third party with respect to the sale between George and Bolesław. If he was unaware that the original sale was void and registered his own deed of sale, rectification of the register entry would not undermine his ownership rights.[44] Albert's only action would then lie against Bolesław.

(c) Portugal

(a) Notaries shall assess the legal suitability of the acts they are asked to realise, namely checking the legitimacy of the submitters and the

[42] See art. 2652 No. 6 ICC. [43] Art. 40 Mortgage Act 1946.
[44] Art. 40 Mortgage Act 1946.

formal and material validity of the documents and the substantial legality of the act required.[45] Since Albert's identity and signature were forged, the deed is null, and the contract between George and Bolesław is void (the contract of sale impinges upon '*bem alheio*'). An act based on a null deed should not in principle attain registration, but if it does, registration does not make it valid. Hence, Albert could apply to a court to declare the sale void as a *res inter alios acta*, and thus cancel the Register entry in Bolesław's name. Whether Bolesław acted in good faith or not is irrelevant. As he was a party to the contract, he does not qualify as a third party whose acquisition would be protected. The only available remedy is to claim restitution of the price and payment of damages from George.

(b)–(d) But Mieszko does qualify as a third party with respect to the sale between George and Bolesław. According to art. 17 LRegC, a declaration of the nullity of the inscription cannot prejudice the rights acquired for consideration by individuals acting in good faith, if the registration of the facts is submitted before the registration of the judicial procedure for declaration of the nullity. Therefore, if Mieszko was unaware that the original sale was void, acquired his right from the owner inscribed in the Land Registry (Bolesław) and registered his own deed of sale, his right becomes enforceable against third parties.[46] Accordingly, Albert's only legal action would be against Bolesław.

This means that in this case registration is again acquisitive. Under the general rules of civil law, since Mieszko was transferred the house from someone who was not an owner, he did not acquire a right. However, registration confers stability and enforceability to his acquisition. In practice, registration in the Land Registry allocates the house to Mieszko.

(d) Greece

(a) According to art. 1033 GCC, transferring ownership of an immovable requires an agreement between the owner and the acquirer

[45] Art. 11 Decree Law 26/2004, of 4 February. Lawyers, paralegals (solicitors), Chambers of Commerc and Industry must also be considered under this duty. See José A. González, *Direitos e Reais e Registal Imobiliário*, 4th edn. (Lisbon: Quid Iuris, 2009), pp. 138–9. In respect of registrars, see Art. 68 LRegC.

[46] See Isabel Pereira Mendes, *Código do Registo Predial – Anotado* (Coimbra: Almedina, 2009), pp. 226–7; José A. González, *Direitos Reais e Direitos Registal Imobiliário*, 4th edn. (Lisbon: Quid Juris, 2009), pp. 245–6.

and registration of the transfer in the Transcription or Land Registry,[47] provided that all the other requirements of a valid transfer have been met.

In this case, there was no valid transfer of ownership as George was not the actual owner of the house and thus could not have made a valid agreement to transfer it to Bolesław. The registration of the contract does not have an effect because registration does not cure the deficiencies of an invalid contract.

So, Bolesław did not acquire ownership and Albert is entitled to ask for recognition of his ownership, recognition of the void registration in order to amend the Registry[48] and the possession of the house.

(b), (c) The only consequence of the fact that Bolesław was aware of the deception is that he cannot acquire ownership of the house by adverse possession in the shortened period of ten years, as good faith is prerequisite in order to benefit from adverse possession.[49] Acquiring ownership through the course of a standard period of adverse possession (twenty years) is always possible.[50]

(d) Given that Bolesław did not have ownership, Mieszko never acquired ownership. Albert is entitled to sue for recognition of his ownership and possession of the house.

4 *France and related jurisdictions*

(a) France

(a) Yes, because by applying of the principle of the relative effect of contracts, the sale of the property by a third party cannot be set against him. The real owner does not even need to claim nullity of the sale (relative nullity reserved by art. 1599 C. civ. for the buyer) and can exercise an action for recovery of property against Bolesław.

Although it seems that this factual scenario is not a known case in French law, a jurisprudential rule called 'theory of appearance' is relevant. This rule confers a title supplying the polluted act when the one who trusted the appearance was under the influence of a common error. That requires that circumstances were such that a person normally

[47] Arts. 1192 and 1198 GCC. [48] Art. 1202 GCC and art. 70 GCCP. [49] Art. 1041 GCC.
[50] Art. 1045 GCC.

informed would have made the mistake, and naturally that the buyer was acting in good faith.[51]

(b) If Bolesław successfully relies on the theory of appearance, Albert cannot claim damages from Bolesław because he committed no fault. On the other hand, George is at fault and therefore liable.

(c) Yes, his *mala fides* excludes the theory of appearance.

(d) Yes, this sub-alienation cannot be set against the real owner, even if Bolesław published his purchase in the land publicity. But we find the same exception: Mieszko can also try to refer to theory of appearance if he bought without *mala fides*.

(b) Belgium

(a) Under the Belgian law, the sale of another's house is considered to be void, as the seller cannot comply with one main obligation of the sales agreement: the obligation to transfer ownership (art. 1599 BCC). However, this voidness is relative because it can only be argued by the person who is protected by this provision – in other words, the buyer. Hence, Albert cannot pursue the voidness of the sale. In this case, George has committed fraud, which is also a ground to render the agreement void. But this voidness is also relative – for instance, it cannot be invoked by Albert.

However, the fact that Albert cannot invoke the voidness of the contract of sale does not prevent him from having remained the owner of the immovable. George has not been able to pass ownership. Indeed, George cannot transfer more rights than he has himself, except if Albert would have given the impression that George has a valid proxy to represent him. This is not changed by the fact that Bolesław was acting in good faith or the registration of the sales agreement. Indeed, the invalidity of the underlying agreement remains notwithstanding the registration of the agreement in the Hypothec Register (see above).

The answer above takes as starting point that Albert or Bolesław can prove that George signed the agreement, and not Albert himself.

(b) Albert will be entitled to claim compensation from George on the basis of a tort claim for the damage he incurred. This claim can be brought both before a criminal court that judges the criminal act and in

[51] See for example Cass. 1ère civ., 12 January 1988, No. 86-12218: *JCP* 1988, éd. N, II, p. 333, note P. Salvage.

a separate civil proceeding before a civil court. However, the loss of ownership will not be considered part of the damage incurred because Albert remained owner of the immovable.

(c) It does not make any difference, as George would already not be able to oppose his title, providing there was good faith (see the answer to question (b)).

(d) Albert can claim restitution of the house, except where Mieszko can claim title because of acquisitive prescription. The fact that Mieszko relied on and was deceived by the Register does not protect him against the obligation to make restitution of the house. Acquisitive prescription requires Mieszko to have acted in good faith, have a valid agreement with Bolesław and ten or twenty years of lawful possession. The term is ten years applies if Albert lives in the same judicial region as the place where the immovable is situated, whereas twenty years applies if he lives in another judicial region (art. 2265 BCC).

As previously noted, title registration does not grant an irrevocable title and it is generally assumed that the fact that one relied on the Registry does not grant protection if it emerges afterwards that the registered rights of the predecessor have been avoided.

5 *England and related jurisdictions*

(a) England

(a) George's transaction with Bolesław seems to have been completed by George forging Albert's signature. The forged signature is void and has no effect on Albert[52] and so the Land Registrar ought not to have registered the transfer of Albert's house to Bolesław pursuant to the forged conveyance. As such, the Registrar made a mistake by registering the transfer and Albert has a *prima facie* right to have the Register altered, thereby reinstating Albert as the registered proprietor of the house.[53] This alteration would amount to rectification of the Register as it is correcting a mistake and it will prejudicially affect Bolesław's title as the registered proprietor.[54] Because the alteration amounts to rectification of the Register, if Bolesław is in possession of the house, the Register cannot be altered without Bolesław's consent, unless (a) the mistake was caused or substantially contributed to by Bolesław's fraud or lack of care;

[52] *First National Securities Ltd.* v. *Hegerty* [1985] 1 QB 850 at pp. 853–4.
[53] Sch. 4, paras. 2 (1) (a) and 5 (1) (a) LRA 2002. [54] Sch. 4, para. 1 LRA 2002.

or (b) some other reason makes it unjust not to alter the Register.[55] Neither exception seems applicable on the facts here and so, assuming that Bolesław is unlikely to consent to an alteration whereby he loses title to the house, Albert is not likely to be able to have the Register altered.

(b) Albert will be entitled to compensation from the Registrar (effectively, the state) because he has suffered loss by reason of a mistake whose correction would have involved rectification of the Register,[56] assuming the loss was not wholly caused by Albert's lack of proper care.[57] He is entitled to be compensated for the value of the estate at the time when the mistake was made (when Bolesław was first registered as proprietor).[58]

(c) If Bolesław was aware of the deception, his complicity in George's fraud means he is unlikely to be able to resist a claim by Albert for rectification of the Register as 'he has by fraud or lack of proper care caused or substantially contributed to the [Registrar's] mistake'[59] and it is 'unjust for the alteration not to be made'.[60] (Nor would Bolesław be entitled to any compensation for the loss caused by rectification.[61])

(d) While Bolesław remains registered as proprietor of the house, he is deemed to have the legal estate vested in him,[62] despite George's forgery, and he is capable of exercising owner's powers in relation to the estate.[63] An owner's powers include the power to make a disposition of the estate,[64] and so Bolesław is capable of selling the house to Mieszko. Therefore, the Registrar makes no mistake when he registers transfer of the estate from Bolesław to Mieszko,[65] and so the Register cannot be rectified to reinstate Albert as the owner. There is no other basis on which Albert could be restored to the Register as proprietor.

If Albert had a right to rectification which was enforceable against Bolesław, that right is a proprietary right which could potentially bind Mieszko,[66] but only if Albert was in actual occupation of the property

[55] Sch. 4, paras. 3 (2) and 6 (2) LRA 2002. [56] Sch. 8, para.1 (1) (b), LRA 2002.
[57] Sch. 8, para. 5 (1) (b), LRA 2002. [58] Sch. 8, para. 6 (b), LRA 2002.
[59] Sch. 4, para. 3 (2) (a), LRA 2002. [60] Sch. 4, para. 3 (2) (b), LRA 2002.
[61] Sch. 8, para. 5, LRA 2002. [62] Sch. 58 (1), LRA 2002. [63] Section 24 (a), LRA 2002.
[64] Section 23 (1) (a), LRA 2002.
[65] *Barclays Bank Ltd* v. *Guy* [2008] EWCA Civ. 452, [2008] 2 EGLR 74.
[66] *Malory Enterprises Ltd.* v. *Cheshire Homes (UK) Ltd.* [2002] EWCA Civ. 151, [2002] Ch. 216 at [68].

at the time of the sale to Mieszko. In such a case, Mieszko may be entitled to indemnity for his loss when the Register is rectified.[67]

(b) Scotland

(a) As George neither owned the house nor was authorised to sell it by the person who did (i.e. Albert), he cannot transfer ownership to Bolesław. Albert thus does not need to get the house back because he never actually lost ownership of it.[68] It is true that, for the moment, the Land Register shows the wrong person as owner (i.e. Bolesław instead Albert), but this does make Bolesław the owner. Provided Albert can prove George's fraud, Albert is able to have the Register corrected ('rectified') and his own name restored as the owner.[69]

(b) A state compensation scheme does indeed exist for cases (notably in question (d) below) where an owner loses his property to a person acquiring from a non-owner but in good faith.[70] The compensation scheme is administered by the Keeper of the Registers. However, in the present case, Albert has not lost his property and so has no need for compensation.

(c) No. Unlike (d) below, this is not a situation in which the law protects a good faith acquirer. Bolesław is unprotected whatever the state of his knowledge.

(d) In a rule designed to facilitate a ready market in land as well as reduce transaction costs, purchasers are entitled to rely on what they see on the Land Register.[71] So, if the Register says that Bolesław is the owner then – even if he is not the owner (as indeed he is not in the present case) – Mieszko can assume that Bolesław is the owner and proceed to buy the house from him. But some conditions have to be met before Mieszko can take advantage of this rule. One is that he must be acting in good faith. Another – which is unlikely to be satisfied in the present case – is that Bolesław must have possessed the house for a year.[72] If these conditions are met, Mieszko becomes

[67] See David Fox, 'Forgery and Alteration of the Register under the Land Registration Act 2002', in Elizabeth Cooke (ed.), *Modern Studies in Property Law: Vol III Property 2004* (Oxford: Hart Publishing, 2005), p. 25.

[68] Section 50 (2), Land Registration etc. (Scotland) Act 2012.

[69] Section 80, Land Registration etc. (Scotland) Act 2012.

[70] Sections 94 and 95, Land Registration etc. (Scotland) Act 2012.

[71] Section 86, Land Registration etc. (Scotland) Act 2012.

[72] If Bolesław is in possession, but not for a year, Mieszko becomes the owner if, still in good faith, he possesses in turn for the missing weeks or months.

the owner on registration and Albert loses the house;[73] if they are not met, Albert remains the owner.

(c) Ireland

(a) Albert has a right to have the transaction set aside for fraud, which is referred to as a 'mere equity'. If the house is not registered in the Land Registry, Albert will succeed against Bolesław unless Bolesław was a *bona fide* purchaser for value without notice of Albert's equity.[74] Bolesław was unaware of the deception, but to benefit from the doctrine of notice[75] he must have inspected the land and checked if anyone in occupation of the house had an interest in the property.[76] The doctrine also requires Bolesław or his solicitor to adequately investigate the title to the house to ensure that the seller is entitled to it. Albert would succeed in having the transaction set aside if Albert was living in the house at the time of the transaction and Bolesław or his solicitor failed to check whether he had an interest in the property, or if there was anything suspicious in the false documents produced by George which should have alerted a purchaser or his solicitor to the possibility of fraud. Otherwise, Albert's 'equity' is defeated by the transaction in favour of Bolesław. The fact that Bolesław registered his deed in the Registry of Deeds will not make any difference.

If the house is registered in the Land Registry and the transfer to Bolesław has been registered so that he now appears as the registered owner, Albert will have to apply to court to have the register rectified on the grounds of fraud.[77] The jurisdiction of the court to order a rectification is restricted to circumstances in which it can be done without injustice to any person. As Bolesław purchased the property in good faith and without notice of the fraud, the court is unlikely to order a rectification.[78]

(b) If the house is registered in the Land Registry, Albert, as 'a person suffering loss as a result of an entry in a folio … caused or obtained

[73] In which case, as mentioned in the answer to question (b), Albert is entitled to financial compensation from the Keeper of the Registers.

[74] *Allied Irish Banks* v. *Glynn* [1973] IR 188.

[75] See section 85, Conveyancing and Land Law Reform Act 2009.

[76] *Hunt* v. *Luck* [1902] 1 Ch. 428.

[77] See sections 31 (1) and 32 (1) (b), Registration of Title Act 1964.

[78] Brendan Fitzgerald, *Land Registry Practice*, 2nd edn. (Dublin: Sweet & Maxwell, 1995), p. 446.

by forgery or fraud' may claim compensation from the Property Registration Authority.[79] Albert will not succeed if his loss was caused or substantially contributed to by the act, neglect, or default of himself or his agent.[80] This does not appear to be the case here.

(c) As outlined in (a), if Bolesław knows about the deception, Albert will succeed in having the transaction set aside or the Land Register rectified. In such circumstances, Bolesław would not be entitled to compensation for the loss suffered as a result of the rectification of the Land Register,[81] as he would have caused or substantially contributed to that loss.

(d) If Bolesław was a *bona fide* purchaser for value without notice of the fraud, Albert's right to have the transaction set aside is extinguished completely by the transaction in favour of Bolesław and cannot be revived by the subsequent transaction in favour of Mieszko.[82] Therefore, Albert will not be able to get the house back, even if Mieszko was aware of the earlier fraud when he purchased the house.

If the house is registered in the Land Registry and Bolesław was a purchaser for value and registered as the new owner, Mieszko is entitled to treat this as conclusive evidence of Bolesław's title and will take good title from him. A rectification would not be ordered by the courts in such circumstances. However, if Albert had a right to seek a rectification of the register (e.g. if Bolesław was aware of the deception) and Albert was in actual occupation of the house when Mieszko purchased it, Albert's right will constitute an overriding interest and Mieszko will be bound by it.[83]

[79] Section 120 (1) (c), Registration of Title Act 1964.
[80] Section 120 (2), Registration of Title Act 1964.
[81] Section 120 (1) (a), Registration of Title Act 1964.
[82] *Wilkes* v. *Spooner* [1911] 2 KB 473.
[83] *Blacklocks* v. *JB Developments Ltd* [1981] 3 All ER 392; *Boyle* v. *Connaughton* [2000] IEHC 28.

Case 7

Henry wants to buy a new house. He finds a new development, in an area he likes; X Ltd owns the site and had planning permission to build thirty houses. Henry likes their plans so much that he wants to buy one now, even though the houses have not yet been built. What should he do?

(A) Foundational Concepts For Understanding Case 7

When the object of the transfer is not the immovable itself but a future flat or house, there are special problems like the risk of completion of the construction works or repayment of the money in case of the builder's insolvency.

It seems that the solutions offered by the different legal systems vary considerably. In these kinds of contracts the seller is usually interested in receiving payments prior to the completion of the construction. This situation is very risky for buyers, especially in the common case of a consumer buyer.

1 *The Existence of a Special Regulation*

Some legal systems reported have special statutes to deal with some or most of the risks associated with 'off the plan' sales. For instance, there are special rules in Austria, Belgium, France, Germany, Greece, Italy and Spain. These special regulations do not avoid the application of the CC to legal questions not covered by these acts. Sometimes special mandatory provisions have been integrated in the CC, as it is the case in the Netherlands

There are some similarities in the Belgian, French and Spanish approaches, on the one hand, and the Austrian and German approaches on the other.

In other legal systems, these sales are regulated by the same laws as an ordinary conveyance applying contract rules for services (as in England, Greece, Italy or Scotland). Especially in England and Scotland, each building company uses its own standard-form contract, but many builders are members of the National House-Building Council (NHBC), which provides a 'Buildmark' warranty.[1]

2 *The Transfer of Ownership*

During the transfer, in most of these countries, ownership is transferred only after construction is complete and payment is made (e.g. England, Germany, Greece, Scotland and Spain). Alternatively, in Belgium, France, Portugal, Finland and Sweden, the seller transfers his land and property rights to the buyer during construction. Future parts of the building automatically become the property of the buyer once complete. In Germany the future ownership of the buyer is protected by entering a notice in the Land Register (*Vormerkung*). The same could be applicable in Austria.

3 *Legal Defects of the Title*

The risk of encumbrances or legal defects of the title are covered in some legal systems by the participation of the notary, solicitor, or other lawyer (England, Greece, Netherlands and Scotland).

There are also external guarantees that cover construction completion in France, Sweden (in the case of a single-family house) and Belgium (where some sellers and building contractors are obliged to pay a security deposit of 5 per cent of the building's total value; other sellers have to pay a deposit of 100 per cent) and also mandatory guarantees for repayments in Spain.

4 *The Risk of Bankruptcy*

In some jurisdictions, the buyers are protected from the insolvency of the seller under certain circumstances. For instance, in Germany the obligation to register a priority notice protects the buyer from the builder's insolvency. In this case, the insolvency administrator must

[1] Cf. www.nhbc.co.uk/ (last consulted July 2013). 'NHBC (National House-Building Council) is the leading warranty and insurance provider and standards setter for UK house-building for new and newly converted homes. As a non-profit distributing company, it reinvests all income in achieving its primary purpose; improving quality in housebuilding to protect homeowners.'

execute, from the insolvency estate, the claim secured by the priority notice. In Scotland, a more direct solution is for the builder to grant a security right ('standard security') over the land in respect to the buyer's instalments, that in order to be effective must be registered in the Land Register. In Ireland, there is an institution called the HomeBond, created in 1978, which will repay lost deposits or contract payments resulting from the bankruptcy or liquidation of registered builders, subject to some limitation on amounts and also some time limits.

In most countries, the buyer can participate in the bankruptcy proceedings as a bankruptcy creditor (Spain). Of course in this case, the possibility of recovering the price paid depends on the existence of assets on the part of the seller.

(B) The Jurisdictions (Presented by Related Jurisdictions)

1 *Germany and related jurisdictions*

(a) Germany

Henry might conclude a so-called '*Bauträgervertrag*'. This is a special kind of contract that combines elements from both a sales and building contract. As this contract contains the obligation to transfer landownership, it must be authenticated by a notary.[2]

The conclusion of such a contract must solve a conflict of interest between the developer and the purchaser. The developer wants to receive payment from the purchaser as soon as possible to allow him to finance construction while the buyer needs protection from bankruptcy. To safeguard these interests, a special statutory instrument regulating the duties of estate agents and developers (*Makler- und Bauträgerverordnung*, hereafter, 'MaBV') is applied.

The MaBV allows the builder to receive instalments in correlation to the progress of the construction if certain conditions are fulfilled.[3] These include, in particular, the following: a notary has confirmed that the contract is valid and all necessary permissions have been granted, a priority notice to transfer ownership to the buyer has been registered in the Land Register, there are no liens on real estate with priority against the priority notice and the building licence has been granted. The builder may demand advance payment before these conditions are fulfilled if he provides a security.

[2] § 311b, para. 1 BGB. [3] See § 3 MaBV.

The obligation to register a priority notice protects the buyer from the builder's insolvency. In the case of X Ltd's insolvency, the registration of the priority notice dictates that the insolvency administrator must execute, from the insolvency estate, the claim secured by the priority notice (i.e. he must transfer the land with the unfinished building[4] to Henry[5]). Regarding the developer's obligation to build the house, the opening of the insolvency proceedings would dictate that the claims for performance (i.e. completion of the house and payment of the outstanding instalments) could no longer be enforced by the parties[6] and the insolvency administrator could obtain a right to opt for performance or non-performance.[7] The original, coherent contract with the developer would be divided into an element of sale secured by the priority notice and an element of construction remaining unsecured.[8] If the insolvency administrator opts for performance, he must complete the development to the credit of the insolvency estate's assets.[9] If the insolvency administrator chooses not to honour the obligation to build the house, Henry could claim damages for non-performance of the contract as a creditor in insolvency obtaining an insolvency quota only.[10] Henry could avoid this disadvantageous result by acquiring a surety for performance of the contract (*Vertragserfüllungsbürgschaft*) from the bank that financed the developer. Such a surety obliges the bank to finance the completion of the building by other builders in case of the developer's insolvency. Alternatively, the developer could have taken out insurance for the completion of the building.

(b) Austria

Henry won't pay the total price in advance. He will, instead, enter into a building developer's contract (*Bauträgervertrag*) with X Ltd, which is determined by a special act, the *Bauträgervertragsgesetz* (BTVG).[11] This type of contract (*inter alia*) is used if propriety rights should be obtained

[4] As the building is an essential part of the plot of land the ownership of the land includes the building (§§ 93 and 94 BGB).
[5] See § 106, para. 1 InsO.
[6] BGHZ (the official reports of the decisions of the Federal Court of Justice), vol. 150, pp. 353ff. (359).
[7] § 103 InsO. [8] See, e.g., BGHZ, vol. 79, pp. 103ff.
[9] §§ 103, para. 1, 55 para. 1, No. 2 InsO. [10] § 103, para. 2 InsO with § 281 BGB.
[11] BGBl I 1997/7 as amended by BGBl I 2008/56 (see Raimund Pittl, 'Die Novelle zum Bauträgervertragsgesetz', *Wohnrechtliche Blätter*, 21 (7) (2008), pp. 186–96).

on buildings that are not yet constructed (§ 2, para. 1). The act is only applicable if Henry is to pay more than €150 per m^2 usable floor space (§ 1, para. 1) before the building's completion. If Henry is a consumer, the rules of the BTVG are obligatory and can't be contracted out to his disadvantage (§ 1, para. 2). The contract must be closed in written form (§ 3) and, since the acquirer can't inspect the building in its final shape, has to bear a certain minimum content (cf. § 4) in order to demonstrate the whole project.[12] Non-compliance with these requirements will see a monetary penalty imposed (§ 17 No. 1).

Should the terms of the contract fail to be sent within one week, at the latest, after the contractual agreement to Henry or if certain information about the security obligation is not timely given to him, he has a right to withdraw (§ 5, para. 1). The same applies if a requested housing subsidy is not granted (§5, para. 3).

Unfortunately, it often occurs that the construction comes to a standstill due to financial difficulties and, as a result, the developer goes bankrupt. If that happens in this case, it must be verified that the contract with Henry is entirely fulfilled on his side. If so, Henry can insist on completion or withdraw from the contract.[13] If the contract is unfulfilled on both sides, the insolvency administrator has the right to both fulfil and claim the outstanding payment or withdraw from the contract (§ 21 KO). This decision will normally be subject to a permission of the committee of creditors if the value exceeds €100,000 (§ 116, para. 1 No. 4 KO). In the first case mentioned, Henry will not suffer losses (since that claim is a privileged one according to § 46, para. 1 No. 4 KO). In the latter case, he will claim damages for non-performance (cf. § 21, para. 2 sentence 3 KO) and will have to refer to his securities (see below) due to the fact that this claim is not generally privileged.

The BTVG aims to protect Henry, in the case of X Ltd's bankruptcy, from losing the money he has paid up to that point.[14] § 7 determines that certain securities must be provided for this purpose. The BTVG lists securities *in personam* (§ 8: *schuldrechtliche Sicherung*) and mentions a (bank) guarantee or an appropriate insurance, the registration in the Land Register (§ 9: *grundbücherliche Sicherstellung* – e.g. the *Anmerkung der Einräumung von Wohnungseigentum*) in connection with a payment

[12] Helmut Böhm and Wiltrud Priglinger, '"Merkzettel" für den Bauträgervertrag', *immolex*, 2002, pp. 273ff.

[13] Helmut Böhm, 'Der einseitig erfüllte Bauträgervertrag im Konkurs des Bauträgers', *wobl*, 1999, p. 69 (78f.).

[14] Christian Degelsegger, 'Das Bauträgervertragsgesetz – in Überblick', *wobl*, 1997, pp. 1ff.

plan (§ 10) and finally, the possibility of creating a mortgage (§ 11: *pfandrechtliche Sicherung*). The Act also allows the combination of the different security forms with each other.[15] By all means, it has to be considered that the registration in the Land Register (§ 9) only secures the main performance claim and not the reclamation of overpayments. However, thanks to the payment plan (§ 10), advanced/further payments are not settled under normal circumstances.

To guarantee and control a sufficient securing in most cases,[16] a fiduciary (notary or lawyer (partnership)) has to be appointed by X Ltd (§ 12).[17] If this is not ensured, the property developer can be adjudged a penalty amounting between €14,000 and €28,000 (§ 17 No. 3).

All in all, Henry will be well protected against a possible insolvency if Austrian law is applied.

(c) The Netherlands

Henry will enter into two separate contracts with X Ltd: a contract of sale of the land and a construction contract. Henry will pay the purchase price for the undeveloped land to the notary who will then make the transfer deed. When the deed has been made and registered the notary will advance the money to X Ltd. There is no risk of insolvency here. Regarding the price for building the house, it would be dangerous for Henry to pay more than the progress of the work justifies. It is therefore, common practice for Henry to pay in instalments according to the progress of the development. As a result of accession, the parts of the house being built will automatically belong to Henry.

Henry will have a contractual right against X Ltd that ensures X will finish the building. He does not lose this right in X Ltd's insolvency. However, there is no way to enforce specific performance. The insolvency administrator might be inclined to have the building finished if it is profitable for the insolvency creditors. Otherwise, Henry will have to file his claim during the insolvency procedure. He will have an unsecured claim. If the administrator in insolvency sells X Ltd's enterprise to Y, the latter will not be bound by X Ltd's obligations. Company X Ltd will be liquidated and dissolved. As a result, all of X Ltd's obligations fall away.

[15] Herbert Gartner, 'Der Treuhänder nach Bauträgervertragsgesetz – Haftungen und Risiken', *immolex*, 2002, p. 265 (p. 269f.).

[16] It is not compulsory to appoint a fiduciary if X Ltd only grants a security in personam. See also § 7, para. 6.

[17] Gernot Fellner, 'Die Sicherung des Erwerbers durch Bestellung eines Treuhänders', *NZ*, 1999, pp. 3ff.

If X Ltd does not finish the building, the more practical solution is to hire a different company to finish it.

Many new houses are built on the basis of a contract in which the builder's obligations have been guaranteed by a private company called Woningborg. The company will pay compensation in the case of the builder's insolvency.

(d) Turkey

The parties can sign a promise of sale for Henry's future house in front of a notary public. This type of contract would be valid. However, a promise of sale is not sufficient enough to transfer an immovable, the parties have to draft a sale contract before the Land Register officer.[18] Also, Henry should have his right annotated in the Land Register,[19] on the page stating where the house is going to be built. Otherwise, X Ltd can readily sell Henry's future house to a third party and Henry would not succeed since, according to the Turkish law system, the legal relationship between the partner of a contract is relative and binds only the partners involved.

2 *Scandinavian jurisdictions*

(a) Finland

The development situation described in this case is uncommon in Finland. There is no specific regulation that applies to this kind of case or practice. Normally, these kinds of development projects refer to the establishment of housing corporations (normally special kinds of limited companies). A housing share confers the right of possession to a residential apartment on the owner of the share.[20] Shares (apartments) are often sold with suspension and instalment clauses during the construction stage. The vendor (X Ltd) is the founding shareholder who is, at the same time, the constructor and assigned his title to the shares when the corporation was established. There are many mandatory provisions

[18] See M. Kemal Oğuzman, Özer Seliçi and Saibe Oktay-Özdemir, *Eşya Hukuku, Gözden Geçirilmiş 11. Bası* (İstanbul: Filiz Kitabevi, 2006), p. 311.

[19] See art 1009, para. 2 TCC; Ivy Williams, Siegfried Wyler and Barbara Wyler, *The Swiss Civil Code, Version II* (Zürich, 1987), art. 959, para. 2; Oğuzman, Seliçi and Oktay-Özdemir, *Eşya*, pp. 209–11; Lale Sirmen, *Eşya Hukuku Dersleri* (Ankara: Savaş Yayınları, 1995), pp. 206–8; Ertaş, *Eşya*, p. 169.

[20] 1:1.1 Housing Companies Act (2009) and 1:2.1 Housing Transactions Act (1994), www.finlex.fi/en/laki/kaannokset/1991/en19910809.pdf and www.finlex.fi/en/laki/kaannokset/1994/en19940843.pdf.

protecting the legal and financial status of purchasers of the shares in the Housing Transactions Act. Purchasers are treated as customers according to this law. Both block and terraced houses are built in this way. It could be a way to construct detached or separate family houses as well, but it is seldom used in Finland.

Developers or building companies have not been interested in buying large areas to construct many detached or separate family houses in order to sell them in Finland. In practice, a person or couple who want to build a house and live in it buy or lease a site, most often from the local municipality. These people can enter into a construction agreement with a small construction company or they can employ workers. In addition, it is very popular to order a ready-made house from a house factory. Today, most of the houses are made in this way. The main parts of the house will be erected as parts of a house or of precast elements in a matter of days. Even in this case, there are mandatory rules protecting purchasers as customers.[21] This practice, as well as establishment of housing corporations is, however, out of the sphere of the case and the question.

The house being built can be a part of a piece of real estate. In this case, Henry buys both a house and the land under and around it. The house can be a leased house as well. In the latter case, Henry buys the house but, nevertheless, X Ltd will be the landowner and landlord. I restrict my answer to the previous case.

There is a preceding question. If X Ltd owns the whole site as a parcel or register unit, the area has to be divided into plots for each house by an official land survey. X Ltd can take care of it and, hence, Henry will buy a house and a plot as a ready-made register unit. Alternatively, X Ltd can sell the houses being built as well as the parcels. In this case, Henry will order and pay the land survey.

The crucial matters are the ways in which to finance construction and the sale of the house and the possible means to protect the purchaser against the possible insolvency of X Ltd.

It is possible that X Ltd does not need the purchase money until the houses are finished. In that case, the sale of a piece of real estate can be made including a cancellation and a payment clause. According to the clauses, a purchaser has the right to cancel the sale if the house is not finished by the fixed date, and the payment will not take place before the house is finished. This is an easy arrangement for Henry. He has plenty

[21] Chapter 9, Consumer Protection Act (1978), regulating the sale of building elements and construction contracts, www.finlex.fi/fi/laki/kaannokset/1978/en19780038.pdf.

of time to sell his previous house or apartment and it is easier to get a residential loan when a ready-made house can be used as a mortgage security. One should remember, however, that the cancellation clause can be valid for no more than five years.[22]

A precontract can be made in the same way. According to a precontract, the parties agree to make the final sale when the house is finished. The purchase money will be paid when the parties sign the final purchase contract (the deed). In order to be legally binding, the precontract has to be made in accordance with the form regulation that applies to a normal sale of a piece of real estate.[23] The precontract can be made either with the help of a paper document witnessed by a notary or as an electronic conveyance with the help of official websites.[24] The precontract creates, however, merely rights *in personam*. As a rule, a precontract does not legally bind third persons. It is possible that a precontract will lapse if the house is sold to another purchaser as a final sale, or if the vendor becomes insolvent. In this case, the purchaser has a right to due compensation for breach of contract.[25] However, the right to the unsecured compensation is, in most cases, normally valueless in the case of insolvency. Down payments are often connected with precontracts.

X Ltd, most likely, wants to finance construction, at least in part, by the purchase money already spent during the construction time. This is normally the case when establishing housing corporations. Moreover, it is probable that X Ltd does not accept any cancellation clauses for the benefit of the purchasers. In these kinds of situations, constructors have greater influence and power over the content of agreements than purchasers. They will draw up the agreements.

Following the model of establishing housing corporations, the purchasers and X Ltd can agree that the sales are arranged with suspension clauses on the instalment plan and for the benefit of X Ltd and on the instalment plan. X Ltd will maintain possession of the houses and will retain titles until the full prices have been paid and the houses are finished. Each part of the purchase money will correspond to the stages of construction. These clauses secure the position of X Ltd but there is no security for Henry. The problem is his possible claim for repayment of the paid purchase money and for damages if X Ltd becomes insolvent and does not finish the houses. In this respect, however, no mandatory rules protecting purchasers as customers are provided. There are some rules in

[22] See 2:2.2 Code of Real Estate. [23] 2:7.1–2 Code of Real Estate.
[24] See the answers to questions 1 and 2 (b). [25] 2:2.3 Code of Real Estate.

the Code of Real Estate protecting purchasers against merchants who develop or sell residential pieces of real estate professionally.[26] They protect Henry, merely, against defects in quality and in some other respects but they do not help Henry with the problem at hand. Registration cannot provide any protection for Henry either. Possible guarantees or other securities for Henry depend on the agreement terms. In this case, Henry has to finance construction before receiving possession of the house being built and before he can sell his current house or apartment. This is not a favourable situation in order to get a residential loan.

(b) Sweden

Even if the house is built on another's property, the house belongs to Henry, and also when the owner of the property and the builder are the same.[27]

If Henry is a consumer, he does not have to pay in advance. Prepayment is contrary to mandatory law, but it is possible for the parties to agree that the consumer pay in instalments as the project advances, as long as the instalments truly correspond to the work that has been done.[28] Henry will probably have a right to claim return of payments not due, unless he voluntarily refrains from this aspect of his legal protection.

In disputes about what has been agreed upon at the time of payment, the burden of proof lies on the building contractor.[29]

If the parties have agreed that there will be a final inspection of the building project, Henry is entitled to withhold 10 per cent of the contract sum until the house has been approved by the inspector.[30]

The sale of the house might include the surrounding land. Henry has priority over X Ltd's creditors once the sale concludes, provided that the formal requirements for a valid conveyance are fulfilled (see question 2). The conveyance will then include all that has been built and his property will accumulate more value as the work proceeds.[31] He will also have a right to all building materials brought to the building site.[32]

[26] See 2:10 and 2:26 Code of Real Estate.

[27] Supreme Court judgments *NJA* 1982, 773 and *NJA* 1984, 562. Cf. also *NJA* 1985, 365 and *NJA* 2015, 961.

[28] § 52 (1) Consumer Services Act; *compare* § 41. Governmental proposal *prop. 2003/04:45, Stärkt konsumentskydd vid småhusbyggande*, p. 135.

[29] § 51 (3) Consumer Services Act.

[30] § 52 (2) Consumer Services Act.

[31] Supreme Court judgments *NJA* 2007, 652 and *NJA* 2002, 561.

[32] Supreme Court judgment *NJA* 1960, 221.

(c) Denmark

Henry should ensure that he is protected against X Ltd's contractual parties as well as creditors in case of X Ltd's insolvency.

In these respects, Henry can only fully protect his proprietary rights if the development has been broken up into individual plots that may be entered into the Land Register under their own title number. For this reason, such developments in Denmark are broken up into individual plots from the outset. In this case, X Ltd still owns the whole development. Thus, the first thing Henry should do is to demand that a specific part of the development is broken up and registered in his name at the Buildings and Dwellings Register in the Land Register. If this is done, the building will enter into Henry's proprietary sphere as it is being built.

If X Ltd does not allow this, the good lawyer should advise Henry to reconsider the situation. If Henry still wishes to continue, he should be aware that he has bought 'a project'. Thus, he has no *right to an identified property* that may be registered in the Buildings and Dwellings Register in the Land Register. This means that, in the case of the subsequent bankruptcy of X Ltd, Henry's claim on the property is not protected against X Ltd's creditors and X Ltd's subsequent contractual parties may extinguish Henry's rights to the plot. Henry may register a conditional deed, conditional upon the subsequent breaking up of the property within a certain time.[33] However, this will not offer Henry any protection if the condition is not fulfilled. Nevertheless, in case the condition is fulfilled, the 'early registration' will offer Henry protection against X Ltd's creditors and contractual parties from the time of the initial registration.

Bearing this in mind, Henry should be very careful in drafting the sales contract with X Ltd. Firstly, the sales sum should only be paid in stages, corresponding to the progression of the building site. Secondly, Henry should (if possible) ensure that a large quantum of the sales sum is reserved to be paid after the house is completed and Henry has been registered as the owner of the house and the land.

(d) Norway

The contractual relationship between X Ltd and Henry – a consumer – is governed by the Housing Construction Act (*lov om avtalar med forbrukar*

[33] Section 15 (3), LRA.

om oppføring av ny bustad, 13 June 1997 No. 43). Normally, X Ltd will offer an agreement under which the house, including the land, will be transferred to Henry against payment when the house is finished. Sometimes the buyer will have to pay part of the price in advance. This is only allowed if Henry's possible claim for repayment of the advance is secured with a bank guarantee or similar.[34] Should Henry, in spite of this mandatory rule, make an unsecured advance payment, he may claim the money back and this will not affect the remaining part of the contractual relationship. Henry's right to the house (or the land) is not protected against the builder's creditors up to registration of his purchase in the Land Register. That may be annoying but not dramatic, as his money is secured.

If X Ltd wants Henry to buy the land at once or at a later stage, but before the house is finished, this may also be done without Henry incurring unacceptable risks. Before Henry pays anything (apart from any sum being secured by a guarantee), he should have the registered title to the relevant part of the land transferred to him. This follows the prohibition against unsecured payment already mentioned. When the registered title is transferred, Henry's right to the land and unfinished building (and even to materials brought to the site, if they are paid for) is protected.[35] It is not permissible for X Ltd to claim instalments that do not correspond to the value of work performed on the land unless they are secured with a bank guarantee or the like.[36] Should Henry pay more than this, he may claim the money back, and this will not affect the remaining part of the contractual relationship.

Henry's claim for repayment of unsecured advance payments (under both scenarios described) has no special protection against the builder's creditors. The point is that a claim for repayment can be presented and enforced at any time, preferably while the builder is still solvent.

It should also be mentioned that the builder is supposed to procure a bank guarantee (or similar) securing Henry's claims, as a result of the builder's non-performance of the contract. In this case, the claim will include possible damages in addition to the return of any advance payment.[37] This guarantee is rather small (before the house is delivered, typically 5 per cent of the total payment; more detail is left aside).

[34] Section 47 (2), Housing Construction Act.
[35] Section 58 (3), Housing Construction Act.
[36] Section 47 (1), Housing Construction Act.
[37] Section 12, Housing Construction Act.

3 *Romanic–Mediterranean jurisdictions*

(a) Italy

In order to acquire the house that has not yet been built, Henry must first enter into an agreement with the developer that allows him to acquire ownership of the property as soon as it comes into existence. Normally, this type of agreement will take the form of a preliminary contract of sale of immovable property to be built, but can also be any other act or contract which does not grant an immediate transfer of ownership over it.[38] It is preferable if the preliminary contract takes the form of a notarial deed, so it can be registered.[39] The transcription of the preliminary contract has a so-called 'booking effect': the subsequent conclusion and registration of the final contract of sale, at the time when the house has been completed, will have the effect of transferring ownership retroactively to the time of transcription of the preliminary contract. The possibility to register the preliminary sale of buildings under construction was provided by Legislative Decree 31 December 1996 No. 669, which introduced the new art. 2645, para. 4 ICC in order to protect the promisee buyer of property, built if the builder should become bankrupt before the final transfer of the immovable property. The registration of the preliminary contract will allow Henry to oppose the inclusion of the immovable property from the bankruptcy proceedings by relying on the registration of the preliminary contract.

The protection accorded to the promisee buyer was later extended by Legislative Decree No. 122/2005 of 20 June 2005, which provides rules concerning the protection of property rights of a person who acquires an immovable property 'under construction'. In particular, it is worth underlining that the abovementioned Legislative Decree introduces rules that aim to prevent the buyer from losing money paid in advance, in the event of the building contractor getting into financial difficulties.

Besides setting out specifically, and in minute detail, what the content of a 'Preliminary contract' or any other agreement for the future transfer of ownership in favour of the buyer should be,[40] art. 2 Legislative

[38] There are other contracts, which do not grant immediate transfer of rights of ownership such as in the case of a 'sale of future goods' (*vendita di cosa futura* – art. 1472 ICC), an 'exchange' (*permuta*) of actual goods with future goods, a 'sales contract under condition precedent or under starting date' (*contratto di vendita sottoposto a condizione sospensiva o termine*), 'unilateral promise to buy' (*promessa unilaterale di acquisto*) and a 'leasing'.

[39] See above, case 2.

[40] Art. 6 LgsD No. 122/2005 requires that the contract should mention the following: indication of the parties' identity (art. 2651 (1) ICC) and the data of the immovable

Decree No. 122/2005 states that the building contractor is obliged to provide a surety (*fideiussione*) 'on pain of nullity of the contract', the guarantor of which has to be – according to art. 3 (1) Legislative Decree No. 122/2005 – a bank, an insurance company, or a financial broker registered in the special list under art. 107 Legislative Decree No. 385/1995 (Consolidated Bank Act), to guarantee the repayment of amounts paid prior to the stipulation of the definitive sales contract (art. 2 Legislative Decree No. 122/2005).[41] If the building contractor does not provide the buyer with a surety, the preliminary contract is void, and such a case of nullity can only be asserted by the buyer (art. 2 (1) Legislative Decree No. 122/2005).

The buyer, who is protected by guarantee, can exercise his right *vis-à-vis* the guarantor as soon as the buyer realises that the building contractor is encountering financial difficulties (art. 3 LgsD No. 122/2005).[42] The guarantor has to reimburse the buyer within thirty days after the latter has delivered, by registered post, the documents proving the sums

property entered in the land registry where the immovable property is mortgaged (art. 2826 ICC); identification and description of the immovable property, its annexes, its structural elements, the material to be used for the building as well as the project under which planning permission was applied for; indication of potential obligations or agreements with the local authority in order to obtain planning consent; an indication of the period required for construction; indication of the price, the conditions of payment, and whether the parties agree upon the deposit of earnest money. Moreover, the price has to be paid by means of payment or money transfer to the seller's personal bank/postal account or by any means of payment able to provide concrete evidence of payment; indication of the guarantee (*fideiussione*) under art. 2 LgsD No. 122/2005; indication of another person's right *in rem* for security purposes, its economic value, its title as well as whether the building contractor has to fulfil the obligations deriving from this title before or after the stipulation of the sales contract; indication of the data concerning either the permission to build or the application for permission.

41 The provision of art. 2 LgsD No. 122/2005 does not apply where the buyer pays by virtue of money that he received as housing loan, since the loan is independently secured (usually the lender will transfer the money after the mortgage on the immovable property is consolidated).

42 Indicators of the building contractor's financial difficulties are:
the registration of the foreclosure of the immovable property under construction; publication of the court decision which declares the building contractor's bankruptcy; publication of the building contractor's application to open bankruptcy proceedings; publication of the court decision which declares the building contractor's state of insolvency and allow the compulsory winding-up or the extraordinary administration proceedings.
In the case of registration of the foreclosure, the buyer can exercise his security right only after having informed the building contractor about his intention to withdraw from the contract (art. 3 (3) LgsD No. 122/2005). In the other cases, the buyer is entitled to exercise his security right only if the trustee in bankruptcy has communicated his intention not to fulfil the obligation deriving from the contract to be concluded.

of money already cashed by the building constructor. In addition, he cannot object that the building contractor did not pay the premium or the fee for the issue of the surety.

Moreover, in the event of the contractor's bankruptcy, the buyer has a preemptive right to purchase the house, where it will be auctioned off to satisfy the former's creditors (art. 9 LgsD No. 122/2005). The buyer can exercise his right, through a bailiff, within ten days from the date of notification of the auction sale.[43]

Finally, in order to safeguard the purchaser, art. 4 LgsD No. 122/2005 requires the builder/developer to provide him with an insurance that covers the buyer for damage caused by total or partial destruction of the building or defects in construction.

(b) Spain

In Spanish law, this matter is subject to *Real Decreto Legislativo 1/2007*, enacting the consolidated text of the *Ley General para la Defensa de los Consumidores y Usuarios* ('Consumer Protection Act 2007'). It is also subject to related statute law, *Real Decreto 515/1989*, concerning consumer protection in regards to mandatory disclosures in sale and lease of dwellings, to the Urban Development Act 38/1999, amended by Act 20/2015 and to the *Ley 34/1988, de 11 de noviembre, General de Publicidad* ('Advertising Act').

Henry should first send a query to the *Registro Mercantil*, the Spanish Registrar of companies – in person, or online, for a fee payable by credit card – to check that X Ltd really exists, that the person who is to sign the contract on its behalf has the authority to do so, that the building site is registered in the name of X Ltd, and that X Ltd holds a licence to build the planned houses. If the *Registro Mercantil* has no details about the licence, Henry can ask the local council, the *Ayuntamiento*.

Next, Henry should make sure that X Ltd provides him with all the mandatory disclosures (some of which he will already have obtained for himself from the *Registro Mercantil*): the company's registration details; general and detailed plans of the house he's interested in; a specification of the construction materials and standards; instructions on use and

[43] However, where the court omits to inform the buyer about the auction sale, no remedy *in rem* (such as a redemption right) is granted to the buyer: indeed, the buyer cannot redeem the immovable property from the person to whom it has been assigned (art. 9 (5) LgsD No. 122/2005). The buyer has only a remedy in tort, since the violation of the pre-emption right can give rise to an action for damages *vis-à-vis* the authority that undertook the sale of the immovable property.

maintenance of the facilities; the total price and terms of payment for the house and so forth.[44] Henry should keep any advertising given to him about the house. X Ltd is bound by an obligation to fulfil all the claims it makes about the development in its advertisements and brochures.[45]

It is likely that, before building the house, X Ltd will require Henry to sign a private contract and pay a down payment. Henry needs to bear in mind that the contract should be worded very clearly and simply and meet all the requirements of consumer protection law. Any abusive clause, even if signed by the buyer, is treated by the law as absent.[46] The contract must specify the price and the terms of purchase – the instalments Henry must pay, and any warranty he has of recovering paid instalments if, for any reason, construction never begins or is not completed within the agreed period.[47] These warranties are statutory and oblige the seller to arrange insurance or a bank guarantee to assure the refunding of down payments, plus the legal rate of interest.[48] The warranty implies that the insurer or bank has scrutinised the development project and has found it sound and viable. The private contract should also specify the account into which Henry should pay the agreed instalments. The account must be kept separate from the rest of X Ltd's funds and X Ltd may use the money only for the purpose of building the house.[49]

Henry has no ownership right to the house until it is built and delivered. His right to the house is thus unprotected against X Ltd's creditors during construction.[50] On the other hand, if the house is not

44 Art. 4 *Real Decreto 515/1989*.

45 Art. 3 (2) *Real Decreto 515/1989* and art. 8 (1) Consumer Protection Act 2007 on incorporation of advertising in the contract (subject to the prevalence of whichever clause best serves the consumer); no detailed commentary is necessary here.

46 Art. 10 *Real Decreto 515/1989*.

47 1st Additional Disposition Urban Development Act 38/1999.

48 1st Additional Disposition Urban Development Act 38/1999.

49 1st Additional Disposition Urban Development Act 38/1999.

50 If Henry has bought not a house but a flat, under the law of horizontal property, then some legal doctrine and case law allows that the buyer holds a right in the flat if the legal act of transfer is formalised as a notarial act and contains a description of the flat as a duly delimited individual property. The buyer's position would then be more protected against third parties, and Henry could bring actions known as *tercerías de dominio* (a third-party action in connection with ownership). This is the view held by the *Tribunal Supremo* in a case concerning the exchange of a plot of land for flats to be constructed in future (decision of 18 May 1994 (RJ 1994/4094)) and by the *Dirección General de Registros y del Notariado*, the government body supervising official registers and notaries, in its decision of 16 May 1996 (RJ 1996/3950).

completed within the agreed term, he is entitled to a refund of any payments made, plus the legal rate of interest.

If Henry needs to finance his down payments, he will have to apply for a personal loan because he's not yet the owner of the house and can't apply for a mortgage. If Henry were his own developer and X Ltd were simply the builder, Henry could apply for a self-development loan, for which he would need to acquire ownership of the land.

(c) Portugal

In Portugal, real rights can only be created or transferred over existing things, not over future things (art. 408 (1) CC). Hence, before the construction of the house is concluded, X Ltd is only entitled to transfer personal rights over it. If X Ltd sells houses off the building plans before completion of the building, the contract of sale will not be void. Transfer of property, however, will take place only after the building is complete (arts. 408 (2) and 880 (1) CC).

Normally, in such a situation, X Ltd and Henry would acknowledge a preliminary contract (*contrato promessa*). After completion of the house, X Ltd would then be entitled to acknowledge the contract of sale of the house and, therefore, comply with the promise.

If X Ltd becomes insolvent and does not finish the building, Henry would have a credit against the insolvent estate (see question 3). The declaration of insolvency causes all the obligations of the insolvent party, which are not subject to a condition precedent, to become due for settlement. Regarding the debtor's assets, the effect of the declaration of insolvency is to deprive the debtor immediately – either directly or through his directors – of the power to administer and dispose of the assets making up the estate. From that moment on, those powers are vested in the administrator who is the debtor's representative for all financial issues relating to the insolvency. As a rule, acts undertaken by the insolvent party in breach of these arrangements are ineffective.

Four types of claims against the insolvent are categorised in the insolvency proceedings: secured, preferential, subordinated and unsecured. Secured claims are those with a security right *in rem* over assets in the estate, up to the value of such assets. Preferential debts are general creditors' preferential claims over assets in the estate, up to the value of the assets over which such preferential claims exist. Subordinated claims (e.g. claims of persons with a special relationship with the debtor – such as the spouse, ascendants, descendants or siblings of the debtor (where a physical person is involved) or the shareholders, partners or persons who have been in a controlling or group relationship with the debtor (where it is a legal person)) are those which will be settled only when the unsecured creditors have been paid in full. Unsecured claims, by default, are those not covered by the above categories.

Under the Portuguese law, special protection for the acquirers of a dwelling is not foreseen, so Henry would have a mere unsecured claim. Accordingly, within thirty days after the insolvency is declared, he must apply for his claim to be admitted. Unsecured creditors, whose rights have been acknowledged by the court, will be paid on a *pro rata* basis, depending on the value of the insolvent assets and only provided that all secured and preferential debts of the insolvent estate have been paid.

(d) Greece

In accordance with law 1024/1971, the owner of a plot of land has the right to create and register titles of independent properties that will be erected on the plot in the future. Following such registration the owner can then sell and transfer the titles of each independent property. Both the deed for the creation of the titles[51] and the purchase contract must be drafted by a notary.[52] The future houses are considered to exist after the contract of creation of titles has been registered in the Transcription or the Land Registry.[53]

Only after X Ltd has created and registered those titles can Henry proceed with purchasing the future house following the same steps that are needed in order to buy a house that already exists (a registered notary deed is needed).[54]

Once the property corresponding to the house that will be built for Henry has been sold and the contract has been registered in the local Transcription or Land Registry, potential creditors of X Ltd will not be able to claim the specific property.

4 *France and related jurisdictions*

(a) France

If Henry wishes to buy one of these houses before its completion, he will have to conclude a special contract recognised and regulated by

[51] 13 § 1 law 3741/1929.
[52] Arts. 369 and 1033 GCC. A precise description of the future houses is needed for the validity of the contract (*principle of particularity*).
[53] 13 § 1 law 3741/1929. [54] Arts. 1033, 1192 and 1198 GCC.

the C. civ.[55] and by the Code de la construction et de l'habitation[56] with X Ltd. In practice, the parties conclude a contract called a 'sale in future state of completion'[57]: the property and its possible equipments is transferred at once to the buyer, who then acquires, gradually, the construction by accession as it is built. At the same time, to contribute to the financing of the construction, the buyer pays the price in fractions.

The conclusion of this type of contract is compulsory when the sale concerns a residential building, and obliges the buyer to make payments or deposits before the completion of the construction. The contract must be then drafted by a notary and contain numerous mentions and documents intended, in particular, to clarify the exact consistency of the building sold. Besides protecting the buyer against the risk of incompletion of the building or even the diversion of the sums advanced to the seller, the law forbids any payment or deposit before the conclusion of the contract. It then defines, for every key stage of the construction (foundations, roof, completion), the maximal percentage of the price that can be paid at this stage (for example, 35 per cent for the completion of the foundation). This supervision is strengthened by the requirement of guarantees given by banking or insurance institutions.

No agreement to sell or to buy can, in principle, be concluded. But the law authorises the conclusion of a preliminary contract allowing the interested candidate to reserve the acquisition of the real estate for the payment of a deposit that can't exceed 5 per cent of the projected price.[58] The shape and the contents of this preliminary contract are also regulated in interest of the future buyer. It is doubtless the preliminary contract that X Ltd will at first make to be signed for Henry. The conclusion of the preliminary contracts does not oblige the developer to sell but allows him to make sure of the existence of future buyers, before making them agree upon the definitive contracts of sale.

(b) Belgium

This situation is, according to the Belgian law, governed by the specific provisions of the Building Construction Act of 9 July 1971.[59] This Act contains several provisions in order to protect the buyer against

[55] Arts. 1601-1 to 1601-4, 1642-1, 1646-1 and 1648.
[56] Arts L. 261-1 to L. 261-22, L. 263-1 and R. 261-1 to R. 261–33.
[57] 'Vente en l'état futur d'achèvement' in French.
[58] Art. L. 261-15 of the Code de la construction et de l'habitation.
[59] *Belgian Official Gazette*, 11 September 1971.

contractual non-compliance and insolvency on behalf of the seller. It applies in the case of a 'sale on map' (e.g. sale of a house or apartment which has not yet been constructed or of which the construction has not yet been finalised). The provisions of this Act are mandatory, in such a way that they cannot be contractually excluded in favour of the seller (developer).

The Act applies independent of whether or not the parties have qualified this agreement as a building or as a sales agreement.

We limit ourselves to the provisions relating to the issues which are dealt with in this questionnaire:

- The ownership of the building materials will pass to Henry at the moment the materials are incorporated in the ground (art. 4). This entails that, in case of the insolvency of the developer, the parts of the building that have already been erected belong to the buyer.
- The agreement must mention a term for the realisation of the construction works or a date at which the construction of the building has to be finished.
- The payment of the purchase price must be effected according to a fixed scheme:
  - Henry is allowed to pay, at most, 5 per cent of the purchase price at the moment the private deed is signed.
  - Henry is allowed to pay the price of the purchased parcel of ground at the moment the notarial deed is signed. He can, at the same time, pay the price of the works that have already been executed.
  - Payment of the other parts of the price for the construction works can only be effected after the execution of the corresponding parts of the works.
- X Ltd must guarantee the execution of the construction work. In order to do so, it must provide a deposit that equates the total amount to be paid if X Ltd is not recognised by public institutions as a recognised constructor.[60] If X Ltd is a recognised constructor, it will be sufficient to deposit a 5 per cent guaranty.
- It must expressly be mentioned whether or not the sale is dependent upon the condition precedent of obtaining finance by the bank on behalf of Henry.

If one or more of these mandatory rules have not been complied with, the agreement can be declared void. It is, once again, void in the sense that it can only be invoked by the buyer (Henry).

[60] This is an aspect of public law. A constructor can obtain recognition if it complies with all tax duties and social obligations which are imposed by the public authorities.

5 *England and related jurisdictions*

(a) England

Henry needs to be careful about the possibility of X Ltd becoming insolvent prior to the house being built. One option would be for him to buy the land from X Ltd and then partner with them to build the house on it. That way, if X Ltd does become insolvent, Henry at least owns the land and can partner with someone else to build the house.

If Henry opts to contract for the house as built, then he would be best advised not to pay anything until the house has been built. However, in developments of this sort, the developer often insists on the purchaser paying intermediate instalments so that the developer has capital with which to build. If Henry agrees, he will be able to assert an equitable lien over the property once he has begun to pay the instalments.[61] This could be important if X Ltd becomes insolvent without having completed the building because it provides protection for the return of the instalments that Henry has paid. Such a lien does not mean that Henry can assert ownership of the land, but rather that he is entitled to treat the land as security for repayment of the instalments which he has paid.[62] This form of lien is available even if specific performance of the contract for sale is not,[63] but it is not available if the right to claim such a lien is excluded by the contract of sale[64] (which is unknown in the facts given) or if the reason that the building development failed was as a result of Henry's own misconduct[65] (which seems unlikely to be the case here). The lien will most likely only affect the parcel of land that was to be conveyed to Henry.[66] The result is that if X Ltd's liquidator sells the land over which Henry has a lien, Henry has first

[61] See *Rose* v. *Watson* (1864) 10 HLC 672 at 678–9 and 683–4; *Hewett* v. *Court* (1983) 149 CLR 639 at 648, 650 and 665; *Chattey* v. *Farndale Holdings, Inc.* (1996) 75 P & CR 298; *Tanwar Enterprises Pty Ltd* v. *Cauchi* [2003] HCA 57 (2003), 217 CLR 315 at [52]; *International Finance Corp.* v. *DSNL Offshore Ltd* [2005] EWHC 1844 (Comm).

[62] See, e.g., *Hewett* v. *Court* (1983) 149 CLR 639 at 665; *International Finance Corp.* v. *DSNL Offshore Ltd* [2005] EWHC 1844 (Comm.).

[63] *Levy* v. *Stogdon* [1898] 1 Ch. 478 at 485–6; *Hewett* v. *Court* (1983) 149 CLR 639 at 664–5; *Chattey* v. *Farndale Holdings Inc.* (1996) 75 P & CR 298 at 307; *Tanwar Enterprises Pty Ltd* v. *Cauchi* [2003] HCA 57 (2003), 217 CLR 315 at [52].

[64] *Chattey* v. *Farndale Holdings Inc.* (1996) 75 P & CR 298 at 309–10.

[65] *Whitbread & Co. Ltd.* v. *Watt* [1902] 1 Ch. 835 at 840–1.

[66] See, e.g., *Chattey* v. *Farndale Holdings Inc.* (1996) 75 P & CR 298 at 317–18. The question of how to give effect to a purchaser's lien in cases in which the relevant building or part does not exist has not yet been resolved.

claim (to the extent of his instalment payments only) over the proceeds from sale of that land.[67]

If X Ltd does become insolvent before the building is complete, Henry cannot force X Ltd's liquidator to complete the house, as the liquidator is able to disclaim the building contract,[68] bringing it to an end. Henry could potentially prove in the liquidation for damages any loss caused by the failure to build the house. But if he has recovered his instalment payments (under the equitable lien) and has no ownership claim to the land, it is not clear that he has suffered any loss.

(b) Scotland

There is no specific legal regulation of this kind of situation, and the parties are free to make whatever legal arrangements they wish. In practice, it is quite common to buy houses 'off-plan' like this. A standard arrangement is that the buyer pays a modest deposit, with the balance of the price not being due until the house is completed and transferred to the buyer. In such a case, the buyer is at risk for his deposit, for if the builder becomes insolvent the deposit will be lost. But the deposit – and hence, the potential loss – is acceptably small.

Far less common, the arrangement may be that the buyer is to pay the price in instalments, typically related to the progress of the building work. In that case, the buyer's potential loss is much greater and it would be advisable to take steps to contain it. One possibility is to obtain an early transfer of the land, but this would put the builder at risk of the *buyer's* insolvency and so is unlikely to be accepted by the builder. A more direct solution is for the builder to grant a security right (known as a 'standard security') over the land in respect to the buyer's instalments. In order to be effective, a standard security must be registered in the Land Register.[69]

(c) Ireland

The dangers in this situation stem from an accepted practice among developers of relying on purchasers' money as well as loans to finance developments. A developer will frequently insist that a prospective purchaser pays a booking deposit in order to secure the purchase. On

[67] Henry could also protect the lien by entry of a notice in the register prior to the liquidator's sale.

[68] Section 178, IA 1986.

[69] Section 11 (1), Conveyancing and Feudal Reform (Scotland) Act 1970.

entering the contract for the purchase of the site and the building agreement, the balance of the deposit (usually 10 per cent of the purchase price) must be paid. Although, in more recent times, the practice has become less widespread, the purchaser may also be required to pay the balance purchase price as a series of stage payments staggered to take place during the period of construction. Usually, a special condition is included in the contract that allows the release of all monies received by the developer's solicitor to the developer to fund the build. There is a risk that X Ltd could become insolvent before the house is completed and Henry, as an unsecured creditor or a creditor whose security ranks behind that of a lending institution, could lose any money he paid towards the purchase price. There are a number of measures that Henry's solicitor can take in order to identify and minimise the risk involved.

First, he must check if the dwelling is registered with the HomeBond scheme, which insures against the possibility of the developer becoming insolvent.[70] Henry will be able to recover his deposit and his stage payments from HomeBond, although financial and time limits apply in respect to the cover provided.[71] Also, booking deposits are not usually covered as, typically, the dwelling will not yet have been registered with the scheme when they were paid. Purchasers are frequently pressured to pay a booking deposit directly to the developer or his agent on site, but if Henry consults his solicitor in advance, his solicitor should insist on sending the booking deposit to the developer's solicitor to be held as collateral until he receives the appropriate HomeBond documentation.

Once Henry enters into a contract for the purchase of the site, he acquires a lien on the land as security for the deposit and any other payments he makes. However, if X Ltd becomes insolvent at this stage, Henry could discover that a lending institution has a prior claim which may prevent him from recovering his money. Most developers have to borrow extensively in the early stages of development and the lending institution will insist on being provided with security for its loan by way of a mortgage or charge on the site and any building in progress. It is very important that Henry's solicitor carries out a number of searches,[72] particularly if the developer is not registered with HomeBond, before he

[70] It also provides a guarantee in respect of certain building defects.

[71] J.C.W. Wylie and Una Woods, *Irish Conveyancing Law*, 3rd edn. (Haywards Heath: Bloomsbury Professional, 2005), para. 4.26.

[72] A Companies Office search, a Judgments Office search and a Land Registry/Registry of Deeds search.

allows Henry to enter into a contract with the developer. These searches will reveal any prior charges so that Henry can at least be advised about the risk of making payments to X Ltd. If Henry's solicitor fails to make these searches or warn him of the dangers involved, Henry may be able to recover his losses by suing the solicitor for negligence.[73]

If Henry is required to make a stage payment that exceeds the level of protection afforded by the HomeBond scheme, his solicitor should insist that ownership of the site, free from any prior charges, is transferred to Henry before the payment is made. If a lending institution is financing Henry's purchase, it will refuse to release the first loan cheque unless such an arrangement has been agreed upon with the developer.[74] The difficulties created by stage payments should be less of an issue in the future as the Code of Practice governing builders who are members of the Irish Home Builders Association precludes the inclusion of provisions for the making of stage or interim payments in contracts entered into after 30 June 2007.[75]

73 *Roche* v. *Peilow* [1985] IR 232.

74 See Law Society of Ireland, *Conveyancing – Volume 2*, 5th edn. (Dublin: Oxford University Press, 2010), para 12.11.6.

75 It is estimated that 80 per cent of home builders are members of this Association. Note that stage payments may continue to be demanded in respect of one-off or specially commissioned houses.

Case 8

Michele and Joanna want to live together and buy a house. They contact an estate agency and are shown a beautiful house near the city centre. They decide to buy the house. Seven days after the completion of their purchase, they discover some cracks in the bedroom wall. An architect explains to them that the construction of the building is seriously defective. Do Michele and Joanna have any remedy and, if so, what is it?

(A) Foundational Concepts for Understanding Case 8

The general rule in almost all European countries is '*caveat emptor*'. This means the seller is liable only for hidden material defects that he knows about. In some systems, like the French or Spanish system, the seller is responsible only in the case of hidden defects in the property that prevent normal use.

Also, in some cases, it is stated that the seller is responsible for all material defects of the property sold, unless the buyer knows about or should have known about them (e.g. §§ 434 and 442, BGB Germany; art. 1490 ICC Italy; art. 911 CC Portugal).

In some countries, it is usual for the prospective buyer to have the house checked by a professional surveyor before signing the sales contract (e.g. England, Finland and Ireland).

(B) The Jurisdictions (Presented by Related Jurisdictions)

1 *Germany and related jurisdictions*

(a) Germany

The existence of the defects does not affect the transfer of ownership. German law strictly separates the obligatory contract of sale (*Kaufvertrag*) from the declaration of conveyance (*Auflassung*).[1] The latter is a real agreement (*dingliche Einigung*) necessary and sufficient for the transfer of ownership to be effectual (together with the registration in the Land Register). The real agreement is abstract and can be used to transfer the ownership arising from all kinds of obligatory contracts (purchase, donation etc.). The underlying contract of sale is only one possible *causa* for the real contract. Its (in)existence or (in)validity does not affect the validity of the real agreement (so-called '*Abstraktionsprinzip*' – principle of abstraction).[2] Nevertheless, there can be an obligation to re-transfer the house following the principles of unjust enrichment if the transfer was made in order to perform a void or an avoided contract (transfer *sine causa*).[3]

A defect of quality, as such, does not make the contract of sale void or voidable but it affects the contract of sale (not the real agreement) following the principles of the seller's warranties[4] dealt with by the law of obligations.

The occurrence of a defect primarily obliges the seller to repair the house at his own expense (subsequent performance (*Nacherfüllung*)).[5] In order to enforce other warranty rights the buyer normally has to give a reasonable period within which the seller is to repair the defects.[6] If this has been done, Michele and Joanna can recover the cost of their repairs, lost profit, etc. as damages.[7] But damages are only available if the seller is responsible for selling the house with a defect[8] (e.g. when he does not disclose known defects). Otherwise, Michele and Joanna can rescind the contract or claim reduction of the purchase price.[9] In the latter case, the purchase price is reduced in the ratio that the value of the house free of defects would, at the time of the conclusion of the contract, have had to the actual value. If Michele and Joanna choose to withdraw from the contract, the original sales contract alters into an obligation of restitution that obliges them to re-transfer the house to the seller (this requires a separate real agreement) where the seller must pay back the purchase price.[10]

[1] See above case 3, question (a).
[2] There is no express mention of the principle of abstraction in the BGB but it underlies its provisions and is unanimously acknowledged.
[3] § 812, para. 1 BGB. [4] See § 437 BGB. [5] §§ 437 No. 1, 439 BGB.
[6] There are however exceptions which will not be dealt with here.
[7] §§ 437 No. 3, 281, para. 1 sentence 1 BGB.
[8] This is legally presumed (see § 280, para. 1 sentence 2 BGB).
[9] §§ 437 No. 2, 440, 323, 326, para. 5, 441 BGB. [10] §§ 346ff. BGB.

In practice, however, the seller's warranty rights are normally largely excluded in the contract of sale when an older house is sold.

(b) Austria

A person leaving an object to another for money is accountable for the quality as agreed upon in the contract.[11] Therefore, under the principles of warranty law,[12] the seller is responsible for defects in substance or law (*Sach- oder Rechtsmängel*) present at the moment of the purchase.[13] If the defect is discovered within the first six months after the transfer of property it is presumed, by law, that the defect existed at the time the product was purchased.[14] As a consequence, the buyer can primarily claim either that the product be exchanged (*Austausch*) or repaired (*Verbesserung*). Secondly, he can claim reduction of the purchase price (*Preisminderung*) or is entitled to withdraw from the contract (*Wandlung*) (if the defect is not considered insignificant).[15]

If the defect already existed at the time of the conclusion of the contract (which seems reasonable in the case given) the buyer can also claim that he was mistaken concerning the quality of the product (*Eigenschaftirrtum*) and claim annulment (*Aufhebung*) on the ground of error (*Irrtum*) if the error is significant[16] and was induced by the seller.[17] In the case of an insignificant error,[18] he can claim adaption of the contract.[19] In the case of wilful deceit[20] on the part of the seller, the buyer can choose to go for an annulment of the contract, even in the case of an insignificant error.[21]

In this case, Michele and Joanna can claim[22] that the object be repaired (*Verbesserung*). Furthermore, if the cracks in the bedroom wall are just

[11] § 922 Abs 1 S 1 ABGB.

[12] See for general rules on the law of warranty Helmut Koziol and Rudolf Welser, *Bürgerliches Recht, II*, 13th edn. (Vienna: Manz Verlag, 2007), pp. 63ff; Silvia Dullinger, *Schuldrecht Allgemeiner Teil*, 3rd edn. (Vienna and New York: Springer Verlag, 2008), Rz 3/66ff.

[13] § 924 S 1 ABGB. [14] § 924 S 2 ABGB.

[15] § 932 Abs 2 S 1 ABGB. Reduction of price and withdrawal from the contract (*Wandlung*) can be done under the circumstances mentioned in § 932 Abs 4 ABGB.

[16] Knowing about the actual facts the contract would not have been concluded (here presumably the buyer would not have concluded the contract).

[17] One of the reasons mentioned in the respectable provision. Comp § 871 Abs 1 ABGB. On error (*Irrtum*), see Peter Bydlinski, *Allgemeiner Teil*, 4th edn. (Vienna: Springer Verlag, 2007), Rz 8/1ff; Kozlol and Welser, *Bürgerliches Recht, I*, pp. 147ff.

[18] Knowing about the actual facts the contract would have been concluded but pursuant to other terms (*unter anderen Bedingungen*).

[19] § 872 ABGB. [20] According to § 870 ABGB.

[21] The avoidance has to be claimed only within thirty years.

[22] The claim has to be brought within three years, § 933 Abs 1 ABGB.

one symptom of the wholly defective construction of the building, they could claim that repairing it (*Verbesserung*) is impossible, was not conducted, or not conducted in time by the seller, would be inconvenient for Michele and Joanna or unacceptable because of the inefficiency or carelessness of the seller.[23] As a result, they can claim reduction of the purchase price and, since the defect can definitely be qualified as essential/significant,[24] withdrawal of the contract. The contract can thus be dissolved *ex tunc* on a contractual basis, meaning that ownership rights of the real estate do not automatically fall back to the seller, but that he can claim re-transferral of the property (out of contract: contractual effect of the annulment of the contract). The contract parties are mutually obliged to return everything they acquired on the basis of the void contract.[25]

If they claim to have mistaken the quality of the house sold, they can claim that the contract is void *ab initio* (*ex tunc* and *in rem*) and annulment of the contract, meaning that the transfer of title can be undone. The ownership falls back to the seller and the parties are mutually obliged to return everything acquired on the basis of the void contract.[26] Claiming adaption of the contract, the purchase price can be reduced.

(c) The Netherlands

Art. 7:17 (1) BW dictates that a thing delivered by the seller should have the properties expected by the buyer on the basis of the sales contract. Art. 7:17 (2) BW adds, among other things, that the thing does not have the properties which the buyer may expect if the thing is not fit for normal use. Whether the defect is visible or latent is irrelevant. Very important in this respect is both the seller's obligation to point out defects that are known or should have been known to him and the buyers' obligation to do any necessary research. Often, the buyers in these cases will have two remedies at the same time. They will have the right to avoid the contract on the basis of error and they will also be able to terminate for breach of contract. The option is theirs. The property effects are different.

[23] § 932 Abs 4 ABGB.
[24] See, for the possibility of getting compensation according to the law of compensation, § 933a ABGB. Under the law of compensation the seller has to be at fault for the action to be granted. This action has to be brought within three years.
[25] According to the rules of unjustified enrichment, § 1435 ABGB.
[26] According to the rules of unjustified enrichment, § 877 ABGB.

If the contract of sale has not yet been followed by a transfer of ownership, the buyer is in a relatively comfortable position. He has not yet paid for the house. Consequently, he is able to withhold payment until the contract has been terminated.

If the sales contract has been followed by a transfer of ownership and the buyer terminates the contract altogether, the buyer will be obliged to transfer ownership back to the seller, and the seller will be obliged to pay back the purchase price and to provide compensation for any additional damage.

Avoidance of the contract, on the other hand, has different property effects. Every transfer of ownership should be based on a valid legal ground – in our example, a valid contract of sale. When the contract is avoided with retroactive effect after the transfer (art. 3:53 BW), ownership automatically reverts to the seller. In the case of avoidance for error (art. 6:228 BW), ownership of the house also automatically reverts to the seller. At first, this seems like a very uncomfortable position for the buyer, for the seller has both the purchase price and ownership of the house; the buyer has a mere unsecured claim against the seller. However, the buyer will be protected because he has a right of retention that works against the seller and the seller's creditors.

Rather than terminating the entire contract, the buyer may opt to terminate part of the contract that leads to a reduction in the price (art. 6:270 BW). The buyer remains owner of the house and can claim a price reduction from the seller, who is then obligated to pay back part of the price to the buyer. A similar effect can be attained when avoiding the contract. Art. 6:230 BW enables the seller to prevent avoidance of the contract by offering to compensate for the defects of the house. By paying back part of the purchase price, he may prevent avoidance provided this is an adequate solution for the buyer. Both parties can ask the judge to lower the contract price to compensate for the damage (art. 6:230 (2) BW).

(d) Turkey

If the defect is latent: According to art. 4 Law on Consumer Protection, they shall notify the seller of the defect within thirty days following the date of delivery of the immovable. In such case, they shall be entitled

- to rescind the contract with a refund,
- or a reduction of the price proportional to the defect,
- or repair, free of charge.

The seller shall do whatever the consumer chooses. In addition to this right to select, they shall also be entitled to claim indemnity from the manufacturer-producer in the event that the defective good causes death and/or injury and/or harm to other goods used.

If the defect is visible: The seller is not liable for defects that the buyer had knowledge of at the time of the purchase. The aforementioned provisions, other than those pertaining to responsibility for damages caused by defective goods, shall not apply to the goods purchased with the knowledge that they were defective.

2 *Scandinavian jurisdictions*

(a) Finland

A fundamental (and essential) defect in the quality of the house (and a piece of real estate), as a fundamental breach of contract, entitles Michele and Joanna, as purchasers, to claim the treatment of the contract as discharged (cancelled). Upon discharge, the ownership of the house and land returns to the vendor and Michele and Joanna are entitled to get the payment back. In addition, Michele and Joanna are entitled to damages if the defect has resulted in costs or a reduction of incomes.[27]

A conveyance of a piece of real estate can only, however, be treated as discharged or cancelled by a voluntary agreement complying with the rules of forms applying to a sale of a piece of real estate or by a local court. In the case of a leased house, Michele and Joanna can treat the contract as discharged by their claim on the same conditions, and the discharge can be confirmed by a court.

The vendor is responsible both for latent and visible defects. On the other hand, a purchaser cannot appeal a defect of which he or she must have been aware of when the sale was concluded. A purchaser has to inspect the house before the conclusion of the sale in broad outline. No technical means or other extraordinary measures are required. A purchaser is not entitled to appeal a defect in quality that could have been noticed in a conventional inspection.[28] Parties often agree on a larger inspection of the physical condition of the house.

In addition, the purchaser shall not invoke a defect if he does not give notice of it, and of his claims, to the seller in a reasonable time from

[27] 2:17 Code of Real Estate. [28] 2:22 Code of Real Estate.

finding out about the defect or from the time when it is thought he ought to have found out about it. In any case, the notice shall be given within five years from the transfer of the possession of the real estate in the case of a defect in quality.[29] In this case, it is clear that the notice will be given in time.

Even in the case of a fundamental breach, Michele and Joanna are entitled to other conventional remedies against the vendor if they do not want to treat the contract as discharged. The most important are price reduction and damages.[30] Michele and Joanna can conclude a contract with a construction company in order to repair the defects. The price of the reparation work can establish, as a starting point, the amount of the price reduction. Nevertheless, a possible overcompensation must be taken into consideration.[31] In addition, Michele and Joanna are entitled to damages, as in the earlier case.

As noted above, a vendor is responsible for both latent and visible defects. Hence, cancellation of the sale or a price reduction does not presume negligence on the part of the vendor. However, this is not the case with the damages. They are founded on the negligence of the vendor. On the other hand, the negligence of the vendor is presumed by application of the general principles of contract law.[32]

Michele and Joanna are better protected against defects in quality if the vendor has been a merchant who develops or sells pieces of real estate professionally.[33] In addition, they can make claims, instead of the vendor, against a merchant who has sold the piece of real estate to the vendor, a previous title-holder or against a building element dealer, developer, or other merchant who is responsible for defects.[34] The claim for repayment of the purchase money or damages is unsecured. The law provides no compulsory securities in this case and, normally, no voluntary securities are agreed upon. Hence, the possible claims usually become valueless in the case of insolvency of the vendor or the merchant.

It is possible that an estate agency is liable for damages together with the vendor on the ground of the defect. The agency's liability is founded on its negligence.[35]

[29] 2:25 Code of Real Estate. [30] 2:31.1 and 2:32.1 Code of Real Estate.

[31] KKO 1993:52 and KKO 1999:76 (precedents of the Supreme Court of Finland). See www.finlex.fi/en/.

[32] 2:32.2 Code of Real Estate. [33] 2:10 Code of Real Estate.

[34] 2:26 Code of Real Estate. [35] KKO 1988:64.

(b) Sweden

Whether Michele and Joanna will succeed depends on the existence of non-conformity and which remedy they seek. A buyer may not invoke non-conformity if the defect was (reasonably) detectable for a normally experienced buyer.[36] The buyer has a duty of investigation.[37] If the defect, as such, was not detectable, circumstances – such as the age or the condition of the building and statements of the seller – may deepen the buyer's duty of investigation.[38] In this case, it *might* be determined that Michele and Joanna ought to have detected the defect, which will preclude them from invoking non-conformity.

If the seller was aware, or must have been aware, of the defect that the buyer was unaware of, *and* the defect was of substantial importance to the buyer, but did not reveal the defect, the buyer may invalidate or rescind the contract, even if the defect, or a symptom of it, was detectable.[39]

The possible remedies for non-conformity are price reduction, avoidance and damages.[40] Rescission is possible only when the non-conformity is fundamental,[41] which seems to be the case here.

(c) Denmark

Under the Danish law, this is dealt with by the Law of Obligations. As a starting point, any property law issues arising out of it are only reflexes of the solutions dictated by the Law of Obligations.

Michele and Joanna may only sue the seller if the flaws were present at the time of *delivery* of the house. If the flaws didn't exist until after the delivery of the house (e.g. there has been a small earthquake), the flaws are at the buyers' risk and, as a rule, no claim may be made under the Law of Obligations. The only exception to this would be if the discovery takes place less than six *working days* from the signing of the contract. In that case, Michele and Joanna may simply avail themselves of the cooling-off-period in the consumer protection regarding the Purchase

[36] Governmental proposal *prop. 1989/90:77, Konsumentskyddet vid förvärv av småhus m.m.*, p. 41.

[37] 4:19 (2) Land Code.

[38] Supreme Court judgment *NJA* 1985, 274. Cf. *NJA* 1980, 555, *NJA* 1984, 3 and *NJA* 1998, 407.

[39] Supreme Court judgment *NJA* 2007, 86.

[40] 4:19 (1) Land Code.

[41] 4:19 (1) and 4:12 (1) Land Code.

of Real Estate Act[42] and cancel the contract. They will have to pay 1 per cent of the purchase price as a fee but this may, dependent on how grave the damage is, be preferable. If Michele and Joanna consider this to be the best option, they must rescind the contract immediately as the six *working days* are likely to have already run out since the discovery of the cracks.

If the flaws were already present at the time of the delivery of the house, a distinction should be made between visible and latent flaws. In case the flaw is visible, the *caveat emptor* rule applies and the buyers will, as a rule, be unable to direct a claim against the seller. However, if the flaw was latent, or not so obvious that the buyers ought to have noticed it, Michele and Joanna might successfully sue.

If the damage is substantial, Michele and Joanna may avoid the contract and claim damages. They may also choose to retain the property but claim damages for repair.

If, on the other hand, the damages were not substantial, but it may be proven that the seller knew or ought to have known about the damage or the seller has warranted that the foundations were sound, a claim for damages for the actual cost of repair may be made.

Finally, if the property is proven to be of less value than Michele and Joanna were expected to assume, they may direct a claim for reduction of the price against the seller. The reduction of the price is the difference in the value of the house with or without the flaw. This might not equal the actual cost of repair.[43]

Please note that if the seller has had a certificate of condition made and taken out a 'seller's insurance' (see question 3(c)), no claim may be made against the seller directly. Instead, a claim may be directed against the seller's insurance company.

(d) Norway

Primarily, this is a question of remedies for the lack of conformity of the purchased object. If the defective construction amounts to a lack of conformity – something that must be decided on the basis of the wording of the contract, the information given to the buyers, the character of the defect, the possibility of observing the defect during an inspection of the house, what the buyers could reasonably expect,

[42] Consumer protection regarding Sections 7 and 8, Purchase of Real Estate Act (Consolidation Act No. 265 of 21 March 2014).

[43] H. Peter Rosenmeier, *Mangler ved fast ejendom*, 6th edn. (Copenhagen: Karnov Group, 2013), pp. 301ff.

given the age of the house, type of construction, the general impression of the house, the price, etc. – the buyers will normally be entitled to damages and to a reduction of the price or termination of the contractual relationship (and, in some cases, even to having the lack of conformity remedied).[44]

If the seller is insolvent, Michele and Joanna might prefer to avoid the contract, a claim that may be successful if the seller knew (or even if the seller ought to have known) of the defective wall without informing them.[45] If the money paid by the buyers has not yet been combined with the seller's other assets, it may be argued that they have a right to the money in full, not merely a dividend in the estate of bankruptcy. If the seller is solvent, on the other hand, there is normally nothing to gain by claiming avoidance instead of terminating the contract.

3 *Romanic–Mediterranean jurisdictions*

(a) Italy

Arts. 1476 No. 3 and 1490 ICC establish an obligation of the seller to guarantee the buyer for defects in the goods sold if they make such goods unfit for use or impair its value substantially. However, the buyer can enforce the guarantee only if the defects were latent: that is, if the buyer did not know of the defects at the moment of the contract's conclusion or could not have discovered them using ordinary care (art. 1491 c 1 ICC). In this case, Michele and Joanna could take legal action against the sellers either to terminate the contract[46] or to ask for a reduction of the asset's selling price (art. 1492 c 1 ICC). They may also claim damages if the seller does not prove that, in absence of negligence, he was unaware of the defect (art. 1495 c 1 ICC) The legal action is subject to a period of one year under the statute of limitations, which runs from the time of delivery.[47]

[44] Section 4-8, Act Relating to the Sale of Real Property (3 July 1992), cf. Chapter 3.

[45] Section 33, Act Relating to the Conclusion of Agreements, etc. (*lov om avslutning av avtaler, om fuldmagt og om ugyldige viljeserklæringer*, 31 May 1918 No. 4).

[46] From which will result as a consequence the restitution to the buyer of the price paid and the reimbursement of expenses and payments lawfully made in relation to the sale under art. 1493 c 1 ICC.

[47] To bring the action, however, Michele and Joanna have to notify the seller of the defects within eight days of discovery. The legal action is subject to a period of one year under the statute of limitation, which runs from the time of delivery.

(b) Spain

Michele and Joanna have six months from delivery of the house to sue the seller for any defects in the dwelling that were hidden, or not visible, at the time of the sale which preclude normal use of the dwelling or detract from its use such that, if they had been known, the buyers would not have bought the dwelling or would have paid a lower price.[48] Such considerations include the purpose for the purchase, the buyers' ability to detect the defects in the course of their visit to the house (bearing in mind its location and the buyers' expertise, by reason of their occupations), the age of the house, the information supplied by the seller, the agreed price and so on, This will aid in determining whether the house is unfit for Michele and Joanna's intended use of it and whether, if they had known of the defects, they wouldn't have bought it at that price. If so, Michele and Joanna may choose to cancel the sale, and recover their costs from the seller, or obtain a proportionate discount on the price paid, as assessed by an expert. The seller is liable for the defects even if unknown to him or her at the time of sale; but if he or she knew of the defects and failed to disclose them to the buyer, he or she must also pay the buyer damages.

If the house was built using a licence dated after 6 May 2000, and less than ten years have passed since the delivery of the house, Michele and Joanna have a period of two years, from their discovery of the cracks to sue the developer, the builder and the architect for defects damaging the foundations, beams, floors, load-bearing walls or other structural elements directly compromising the mechanical strength and stability of the building.[49] Developers and builders are required to arrange ten-year insurance against these liabilities; without this insurance, a notarial act of declaration of new building works (*declaración de obra nueva*) cannot be entered in the *Registro de la Propiedad*.[50]

(c) Portugal

The fact that the house has defects does not compromise or alter the transfer of property. However, the fact that the construction is seriously defective might have consequences.[51] I will illustrate three situations:

[48] Arts. 1484 *et seq.* CC.

[49] Art. 17 *Ley 38/1999, de Ordenación de la Edificación* (a statute on building standards).

[50] Arts. 19 and 20 *Ley 38/1999*.

[51] Visible defects (*defeitos aparentes*) are presumed to be known, even if there was no examination of the thing.

where Michele and Joanna had bought a house from a non-professional seller; where they bought the house from a professional seller or developer; where Michele and Joanna are professionals.

If Michele and Joanna had bought a house from a non-professional seller, Arts. 913ff. CC dictate the legal regime for the sale of defective things. Therefore, if the property has a defect that causes a depreciation in value, prevents the fulfillment of its function, or does not have the qualities advertised by the seller, the acquirer has to give notice[52] of the defect within a year after acknowledgement of the defect and within five years of the contract's conclusion. If the buyer gives evidence of the defects affecting the quality of the property, she has the following legal rights against the seller: to have the property repaired (art. 914 CC);[53] reduction of the price (art. 911 CC); rescission of the contract (art. 905 *ex vi* 913 CC); compensation for damages incurred (if the seller is responsible for the defect). If the seller had an intentional fault, he has to compensate the acquirer for damages that he would not have suffered if he had not concluded the contract; if the sale was due to the acquirer's mistake, he is liable only for damages resulting from the contract (arts. 908 and 909 CC). These rules constitute a default legal regime. Therefore, the parties could have agreed otherwise (art. 912 CC).

If Michele and Joanna had bought a house from a professional (normally, a developer), special rules on consumer protection would apply. According to art. 5 Decree Law 67/2003, of 8 April,[54] in a business to consumer (B2C) transaction, the seller is responsible for the defects of the building unless he proves conformity with the contract. Unless proved otherwise, any lack of conformity, which becomes apparent within five years of delivery of the goods, shall be presumed to have existed at the time of delivery. Notice might be given by the owner within one year after knowledge of the defect and compensation within three (art. 5-A (3) Decree Law 67/2003).

If Michele and Joanna were professionals and had bought a house from a developer (the seller is also the builder of the house), art. 1225 CC applies. Art. 1225 CC, which applies to a B2B transaction, dictates that the seller is liable for damages for five years, if he has also constructed, repaired or modified the building. Liability exists if the building collapses completely, partially or has defects, whether or not

[52] Except if there was an intentional fault of the seller (art. 916 CC).
[53] This duty does not exist if the seller did not know the defect of the thing.
[54] As amended by Decree Law 84/2008 of 21 May.

those defects impinge upon the soil or the construction itself. Notice might be given by the owner within one year after the knowledge of the defect and compensation might be asked for within one year after notice (art. 1225 (2) CC).

(d) Greece

Michele and Joanna have bought the house in order to live in it safely. The defective construction of the house gives Michele and Joanna the right to sue the seller for non-fulfilment of the obligation to deliver the property free from actual defects[55] he had undertaken under the contract of sale.[56] While in principle, the issue of whether the defect was latent or visible makes no difference in the above answer, in practice, if Michele and Joanna accepted the house despite the visible defects without protest this could be interpreted as an implied acceptance of the defects.[57]

Furthermore, Michele and Joanna have the right to rescind the contract[58] since the defect is essential. If they do so, both parties of the contract have an obligation of restitution: the seller will be obliged to return the money and Michele and Joanna will have to re-transfer ownership of the house to the seller.

Finally, the buyers can also choose to claim only a reduction of the price of sale due to the existence of defects or repair of the defects, if the former is not impossible.[59]

4 *France and related jurisdictions*

(a) France

The disorders compromising the solidity of the building allow, within ten years from the acceptance of the work done, engagement of the ten-year guarantee of the builder.[60] This guarantee works by rights and benefits, not only to the client, but to the successive owners of the real estate. It allows, in particular, the execution of the repair works. The effectiveness of this legal guarantee is assured by a system of compulsory insurances: insurance of damages signed by the client, and insurance of liability contracted by the builder.[61]

[55] Arts. 534, 537 and 540 GCC. [56] Arts. 534, 535, 537 and 540 GCC.

[57] If the defect is discovered within the first six months after the transfer of property, it is presumed by law that the defect existed at the time the product was purchased (art. 537 § 2 GCC).

[58] Art. 540 GCC. [59] Art. 540 GCC. [60] Arts. 1792 and 1792-4-1 C. civ.

[61] Art. L. 241-1 *et seq.* of the Code des assurances.

The possible guarantee of the builder excepted, Michele and Joanna can try to sue their seller for the guarantee of the hidden defects.[62] But this guarantee does not apply to the conspicuous defects that the buyer could notice during the visit of the building, which is probably the case with cracks. Furthermore, in practice, this guarantee is spread almost always by a clause according to which the buyer takes the building as it is. This clause is valid except when the buyer proves the *mala fides* of the seller, who had knowledge of the hidden defect. This guarantee offers an option between the reduction of the price or the avoidance of the sale, in addition to the liability of the *mala fide* seller.

Finally, it is possible to look for the liability of the real estate agent, even the notary if, because of their experience, it was possible to detect the defect. They are, indeed, held by an obligation of information and advice.

(b) Belgium

In the Belgian law, the answer to this question depends upon the factual issue as to whether or not these cracks were already visible at the moment the purchase agreement was completed.

The seller is liable for the latent defects of the house, which makes the house defective for the function to which it was built or diminishes the value of the house in such a way that Michele and Joanna would not have bought the house if they had known of the defect (art. 1641 BCC). The seller will even be liable for these defects if he did not know that the house was defective. However, he can, in the latter case, insert a clause in which he exonerates himself from this contractual liability. A clause, exonerating him from his liability for defects that he knew of will remain ineffective.

The seller, however, is not liable for the defects that are visible and could be observed by Michele and Joanna (art. 1642 BCC). If the cracks were already visible at the moment of the purchase, Michele and Joanna will not be entitled to sue the seller.

The question does not address the issue of whether the construction company can be sued by Michele and Joanna. In the Belgian law, it is possible that Michele and Joanna can directly sue the construction company within ten years after the delivery of the construction works, on the basis of a direct contractual claim. According to art. 1792 BCC, a building constructor is liable for a period of ten years from the moment of the

[62] Art. 1641 *et seq.* C. civ.

delivery in relation to the contracting party. This is a claim connected to the quality of the owner of the house ('qualitative right'). If this quality is transferred (e.g. if ownership of the house passes) the claim passes immediately and, by operation of law, also to the buyer, even if each party has not expressly agreed. This is an application of the '*accessorium sequitur principale*' principle.

5 *England and related jurisdictions*

(a) England

If the seller made a misrepresentation regarding the state of the property, Michele and Joanna have an equity to rescind the contract *ab initio*, allowing them to set it aside.[63] The transfer of title can then be undone. However, without any such misrepresentation, Michele and Joanna are expected to inform themselves of the quality of the property prior to purchase,[64] with the consequence being that the defect does not allow them to undo the transfer of title.

Alternatively, Michele and Joanna can sue the seller for damages to recover the cost of repair if there was an express term in the contract regarding the quality of the premises and the seller was in breach of that term. Also, if the seller made representations regarding the cracks that the seller knew to be false or had no reasonable grounds to believe were true.[65] However, in the absence of any such contractual term or misrepresentation, they have no right to recover the cost of repair from the seller, unless the seller built the house.[66]

(b) Scotland

Although some older authorities may suggest otherwise,[67] modern law dictates that there is no *implied* term in a contract of sale that guarantees the physical condition of the building, nor would such a term normally be expressed. So, in the absence of actual misrepresentation, Michele and Joanna would have no remedy against the seller.

[63] See, e.g., Charles Harpum, Stuart Bridge and Martin Dixon, *Megarry & Wade's The Law of Real Property*, 7th edn. (London: Sweet & Maxwell, 2008), paras. 15-112 to 15-113.

[64] See Kevin Gray and Susan F. Gray, *Elements of Land Law*, 4th edn. (Oxford University Press, 2005), para.12.9

[65] See Harpum, Bridge and Dixon, *Megarry & Wade's The Law of Real Property*, para.15-104.

[66] As to which, see W.V.H. Rogers, *Winfield & Jolowicz on Tort*, 17th edn. (London: Sweet & Maxwell, 2006), para. 9-32.

[67] Robert Black, 'Practice and Precept in Scots Law', 27 *Juridical Review* (1982), pp. 47ff.

As mentioned in the answer to question 2, all houses offered for sale must have a home report that includes a property survey. Although Michele and Joanna do not have a contract with the surveyor, the surveyor is nonetheless liable to them in delict (tort) if the report has not been prepared with reasonable skill and care.[68] Their claim would be for damages. In addition, if Michele and Joanna instructed a survey of their own, they would have a contractual claim in the event that the survey was carried out negligently.

(c) Ireland

There is no obligation on the vendor's part to disclose physical defects in the property and the general rule in conveyancing transactions is '*caveat emptor*'. However, if the vendor, knowing of the defect, misrepresented the house as structurally perfect and this statement caused Michele and Joanna to enter into the contract[69] or if the property was misrepresented as structurally sound in the contract for sale,[70] they will be able to apply to court to have the conveyance set aside. Alternatively, Michele and Joanna have the option of suing for damages to cover the cost of the repairs. If the seller built the house himself he may be liable for negligence for damages to cover the cost of the repairs.[71] Michele and Joanna's solicitor should have advised them to arrange for an architect/engineer to carry out a structural survey of the house before they entered into a contract and, if he failed to do so, they may be able to sue their solicitor for negligence.[72]

[68] Housing (Scotland) Act 2006 (Consequential Provisions) Order 2008, SI 2008/1889.

[69] If the vendor honestly believed his representation, once the deed of conveyance has been executed, it cannot be rescinded. See *Brownlie* v. *Campbell* (1880) 5 App. Cas. 925 at 937; *Lecky* v. *Walter* [1914] 1 IR 378 at 385–6.

[70] This remedy will be available if the vendor knows that the description is false or if it is a substantial misdescription so that the purchaser is not getting what he was entitled to under the contract, see *Flight* v. *Booth* (1834) 1 Bing. NC 370 at 377; *Linehan* v. *Cotter* (1844) 7 Ir. Eq. R. 176 at 179.

[71] See *Ward* v. *McMaster* [1985] IR 29. Other remedies may be available to purchasers who entered into a building agreement with the seller, but that does not appear to be the case here.

[72] In *O'Connor* v. *First National Building Society* [1991] ILRM Lynch J held that there is a *prima facie* duty on the purchaser's solicitor to advise his client that he ought to have an independent survey by a suitably qualified person and the onus is on the solicitor to show why this duty should not apply in the particular case.

Case 9

Oliver has agreed to buy a house in a residential area from Polly but has not yet paid the price. Polly has not yet moved out and Oliver has not yet moved in. A week after the agreement, a young mother was walking past the house pushing her baby in a pram. A plant fell off the balcony and injured the child.

(a) Who would be responsible for the damages?
(b) Would your answer differ if what fell was not a plant but part of the roof?

(A) Foundational Concepts for Understanding Case 9

The rules about the transfer of ownership are also important in answering a significant question in relation to the process of circulation of immovables such as who should be responsible for the damage caused to a third person due to the fall of a part of the immovable or the furniture inside it.

Nevertheless, according to the reports, the most important issue in determining the person responsible is not who the owner is but who is in possession of the immovable. Another thing to consider is if there is any difference between a plant on the balcony falling versus a part of the roof. Because in some systems, in part (b) of the question, the responsibility lies with the owner, independent of negligence (objective responsibility) or, alternately, depending on it (subjective responsibility), while in part (a) of the question, the one who is in possession is the one who pays compensation in the case of negligence.

For instance, in the case of Germany, it is not important who the owner is, but who the possessor is, and there are differences among the two subquestions. The situation is similar in Austria. In the Netherlands, in part (a), no matter who owns or is in possession of the house, it is usually the occupier who creates the danger. In part (b), the possessor would be also responsible.

In the Nordic countries, liability lies with the owner, if the owner has taken possession. A possessor could also be liable, if it should keep the property in good repair, such as a long-term leaseholder. In Finland, Sweden and Denmark liability requires negligence; however, in Denmark a low threshold for negligence is applied. In Norway strict liability for damage caused by immovable property is, to a certain extent, established by case law, and a distinction as to the liability for immovable and movable parts can therefore be drawn. In the other Nordic countries, such a distinction is less clear.

In Italy, if the plant is not considered an annex element (*pertinenza*) of the house, the claim will be brought against the person who has acted negligently. In part (b), there would be a difference, as the one who has obtained the legal title of the house remains generally liable for damages that may result from those structures that are within his legal control and which he has a duty to supervise, among which are the walls, including the roof and ledges.

In Spanish law, under the CC, the head of the household inhabiting a house or a part of it is liable for any damage caused by objects thrown out of or falling from that house. In the case of part (b), if the damage is caused by part of the roof falling, the owner would be responsible. The situation is similar in Belgium, France, Greece, Portugal and Turkey.

In England, if the claim is brought in negligence, it will be brought against the person who has acted negligently. According to this, the one who is in occupation of the house would be responsible, regardless of whether or not he or she is the owner. Part (a) has to be solved according to who is in possession of the immovable. There is no difference from part (b). In Scotland, the one who is occupying the house is liable in delict (tort) if the accident results from her negligence. There is no difference at all from part (b). In Ireland, the answer to part (a) does not differ much, but there is a difference from part (b) if the roof collapsed due to a defect in the original construction. In that case, the builder may be liable for negligence. However, if the deterioration was due to inadequate maintenance, the negligence action should be brought against Polly.

(B) The Jurisdictions (Presented by Related Jurisdictions)

1 *Germany and related jurisdictions*

(a) Germany

(a) If somebody has acted culpably (intentionally or negligently) and unlawfully this would constitute a tortious act and this person would be liable for the damages.[1] The responsibility can result from neglecting the general duty of care to safeguarding the public in general (*Verkehrssicherungspflicht*) to ensuring that (potential) danger doesn't result in damage to third parties.

As long as Polly is still owner and in possession of the house it is her duty to safeguard the house. Failure to do so could result in responsibility for the damages. Oliver cannot be made responsible for the damages unless he takes possession of the house or becomes sole owner of the house by agreement registration.

(b) The answer is basically the same. The difference is that §§ 836 and 837 BGB provide for a special liability in damages of a possessor of the land or the building due to the severing of parts of the building in consequence of defective construction or inadequate upkeep. Compared to the general rules of delict, the aforementioned provisions contain a reversal of the burden of proof in favour of the victim. Therefore, it is more difficult for Polly to escape liability resulting from §§ 836 and 837 BGB than from the general rules of delict applicable in the part (a) of the question.

(b) Austria

(a) The child, who is legally represented by his parents, will not be successful with a claim against Oliver. He has to sue the occupant of the house, which is still Polly. It is not necessary that she be the owner of the house as well.[2]

The relevant cause of action is laid down in § 1318 ABGB. According to this provision, the occupant who has the actual power of control over the building is (*inter alia*) liable if someone suffers damage due to the dropping out of a dangerously placed or overhanging object.[3] The liability can be expanded to rooms or places that belong to the

[1] § 823, para. 1 BGB. [2] OGH 18.2.1986, 2 Ob 657/85, JBl 1986, 523.

[3] See also Friedrich Reischauer, in Peter Rummel (ed), *Kommentar zum ABGB, II*, 3rd edn. (Vienna: MANZ Verlag, 2004) § 1318 mn 3.

immovable (such as a balcony of a house or flat, outdoor area or a roof garden).[4] A mere spatial connection is deemed to be adequate. It is legally assumed that there is a certain chance of loss. Fault is not generally required, although the blame of default (omission) remains central. The plaintiff is supposed to avert damage, causation and dangerousness.[5]

Polly could exonerate herself from liability by giving proof of the fact that she acted carefully. For this purpose, she would have to demonstrate (for instance) that the plant was fixed on the balcony or something to that effect.

Polly's special liability does not exclude the general liability (laid down in §§ 1295ff. ABGB) of other persons. But yet, Oliver can't be made responsible because they have made a purchase agreement on the house.

(b) By answering the alternative question, we have to apply § 1319 ABGB since this time, pieces of the building (roof tile, parts of cornice)[6] have detached. Parts of the roof are not 'hanging' within the meaning of § 1318 ABGB.

The aggrieved party has to provide proof of the impairment and highlight the fact that the defendant has been the occupant of the defectively constructed building at the time of injury.[7] The injured child does not have to substantiate Polly's fault that means a shifting of the burden of proof.[8] § 1319 ABGB constitutes, not an absolute, but a fault-based liability. It is likely that, in our case, the child will be entitled to a compensation claim. But Polly can again try to furnish a proof of exoneration by arguing that she took reasonable care to avert any kind of danger[9] (e.g. by ensuring that periodic reviews of the roof have been undertaken by a master roof tiler).[10]

(c) The Netherlands

(a) If it is a small plant and the plant falling over is not caused by a defect in the building, the question of who is liable for the damage is,

4 Cf. OGH 23.4.1998, 2 Ob 90/98v, ZVR 1999/23; OGH 26.1.1999, 4 Ob 179/98x, NZ 2000, 42.

5 Friedrich Harrer, in Michael Schwimann and Georg E. Kodek (eds.), *Praxiskommentar zum ABGB, VI*, 3rd edn. (Vienna: LexisNexis, 2006), § 1318 mn 17.

6 See judgments OGH 8.9.1931, 1 Ob 718, ZBl 1932/43; OGH 15.10.1964, 6 Ob 99/64, EvBl 1965/256 = RZ 1965, 28.

7 Reischauer, *Kommentar zum ABGB, II*, § 1319 mn 16.

8 Herbert Schimetschek, *Schadensfälle rund um das Haus* (Vienna: MANZ Verlag, 1981), p. 369 (370).

9 Harrer, *Praxiskommentar zum ABGB, VI*, § 1319 mn 15.

10 OGH 4.2.1930, 4 Ob 59/30, SZ 12/94 = JBl 1930, 322.

in principle, unrelated to questions of property law, such as the passing of ownership and possession. The person who placed and maintained the plant in its dangerous position can be held liable, if all requirements for liability are met. This will normally be the last occupant of the house. Only after the transfer of possession can the new possessor be held liable from the moment that he should have realised there was a plant in a dangerous position.

Under art. 6:174 BW, the possessor of a building can be held liable for damage caused by the building if the requirements for liability are met. The article will be relevant if the fall of the plant is caused by a defect in the building or if the plant box is so large and heavy that it should be regarded as part of the building. Normally, the possessor of the building will be the owner. The sales contract obliges the seller not only to transfer ownership of the land and building but also to transfer possession of it to the buyer. Ownership passes only when the transfer deed has been registered. In principle, the moment when possession is transferred can freely be decided by the parties. Commonly, however, the parties do not make any express agreement as to the passing of possession. For the application of art. 6:174 BW this will not pose any problems, as art. 6:174 (5) BW presumes that the person who is registered as owner of the building is the possessor of the building.

(b) If, during a storm, a roof tile properly fastened onto the roof falls off and causes damage, the possessor of the building is not liable under art. 6:174 BW, nor under any other legal norm. A roof tile falling off the roof may be considered a defect if it has not been fastened properly or if, for example, the tile was loose after a storm and the possessor did not repair the roof within a reasonable period of time.

In the above example, the seller is still the owner and possessor of the land. Signing the transfer deed and transferring possession will take place only after the buyer has paid the purchase price in the hands of the notary. If, in our example, anyone is responsible for the injury at all, it is the seller. He is still the possessor of the building.

(d) Turkey

(a) According to art. 49 TCO, whoever unlawfully causes damages to another, whether wilfully or negligently, shall be liable for damages. Thus, Polly would be liable for the damages. Oliver would not be liable.

(b) After the realisation of the sale contract and the registration in the Land Register, the new owner would be responsible since the owner of a building shall be liable for the damage that it causes due to its faulty design or construction or inadequate maintenance.[11] In this case, Oliver would be liable.

2 *Scandinavian jurisdictions*

(a) Finland

(a) A house has to be kept in such a condition that no accidents or harm are caused to persons passing the house. Things falling down from the house are typical reasons for damages. Accidents or harm caused in this way are indications of negligence and negligence, here, means a tort. Negligence, as a tort, is a reason for damages.[12] The negligence in these kinds of cases is, however, presumed (as in contractual relations). In addition, it is difficult to be excused from the liability.[13]

The person who is responsible for taking care of the house is liable for the damages as well. If no one else has taken care of the house, the owner who has the possession of the house is liable.[14] In addition, there can be many liable persons. If the house is a part of a piece of real estate, the date the valid contract (deed) was signed is normally decisive when the house is sold. Oliver is liable if the possession of the house is his at the moment of the accident.

The possession of the house might belong to the vendor even after contracting. The parties can agree on the vendor withholding possession. Moreover, a purchaser's breach of contract can entitle the vendor to withhold possession if the purchaser has not yet received the possession. In these cases, Polly as a possessor of the house may still be liable. It is even possible that Polly and Oliver are both liable.

In this respect, paying the price, as such, does not make any difference. Even a suspension clause, together with a term of payment, does not make any difference. Agreed suspended paying or a suspension clause of ownership does not entitle a vendor to withhold possession of the house.

[11] See art. 69 TCO; Georg Wettstein, *The Swiss Code of Obligations with Turkish Alterations* (Zürich, 1928), art. 58; M. Kemal Oğuzman and M. Turgut Öz, *Borçlar Hukuku: Genel Hükümler, Gözden Geçirilmiş ve Genişletilmiş Dördüncü Bası* (İstanbul: Filiz Kitabevi, 2005), p. 613.

[12] 2:1.1 Tort Liability Act, www.finlex.fi/en/laki/kaannokset/1974/en19740412.pdf.

[13] KKO 2004:50 and KKO 2001:1.

[14] KKO 2007:62, KKO 1962 II 46, KKO 1968 II 98, KKO 1972 II 10, KKO 1983 II 105, KKO 1997:151 and KKO 1998:146.

In the case of a lease house, the rules applied are similar.

(b) There is no difference in the principles or rules regulating the responsibilities of owners of houses or other persons mentioned above. The quality of the fallen thing may influence the consideration of the level of required diligence. It seems that the duty to install a plant carefully does not differ, in this respect, in a significant way from the duty to maintain a roof in proper condition. The same rules are applied in the cases of snow or ice falling down from the roof.

(b) Sweden

(a) Anyone who has negligently caused a personal injury to another is liable.[15] Liability may, however, also follow from non-delegable duties. Owners and other possessors of real property have a duty to keep the property reasonably safe for visitors and passers-by.[16] If the owner or the possessor does not tend to deficiencies of the property that may cause harm, he or she may be liable. One may say that keeping the property safe is a form of a non-delegable duty.[17]

However, this does not mean that liability rises independently of fault, and it cannot be said that a possessor of real property is always liable when someone else has negligently made the property unsafe.[18]

As a rule, there is no vicarious liability outside of contractual relationships. Vicarious liability means that a person is responsible for someone else's actions. In accordance with the general rule, owners or possessors of real property do not bear any vicarious liability towards third parties for hired independent helpers' negligence.[19] This may, however, be the case when the legally independent helper is under the supervision of the owner or possessor.

(b) It may be negligent by the owner and possessor, Polly, to have plants on a balcony in such a manner that they may fall down and injure passers-by. Insufficient securing of roof tiles or other parts of

[15] 2:1 Tort Liability; *skadeståndslagen (1972:207).*

[16] 3:3 and 3:5 Orderly Act; *ordningslagen (1993:1617).*

[17] Cf. Jan Hellner and Marcus Radetzki, *Skadeståndsrätt*, 9th edn. (Stockholm: Juristförlaget, 2014), p. 158f. and the analysis of the Supreme Court judgment *NJA* 1947, 23. Cf. also Supreme Court judgments *NJA* 1963, 415 and *NJA* 2005, 372.

[18] Hellner and Radetzki, *Skadeståndsrätt*, p. 158. Supreme Court judgment *NJA* 1940, 550.

[19] Hellner and Radetzki, *Skadeståndsrätt*, pp. 144ff.

buildings may also be deemed as negligent behaviour. Oliver can hardly be found liable before taking possession.[20]

(c) Denmark

(a) Under the Danish law, the owner of a property has a duty to keep the building in good order and repair so that it does not cause harm to third parties or the general public. This duty passes with the delivery of the property – that is, the day that Oliver takes over the possession of the property from Polly, even if the agreement to sell the house is made (considerably) before that date.[21]

There is no strict liability for owners of a property for damage caused by the property (pollution cases excepted). Instead, there is a duty of care and the liability is based on negligence. However, the duty of care is extensive and even slight negligence will tend to suffice.

Polly (not Oliver) is, thus, potentially liable for the injury.

(b) The answer would not differ if what fell was a part of the roof.

(d) Norway

(a) If the plant fell down because someone acted negligently, that person will be liable.

Strict liability for damage caused by immovable property is, to a certain extent, established by case law. Such liability covers, for example, situations where parts fall from a house and injure someone passing by.[22] A buyer of a house is hardly liable under such rules before he has taken control of the house or, at least, could have taken control according to the contract. There is no legislation or clear case law regarding this question but it can be argued that an analogy can be drawn from the rule on passing of 'risk' (i.e. the rule on consequences for the obligation to pay the price when the property is damaged by chance).[23]

20 Hellner and Radetzki, *Skadeståndsrätt*, p. 160 discusses liability for previous owners' negligence, but it seems that such a responsibility requires that the new owner has taken possession.

21 Bo Von Eyben and Helle Isager, *Lærebog i erstatningsret*, 8th edn. (Copenhagen: DJØF, 2015), p. 107f.

22 See, e.g., Supreme Court judgments *Norsk Retstidende*, 1939, 766 and 1972, 965.

23 Section 2-4, Act Relating to the Sale of Real Property (3 July 1992).

(b) Arguably, strict liability should be the same for plants falling down if the plants are more or less permanently placed as parts of the decoration of the building. It seems doubtful, however, that the same rule should apply for plants that are placed more occasionally on a windowsill or a balcony. The reasoning in case law concerning building parts falling down is that these parts represent a 'characteristic and extraordinary risk', the consequences of which should not be borne by the person that happens to pass by.

3 *Romanic–Mediterranean jurisdictions*

(a) Italy

(a) If the plant is not considered an annex element (*pertinenza*) of the house, the claim will be brought against the person who has acted negligently, under art. 2043 ICC. So in this case, Polly could be found liable for negligence, regardless of whether the property had been transferred or not.

However, if the plant is considered part of the house, as an accessory firmly fixed to it, and has then fallen due to a defect in the house itself, the ICC identifies the legal owner strictly liable for the damages.[24] Oliver should be considered liable for any such damage arising from the house since, at the time the damage occurred, ownership of the house had been transferred to him[25] even though he had not yet taken material possession of it.

However, under certain circumstances, Polly could be considered liable. Indeed, even though the ownership of the house had been transferred at the time of the sale (arts. 1376 and 1470 ICC),[26] the absence of physical delivery will implicitly transform Polly into the holder (*detentore*) of the house in the interest of Oliver.[27] As such, Polly

[24] Art. 2053 ICC that states that the owner of a building is liable for damage caused by its dilapidated condition.

[25] Arts. 1376 and 1470 ICC provide that ownership of an immovable property is transferred at the moment of the conclusion of the contract, provided it is done in writing, although there was no registration nor delivery.

[26] The payment of the price and the delivery, in the Italian law, are considered merely ancillary obligations. See arts. 1476 and 1477 ICC regarding the duty to deliver the thing sold and art. 1489 ICC for the payment of the price.

[27] This conclusion follows from art. 1477 c 1 ICC that from the obligation of the seller to deliver the thing sold in the condition at time of sale, implicitly requires an obligation for him to take care of the immovable property in the interests of those who bought it. Indeed if the thing sold and not yet delivered perishes because of the seller's act, he will be considered liable in contract. This will relieve the buyer of

has a duty of care towards the object on behalf of the buyer for damages that could arise from the immovable property to a third party under art. 2051 ICC.[28]

(b) According to case law, in the case of the liability of bailees, the person in the best position to control the risks deriving from the thing should be considered liable.[29] So Oliver, by obtaining the legal title of the house, remains generally liable for damages that may result from those structures that are within his legal control and which he has a duty to supervise among which are the walls, including the roof and ledges under (b).[30] Whereas Polly will be held liable for all the things that are in her immediate control and over which she can intervene to prevent damage, as in the case of the plant under (a).[31]

(b) Spain

(a) Under the CC, the head of the household inhabiting a house, or a part of it, is liable for any damage caused by objects thrown out of or falling from that house.[32] The child (or, rather, his parents, as legal guardians) is thus entitled to recover damages caused by the falling plant from Polly, the occupant of the house. There is no action lying against Oliver, who neither inhabits the house nor has been placed in possession of it (there is no indication that he has received the keys or that the notarial act of sale has been executed (see answer to case 3)). If Oliver had already received the house, even if he hadn't yet moved in, the child – properly represented – could sue him, provided that the child showed that the plant fell owing to the ruinous state of the building as a result of a lack of necessary repair.[33]

the obligation to pay the price (art. 1465 c 1 ICC). See Rodolfo Sacco and Raffaele Caterina, *Il Possesso* (Milan: Giuffrè, 2000), pp. 243ff.

28 Art. 2051 ICC held liable for damages resulting from the thing everyone who should take care of them.

29 See Court of Cassation United Section, 11.11.1991, No. 12019, in *Giur. It.*, 1992, I, 1, 2218.

30 See Court of Cassation, 15.09.2008, No. 23682, in *Quotidiano Giuridico Ipsoa*, 2008.

31 See Court of Cassation United Section, 11.11.1991, No. 12019, in *Giur. It.*, 1992, I, 1, 2218.

32 Art. 1910 CC.

33 Art. 1907 CC. In its decision of 4 December 2007 (JUR 1243/2007) the *Tribunal Supremo* ruled on the liability of the tenant, the heirs to the property and the insurance company for damages caused to a pedestrian by a falling plant pot. The court confirmed the liability of the tenant, as occupant of the dwelling, under art. 1910; but with regard to the owner's liability under art. 1907 further ruled that, '[T]he proved facts contain not the slightest indication that the building was ruinous for lack of necessary repair, and the poor condition of the hoop holding the plant-pot, presented merely as an

(b) If the damage is caused by part of the roof falling, the child may again sue Polly, not as occupant of the house but as an owner failing to make the necessary repairs to prevent the ruin of the building. If the fragment of roof falls, not because of defective maintenance, but because of faulty construction, the child must sue the architect or the builder.[34]

The liability of the head of the household inhabiting a house, for objects falling from or thrown out of that house, and the owner's liability for the ruin of a building, are both 'objective' (i.e. strict). The victim needn't prove a lack of due diligence.

(c) Portugal

(a) If the plant fell off the balcony due to lack of diligence by Polly, she would be held liable for the injuries of the child on the basis of her wrongful negligence in the placing or securing of the plant (art. 483 CC). On the other hand, if the plant fell off the balcony due to a *force majeure*, Polly will not be held responsible. In respects to the plant, there is no action lying against Oliver, who neither inhabits the house nor has been placed in possession of it (there is no indication that he has received the keys).

(b) If the roof collapsed, and the deterioration was due to inadequate maintenance, the negligence action should be brought against Polly. Art. 492 CC presumes that the collapse of the roof was Polly's fault. It sets a reversal of the burden of proof: it rests with Polly to submit evidence that she had no fault in the accident.[35] Although Oliver becomes the beneficial owner once he enters into an enforceable contract for sale, this does not affect the obligation of Polly to maintain the property so long as she retains possession of it.

(d) Greece

(a) The injury of the child is a direct result of Polly's negligence in placing the plant on the balcony, in a place where it could fall off.

unconfirmed hypothesis within another hypothesis, cannot be simply ascribed to the owner of the building in the absence of further particulars on who installed the hoops the owner or the tenant – and at what time.'

34 Art. 1909 CC.

35 Decision of the Supreme Court of 10 May 2012, www.dgsi.pt (www.dgsi.pt/jstj.nsf/954f0ce6ad9dd8b980256b5f003fa814/9cb425625bbd959e80257a06003ded47?OpenDocument, last visited 28 November 2012).

Polly, as the owner of the house (the oral sales agreement has no effect and the ownership hasn't yet been transferred), has a duty to safeguard the house due to general duty of care and thus, is responsible for potential damages to third parties provoked by her possessions.[36]

Oliver can't be held responsible for the damages though, since he is not the owner of the house and there is no action or omission of Oliver that could be causally linked to the injury.

(b) If the injury was caused by a part of the roof, then the person responsible to restore the damages from the child's injuries is the lawful owner or occupant of the house, unless he proves that the fall is not a consequence of defective construction or inadequate upkeep (reversal of the burden of proof in favour of the victim).[37] In this case, the responsbility to repair the roof and ensure safety will (again) be attributed to Polly and not to Oliver (as long as Oliver has not moved in the house).

4 *France and related jurisdictions*

(a) France

(a) This case comes under the general regime of occupiers' liability, based by jurisprudence on art. 1384, para. 1 of the C. civ. It is Polly who is liable because she had custody of the plan.[38] This liability is totally independent of the identity of the owner of the house.

(b) Yes, because, according to art. 1386 of the C. civ., the owner of a building is liable for the damage caused by its ruin when it results from defective maintenance or structural fault. If the transfer of property has already taken place between the parties, Oliver is liable in his owner's quality. It doesn't matter whether he is not in possession and had not yet paid the price. However, we can assume that Polly is liable too because she kept custody of the plant, still in application art. 1384, para 1 C. civ., the accumulation of which the Court of Cassation admits from now on with art. 1386.[39] And if the cause of the fall is

[36] Any person who had put and maintained the plant in a dangerous position could be held liable if all the requirements for liability are met. In this case, ownership of the house is an unrelated issue.

[37] Art. 925 GCC.

[38] Cass. ch. réunies, 2 December 1941 (Franck): D. 1942, p. 25, note G. Ripert.

[39] Cass. 2ème civ., 23 March 2000, No. 97-19991: Bull. civ., II, No. 54 – Cass. 3ème civ., 8 February 2006, No. 04-19731: *Gaz. Pal.* 2006, jur. p. 2613, note A. Paulin.

neither defective maintenance nor a structural fault, Polly will be the only one responsible in application of art. 1384, para. 1.[40]

(b) Belgium

(a) As we have already pointed out above, ownership normally immediately passes to Oliver, except if the parties have postponed passing of ownership. It is frequent legal practice to contractually postpone the passing of ownership until the moment that the notarial deed is signed and the price is paid.

In this regard, Oliver is considered the owner from a theoretical point of view, but in legal practice Polly will frequently be the owner of the immovable.

The answer to the question depends upon the reason for the falling of the plant. If it is due to a lack of diligence by Polly, Polly will be held liable on the basis of her wrongful negligence for the injuries of the child. If Polly has not been negligent, it is possible that the falling of the plant is due to a defect in the plant or the balcony. As Oliver still controls the plant, he will be held liable on the basis of a non-wrongful liability (art. 1384, para. 1 BCC). This would be the case if there is a defect, even if Polly has not committed a wrongful act at all.

(b) If part of the roof collapsed and fell on the child, art. 1386 BCC should be applied. According to this provision, the owner of the good is liable for the damage pursuant to the collapse of a building when this collapse is due to lack of maintenance or to a defect in the building. There is a presumption that the collapse is due to one of these reasons. This would make Oliver liable if the parties did not contractually postpone the transfer of ownership. The owner will be strictly liable, meaning that he will be liable even if he did not commit any wrongful act. However, it is possible that the sales agreement stipulates that Polly must compensate Oliver for the responsibilities he would encumber against third parties.

5 *England and related jurisdictions*

(a) England

(a) If the claim is brought in negligence, it will be brought against the person who has acted negligently. Polly has remained

[40] Cass. 2ème civ., 22 October 2009, No. 08-16766: Bull. civ., II, No. 211.

in occupation of the house and so is the only person who could have acted negligently (Oliver cannot have any duty to take care of Polly's belongings). If Polly was negligent in the way she left the plant on the balcony, she will be liable in damages for the injury caused to the child.

Similarly, any liability that might arise under the Occupiers Liability Act 1957 (which seems unlikely given the young mother and child did not enter the house), would rest on the occupier rather than the owner and so could only affect Polly.

(b) The answer does not change in any material respect.

(b) Scotland

(a) Polly, as owner (and presumably occupier) of the house, is liable in delict (tort) if the accident was a result of her negligence in the placing or securing of the plant.[41] In a case like this, it is possible that negligence would be presumed on the principle of *res ipsa loquitur*.

As Oliver neither owns nor occupies the house, he has no liability for the accident.

(b) The answer would be the same: Polly would be liable if it could be proved that the disrepair in the roof was a result of her negligence.[42]

(c) Ireland

(a) The claim will be in negligence against the person who acted negligently.[43] As Oliver has not yet moved in and Polly is still residing in the house, Polly was most likely responsible for placing the plant on the balcony and would owe a duty of care to anyone who is likely to be injured as a result of it being inadequately secured. If it can be proved that she was in breach of that duty of care, she will be liable in damages.

[41] A possible alternative basis of liability is the *actio de posito vel suspensis* of Roman law, although there is some uncertainty as to whether this has been received into Scots law. See, e.g., *McDyer* v. *Celtic Football and Athletic Co Ltd* 2000 SC 379; Willam Gordon, *Roman Law, Scots Law and Legal History* (Edinburgh University Press, 2013), Chapter 13. Again liability requires fault.

[42] *MacColl* v. *Hoo* 1983 SLT (Sh. Ct.) 23 (car damaged by a slate which had blown off a roof).

[43] See Eoin Quill, *Torts in Ireland*, 4th edn. (Dublin: Gill & Macmillan, 2014).

(b) If the roof collapsed due to a defect in the original construction, the builder may be liable in negligence. However, if the deterioration was due to inadequate maintenance, the negligence action could be brought against Polly. Although Oliver becomes the beneficial owner once he enters into an enforceable contract for sale,[44] this does not affect the obligation of Polly, as vendor, to maintain the property so long as she retains possession of it.[45]

[44] Section 52 (1), Land and Conveyancing Law Reform Act 2009.

[45] Section 52 (2) (a), Land and Conveyancing Law Reform Act 2009. Note, also, that under the general law the purchaser must bear any loss or damage caused to the property by such things as fire, flood, or storm between the date of the contract and completion of the transaction and, if the general law applies, the purchaser should be advised to insure the property to cover that period. However, usually, the Law Society General Conditions of Sale (2017 edn.) apply and general condition 43 reverses the general law and provides that the vendor is liable for such losses during this period.

Case 10

Charles has a ten-year lease of a flat owned by David. Five years after the commencement of the lease, David sells the flat to Edward, who wants to move in immediately.

(a) Can Edward move into the flat?
(b) Would your answer differ if this was a business lease?

(A) Foundational Concepts for Understanding Case 10

The information required in this question was whether or not an acquirer of the immovable is bound by a lease that has the immovable as object. In some countries, there are special rules if the lease is a business one.

We could generally say that in most European legal systems, leases only create obligations. But in Germany, for instance, the lease contract confers the lessee a right of possession against the acquirer of the immovable. In Austria, Italy and Spain, such contracts may, if certain conditions are fulfilled, be entered in the Land Register and this would produce proprietary effects '*erga omnes*'. In Greece, the effect of protecting the lessee is obtained even though there is no inscription in the Land Register but only if the deed of lease had a certified date (bearing an official state stamp). The situation is similar in France and Belgium. In the latter, the lease contract could be registered at the Registration Office, which is a special tax administration.

In the Netherlands, the transfer of possession normally happens when the transfer deed is signed. The buyer will then become the possessor despite the existence of the lease. However, this does not entitle him to terminate the lease. He will be bound by the lease and will be unable to live in the flat himself. Alternately, in Turkey, the new owner is not bound by the lease contract. The situation is similar in Portugal where the CC contains the rule '*emptio non tollit locatum*'. According to this, the acquirer of the right of the landlord will succeed in his rights and duties without prejudice of registration provisions.

In the Nordic countries, it is possible to register the lease in the Land Register so that it would be opposable to the new acquirer. Registration is rather unusual, however, in Sweden, Denmark and Norway, as a buyer has to respect any tenant's rights within the limits of mandatory legislation leases even if the lease has not been registered. Registration is a means of protection for more comprehensive rights of the lessee, for example a long-term contract.

In England, Ireland and Scotland, leases are regarded as constituting a proprietary right and could be registered under certain conditions. Nevertheless, in England, if the lease was not registered, it will be a mere equitable lease. As such, it will only bind the acquirer if the lessee was in actual occupation of the property at the time of the sale contract.

The information required in this question was, basically, if an acquirer of the immovable is bound by a lease that has the immovable as object. In some countries, there are special rules if the lease is a business one.

(B) The Jurisdictions (Presented by Related Jurisdictions)

1 *Germany and related jurisdictions*

(a) Germany

(a) No, Edward cannot get possession of the flat because the lease gives Charles a right of possession against Edward.[1] The lease is an obligatory contract normally effective only between its parties. But if the lessor sells the flat after surrender[2] to the lessee, the acquirer of the leased flat enters into the rights and obligations emerging for the duration of the acquirer's ownership under the lease.[3]

The lease can only be terminated if Edward gives notice of termination (*Kündigung*) to Charles. As Charles has a ten-year lease, and not a lease for an indefinite period of time, the rules regarding ordinary notice on

[1] §§ 985, 986, para. 1, 566 para. 1, 535, para. 1 BGB.

[2] In special cases the same applies even if the lessee is not yet in possession of the flat (§ 567a BGB).

[3] § 566, para. 1 BGB.

termination do not apply.[4] Before its expiry, the lease can only be terminated for cause in legally permissible cases.[5] An example of such a case would be that Charles is in arrears for two successive dates with payment of the rent.[6]

(b) No, the answer would not differ.

(b) Austria

(a) With the transfer of the ownership right, the new owner gains the legal status of the previous owner.[7] But, according to the ABGB, the new owner can terminate the contract according to the applicable statutory rules.[8] The new owner is not bound to the period of notice agreed upon in the contractual agreement and can terminate the contract[9] regardless of whether or not a ten-year period was agreed upon as binding.[10] If the contract (*Bestandvertrag*) was registered in the Big Book,[11] the buyer/new owner is bound to the right resulting from the tenancy agreement and does not have a special right of termination.[12]

The case has to be resolved differently if the Austrian Code on Tenant Law (MRG)[13] is applicable[14] to the contract. According to the respective

[4] In that case it would suffice that Edward needs the space as residence for himself or members of his family (see § 573, para. 2 No. 2 BGB).

[5] § 542, para. 2 BGB. [6] §§ 542, para. 2; 543, para. 2 No. 3 BGB.

[7] See further Gert M. Iro, *§ 1120 ABGB*, in Helmut Koziol, Peter Bydlinski and Raimund Bollenberger, *Kurzkommentar zum ABGB*, 2nd edn. (Vienna: Springer Verlag, 2007), Rz 5.

[8] § 1120 S 1 ABGB. See further Peter K. Apathy and Andreas Riedler, *Schuldrecht Besonderer Teil*, 3rd edn. (Vienna: Springer Verlag, 2008), Rz 8/78; Helmut Koziol and Rudolf Welser, *Bürgerliches Recht, II*, 13th edn. (Vienna: MANZ Verlag, 2007), p. 242.

[9] Contracts of limited duration are transformed into contracts of unlimited duration. Edward can therefore terminate the contract on the basis of the provisions for ordinary termination as applicable to contracts not limited in duration. Statutory provisions hold that it can be terminated within the notice period and contractual date as agreed upon in the contract or if none such was agreed upon according to the respective provisions (§ 1116 ABGB, § 560 ZPO). Furthermore Edward can terminate the contract if an extraordinary reason (*außerordentliche Kündigung*) according to the respective provision in the code (as stated in § 1118 ABGB) is given in the case at hand. He can do so without notice period (*Kündigungsfrist*) or upholding a contractual date for termination of the contract (*Kündigungstermin*). See further Koziol and Welser, *Bürgerliches Recht, II*, pp. 237, 242.

[10] See further Apathy and Riedler, *Schuldrecht Besonderer Teil*, Rz 8/78; Koziol and Welser, *Bürgerliches Recht, II*, p. 242.

[11] As according to § 9 GBG and § 1095 ABGB. See further Apathy and Riedler, *Schuldrecht Besonderer Teil*, Rz 8/80; Koziol and Welser, *Bürgerliches Recht, II*, p. 242f.

[12] See § 1120 S 1 ABGB.

[13] See for the application of the MRG in general Apathy and Riedler, *Schuldrecht Besonderer Teil*, Rz 8/7ff.; Koziol and Welser, *Bürgerliches Recht, II*, pp. 218ff.

[14] Application according to § 1 MRG.

provisions of the MRG, the new owner is generally bound to the contract as concluded by the buyer and the pre-owner.[15] Therefore, the new owner virtually enters into the contract (*Vertragseintritt*) which means that he is permanently bound to the contract as concluded by David and the restrictive provisions on termination that the MRG apply.[16] This applies even if the contract (*Bestandvertrag*) was not registered in the Big Book.[17]

(b) The applicability of the provisions of the MRG has to be established.[18]

(c) The Netherlands

(a) As a preliminary remark, it should be noted that the Dutch law does not acknowledge temporary ownership as such. A transfer of ownership for ten years will automatically be converted, by statute, into a grant of a usufruct for ten years (art. 3:85 BW).

As said before, the seller of a building is under an obligation to transfer possession of the building to the new owner. The transfer of possession normally happens when the transfer deed is signed. The buyer will become the possessor despite the existence of the lease. However, this does not entitle him to terminate the lease. He will be bound by the lease and will be unable to live in the flat himself.

Where the lease is contractual (*huur*), art. 7:226 BW provides that the new owner is bound by any lease agreement and automatically becomes the landlord. This applies, equally, to residential and business leases. If the lease is a limited real right (*erfpacht* or *opstal*), the new owner is bound because the limited real right works against the world and, hence, also against the new owner.

(b) The above answer would be the same in the case of a business lease.

15 Apathy and Riedler, *Schuldrecht Besonderer Teil*, Rz 8/81; Koziol and Welser, *Bürgerliches Recht, II*, p. 243. Apart from collateral/subsidiary agreements with exceptional content (*Nebenabreden ungewöhnlichen Inhalts*) to which he is bound only if he knew or had to know about them, or if the contract was registered.

16 § 30 MRG. Koziol and Welser, *Bürgerliches Recht, II*, p. 243.

17 See further Apathy and Riedler, *Schuldrecht Besonderer Teil*, Rz 8/81; Koziol and Welser, *Bürgerliches Recht, II*, p. 243. If the contract (*Bestandvertrag*) was registered, the new owner is additionally bound to collateral/subsidiary agreements with exceptional content (*Nebenabreden ungewöhnlichen Inhalts*).

18 § 1 MRG.

(d) Turkey

(a) This lease will be considered as a lease of residential and commercial premise, which is why art. 351 TCO will be applied. If the new owner wishes to get possession of the rented immovable and the renter objects to it, the new owner will have to sue for the evacuation. In order to do that, the new owner must first notify the renter within a month, starting with the acquisition date of the immovable. Edward must then wait six months before suing for the evacuation.[19] The new owner, if he wants, can exercise his right, within a month starting from the expiration of the term fixed in the contract, by suit. To be able to move in, the new owner must prove that his need for residence is real and true.

(b) No, it would not change.

2 *Scandinavian jurisdictions*

(a) Finland

(a) Agreements on residential lease are, most often, in force for an unspecified term (until further notice) in Finland. It is possible to agree on a fixed term but it is seldom as long as ten years. There is, nevertheless, no time limit imposed by the law.[20]

Rules regulating permanence of a lease agreement, when the object of the lease is conveyed, are given in the Code of Real Estate when the object is a piece of real estate. They are partly common and similar to the rules regulating double sale of a piece of real estate (see question 5). In this case, rules of the Act on Residential Lease supplement the rules of the Code.

The point of a departure is the priority in time. According to the major rule, Charles has priority.[21] It is possible, nevertheless, that Edward takes precedence. This exceptional solution presupposes, first, that Edward applies for the registration of the title in the Title and Mortgage Register before Charles applies for the registration of his lease. Second, Edward should not have known of the lease.[22] Edward cannot, however,

[19] Cevdet Yavuz, *Borçlar Hukuku Dersleri (Özel Hükümler), 6098 Sayılı Türk Borçlar Kanunu'na Göre Güncellenmiş ve Yenilenmiş 11. Baskı* (İstanbul: Beta, 2012), pp. 305–7; Mustafa Alper Gümüş, *'Yeni' 6098 Sayılı Türk Borçlar Kanunu'na Göre Kira Sözleşmesi (TBK. m. 299–356)* (İstanbul: Vedat Kitapçılık, 2011), pp. 364–8; Murat Aydoğdu and Nalan Kahveci, *Türk Borçlar Hukuku Özel Borç İlişkileri* (İzmir: İleri, 2013), pp. 607–10.

[20] 4.1 Act on Residential Lease, www.finlex.fi/en/laki/kaannokset/1995/en19950481.pdf.

[21] 3:7.1 Code of Real Estate.

[22] 13:3.3 Code of Real Estate.

enjoy the protection of good faith if Charles has taken possession of the apartment before its sale.[23] Hence, Charles has a strong position. He guarantees the permanence of his right by possession or by registration.

This is not, however, the case here according to Finnish law. In addition, these kinds of leases are not common in Finland. Most often, as in this case, the objects are flats and are therefore included in the movable property. In this case, the solution is regulated only by the Act on Residential Lease.

The lease agreement made by David and Charles binds Edward as the new owner of the flat on certain conditions. Charles' tenancy stays in force if he has taken possession of the flat before its sale or the sales contract contains a provision on the permanence of the leasehold.[24] Flats are not units of the system of real estate in Finland. Hence, it is not possible to register a lease or another right concerning a flat in the Title and Mortgage Register. Otherwise, the lease agreement may expire. Normally, the tenant's possession of the residence secures the continuation of the leasehold. Hence, if Charles had possession of the flat when David sold it to Edward or if some other of the conditions mentioned above were fulfilled, the lease agreement continues in effect and Edward will be Charles' new lessor.

The principle is that the original, or a new lessor, may not give premature notice if the leasehold is fixed term. There are, however, certain reasons to terminate even a fixed-term agreement before the end of its term. A local court may permit the lessor to give notice on the agreement that the lessor needs the flat for his own use or for the use of a member of his family for reasons which he could not have been aware of at the time when the lease contract was made or if the agreement's remaining in force until the agreed date would be patently unreasonable from the lessor's point of view.[25] In addition, as a general rule, it is possible to adjust or ignore a stipulation or a whole lease agreement if it proves to be unreasonable.[26]

As the new lessor, Charles naturally has the right to treat the lease contract as discharged on the grounds of the tenant's fundamental breach of contract.[27]

[23] 38.1 Act on Residential Lease 1.
[24] 38.1 Act on Residential Lease.
[25] 55.2 Act on Residential Lease.
[26] 6.1 Act on Residential Lease.
[27] 61.1–2 Act on Residential Lease.

As a rule, Edward cannot get possession of the flat before the end of the lease term. There are, nevertheless, certain exceptional possibilities for an earlier termination, as described above. The period of David's ownership has no significance in this situation.

(b) Agreements on business leases are, most often, in force for a fixed term. There is no time limit. A lease is a non-fixed-term lease unless otherwise agreed.[28]

The rules regulating the permanence of a business lease, when the object of the lease has been conveyed, are the same as in the case of a residential lease.[29] This holds true in the cases of both a piece of real estate and a flat as the objects of a lease. However, the rules permitting premature notice when a leasehold is fixed term are not applied.

(b) Sweden

(a) If David owned the flat it would, in Swedish law, be either an ownership apartment[30] or an apartment in a housing cooperative.[31]

Leases for housing purposes are generally protected with a direct right of prolongation.[32] Due to that, agreed long-term leases are rare, since the tenant has the right to stay in the apartment even if the agreed lease period has run out. However, when the apartment is an ownership apartment or an apartment in a housing cooperative, the tenants' rights are weak. It is enough that the owner of the apartment has an interest in using the apartment – for example, to sell it or to move into it – so that it would not be unfair if the lease would come to an end.[33] In this case, however, the landlord and tenant have agreed upon a lease period of ten years, which is rare but not impossible.[34] Then it would not be a question of prolongation of a rental period, but of a breach of contract on the part of the landlord. Whether the tenant, Charles, would be protected *vis-à-vis* the buyer, Edward, is not already solved by these rules.

If it is an ownership apartment, the sale of the apartment is also a sale of a registered property unit. When a landlord sells property encumbered by tenancy rights, the landlord is obliged to make a

[28] 3.1 Act on Business Lease (1995). Not available in English.
[29] See 31.1 Act on Business Lease. [30] Swedish: '*ägarlägenhet*'.
[31] Swedish: '*bostadsrättslägenhet*'. [32] 12:46 Land Code. [33] 12:46 (6)–(7) Land Code.
[34] 7:3 (1) Land Code. If the apartment was situated in an area under a detailed development plan, the maximum original lease period would be twenty-five years. Outside such areas, the maximum period is seventy years. These rules, however, do not prevent subsequent prolongation.

reservation of the lease in relation to the buyer of the property.[35] If the landlord fails to do so, the tenant might lose the lease. Apart from such reservations, the lease is preserved if either the tenant had taken possession of the apartment *and* the lease contract was made out in writing, or the buyer knew or ought to have known about the lease at the time when the sale was concluded.[36]

If the flat is a housing cooperative apartment, the legal position is unclear.[37] Housing cooperative apartments are not immovable property in a technical sense. The general rule for movable property is that a sale has priority over a lease and this holds even if the buyer knew about the lease. In that case, the buyer, Edward, would have priority over the tenant, Charles. However, it cannot be ruled out that the rules on sale of real property may be used by analogy,[38] whereby Edward's factual or constructive knowledge of the tenancy *or* the existence of a written contract in combination with Charles' possession would give Charles priority.

Even if Charles originally would have priority, the lease might be terminated later due to other rules. In this case, however, the lease period is ten years, which is binding. If the lease is for dwelling purposes, the tenant is given a direct right of prolongation even after that period.[39] That means that the landlord cannot oppose a prolongation of the lease without reasons of considerable weight. If it, however, is a lease of an

[35] 7:11 Land Code. Such a reservation is not necessary if the lease has been registered in the Real Property Register. Registrations of tenancy leases are rare, and lease contracts often contain a waiver clause, whereby the tenant refrains from having the lease registered. Waiver clauses are explicitly accepted in lease contracts, 7:10 (1) Land Code.

[36] 7:13 and 14 Land Code.

[37] Anders Victorin and Jonny Flodin, *Bostadsrätt med en översikt över kooperativ hyresrätt*, 4th edn. (Uppsala: Iustus Förlag, 2016), pp. 187ff.

[38] It would seem that 7:4 Land Code would prevent such an application, since the provision prescribes that the rules on rights of use in the Land Code are not applicable to cooperative leases. *But see* the appeal court decision RH 2002:9, where Chapter 7 of the Land Code was applied by analogy in a case where a tenancy lease from 1967 preceded the establishment of the housing cooperative and the letting of a competing cooperative lease at the end of the 1970s. The cooperative apartment owner later went bankrupt. The court stated that an analogy was appropriate due to the purpose of protecting socially vulnerable parties. Such competing cooperative leases are invalid since 1981, see 4:3 Housing Cooperative Act. A conflict might, however, appear in cases of older leases like the one tried in RH 2002:9, and in cases where an owner of a cooperative lease apartment first sublets to a tenant and then sells to a buyer of the apartment.

[39] 12:46 Land Code *e contrario*.

ownership apartment or a sublease of a cooperative apartment, the general rule is that the landlord is given priority.[40]

(b) If the flat was leased for commercial purposes, it would *prima facie* only differ with respect to the right of prolongation after the ten-year lease period. If the lease is for commercial purposes, the tenant is protected by an indirect right of prolongation.[41] The tenant may not claim the apartment, but compensation for termination without good cause.

However, another difference appears in the case of a commercial lease. Applying the rules on real property, by analogy, to cooperative apartments leased for commercial purposes does not seem as convincing as in leases for dwelling purposes.

(c) Denmark

(a) The contract of lease between Charles and David is made for a specific period of time. According to the Rent Act,[42] in that case, the starting point is that the tenancy expires at the end of the fixed period and not before. Thus, the general rule that a tenant may be given notice does not apply. Besides in a case of breach of the contract by the tenant, the tenancy may only be brought to an end if the contract of lease contains a specific provision to that effect.

As a starting point, a buyer of a flat has to respect any tenants' rights. This is the case regarding all rights protected by the mandatory provisions of the Rent Act. The tenant is protected, outright, by these provisions without registration in the Land Register being necessary. Rights that do *not* follow from the Rent Act's mandatory provisions *must* be registered in the Land Register to be protected against the lessor's creditors and contractual parties.

The Rent Act's standard set up is a lease made until further notice. Such leases may be terminated under certain preconditions. So if the lessee has more far-reaching rights, such as in this case where no notice may be given for ten years, Charles must register his right in the Land Register in order to be sure that he is protected.

Consequently, if Charles has had the tenant agreement registered on the property's gazette in the Buildings and Dwellings Register[43] or if

[40] 12:46 (1), (6) and (7) Land Code. [41] 12:57 and 12:58b Land Code.
[42] Section 80 (1), Act of 9 March 2016, No. 227 on Tenants (Rent Act).
[43] Section 7 (2), Rent Act.

Edward already knew or ought to have known of the conditions of the lease,[44] Edward cannot move into the flat.

Even if Edward was in good faith regarding the non-terminability and it was not registered in the Buildings and Dwellings Register, Edward cannot evict Charles from the flat. Instead, he will have to give notice according to the mandatory provisions of the Rent Act, meaning Charles will have to be given a year's notice.[45]

(b) Business leases are governed by the Business Lease Act, containing specific rules on termination and fixed-period leases.[46] However, the lessor's position is generally the same as for lessors of flats. As a result, this would not make any difference.

(d) Norway

(a) The lease may be registered in the Land Register, and if it is, it is protected against competing rights in the property, including the right of a new owner.[47]

The lease is regarded as a right in the property and the lease is older than Edward's right as a buyer. If Edward knew or ought to have known about the lease at the time when his right was registered he must respect the lease even if it is not registered. If Edward knew that there was a tenant, he would normally also be required to inquire as to the lease period.

Even where Edward was acting in good faith concerning the lease (or, as the case may be, concerning the lease period), Charles has some protection under an unregistered lease if he took possession of the flat before the registered title was transferred to a new owner. In that case, Edward may terminate the lease by giving an ordinary period of notice, which is normally three months. However, Edward must respect the lease until it has been terminated in this way.[48] Furthermore, Charles may invoke the protection of tenants under the Landlord and Tenant Act, implying that a court may set aside a notice of termination if it will have unreasonable effects.[49]

44 According to section 1 (2), LRA, good faith is a general precondition for gaining better title in competition between a transferor's contractual parties. See also the case U 1983.626; Western Court of Appeal.

45 Section 83 (1), Rent Act, in conjunction with section 84.

46 Section 63, Act of 16 December 2010, No. 1714 on Business Leases (Business Lease Act), and the following sections.

47 Section 20, Judicial Registration Act.

48 Section 22 No. 3, Judicial Registration Act.

49 Section 9-8, Landlord and Tenant Act (*lov om husleieavtaler*, 26. March 1999 No. 17).

(b) These rules are the same for residential tenancies and business tenancies.

3 *Romanic–Mediterranean jurisdictions*

(a) Italy

(a) No, Edward cannot take immediate possession of the flat, because Charles' lease takes precedence over Edward's right, provided that the lease is dated prior to the transfer.[50] Edward is bound by Charles' lease and thus he could move in only if legally able to terminate the lease. With regard to residential leases, the lease may be terminated if the reason for so doing arises from the need of the owner or any of his family (spouse, children, parents) or under other circumstances strictly specified by law and only on written notice, served at least six months before.[51]

(b) In the event of a business lease Edward cannot move in, if fewer than six years since the beginning of the lease have elapsed and the contract may still only be terminated on notice of at least twelve months before the end of the lease, motivated by need (for residential as well as business purposes) to use the immovable property for his own or his family's use.

(b) Spain

(a) The Spanish Urban Lettings Act was amended on 6 June 2013. Therefore, this case requires us to distinguish between those leases celebrated before 6 June 2013 and those celebrated after this date.

On the one hand, for those contracts celebrated before 6 June 2013, we would need to know if, when he signed the contract, Charles agreed to leave the flat in the event that David sold it. If not, then, for the first five years of the lease, regardless of whether the lease was known to Edward and whether or not it was registered with the *Registro de la Propriedad*, Charles would be entitled to stay in the flat.[52] If the lease – as is the case here – was agreed for a term exceeding five years, after the first five years Edward must continue to hold the lease for the remainder of the term only if he does *not* satisfy the following requirements (see the

[50] See art. 1599 c 1 ICC. However, as in this case, if the lease lasts more than nine years, Charles could oppose his right, for the entire duration of the contract, only if the contract is registered: art. 2643 No. 8 ICC.

[51] See art. 3 Statute 09.12.1998 No. 431 on residential leases.

[52] Art. 14 (1) *Ley 29/1994, de 24 de noviembre, de Arrendamientos Urbanos* (Urban Lettings Act 1994), before the 2013 amendment.

answer to question 1): acquisition in good faith, for value, from a person named in the *Registro* as entitled to transfer the right; and registration of the acquired right.[53] So, unless Charles registered his lease title with the *Registro*, thus depriving Edward of the ability to invoke unawareness of the existence of Charles' right, Edward is very likely to be able to move into the flat. David will have to indemnify Charles in the amount of five monthly rent payments (one for each remaining year of the lease, above the first five).[54]

If in the lease agreement Charles agreed to leave the flat in the event that David sold it, he would still be entitled to remain in the flat for the first five years; but, after the first five years, Edward could terminate the lease without the need to satisfy any of the above requirements – i.e. even if he were aware of the existence of the ten-year lease.[55]

On the other hand, if the contract was signed after 6 June 2013, the sale of a leased dwelling does not oblige the buyer to hold the lease for the remainder of the term – regardless of when the sale took place – unless the tenant's right was registered with the *Registro de la Propriedad*.[56] Therefore, if Charles did not register his right, and Edward was unaware of the existence of Charles' right[57] and registered his acquisition (see the answer to question 1),[58] Edward could move into the flat, although Charles would be entitled to remain in the premises for three months after Edward notified him of his intention. Charles would also be entitled to the damages he might have suffered because of the breach of the contract.[59] If Charles' right was registered or Edward knew about the existence of the lease, he would have to hold on to it.[60]

(b) If this was a business lease, there would be no legal restrictions in the tenant's favour.[61] Edward could terminate the lease if he acquired the premises for value; he need not have known about the lease;

[53] Art. 34 Mortgage Act 1946.

[54] Art. 14 (2) Urban Lettings Act 1994, before the 2013 amendment.

[55] Art. 14 (3) Urban Lettings Act 1994, before the 2013 amendment.

[56] Art. 14 (1) Urban Lettings Act 1994, amended by *Ley 4/2013, de 4 junio, de medidas de flexibilización y fomento del mercado del alquiler de viviendas.*

[57] It is a problem that Edward was unaware, because, according to art. 25 (5) Urban Lettings Act 1994, the sales deed has to mention whether the dwelling was leased. In any case, Charles would have to prove that Edward was aware.

[58] Art. 34 Mortgage Act 1946. The acquisition also has to be for value (Edward made a purchase) and from a person named in the *Registro* (as entitled to transfer the right) which is presumed since otherwise Edward could not have registered his right.

[59] Art. 14 (2) Urban Lettings Act 1994, after the 2013 amendment.

[60] Art. 14 (1) Urban Lettings Act 1994, after the 2013 amendment.

[61] Art. 29 Urban Lettings Act 1994.

Charles' ownership was registered; and Edward likewise registered his ownership.

(c) Portugal

(a) By a lease contract one party, the lessor, grants the lessee the use of a thing to another party, for a certain period of time, against payment of a rent (art. 1022 CC). The rule *'emptio non tollit locatum'* is set out in art. 1057, which provides that the acquirer of the right of the landlord will succeed in their rights and duties, without prejudice of registration provisions. Therefore, Edward is bound by the tenancy contract concluded between Charles and David and is not entitled to ask Charles to vacate the apartment.

The grounds for termination of a lease are: expiration (*caducidade*), termination by mutual agreement, and notice (here one can find a distinction between an 'ordinary notice' (*resolução*) and a 'specific notice' (*denúncia*). 'Specific notice' supposes that the landlord has an objective and legitimate interest in the termination of the lease contract (e.g. the landlord needs the premises for himself or his family, or has the intention to reconstruct it). Arts. 1101 and 1102 CC provide that the landlord is entitled to give specific notice of the lease contract if he needs the house to reside there, and owned the house at least for five years.

(b) If it was a business lease, the answer would be the same. As a rule, Edward cannot get possession of the flat before the end of the lease term.

(d) Greece

(a) In principle, due to the rule of privity of contract, there is no contractual link between Charles and Edward, and Edward would therefore be entitled to ask for possession of the flat. However, due to art. 615 GCC, Edward can terminate the contract regardless whether it was agreed that the lease would last for ten years, although prior notice has to be given to Charles.[62]

Nevertheless, in accordance with art. 614 GCC, if the lease is evidenced by a deed bearing an officially certified date and the lessor has transferred the property during the currency of the lease, the new owner shall be surrogated to the rights and obligations flowing from the lease. Therefore, if the deed of lease had a certified date (bearing an

[62] Two months prior notice according to art. 615 GCC.

official state stamp by a public servant evidencing the date) then Edward cannot move into the flat.

(b) In theory, the nature of the lease as a private or business lease should make no difference despite the fact of the existence of a special law for business leases.[63] In practice, almost all business leases have a certified date and thus the new owner is surrogated to the rights and obligations stemming from the lease.

4 *France and related jurisdictions*

(a) France

(a) No, in principle. Art. 1743 C. civ. requires that the buyer of a rented building continue the lease, provided that it is an authentic act or has sure date. The jurisprudence also protects the tenant when the buyer bought having knowledge of the lease.[64] The parties can agree otherwise, but only in the lease (not in the bill of sale) and provided that it is not a rural or commercial lease.[65]

(b) The principle is the same but cannot agree otherwise than provided in the law, as indicated above.

(b) Belgium

(a) In the Belgian law, the rule that a sale does not break a lease agreement applies under certain conditions. The lease agreement is enforceable against the buyer, who is obliged to comply with the lease agreement for at least the remaining nine years that are specified in the lease.[66] However, this rule is subject to the condition that the lease agreement has a 'fixed date' before the sales agreement.[67] This 'fixed date' can be accomplished by formalising the lease agreement in a notarial deed or by registering the lease agreement at the Registration Office, which exists for the purposes of tax administration and has nothing to do with the Hypothec Register.[68] This tax requirement thus has major civil law implications. Except if the leasing concerns a premise

[63] Presidential decree 34/1995.

[64] See for example Cass. 3ème civ., 11 February 2004, No. 02–12.76: *Bull. civ.*, III, No. 24.

[65] Art. 1743, al. 2 C. civ. and art. L. 145–15 C. com. [66] Art. 1743 BCC.

[67] In case of a commercial lease agreement or principal building lease agreement, a lease which has been executed since six months is equated to a lease with a fixed date: see art. 12 Commercial Lease Act of 30 April 1951, *Belgian Official Gazette*, 10 May 1951 and art. 9 Principal Building Lease Act of 20 February 1991, *Belgian Official Gazette*, 22 February 1991.

[68] Art. 1341 BCC.

which is used by Charles as his principal residence or a commercial premise,[69] the parties can contractually derogate from this rule by inserting in the lease agreement an 'eviction clause', providing that the lease agreement can be terminated by the new owner of the immovable. In the case of commercial leases, an eviction clause will only have limited effect (see the answer under (b)).

However, the foregoing will merely enable David to stay in the house for the nine-year period in the course of which the house is sold. If David wants to make the tenth year of the lease also opposable to Edward, he will have to ensure that the lease is authenticated in a notarial deed and registered in the Hypothec Register before the immovable is sold (art. 1 Mortgage Act). A lease agreement of more than nine years that is registered has effect in relation to the buyer for its entire duration.

(b) The lessee is even more protected in case of a business lease. A business lease that has been effective for more than six months preceding the transfer of the immovable is identified as a lease with a certain date.

Even if the business lease provides that the contract can be terminated if the immovable is transferred, the purchaser can only expel the lessee under certain conditions, which have to be expressly mentioned, (1) providing one year of notice and (2) within three months of the acquisition.

The conditions justifying the termination of the business lease agreement are:

(1) the fact that the lessee aims to use the immovable for personal purposes or for the use of their family members;
(2) The fact that the lessee aims to use the immovable for non-commercial activities;
(3) The fact that the lessee aims to rebuild the immovable (the expenses must exceed three years' of the lease price);
(4) Gross negligence of the lessee with regard to the lease obligations, including damage to the immovable.

5 *England and related jurisdictions*

(a) England

(a) If David's freehold title is registered with HM Land Registry, Charles' lease would need to be registered in order to be a legal lease as

[69] Art. 9 Principal Building Lease Act of 20 February 1991 and art. 12 Commercial Lease Act 1951.

it is a lease for more than seven years.[70] If Charles' lease is registered, a notice of the lease will have been entered in the Register[71] and so the lease will bind Edward.[72] As such, Charles can resist Edward's desire to take possession for the remaining five years of the lease.

If the lease was not registered, it will be a mere equitable lease. As such, it will only bind Edward if Charles was in actual occupation of the property at the time when Edward bought it from David.[73] Assuming Charles was actually in occupation at that time, the lease will bind Edward unless either (a) Charles' occupation would not have been obvious on a reasonably careful inspection of the flat and was not known to Edward; or (b) Charles was asked about his interest in the property prior to the disposition to Edward but he did not disclose his interest under the lease.[74] If the lease does not bind Edward, he is entitled to evict Charles and take possession for himself.

If David's freehold is not registered, then Charles' lease will bind Edward if it was created by deed so as to be a legal lease. If the lease was not created by deed, such that it was only an equitable lease, then it would only bind Edward if Edward bought David's freehold with notice[75] of the lease. Charles' occupation of the flat would most likely constitute constructive notice to Edward of Charles' rights, if proper investigation would have revealed those rights (which seems likely).[76]

(b) This would not alter the answer in any important respect. The question whether Charles was in actual occupation at the relevant time (the time when the contract between Edward and David was completed[77]) is a question of fact. While it need not necessarily involve the personal presence of the person claiming to occupy (e.g. it is possible for a caretaker to occupy on behalf of his employer), there must be some degree of permanence or continuity, but that should be satisfied by the presence of Charles' business on the premises.[78]

70 Section 27 (1) and (2) (b) (i), LRA 2002.

71 Section 27 and Sch. 2, para. 2 (b), LRA 2002.

72 Section 29, LRA 2002.

73 Sch. 3, para. 2, LRA 2002. An equitable lease cannot bind a purchaser of the land under Sch. 3, para. 1, LRA 2002: see *City Permanent Building Society* v. *Miller* [1952] Ch. 840.

74 Sch. 3, para. 2, LRA 2002.

75 As to which see Charles Harpum, Stuart Bridge and Martin Dixon, *Megarry & Wade's The Law of Real Property*, 7th edn. (London: Sweet & Maxwell, 2008), paras. 8-015 to 8-024.

76 *Kingsnorth Finance Co. Ltd.* v. *Tizard* [1986] 1 WLR 783 at 794.

77 See Sch. 3, para. 2, LRA 2002; *Abbey National Building Society* v. *Cann* [1991] 1 AC 56 at 88.

78 *Abbey National Building Society* v. *Cann* [1991] 1 AC 56 at 93.

(b) Scotland

(a) Assuming that Charles has taken possession of the flat, the answer is no. The position is regulated by the Leases Act 1449, which is one of the oldest acts still in force. Under that Act, a tenant who takes possession before the landlord transfers ownership to a third party can assert the lease in a question with that third party. It is sufficient for someone to possess on Charles' behalf, such as a subtenant or a member of his family.[79]

If the term of the lease had been more than twenty years, it could not have bound Edward without first being registered in the Land Register.[80] But it is not possible for a house to be leased for more than twenty years (although certain statutory protections can have the effect of extending a lease beyond that period).[81] A lease for twenty years or less cannot be registered.

(b) The answer would be the same.

(c) Ireland

(a) First, we will assume that the flat is not registered in the Land Registry. A lease for a term not exceeding twenty-one years where actual possession is in accordance with the lease cannot be registered in the Registry of Deeds.[82] Therefore, if Edward registers his deed of purchase in the Registry of Deeds, this will not automatically afford his deed priority over the earlier lease in favour of Charles. Older rules of priority[83] will determine whether Edward is bound by Charles' lease; it will depend on whether the lease was legal or equitable.

Section 4 of Deasy's Act 1860 provides that any lease exceeding a term from year to year must be in writing and signed by the landlord or an agent who has been authorised in writing to sign on his behalf. If Charles' ten-year lease complies with these formalities his interest will qualify as legal and bind Edward regardless of whether Edward was aware of its existence. This is because 'legal interests bind the world'. If the lease was oral and part-performed (as Charles went into

79 For a full discussion, see Cornelius van der Merwe and Alain-Laurent Verbeke (eds.), *Time-Limited Interests in Land* (Cambridge University Press, 2012), pp. 149–52.

80 Sections 2, 20B (2), Registration of Leases (Scotland) Act 1857.

81 Section 8, Land Tenure Reform (Scotland) Act 1974.

82 Section 32 (1) (ii), Registration of Deeds and Title Act 2006. Note that section 32 (1) (ii) permits the Minister to prescribe that leases for lesser periods are registrable.

83 These older rules applied before the registration of deeds system was introduced.

possession of the flat and paid rent),[84] Charles will be regarded as possessing an equitable lease,[85] which will bind a purchaser for value unless he had no notice of the interest.[86] The doctrine of notice fixes a purchaser with constructive notice of any interests that he would have discovered if he had made the enquiries and inspections that a reasonable purchaser would have made in relation to the property. One element of the doctrine of constructive notice is the rule in *Hunt* v. *Luck*,[87] which provides that a purchaser will be fixed with notice of any rights of a tenant in occupation regardless of whether he made enquiries about whether the tenant had rights in relation to the property. Therefore, if Charles was in occupation of the flat pursuant to an equitable lease when Edward purchased it, Edward will be bound by the lease and unable to get possession provided that Charles continues to comply with the covenants in the lease.

If the property is registered in the Land Registry, a lease for twenty-one years or less, where occupation is in accordance with the lease, cannot be registered as a burden on David's land.[88] However, such a lease constitutes an overriding interest that will bind a transferee for value regardless of registration.[89] Therefore, if Charles was in occupation of the property at the time of the transaction, Edward will be bound by the lease and will be unable to recover possession, provided that Charles continues to comply with the covenants in the lease.

(b) No.

[84] *Babington* v. *O'Connor* (1887) 20 LR Ir. 246. Note that oral agreements in relation to land are unenforceable unless the doctrine of part-performance applies.
[85] Under the Rule in *Walsh* v. *Lonsdale* (1882) 21 Ch. D. 9.
[86] Section 85, Land and Conveyancing Law Reform Act 2009.
[87] [1902] 1 Ch. 428.
[88] See section 69 (g), Registration of Title Act 1964.
[89] Section 72 (1) (i), Registration of Title Act 1964.

Case 11

Philip bought a field from Quentin. The field has direct access onto the main road through a gate; but it was a term of the agreement that Philip would also be allowed to use a road that passes through Quentin's adjoining farm in order to get to another road. Quentin sells the farm to Richard. Richard has put up a gate to prevent Philip from using the road.

(a) Is Philip still entitled to pass through the field?
(b) Would it make any difference if Richard knew about Philip's right before he bought the land?
(c) Would it make any difference if Richard was a close friend of Quentin; Quentin wanted to stop Philip using the road. Quentin and Richard agreed that Richard would buy the farm in order to prevent Philip from using the road, and that Richard would later sell the farm back to Quentin.

(A) Foundational Concepts for Understanding Case 11

In the questionnaire, it was agreed that servitude and easement would be equivalent terms. Nevertheless, there is a difference among them in many European countries. For instance, in Germany, easements are burdens of one piece of land for the benefit of the successive owners of another piece of land. In contrast, the holder of a restricted personal servitude is a particular person. So this difference dictates that the consequence is also divergent. In Germany, the right to use the road must be constituted by agreement and registration in order to be effective as a servitude. To register the servitude, the consent of the owner of the plot of land must be notarised. In Austria, this right to pass should also be registered in the Land Register to be effective '*erga omnes*'. On the contrary, it would not be regarded as a right *in rem*, but only as a contractual settlement that does not bind another party. The situation is similar in the Netherlands, where a notarial deed and registration of the deed in the Land Register is necessary.

In all of the Nordic legal systems, it is possible to register this right in the relevant real estate register so that the third acquirer of the immovable would be obliged to respect this right to pass. If the right is not registered, survival of the right depends on the knowledge of the buyer, however with somewhat differing thresholds of knowledge among the Nordic countries. In Sweden, there is also the possibility that the seller makes a reservation for the right in the sales contract, which *ex lege* has the effect of preserving the right for the beneficiary or for the benefiting property.

In Italy, as in Germany, there is also such a distinction. In order for a servitude to produce effects against third parties, it must be registered in the Land Register. In the other case, the right to pass for the benefit of a person is considered a personal right. To ascertain if that right produces an effect against third people, the agreement has to be interpreted in the sense that if it is a lease, it could also be enforceable against third people. The situation is similar in Spain, where the servitude should also be registered in the Land Register. The distinction also operates in Portugal, where only the real right must be constituted by a formal deed or a certified private agreement and registered. On the other hand, according to the Portuguese law, easements in gross servitudes constituted for the personal benefit of another person are not real rights. Even though they could be agreed upon by each party, they would only have '*inter partes*' effects. According to the Greek legal system, it is necessary to create an easement agreement contained in a registered notarial deed. The situation is also similar in France and Belgium.

In England, for this right to pass to constitute a legal easement, it is necessary that it was created by deed, held forever (i.e. a period equivalent to a fee simple absolute in possession) or for a certain period of time (i.e. a period equivalent to a term of years absolute) and was registered. If any of these requirements were not met, the easement would be an equitable easement. The first one would bind the new acquirer, the second one only if a notice of the easement had been entered in the charges register for the benefit of the farm. This situation is similar in Ireland. At this point, however, Scotland is more closely related to the French jurisdiction, as the servitude is a 'real right' that is constituted by a formal deed signed by the owner of the servient tenement and registered in the Land Register. In other cases, the access right would be no more than a contractual right enforceable against the other party to the contract.

According to part (c) of the question, in many cases, it has been answered that an action in tort could be brought if there was bad faith on the part of either party. Fraud or abuse of right has also been written about in this situation.

(B) The Jurisdictions (Presented by Related Jurisdictions)

1 *Germany and related jurisdictions*

(a) Germany

(a) He is entitled to pass if he can claim a servitude. German law distinguishes between two types of servitudes: the easement (*Grunddienstbarkeit*)[1] and the restricted personal servitude (*beschränkte persönliche Dienstbarkeit*).[2]

Easements are burdens of one piece of land (servient plot of land) for the benefit of the successive owners of another piece of land (dominant piece of land). In contrast, the holder of a restricted personal servitude is a particular person. The restricted personal servitude cannot be transferred to another person.[3] The holder of an easement or a restricted personal servitude is entitled to use a piece of land specifically (positive servitude) to prohibit certain acts on the servient tenement (negative servitude) or to exclude the exercise of a right, which arises out of the ownership of the servient tenement relative to the other tenement.[4]

Like any other land right, Philip's right to use the road must be constituted by agreement and registration in order to be effective as a servitude.[5] Unlike a declaration of conveyance, the agreement to constitute a servitude can be made orally. But in order to register the servitude, the consent of the owner of the plot of land must be notarised.[6]

If Philip did not register the right of way, the agreement is just a contractual right effective only between Philip and Quentin and does not bind Richard.

[1] §§ 1018ff. BGB. For a comparative study on easements and servitudes in German, English and Scots law see Egmont Neubauer, *Easements und Servitudes – Eine rechtsvergleichende Untersuchung zu Grunddienstbarkeiten im englischen und schottischen Recht* (Berlin: Duncker & Humblot Verlag, 2012); for a comprehensive account about German easements and personal servitudes see Claus Ahrens, *Dingliche Nutzungsrechte, Nießbrauch – Dienstbarkeiten – Wohnungsrechte*, 2nd edn. (Berlin: Erich Schmidt Verlag, 2007).

[2] §§ 1090ff. BGB.

[3] § 1092, para. 1 BGB. This does not apply to legal persons if certain conditions are fulfilled (see § 1092, paras. 2 and 3 BGB).

[4] §§ 1018, 1090, para. 1 BGB. [5] § 873, para. 1 BGB. [6] § 29 GBO.

(b) No, it would not make any difference.

(c) If Philip is entitled to an easement or a restricted personal servitude, Quentin and Richard are both bound by the right of way irrespective of the agreement between them.

If the right of way is of a contractual nature, the general rule of good faith (*Treu und Glauben*)[7] might prevent Richard from relying on his right to stop Philip from using the road.

(b) Austria

(a) Philip bought a farm plot from Quentin and was obviously granted[8] a right of way (*Wegerecht*) which had constituted an easement (*Grunddienstbarkeit*).

It is not clear, from the given facts, if Philip has properly registered that privilege (§ 481 ABGB). He is only authorised to keep on using the road that passes through the adjoining farm if the original agreement with Quentin has been recorded in the Land Registry. It is not operative towards Richard without an entry.[9] Then, it is not regarded as a right *in rem* but only as a contractual settlement that does not bind another party.

Therefore, the answer to the question above depends on the fulfilment of the registration requirement. Subsequently, it will be assumed that the correct modus has been complied with.

Philip will bring an action against Richard, refer to § 523 ABGB (*actio confessoria – Servitutenklage*), and state that he is the entitled person of the easement and had actually been aggrieved when the gate was put up. He will point out that the construction hinders him from using the other road and passing the adjoining farm. The claim aims to determine the existence of the servitude, remove the trespass, reconstitute the original state, prevent further disturbances and compensate for any losses.[10]

[7] § 242 BGB.

[8] Possible forms of acquirement are laid down in § 480 ABGB (here: acquisition by contract).

[9] Some authors (e.g. Bernd Schilcher, 'Offenkundige Servituten, Doppelveräußerung und Eintragungsgrundsatz', *JBl* 2005, p. 619) tend to assume that a servitude which is apparent for everybody (*offenkundige Eigentümerservitut*) even has to be effective without any agreement and registration. But obviously that is contrary to the law and not provided for in particular – cf. Helmut Koziol and Rudolf Welser, *Bürgerliches Recht*, I, 13th edn. (Vienna: MANZ Verlag, 2006), p. 429.

[10] Doris Kiendl-Wendner in Michael Schwimmer (ed.), *Praxiskommentar zum ABGB, II*, 3rd edn. (Vienna: LexisNexis, 2005), § 523 mn 3.

By way of exception, Philip could have also been granted an irregular personal servitude (*unregelmäßige persönliche Dienstbarkeit*), which only refers to a special person. In this case, the right is not connected to a piece of land and is, therefore, not subject to a legal successor.

Finally, Philip could consider applying for a right to a way of necessity (*Notwegerecht*) *per curiam*.[11] But this takes for granted that proper land use is impossible, as a connection to public roads is missing or unfeasible. In our case, these are not the circumstances since Philip still has direct access to the main road.

(b) No, it would not make any difference.

(c) Quentin and Richard are both bound by the right of way irrespective of the agreement between them. They can't circumvent the legal consequence of the registration.

If the right of way is only of a contractual nature, the general rule of good faith (*Treu und Glauben*) might prevent Richard from relying on his right to stop Philip from using the road.

(c) The Netherlands

(a) A real right of servitude would bind any subsequent owner of the servient land but, in case 11, no servitude has been created. The creation of a servitude requires a notarial deed and registration of the deed in the Land Register (art. 3:98 read with 3:89 BW). Case 11 speaks about a term of the sales agreement. Philip's right to pass through the field is, therefore, a mere contractual right. As a result, it does not bind third parties such as the new owner of the field.

(b) It makes no difference whether or not the new owner knew about this contract before he bought and acquired the land.

(c) Part (c) of the question is difficult to answer with certainty, as there is no authoritative case law on this point. It seems that in exceptional cases, Quentin may be liable in tort against Philip. In that very unlikely case, damages may be payable, in kind, so that the judge may decide that Quentin should tolerate Philip's use of the road.

(d) Turkey

(a) This term of the agreement cannot constitute a servitude on the field. Thus, Philip is not entitled to pass through the field since, in a

[11] Cf. Notwegegesetz 1896, RGBl 140; Koziol and Welser, *Bürgerliches Recht*, I, p. 428.

contractual relationship, the right accruing to a creditor is regarded as a relative right which may be claimed from the debtor only.[12]

(b) No, it would not make any difference.

(c) In this case, art 49, para. 2 TCO will be applicable. According to this article, every person who, *contra bonos mores*, wilfully causes damage to another is liable for compensation.[13] Consequently, Philip can sue Quentin and Richard for an appropriate compensation. Since the judge can determine the nature and the amount of the compensation, taking into account the circumstances and the degree of guilt, he, instead of compensation, may decide that Philip can use the road according to the clauses of the sale agreement.

2 *Scandinavian jurisdictions*

(a) Finland

(a) Finnish legislation ensures road connections to all pieces of real estate on a large scale. Needful connections, as rights to use existing roads situated in the areas of neighbours or as rights to build new ones onto the areas of neighbours and use them (the private road rights), are often established even *ex officio* and irrespective of possible agreements.[14] This is not the issue here, however. The dispute is not about a matter of necessary road connection, but of a supplementary road founded on a term of an agreement.

It is possible that an official road survey procedure applied by Philip, that includes its registration in the Real Estate Register, has taken place before the sale of the farm. Philip's application can be found on the contract between Philip and Quentin. The finished survey procedure guarantees the permanence of Philip's road right irrespective of possible transfers of ownership of the serving area. The permanence does not depend on the knowledge or good faith of the new owner of the serving land.

Despite the earlier survey procedure, including the establishment of the road right, it is possible to withdraw (cancel) a road right by a new road survey procedure applied by the new owner of the serving land.

[12] M. Kemal Oğuzman and M. Turgut Öz, *Borçlar Hukuku: Genel Hükümler Gözden Geçirilmiş ve Genişletilmiş Dördüncü Bası* (İstanbul, 2005), p. 24; M. Kemal Oğuzman, *Turkey*, trans. Toker Dereli (The Hague, London and Boston, MA: Kluwer Law International, 1996), p. 39.

[13] Oğuzman and Öz, *Borçlar*, p. 535.

[14] Act on Private Roads (1962) (not available in English).

Withdrawing presupposes that the charge of the road right, on the serving land, is disproportionately heavy compared with the benefit to the holder of the right.[15] When the road is merely a supplementary one, it is possible to cancel the road right depending on the charge imposed on the serving land.

A right to build or use a road, founded merely on a contract, differs essentially from a right established in an official survey procedure. The officially established road right exists between the pieces of real estate but the official survey procedure exists between the parties of the contract, and there are no guarantees of its permanency. Such a contract merely binds a party and his or her heir, a person who has accepted the contract and a transferee of ownership of the serving land who knew about the right when the transfer took place.[16] Hence, it is possible that Philip's road right does not bind Richard. It may expire and Richard may have the right to put up the gate. Moreover, it is normally not possible for Philip to apply a road survey in order to establish the expired road right, for a second time, because of its supplementary nature. Philip might be entitled to claim compensation from Quentin for the expiration of the road right founded on the contract.

(b) The legal significance of Richard's knowledge or good faith is given in (a) above.

(c) Collusion is acknowledged in the Finnish legal system. In this case, it would mean that Quentin and Richard made an improper agreement in order to violate or suppress the right of a third person (Philip). Parties have tried to take advantage of the rules governing the permanency of property rights in a way that is treated as an action in violence of *bona mores* (violence of good practice). This kind of agreement is voidable, or without effect, in relation to Philip.

An easier solution is founded on Richard's knowledge. As mentioned above, Philip's road right will stay in force if it is proved that Richard knew about the right when he bought the farm. Nevertheless, one should remember that, irrespective of its permanency against a new land owner, the road right can be withdrawn later by a road survey, as described above.

A term of a sale of a piece of real estate under which the vendor has the right to redeem the real estate at will or under which the vendor has

[15] 84.1 Act on Private Roads (1962).
[16] 21.1 Act on Private Roads (1962) and 3:8 Code of Real Estate.

the right of first refusal before the piece is conveyed to a new titleholder, is invalid.[17] They are two of the invalid clauses given in the Code of Real Estate. On the other hand, a voluntary conveyance of the farm from Richard back to Quentin would result in extra taxes and other transaction costs. Hence, a sale-back arrangement would not, in fact, be a practical solution.

(b) Sweden

(a) Philip is protected if Quentin sold the farm with a reservation as to Philip's right.[18] Even if Quentin did not make such a reservation, Philip's right is protected if it was registered in the Real Property Register[19] or if Richard knew, or ought to have known, about Philip's right.[20] If Richard acted in good faith, and Philip's right was extinguished, Philip is entitled to damages from Quentin.[21] If Philip's right is not extinguished, but Richard does not respect it anyway, Philip may also claim damages from Quentin.[22]

Philip's right might be either an easement,[23] or a right of use.[24] If it is an easement, it is not a personal right of Philip's but a right that is part of Philip's property that cannot be sold separately.[25] Easements must be put in writing by the encumbered owner, and they must state the properties in question and the nature of the easement.[26] Easements must be permanently appropriate for the use of the land.[27] Easements that fulfil these requirements may always be registered.[28] Easements that do not fulfil these requirements are, instead (mostly), rights of use.[29] If it is a right of use, it is Philip's personal right. Such a right may be registered only if the agreement has been made in writing.[30]

(b) As noted above, Philip's right is definitely preserved if Richard knew, or ought to have known, about the right.

(c) If Quentin and Richard intended to extinguish Philip's right, Richard is in bad faith, whereas Philip's right is unaffected.

[17] 2:11.1 Code of Real Estate. [18] 7:11 (1) Land Code.
[19] 7:11 (1), 17:1 and 17:2 (3) Land Code. [20] 7:14 (1) Land Code. [21] 7:18 (1) Land Code.
[22] 7:20 (1) Land Code. [23] Swedish: '*servitut*'. [24] Swedish: '*nyttjanderätt*'.
[25] 14:3 Land Code. [26] 14:5 Land Code. [27] 14:1 (1) and (2) Land Code.
[28] 7:10 (1) Land Code.
[29] Sten Hillert, *Servitut*, 2nd edn. (Uppsala: Iustus Förlag, 1984), pp. 17ff.
[30] 7:10 (1) Land Code.

(c) Denmark

(a) According to Philip and Quentin's agreement, Philip has a limited right over Quentin's property – an easement acquired by express grant. That right may be enforced against Quentin according to the Law of Obligations. However, as it is a right over real property, it must be registered in the Buildings and Dwellings Register at the Land Register to be protected against third parties who enter into subsequent contracts with Quentin in good faith.[31] If this has not been done, Philip cannot invoke the right to use the road against Richard.

(b) According to the Land Registration Act, a transferee claiming to have extinguished an existing right over a property must (1) be in good faith in regards to the conflicting right at the time of registration and (2) must register his own right in the Land Register.[32] The standard of good faith, in the Act, is lenient; only *actual knowledge* of the right or lack of knowledge due to *gross negligence* will suffice in establishing 'bad faith'.[33] As a starting point, Richard does not need to undertake any independent investigations or inquiries as to any conflicting right – all he has to do is check the property's gazette in the Buildings and Dwellings Register. However, if the transferee – Richard – suspects that a third party has an unregistered right over the property, he must undertake further enquiries to assess if his suspicion is true.[34]

(c) As stated above under (b), if Richard is not in good faith regarding the right of way when he files the deed for registration, he will have to respect the right of way even if it has not been registered. Generally, if Richard and Quentin are good friends, it would be considerably easier for Philip to establish that Richard was suspicious of the right and, thus, should have undertaken further inquiries. Alternately, Richard knew of the right and, therefore, must respect it.

In keeping with the above, only a transferee in good faith may extinguish another's right over a property. Thus, the 'construction' intended by Quentin and Richard would not procure the result intended, as both parties knew of the situation beforehand. In any case, the set up would be considered an attempt to evade the law and be invalid.

[31] Section 1, LRA. [32] Section 1 (2), LRA.

[33] Section 5, LRA; Peter Mortensen, *Digital tinglysning – rettigheder over fast ejendom*, 4th edn. (Copenhagen: Karnov Group, 2007), pp. 281ff.

[34] Hans Willumsen, *Tinglysningsloven med kommentarer*, 2nd edn. (Copenhagen: DJØF, 1997), p. 68.

(d) Norway

(a) Philip may register his right in the Land Register and, if he has done so, his right is protected against a new owner.[35]

(b) Philip's right is regarded as a right in the property and the right is older than Richard's right as a buyer. If Richard knows, or ought to know, about Philip's right at the time when his right is registered, he must tolerate Philip's right even if the right is not registered.

However, if Richard, at the time his right was registered, was in good faith – he did know, and ought not to have known, about Philip's right – he does not have to tolerate Philip's unregistered right. Richard's good faith depends on the circumstances; he may be in good faith even if he could see the road and the gate and they could be held to serve another purpose other than as access to Philip's field.

(c) If the sale of the farm is a mere sham, it will not affect Philip's right because, in that event, Richard would not be in good faith regarding Philip's right. Even apart from that (Richard might not know about Philip's right, but Richard and Quentin agree on a mere *pro forma* sale for some other purpose), a formal transaction without substance will not entail consequences of this kind.

The object of the agreement between Philip and Quentin is characterised as a *servitutt* where Philip is either the holder of the right or where the right lies with any owner of the field (Philip and subsequent owners).[36] Decisive for the possibility of Philip's registering the right is whether or not it is meant to bind, not only Quentin, but also new owners. This is, in principle, a question of interpretation of the agreement. There is no *numerus clausus* of rights that may be registered in the Land Register.

3 *Romanic–Mediterranean jurisdictions*

(a) Italy

(a) The answer depends on the identity of the right to pass granted by Quentin to Philip. By general principle, if the right to pass over Quentin's property is for the benefit of the field bought by Philip, it is

[35] Section 20, Judicial Registration Act.

[36] This is the terminology in legal doctrine and in some acts referring to such rights, but *not* in the main act governing the relationship between the owner of the property and the holder of the right, Act Relating to Restricted Rights of Use of Another's Property (*lov um særlege rådererttar over framand eigedom*, 29 November 1968 No. 1).

considered an easement (*servitù*) that, as a real right, is enforceable against any succeeding owners of Quentin's property. This is only the case, however, if they have been in a position to know that the property was burdened by the easement. This situation occurs only when the agreement establishing the servitude on the property still owned by Quentin has been registered before Richard's acquisition[37] or, in the case it has not been registered, whether the easement is clearly and explicitly mentioned in the deed of Richard's purchase of the property. In both cases, the easement could be enforceable against Richard.[38]

If, on the contrary, the right to pass is for the benefit of Richard, it is considered a personal right. To see if that right survives the transfer of the burdened property, the agreement has to be interpreted. If the agreement is interpreted as a lease (which, in Italy, is a contract) or similar contract, Richard's right to pass could be also enforceable against Richard.[39]

(b) To be enforceable against Richard, the easement must be registered or expressly mentioned in the sales contract in favour of Richard. The fact that Richard's knowledge of the existence of the easement may have come from different sources than those mentioned above is irrelevant.[40]

(c) It does not make any difference if the easement is registered, or expressly mentioned, in the sales contract in favour of Richard. On the contrary, Philip may rely on the absolute invalidity of the sham transaction, ex art. 1415 c 2 ICC, in order to reaffirm his right to pass.

(b) Spain

(a) The main difficulty is to ascertain whether Quentin created the right of way over his farm for the benefit of the field bought by Philip, whoever might acquire it subsequently (a 'real servitude'), or for the benefit of Philip. And, if for the benefit of Philip, whether Quentin and Philip intended to make that right of way a right *in rem* ('personal servitude') or a right *in personam*. All of this creates the problem of how to interpret the legal transaction. If the parties intended to create a right *in rem* – a right constraining Quentin's powers over his farm – that right

[37] See art. 2644 ICC.

[38] See Court of Cassation, 16.07.1997, No. 6485, in *Giur. It.*, 1998, p. 420.

[39] For the possibility of the third buyer of property enforcing the contract lease see case 10 above.

[40] The case law is crystal clear on that point. See for the most recent decision Cassazione 31.07.2006, No.17301, *CED Cassazione*, 2006.

affects any person succeeding Quentin in the ownership of the farm. But, if they intended to create a right *in personam*, the constraint applies only to Quentin and his heirs.

If, as would be most common, the right was created for the benefit of the field, then Richard would not be bound by the agreement between Quentin and Philip, but only if he acted in good faith. He must not have known of Philip's right at the time he bought the land. If Philip's right to pass through the sold farm was entered in the *Registro de la Propiedad* (together with the property itself), or was a right recognisable to Richard (e.g. because Philip used the road regularly),[41] Philip could oblige Richard to continue the observance of his right.

(b) If Richard knew about Philip's right before he bought the land, then even if the right were unregistered and there was no outward sign making such right recognisable, Richard would have to allow Philip to continue exercising his right.

(c) If Quentin and Richard agree to feign a sale to Philip's detriment, Richard is not acting in good faith. Philip could, if he manages to prove the existence of deception, continue to exercise his right.

(c) Portugal

(a) It is not clear whether the agreement between Philip and Quentin gives rise to a real right or to a mere personal right.

Under Portuguese law (art. 1534 CC), a servitude (easement in appurtenance) is a real right created by the owner of a piece of land, the servient land (*prédio serviente*), to benefit the successive owners of another piece of land, the dominant land (*prédio dominante*). The distinctive feature of this institution is that the charge is imposed on

[41] The case law is consistent in its view that a third-party acquirer is not protected if from the outward appearance of the acquired property he could perceive the defining elements of the state of affairs that might affect him. The *Tribunal Supremo*, in its decision 223/1993 of 15 March 1993 (RJ 1993/2277), ruled as follows: 'The statutory rule giving rise to the case and preventing the unregistered servitudes from having effect against third parties has been construed by this Court in the proper sense of depriving it of absolute and definitive force, because, even if such an encumbrance upon property is unregistered, when the third party is aware of it – because, as in this case, it is permanent, or because it is proved by other means – such third party may not rely on that lack of express registration [decisions SS. 8-5-1947 (RJ 1947\760) and 20-5-1992 (RJ 1992\4915)]: when the signs of a servitude are apparent, permanent and wholly outward, such undoubted appearance creates a publicity resembling registration [decisions SS. 17-5-1927, 5-4-1986 and 21-12-1990 (RJ 1990, 10591)].'

an estate to serve the estate belonging to another holder. Under this scope, commodities can be future or eventual. The holder of an easement is entitled to a limited use of a piece of land, e.g. passing through (positive servitude), or to prohibit certain acts on the servient tenement (negative servitude). Like any other land right, Philip's right to use the road must be constituted by a formal deed or a certified private agreement (art. 23 Decree Law 116/2008, of 4 July) and registered (art. 2 (1) (a) LRegC) in order to be effective as a real right enforceable against third parties. If Philip and Quentin have complied with these formalities, Philip has a right *in rem*, i.e. enforceable against third parties, to use the road that passes through the farm.

Under Portuguese property law, easements in gross (*servidões pessoais*), that is to say, to a personal benefit of another person, are not real rights. Restricted personal servitudes might be agreed upon by each party, but they will only have *inter partes* effects, according to the *numerus clausus* principle of property law (art. 1306 (2) CC). Unlike a declaration of conveyance, the agreement to constitute a personal servitude can be made orally or in a written deed. If the agreement between Philip and Quentin only constitutes a contractual right, it is effective only between them and does not bind Richard. Quentin, however, may be held liable before Philip for breach of contract.

(b) I will consider, first, the hypothesis where a real servitude has been created. Normally, Philip would know about Richard's right since the servitude should have been registered in order to be enforceable against third parties. If Philip had bought the land, and was unaware of the servitude, art. 905 CC applies. According to this provision, if the property is burdened, the contract is voidable, by reason of mistake or intentional fault. Cancellation of the burden would validate the contract, except if the existence of the burden had caused prejudice to the buyer or the buyer had already claimed the declaration of nullity of the contract. If there was intentional fault, the seller might compensate the acquirer for the damages he would have suffered if he had not concluded the contract (art. 908 CC). Mistake is also grounds to invalidate the contract and the seller is liable for damages resulting from the conclusion of the contract (art. 909 CC). Those rules constitute a default regime. Therefore, the parties might have otherwise agreed (art. 912 CC).

If Quentin and Philip had celebrated a mere personal right, Richard is not bound by it. It is not clear whether Richard is considered to be abusing his right (art. 334 CC) in putting up a gate to prevent Philip from using the road.

(c) As the servitude can be opposed against Richard, such a construction would normally not enable Richard and Quentin to prohibit Philip from exercising the road nearby the farm. If the servitude was not registered, or if Quentin had granted Philip only a personal right, Philip's right is not enforceable against Quentin. However, in such a scheme, Philip could certainly claim that Quentin was abusing his right (art. 334 CC).[42]

(d) Greece

(a) Greek law distinguishes between two types of servitudes: the praedial (real) easements[43] and the gross (personal) easements.[44]

The praedial easement is a real right (albeit, limited) created by the owner of a piece of a land (*servient estate*) to benefit another piece of land (*dominant estate*) and its successive owners. The burden lies on the piece of the land (right *in rem*). It is not important who the owner is. The successive holder is entitled to a limited use of an immovable, e.g. passing through (*positive servitude*) or prohibiting certain acts (*negative servitude*).

Similar to the real easement, art. 1012 GCC foresees the right to a way of necessity if a connection to a public road is missing from a plot of land.

Gross easements are real rights (although limited) as well. However, the holder is a particular person (right *in personam*) and his right cannot be transferred to another person merely by acquiring ownership to the property.

Like any other land right, servitudes can only be obtained by virtue of an agreement contained in a registered notarial deed in order to become public.[45]

Philip has validly obtained a right to pass from the field belonging to Quentin. If this right is the result of just a contractual agreement between Quentin and Philip, in accordance with the principle of privity of contract, this agreement has no effect on Richard. If, however, Philip validly obtained and registered the easement before Richard's acquisition, then it also binds Richard and all of the potential owners

[42] Mário J. de Almeida Costa, *Direitos das Obrigações* (Coimbra: Almedina, 2016), p. 83, and Luís M. Menezes Leitão, *Direito das Obrigações I*, 13th edn. (Coimbra: Almedina, 2016), p. 101.

[43] Art. 1118 GCC. [44] Art. 1142 GCC. [45] Arts. 1121, 1033 and 1192 GCC.

of the adjoining farm (since it is real easement and a right *in rem*). If, however, the parties intended to only create a right *in personam*, the constraint applies only to Quentin. Art. 1132 GCC provides Philip an *actio confessoria*; Philip can bring in an action against Richard asking for his right to be recognised and the original state to be reconstituted, to prevent further disturbances and compensate for any losses.

(b) The element of knowledge bears no importance in this case.

(c) The true intention of Richard and Quentin bears no importance.

4 *France and related jurisdictions*

(a) France

(a) The answer depends on the qualification of the right of passage granted by Quentin to Philip; what comes under the appreciation of the inferior jurisdictions. If the parties created it as an easement, it is likely that a real right is enforceable against the successive owners of the subjected real estate. Philip can, thus, require the demolition of the obstacle to his right of passage. If, on the contrary, the parties stipulated only a simple personal obligation, Richard benefits from the principle of the relative effect of the contracts, unless he obliged himself in his turn.

(b) No. If it is only about a personal obligation, it is, in principle, not transferred to the buyer, even if it arose in relation to the real estate.[46] Thus, Richard is not in connivance with the debtor in the breach of the obligation.

(c) This is a fraud intended to release Quentin of his obligation to leave the passage. It is ineffective if the right of passage has the nature of an easement. If it is a personal obligation, French law does not recognise it. We can think of the Paulian action, which would allow Philip to declare the transfer inoperative against Richard because of the fraud. The civil liability could also protect Philip: if Richard is a third party, he is collusive in the breach of contract, which pulls his tortuous liability at the same time as the contractual liability of Quentin. The right of passage could then be imposed on both people in charge by way of compensation in kind.[47]

[46] See for example Cass. 3ème civ., 16 November 1988, No. 88-11298: *Bull. civ.*, III, No. 163; D. 1989, p. 157, note Ph. Malaurie.

[47] We can even wonder if the obligation does not become again enforceable as Philip becomes again the owner, because the transfer to Richard is in this analysis only a temporary obstacle to the execution and not a cause of extinction.

(b) Belgium

(a) Philip will succeed on the condition that the sales agreement, containing the right of way, has been registered in the Hypothec Register. The right of way is a conventional servitude. With each property right, a servitude can be opposed against the buyer of the land which is the object of the servitude. A servitude is attributed with a right to follow the object into whosever hands it may pass.

(b) If the servitude has been registered in the Hypothec Register, it does not make any difference whether Richard had actual knowledge of the existence of the right. He is deemed to have 'objective knowledge'. If the public notary, who will, in legal practice, obtain the information from the Hypothec Register, did not inform Richard, he will be subject to a risk of liability.

If the servitude had not been registered,[48] the servitude could be opposed against Richard if the latter had knowledge, or ought to have had knowledge, of the existence of the servitude. Once again, art. 1 Mortgage Act comes into play: property rights can be opposed against third parties with a competing right, on the condition that they are in good faith.

It is questionable whether the fact that the way is visible renders Richard in bad faith. The fact that there are external signs of the existence of the servitude could be proof of Richard's bad faith if the external signs unequivocally point to the existence of a right of way.[49]

(c) As the servitude can be opposed against Richard, such a construction will normally not enable Richard and Quentin to prohibit Philip from exercising the road nearby the farm. If the servitude was not registered, it is clear from the facts that Richard is in bad faith and that the existence of the right will, therefore, be opposable against him.

5 *England and related jurisdictions*

(a) England

(a) The response to this question assumes that the title to Quentin's farm has been registered at all times and that both the transfer of

[48] Because the sales agreement had not been registered if the servitude was part of the sales agreement or because the separate agreement vesting the servitude was not registered.

[49] Belgian Supreme Court 13 December 2002, Pasicrisie 2002, 2412 and *Rechtskundig Weekblad*, 2002-03, 1384, note V. Sagaert.

the field to Philip and the transfer of the farm to Richard occurred after 13 October 2003.[50]

Philip's right to pass over Quentin's land is a right of way. It was created by way of express grant. As such, it is a legal easement if, and only if, (i) it was created by deed[51] and (ii) it was held forever (i.e. a period equivalent to a fee simple absolute in possession) or for a certain period of time (i.e. a period equivalent to a term of years absolute)[52] and (iii) it was registered.[53] If any of these requirements were not met, the easement is an equitable one.

If Philip's right of way is a legal easement, it will bind Richard when he purchases Quentin's farm,[54] as the easement will appear in the charges register for Quentin's farm.[55] If Philip's right of way is an equitable easement, it will not bind Richard when he purchases Quentin's farm unless Philip had entered a notice of the easement in the charges register for Quentin's farm.[56]

If the easement is binding on Richard, Philip remains entitled to pass through the field.

(b) This would not affect the preceding analysis.

(c) This would probably not affect the preceding analysis. The mere fact that the vendor and purchaser conspire together to render someone else's rights unprotected does not cause those rights to become protected.[57] Hence, assuming that Philip's easement would not otherwise be binding on Richard after he buys Quentin's farm, Richard is able to sell the farm back to Quentin free of the easement.

This is subject to one caveat. Richard's conduct could potentially constitute the tort of inducing a breach of contract, in which case Philip could sue Richard.[58] Richard will only be liable if he entered into the transaction with Quentin knowing that it would be inconsistent with

50 This is the date on which LRA 2002 came into force. The assumption is made so as to avoid the impact of complicated transitional provisions.

51 Section 52 (1), LPA 1925. 52 Section 1 (2) (a), LPA 1925.

53 Section 27 (2) (d), LRA 2002. 54 Section 29 (2) (a) (i), LRA 2002.

55 Registration of an easement requires that a notice be placed in the servient tenement's (i.e. Quentin's) Charges Register and that the easement be placed in the dominant tenement's (i.e. Philip's) Property Register: sections 38 and 59 and Sch. 2, paras. 7 (2) (a) and (b), LRA 2002 and Rule 5 (b) (ii), Land Registration Rules 2003.

56 Under section 32, LRA 2002.

57 *Midland Bank Trust Co. Ltd.* v. *Green* [1981] AC 513 at 527–8.

58 *Midland Bank Trust Co. Ltd.* v. *Green* [1980] Ch. 590 at 626.

contractual obligations that Quentin owed to Philip.[59] If so, a court can potentially order Richard to return the farm to Quentin so that the contract can be performed;[60] the court cannot order that Richard be bound by the easement itself.[61] Ordering re-transfer in this way is very unusual, although it might be justified here on the basis that Quentin and Richard are only entering into the transaction as a contrivance to free Quentin from his obligations. The argument might fail, in the present scenario, on the basis that the contract to create the easement merges into the easement once it is granted[62] and, as a result, Richard's conduct does not induce Quentin to breach any contract. Alternatively, Philip could potentially sue Richard for the tort of conspiracy,[63] but the remedy is likely to be a claim in damages for the loss suffered by Philip as a result of losing the right to pass over Quentin's farm.

(b) Scotland

(a) In order for a successor, such as Richard, to be bound, it would be necessary for the access right to be constituted as a right of servitude. A servitude is a property (i.e. 'real') right which, in this context, allows the owner of one property (known as the 'dominant tenement') to make use of a different property (known as the 'servient tenement'). A servitude is constituted by a formal deed signed by the owner of the servient tenement (Quentin) and registered in the Land Register against both the dominant tenement (Philip's field) and the servient tenement (Quentin's farm).[64]

In the absence of registration, the access right would be no more than a contractual right enforceable against the other party to the contract (Quentin). Not being a party to the contract, Richard would be under no obligation to allow Philip to pass through the field. Philip's only remedy against Quentin is for breach of contract – and only then

[59] *D.C. Thomson & Co. Ltd.* v. *Deakin* [1952] Ch. 646 at 694; *OBG Ltd.* v. *Allan* [2007] UKHL 21 at [39]–[43]; Anthony M. Dugdale and Michael A. Jones (gen. eds.), *Clerk & Lindsell on Torts*, 19th edn. (London: Sweet & Maxwell, 2006), paras. 25–49.

[60] *Esso Petroleum Co. Ltd.* v. *Kingswood Motors (Addlestone) Ltd* [1974] QB 142 at 156.

[61] *Law Debenture Trust Corp.* v. *Ural Caspian Oil Corp. Ltd* [1995] Ch. 152 at p. 166.

[62] As to merger, see Roderick P. Meagher, John D. Heydon and Mark J. Leeming, *Meagher, Gummow & Lehane's Equity: Doctrines and Remedies*, 4th edn. (Sydney: Butterworths LexisNexis, 2002), paras. 40-050 to 40-055.

[63] *Midland Bank Trust Co. Ltd.* v. *Green (No. 3)* [1982] 1 Ch. 529 at p. 539.

[64] Section 75 (1), Title Conditions (Scotland) Act 2003.

if the contract contains a term, express or implied, which guarantees a permanent right of access.

(b) If the access right was constituted as a servitude, knowledge – or lack of it – would make no difference. Philip would be entitled to pass through the land.

The position is, or may be, different if the access right was merely a contract. Admittedly, knowing about a contract to which one is not a party is not, under normal circumstances, sufficient to make one bound by its terms. But if the contract contained an obligation to grant a servitude to Philip, and if Richard acquired the land knowing that that obligation was unfulfilled, Richard is now bound to do what Quentin did not (i.e. grant the servitude).[65]

(c) It would make no difference if the access right was constituted as a servitude.

If the access right was only contractual, the key question would be: did the contract fall when Quentin transferred the land to Richard? Unless this was the subject of an express term, it is hard to see why it should. Assuming the contract survived, Philip's remedy against Quentin will depend on the location of ownership. For as long as the farm belongs to Richard (and subject to the effect of bad faith discussed in (b) above), Philip's remedy will lie in damages for breach of contract because the access right can no longer be exercised. But if ownership reverts to Quentin, then Philip can require performance of Quentin's obligations – or, in other words, he can reassert his right to take access.

(c) Ireland

(a) It can probably be assumed that Quentin's land was registered in the Land Registry at the time he sold the field to Philip, as nearly all agricultural land in Ireland is registered.[66] Philip and Quentin clearly intended that Philip would have a right of way over a road through Quentin's adjoining farm. The Deed of Transfer, which Philip received when he completed the purchase of Quentin's field, should have

[65] This is another example of the application of the rule against 'offside goals', mentioned in the answer to case 5.

[66] This is because towards the end of the nineteenth century the Land Purchase Acts were enacted which enabled tenant farmers to purchase their holdings from their landlords and section 22, Local Registration of Title (Ireland) Act 1891 triggered a compulsory first registration of the land purchased under such schemes.

included a grant of a right of way over Quentin's farm and his assent to the registration of the right of way as a burden on the rest of his land.[67] Normally, Philip's application to register his ownership of the field would have included an application to register the right of way over Quentin's farm. If the right of way was registered as a burden on Quentin's farm when Richard purchased it, Richard will be bound by it and Philip will be entitled to use the road.[68] If a formal grant of a right of way was never executed or if a grant was executed but it was not registered as a burden on Quentin's folio Richard, provided he has registered his Deed of Transfer, will not be bound by it. In such circumstances, Philip would no longer be entitled to use the road.

Although an unregistered grant of a right of way or a specifically enforceable agreement between Philip and Quentin to grant Philip a right of way gives rise to an equitable interest in Quentin's land (known as an equitable easement), it will not bind Richard unless Philip protected this interest by registering a caution or an inhibition on Quentin's folio.[69] Such an interest does not amount to an overriding interest, which binds a transferee for value even if unregistered. Only easements, created by grant before Quentin's land was registered for the first time in the Land Registry or certain easements that arise by prescription or implication, are overriding interests that will bind Richard regardless of whether they are registered.[70] As Quentin's land was probably registered in the Land Registry many years ago, the right of way could not have been created before the first registration of the land. Also, it was a term of the agreement that Philip was to have a right of way over Quentin's farm, which rules out the possibility of an easement by prescription[71] or an

[67] Section 69, Registration of Title Act 1964 sets out a list of burdens which may be registered as affecting registered land. It includes any easement that was created by express grant after the first registration of land.

[68] Section 52 (1), Registration of Title Act provides that on registration pursuant to a transfer for valuable consideration, the transferee takes ownership subject to all registered burdens and any unregistered section 72 burdens (or overriding interests).

[69] Sections 97 and 98, Registration of Title Act 1964.

[70] Section 72 (1) (h), Registration of Title Act 1964.

[71] An easement by prescription can only be acquired through 'user as of right', which requires use without force, secrecy and without Quentin's consent. See sections 33–38, Land and Conveyancing Law Reform Act 2009, as amended by sections 37–38, Civil Law Miscellaneous Provisions Act 2011, for the new rules which govern the acquisition of easements by prescription. Note that from 1 December 2021 it will be necessary to register implied easements or easements by prescription to prevent their automatic extinguishment through twelve years' non-user.

implied easement.[72] If Quentin failed to comply with an obligation, set out in a specifically enforceable contract to provide a grant of a right of way, Philip may be able to sue Quentin for damages for breach of contract.[73]

(b) Such knowledge will usually be irrelevant, as a right of way must be registered to bind a registered transferee for value.[74] However, Richard's knowledge may be relevant if neither Richard nor Philip had registered their interests in the Land Registry. In such circumstances, unregistered principles will be applied in order to determine priority.[75] If Philip's right of way was made by deed, it will bind Richard regardless of whether he knew about it as 'legal interests bind the world'. If Philip's right of way only amounted to an equitable easement, it will bind Richard if he knew about the interest or if he had implied or constructive notice of it (e.g. if it was obvious that it was being used by Philip).[76]

(c) Assuming the farm is registered in the Land Registry and Philip's right of way has not been protected by registration, once the transfer to Richard is registered, Philip's right will be defeated unless fraud was involved.[77] Fraudulent dispositions or entries in the Register are deemed to be void[78] and there is provision for the Register to be rectified in such circumstances.[79] However, it is unlikely that the courts would treat this plot, whereby Quentin and Richard sought to take advantage of the effect of registration and Philip's folly in not registering, as fraud.[80]

[72] Implied easements arise by way of necessity, to give effect to the common intention of the parties or under section 40, Land and Conveyancing Law Reform Act 2009 (where an owner disposes of part of his land and an implied easement was necessary for the reasonable enjoyment of the part disposed of and it was reasonable to assume that it would be included in the grant).

[73] Provided the doctrine of merger does not defeat any remedies he has for the enforcement of the contract, see J.C.W. Woods and Una Wylie, *Irish Conveyancing Law* (Haywards Heath: Bloomsbury Professional, 2005), Chapter 21.

[74] Section 31 (1), Registration of Title Act 1964.

[75] *Tench* v. *Molyneaux* (1914) 48 ILTR 48. [76] *Hervey* v. *Smith* [1856] 52 ER.

[77] Section 31 (1), Registration of Title Act 1964.

[78] Section 30, Registration of Title Act 1964.

[79] Section 31 (1), Registration of Title Act 1964.

[80] *De Lusignan* v. *Johnson* (1973) 230 EG 499; *Midland Bank Trust Co. Ltd* v. *Green* [1981] AC 513 at 530A.

Case 12

Dodgy Dealings Ltd owns a large piece of land, Blackacre. Blackacre is its only asset. It has failed to pay a substantial debt to Z Ltd. Z Ltd sues the company in order to recover the debt. On 1 September, Dodgy Dealings Ltd agrees to sell Blackacre to Victoria. On 1 October, an order is made, charging Blackacre with the debt. On 1 November, Victoria registers her purchase of the land. Can Z Ltd enforce its debt against the land?

(a) Would it make any difference if Victoria knew about the proceedings?
(b) Does Z Ltd have any other rights against the land?

(A) Foundational Concepts for Understanding Case 12

This question explains, as a starting point, that there is no unique moment in which transfer occurs but better that transfer is a process in which the different attributions of the property pass separately from the transferor to the acquirer. In the meantime, it could happen that one of the parties becomes insolvent, so that the question is if, at this point, the good constitutes a guarantee for the creditors of the transferor or the acquirer.

Also, the legal terminology is complicated in this question when it states that 'an order is made, charging Blackacre with the debt'. The German report, for instance, talks about the inscription in the Land Register of a compulsory mortgage (this is the same as in both the Irish and Finnish order reports). In that case, what's most important is the moment in which this mortgage was registered. If it was previous to the application of the new acquirer to be registered as owner, then he acquires the land charged with the mortgage. If the registration of the mortgage occurs after that moment, it cannot be enforced against the new acquirer. In a similar way, the Austrian reporter answers this question: the main issue here is the date and time of the arrival of the application for registration at the responsible court. The acquirer can ask for an annotation (*Anmerkung*). By doing so, he receives a court order of precedence (*Rangordnungsbeschluss*) that is valid for a year. On the other hand, in the Netherlands, in order to produce effects against third parties, the seizure should be registered in the Deeds Register. This does not impede the owner from transferring the immovable, but this transfer does not work against the seller's creditor who seized the land in execution. Without this seizure, there is no prejudice for the acquirer. Alternatively, if the acquirer has registered the sales contract before the execution of the seizure, the seizure does not produce effects against her.

In Nordic law, the registration of a charge encumbers the property from the date of registration. The charge is registered shortly after the charge has been issued. In the period between the charge and the registration of the charge, priority might be given to a buyer in good faith of the (unregistered) charge. In Denmark and Norway priority is given to the first registration, whichever comes first – the title or the charge. In Finland and Sweden, the buyer's acquisition in good faith is protected irrespective of the buyer's registration of title, as long as the charge was not registered when the sale was concluded.

The terminology changes in the Italian report, but the situation is similar, as the conflict should be resolved according to the general rules on registration. Also similar is the situation in Portugal and Greece. On the other hand, in Spain, it is more complicated as the transfer of ownership requires a valid legal act that conveys the acquirer's ownership and possession of the property. If, at the time the charge was ordered, the acquirer had already taken possession of the property but hadn't yet registered ownership, his right of ownership cannot be affected by a charge order issued subsequently.

In the French legal system, if the mortgage or the seizure was registered before the transfer, the new acquirer can purge the real estate only by depositing the price for the benefit of the creditors. In Belgium, the seizure of an immovable has to be registered in the Hypothec Register. The question of whether or not enforcement by the creditors of the transferor will be effective in relation to the acquirer depends upon the priority rule, taking into account the moment of the registration.

In England, if the transferor had his property registered, the creditors should have protected the priority of their charging order by entering a notice of it in the Register (in particular, in the Charges Register) for the immovable. If the creditor failed to apply for such a notice to be entered before the acquirer applied for registration of his interest in the property, the charging order would not bind him when registered as freehold proprietor of the land. If it is the case, the charging order does not bind the acquirer. So what is important is the date of the registration in the Land Register (according to the principle '*prior tempore potior iure*'). In Scotland, ownership is not acquired until registration in the Land Register. Equally, the order does not attach the land until it is registered. In Ireland, there was a modification of this point by the Land and Conveyancing Law Reform Act 2009. According to this regulation, it is necessary for a creditor, who has obtained a judgment against a debtor, to apply to the Property Registration Authority to register a judgment mortgage against the debtor's estate or interest in land. A judgment mortgage takes effect subject to any registered or unregistered right or incumbrance affecting the immovable at the time of its registration.

In part (b) of the question, many reports are referring to the so-called *actio Pauliana*. The normal consequence in these cases would be that after avoidance of the sale and transfer, ownership of the land reverts to the transferor with retroactive effect so that creditors can seize the land in execution.

(B) The Jurisdictions (Presented by Related Jurisdictions)

1 *Germany and related jurisdictions*

(a) Germany

When Z Ltd succeeds with its claim against Dodgy Dealings Ltd, it will obtain a court order that obligates Dodgy Dealings Ltd to pay the debt. If Dodgy Dealings Ltd does not pay the dept voluntarily, Z Ltd must enforce the court order by compulsory execution (*Zwangsvollstreckung*). In relation to Blackacre, this can be done in three – cumulative or alternative – ways by Z Ltd: by registration of a compulsory mortgage (*Zwangshypothek*) in the Land Register, compulsory auction (*Zwangsversteigerung*), or by enforced administration (*Zwangsverwaltung*).[1]

By charging Blackacre with a compulsory mortgage (which is a debt-securing mortgage (*Sicherungshypothek*), i.e. it is strongly dependent on the existence of the debt), Z Ltd only obtains a real security for its debt

[1] See § 866 ZPO.

that it can later enforce by compulsory auction or enforced administration without the need of a further court order. The mortgage does not arise until it is registered in the Land Register on the application of Z Ltd.[2]

If the mortgage is registered before Victoria made the application to be registered as owner, she acquires the land charged with the mortgage and Z Ltd can enforce the mortgage. If the registration of the mortgage occurs after Victoria made the application to be registered as owner, it cannot be enforced if Victoria did not know about the proceedings. In this case, Victoria receives the land free of charge by acquisition in good faith.[3] As the acquisition in good faith is only applicable for a transfer by legal transaction, not by compulsory execution, Z Ltd cannot rely on this principle.

If Z Ltd chooses to enforce the debt by compulsory auction or by enforced administration, the land will be sequestered and a notice (*Versteigerungsvermerk*) is entered in the Land Register of the land.[4]

The sequestration of the property dictates that Dodgy Dealings Ltd is no longer allowed to alienate the land. If, nevertheless, a transfer is made, it would be ineffective in the case of Z Ltd.[5] That is to say, as long as Z Ltd does not invoke the relative ineffectiveness of the sale, the transfer to Victoria is effective.

But the transfer to Victoria is not relatively ineffective if the sequestration does not affect her or if she acquired the property in good faith. In these cases, Z Ltd cannot enforce its debt against the land because Victoria can prevent the compulsory execution by taking action against it.[6] Only if Z Ltd has secured its debt by a land charge or mortgage (including the abovementioned compulsory mortgage) can it enforce its debt against the land despite the wholly effective transfer of the land to Victoria.[7]

[2] § 867, para. 1 ZPO.

[3] See § 892 BGB. In this case Victoria is entitled to apply for deletion of the mortgage from the Land Register (see § 894 BGB) and to prevent a compulsory execution by taking action against it (§ 771 ZPO).

[4] §§ 15, 19 German Statute for the Compulsory Auction and the Compulsory Administration (*Zwangsversteigerungsgesetz*, ZVG).

[5] §§ 20, para. 1, 23 para. 1 ZVG; §§ 135, para. 1, 136 BGB.

[6] See Kurt Stöber, *Zwangsversteigerungsgesetz*, 21st edn. (Munich: C.H. Beck Verlag, 2016), § 28, note 4.5; Roland Böttcher, *ZVG*, 6th edn. (Munich: C.H. Beck Verlag, 2016), § 23, notes 5 and 6; § 26, note 4.

[7] See § 26 ZVG.

The prohibition of alienation conferred by the sequestration would not affect the transfer to Victoria if, before the sequestration has become effective, the agreement to sell Blackacre has already become binding on Dodgy Dealings Ltd and the application for registration has been made to the Land Registry.[8] The parties are bound by the agreement to transfer the ownership of Blackacre as soon as the declarations are recorded by a notary, made before the Land Registry or submitted to the Land Registry; or, alternately, if Dodgy Dealings Ltd has delivered Victoria a notarised approval of registration.[9] Insofar, it is neither relevant whether Victoria knew about the proceedings nor whether at what time the notice about the compulsory auction or administration was entered in the Land Register.

Victoria could have acquired the property in good faith if the notice is not entered in the Land Register until she is registered as owner of the land and does not know about the sequestration or Z Ltd's application for compulsory auction or administration at the time of her application for registration as the owner.[10] If the notice is registered before Victoria is registered as the owner of the land, she cannot acquire the property in good faith.[11]

Apart from the fact that the debt is secured by a land charge or a mortgage, and assuming that Victoria did not know about the proceedings, Z Ltd can only enforce its debt if Victoria has made the application to be registered as the owner after the sequestration became effective.[12] Also, this is only the case if the compulsory auction or administration is registered before Victoria is registered as the owner.[13]

(a) In the case of the registration of a compulsory mortgage, Victoria's knowledge of the proceedings prevents her from acquiring the land free of charge in good faith. Z Ltd can enforce the debt secured by the mortgage even if it is registered after Victoria made her application to be registered as the owner.

In the case of the sequestration of the land, Victoria's knowledge of the proceedings is relevant only if the notice about the compulsory auction or administration is entered in the Land Register after Victoria is registered as the owner of the land. If, under these circumstances, she obtained knowledge about the sequestration or Z Ltd's application

[8] See § 878 BGB. [9] See § 873, para. 2 BGB.
[10] See §§ 135, para. 2, 892 para. 1 sentence 2, para. 2, § 23, para. 2 ZVG.
[11] See §§ 135, para. 2, 892, para. 1 sentence 2 BGB. [12] § 878 BGB is not applicable.
[13] No acquisition in good faith is possible.

for compulsory auction or administration up to the time of her application for registration as owner, no acquisition in good faith would be possible.[14]

(b) No, she does not have any other rights against the land.

(b) Austria

In general, the first party to claim registration of a property right prevails over any subsequent third parties claiming the same.[15] Various rights are classified according to the order of precedence. This order of precedence is formed according to the date and time of their creation, more explicitly, according to the date and time of the arrival of the application for registration (*GB-Gesuch*) at the responsible court.[16]

The reason for precedence is to temporarily secure the rank of a property right. The owner of the real estate – wanting to sell or encumber his land – can ask for an annotation (*Anmerkung*).[17] In doing so, he receives a court order of precedence (*Rangordnungsbeschluss*), which is valid for a year. Within that year, only a person showing that order can ask for an annotation in the rank discussed.[18]

Therefore, the important question here is whether it was Victoria or Z Ltd who asked for an annotation of their rank (*Anmerkung*) first. According to § 137 Austrian Act on Execution (EO), the court authorising the compulsory sale (*Bewilligungsgericht*) is obligated to order that the authorisation of the compulsory sale (*Zwangsversteigerung*) is registered in the Big Book (annotation of the commencement of the sale procedure – *Anmerkung der Einleitung des Versteigerungsverfahrens*). If Victoria applied for annotation first, Z Ltd cannot enforce any right against Blackacre.

(a) According to § 1 Austrian Statute on Rescission (AnfO), all legal actions concerning the assets of a debtor can be contested and declared to be void under the circumstances mentioned in the statute. Victoria's knowledge of the facts can be of importance in two case scenarios: if Victoria knew, or had to know, about discriminatory intent

[14] See §§ 135, para. 2, 892, para. 1 sent. 2, para. 2, § 23, para. 2 ZVG.

[15] Comp § 440 ABGB. See further Gert M. Iro, *Sachenrecht*, 3rd edn. (Vienna: Österreich Verlag, 2008), Rz 6/43.

[16] § 29 GBG.

[17] §§ 53ff GBG. See further Iro, *Sachenrecht*, Rz 3/30f; Helmut Koziol and Rudolf Welser, *Bürgerliches Recht, I*, 13th edn. (Vienna: MANZ Verlag, 2006), p. 359f.

[18] Also Koziol and Welser, *Bürgerliches Recht, I*, p. 367; see further Iro, *Sachenrecht*, Rz 3/51ff.

(*Benachteilungsabsicht*) on the part of the debtor[19] (Dodgy Dealings Ltd) or if Victoria knew, or had to know, about the fact that Dodgy Dealings Ltd was squandering assets (*Vermögensverschleuderung*).[20] If so, the contract with Victoria can be contested by Z Ltd according to the rules stated in the AnfO.

Furthermore, it could be argued that § 1409 ABGB has to be applied to this case, in that a person taking over property knowing, or having to know, about the debts pertaining to the assets has to take over these debts. This provision is to be applied if the acquired property represents the whole asset of the seller, which could be the case as Blackacre is said to be the only asset of Dodgy Dealings Ltd. As a consequence, Z Ltd could enforce its debt against Victoria.[21]

(b) No.

(c) The Netherlands

(a) In the Dutch law, an order charging the land with the debt is called *beslag* (seizure in execution). The seizure should be registered in the Deeds Register (arts. 505 and 726 Rv[22]). The seizure works against third parties. The seller is still able to transfer ownership of the land to the buyer but this transfer does not work against the seller's creditor, who seized the land in execution. The transfer is said to be relatively void, namely void in relation to the seller's creditor (arts. 505, para. 2 and 726 Rv).

In case 12, no seizure has taken place. The judgment in which the debtor is ordered to pay his debt does not constitute a seizure. Without seizure, the transfer to Victoria is also valid against Z Ltd, so that Z Ltd can no longer seize the land.

Although the mere sales contract does not pass ownership, registration of the sales contract in the Land Register is possible. It protects the buyer against subsequent buyers but also against the seller's bankruptcy and individual creditors. If Victoria has registered the sales contract before the seizure's execution, the seizure does not work against her (art. 7:3 (3) (f) BW). It makes no difference whether or not the buyer knew of the proceedings. It is simply a question of what has been registered first: the sale or the seizure. Similarly, if the sale had

[19] § 2 Z 1 and 2 AnfO. [20] § 2 Z 4 AnfO.

[21] See further Koziol and Welser, *Bürgerliches Recht, II*, p. 132f; Silvia Dullinger, *Schuldrecht Allgemeiner Teil*, 3rd edn. (Vienna and New York: Springer Verlag, 2008), Rz 5/87ff.

[22] Rv stands for *Wetboek van burgerlijke rechtsvordering* (Code of Civil Procedure).

already been followed by a transfer of ownership (registration of the transfer deed) before the registration of the seizure, the seizure would be void.

(b) Z Ltd has no other rights against the land other than the abovementioned right of seizure, provided the land has been sold for the market value. If it was sold under the market value, Z Ltd may be able to nullify the sale and transfer of ownership with the so-called *actio Pauliana* (art. 3:45 BW). Afterwards, avoidance of the sale and transfer ownership of the land reverts to Dodgy Dealings Ltd with retroactive effect (art. 3:53 BW) so that Z Ltd can seize the land in execution.

(d) Turkey

No, Z Ltd cannot enforce its debt against the land since the immovable has been transferred to a third party. A contractual relationship is relative and, as a principal rule, the creditor can only sue the debtor and demand sequestration for the debtor's properties.

(a) Yes, if Victoria knew about the proceedings, Z Ltd's creditors could bring an action for the nullity of the sale contract depending on art. 280 Execution and Bankruptcy Code. According to art. 280 if an insolvent debtor enters into a legal transaction, for instance, transfers his or her immovable properties with the wilful intention to damage his or her creditors, and the other parties of the contract have recognisance of his or her insolvency and wilful intention to damage, the creditors of the debtor can bring an action for the cancellation (*actio Pauliana)* of the legal transaction, such as the transferring of the immovable. Where a third person acquires the only, or most important, asset of a company, the third party is deemed to have recognisance of the economic situation and the wilful intention to damage of the debtor.[23]

If Z Ltd demands sequestration or bankruptcy within five years of the legal transaction, it will succeed. The immovable will be sold for the debts of the transferor, Dodgy Dealings Ltd.[24]

(b) No, Z Ltd does not have any other rights against the land.

[23] See Baki Kuru, *İcra ve İflâs Hukuku, İkinci Tıpkı Baskı* (İstanbul:Türkmen Kitabevi, 2006), p. 1207.

[24] See Kuru, *İcra*, p. 1208.

2 *Scandinavian jurisdictions*

(a) Finland

According to the Finnish legal system, a district court can confirm a debt and order a debtor to pay it. However, as a rule, a court does not charge any piece of real estate or parcel in connection with its judgment without a mortgage.[25] At this stage, a debt is a creditor's unsecured and personal (general) claim. It has to be adjusted (individuated and directed to a certain piece of property) in order to charge Blackacre *in rem*. A debt can be adjusted by a mortgage before or after a trial. After a trial, adjustment can be a part of a bailiff's attachment procedure founded on a creditor's application and a judgment. Alternatively, the debtor's bankruptcy can be adjudicated or precautionary measures can be directed.[26]

Adjustment in the form of attachment means, in this case, that an owner is not allowed to sell, mortgage, or dispose of his or her property in another way.[27] Attachment can be seen, in this case, as charging Blackacre. Basically, charging takes place in the enforced and public sale carried through by the bailiff as part of the attachment procedure.[28] The creditors' shares of the price are determined by the creditors' order.[29] A private person cannot charge a piece of real estate on his or her own without an official procedure. The same applies to leaseholds.

Before charging and adjustment (i.e. before the beginning of attachment, bankruptcy, or precautionary measures) Dodgy Dealings Ltd is free to sell Blackacre. Afterwards, charging a valid conveyance made by the company is not possible any more. Hence, Z Ltd cannot enforce its debt against Victoria (as the new owner of the land, that is, 'against the land') without a mortgage in a normal way. Registration of Victoria's title has no significance in this situation.

(a) The voidable conveyance made after charging can be improved by the good faith of the transferee (Victoria did not know, nor should

[25] 4:30.1 Enforcement Code and 10:8.2/2 Code of Judicial Procedure, /www.finlex.fi/en/laki/kaannokset/1734/en17340004.pdf.

[26] 2:2 Bankruptcy Act (2004), www.finlex.fi/en/laki/kaannokset/2004/en20040120.pdf. 7:1 Code of Judicial Procedure.

[27] 4:37 Enforcement Code. [28] 5:1.1 Enforcement Code.

[29] Act on the Payment Order of Creditors (1992, the general order, not available in English) and 5:47 Enforcement Code (the special order applied to pieces of real estate and leased houses).

have known, about the adjustment).[30] There are, nevertheless, limited possibilities for that. The full legal effect of charging (beginning of an attachment, bankruptcy, or precautionary measures) takes place by entering a notice of it into the Title and Mortgage Register. A piece of real estate can be conveyed after the beginning of such a procedure, but before its registration. A transferee can act in good faith only before the registration. In this case, however, there is no need for such protection. Registration of a transferee's title has no significance here.

(b) Z Ltd can have a claim, however, against Victoria and Blackacre even if it cannot charge Blackacre in the normal way described above. A general creditor can claim a recovery against a transferee of any kind of property in a general court, on certain conditions (*actio Pauliana*, *takaisinsaanti* in Finnish).[31] First, the transferor, Dodgy Dealings Ltd, has been insolvent or has become insolvent because of the transaction. Second, the recovery is possible if the transfer has been improper in relation to a creditor or creditors. 'Improper', here, means violating legal interests of creditors. Third, the transferee has known, or should have known, about the impropriety of the transaction. In other words, he or she has been acting in bad faith. Fourth, the beginning of an attachment made by a bailiff or a bankruptcy against the transferor must have taken place and a fixed term after the transfer, as a rule, must not have terminated before the application for the bailiff's attachment or bankruptcy. A recovery is possible, even in connection with an official reorganisation of the debtor's debts. On the other hand, the conveyance of Blackacre can take place many years before it is claimed by creditors. There are various fixed terms with various preconditions for different situations. As the result of a successful recovery, Blackacre is again treated as a property of Dodgy Dealings Ltd and Z Ltd can enforce its debt against Blackacre.

In addition, it is possible to treat the conveyance of Blackacre as a fictitious transaction (simulated or *pro forma* transaction) in connection with a bailiff's attachment, or in a trial.[32] In practice, these procedures, attachment and appealing to the fictitious nature of the transaction, are important means for creditors. The registration of Victoria's title has no significance here either.

[30] 10:3 Code of Real Estate.
[31] Act on Recovery to a Bankruptcy Estate (1991, not available in English).
[32] Connected with bailiff's attachment procedure: 4:14 Enforcement Code.

(b) Sweden

A registered mortgage cannot be extinguished by an acquisition in good faith[33] but we may assume that the claim is not secured by a mortgage.

A creditor may apply for a distraining order against a debtor in default, notwithstanding that the creditor has no prior (consensual) security right. A distraining order presupposes that the creditor has a title of execution. Such a title may, *inter alia,* be acquired through a decision of a court, a settlement confirmed by a court, an arbitral award, or a decision of the enforcement authority after an uncontested summary procedure.[34]

The enforcement authority[35] decides what measures should be applied. If the enforcement authority decides to distrain upon some of the debtor's property, it is forbidden for the debtor to make dispositions with the property that harm the applicant.[36] A distraining order on real property will immediately be noted in the Real Property Register. A distraining order will not charge real property unless the applicant is a mortgagee[37] or has explicitly applied for that.[38]

Real property is distrainable if it belongs to the debtor. If the debtor has registered title in real property, he or she is assumed to be the owner.[39] This presumption is rebuttable.[40] If the enforcement authority is not convinced by a person who claims to be the rightful owner, the enforcement authority is to direct that person to bring an action before court.[41] If the sale is conditional, the property is distrainable for Dodgy Dealings Ltd's debts.[42] But, the order will not be enforceable until it is

[33] Supreme Court judgment *NJA* 1985, 97.

[34] 3:1 Enforcement Code; *utsökningsbalken (1981:774).*

[35] Swedish: '*Kronofogdemyndigheten*'.

[36] 4:29 Enforcement Code. This does in itself not prevent the owner from making pledges of mortgage deeds in the owners' possession, 4:29 (2) Enforcement Code, which may have the effect that good faith acquisitions of mortgages would be possible, but the enforcement authority may take measures to prevent that, for instance by taking the deeds in custody, 12:5 Enforcement Code. Usually, the enforcement authority would distrain upon such deeds, 4:2 (2) Enforcement Code. *See* Ulf Jensen, *Panträtt i fast egendom,* 10th edn. (Uppsala: Iustus Förlag, 2016), p. 118.

[37] 4:4 Enforcement Code. [38] 4:5 Enforcement Code. [39] 4:24 Enforcement Code.

[40] Gösta Walin, Torkel Gregow, Peter Löfmarck, Göran Millqvist and Annina H. Persson, *Utsökningsbalken*, 4th edn. (Stockholm: Norstedts Juridik, 2009), p. 186f. Anders Victorin and Richard Hager, *Allmän fastighetsrätt*, 7th edn. (Uppsala: Iustus Förlag, 2015), p. 225f.

[41] 4:26 Enforcement Code. [42] 4:25 Enforcement Code.

decided whether the condition will be fulfilled or not.[43] However, if the condition is fulfilled, the distraining order will cease to charge the property. Victoria will not be able to register title as long as the property is under a distraining order.[44]

The facts of this question state that Dodgy Dealings Ltd 'agrees' to sell Blackacre to Victoria. If this is to be understood, so that the parties had reached an agreement satisfying the formal requirements on 1 September, and that the sale was made unconditional or conditional (but the condition is later fulfilled), Z Ltd's charge is of no effect against Victoria's ownership.

(a) Victoria's possible knowledge of the proceedings does not affect her right. If there was a valid, and formally correct sales deed before 1 October, Victoria's ownership is unaffected.

If Dodgy Dealings Ltd declared bankruptcy within five years after the sale, Victoria's knowledge of the proceedings could become relevant. A legal disposition of the debtor may be recovered if the disposition led to an evasion of the debtor's property in an unconscionable manner, but only if the disposition was made when the debtor was insolvent or if the disposition caused the insolvency *and* the counterpart knew, or ought to have, about the circumstances that rendered the disposition unconscionable.[45] If this happened, Victoria would be entitled to regain the payment.[46]

(b) Z Ltd has no other rights against the land.

(c) Denmark

In general, the one who acquires a right or a claim on a property first, prevails over any subsequent third parties claiming the same. This may not be the case if the subsequent holder of a right or claim protects his right or claim against third parties before the original holder does. In this case, an order has been made by the Bailiff's Court charging Blackacre with Dodgy Dealings Ltd's debt. Such an order will be immediately sent to the Buildings and Dwellings Register and will be registered immediately after 1 October. As Z Ltd is the first to register their right, it may enforce the debt against the land. Therefore, effectively, Danish law has a 'first to the post' system for registration.

[43] 4:33 (1) Enforcement Code. [44] 20:7 (3) Land Code.
[45] 4:5(1) and (3) Bankruptcy Act; *konkurslagen (1987:672).* [46] 4:14 (2) Bankruptcy Act.

(a) Z Ltd may enforce its right against the land irrespectively of whether or not Victoria knew about the debt.[47]

(b) As Z Ltd has already acquired the right to enforce the debt against the land, the answer is no.

(d) Norway

The order charging Blackacre with the debt (i.e. a compulsory security right in the property) should normally be registered in the Land Register. If that is done prior to the registration of Victoria's right as a buyer, the compulsory security right has priority over Victoria's right and she must respect it. Z Ltd's possible knowledge of the sale is not relevant.[48]

(a) If the compulsory order is *not* registered prior to the registration of Victoria's purchase, Victoria's right as a buyer has priority over the order, i.e. she does not have to tolerate the compulsory security right. That is the case even if Victoria knew about the order, as her right is regarded as already established at the conclusion of the sale contract, thus being the older right.

(b) Z Ltd has no other rights against the land.

A compulsory security right is created by a public officer if the creditor's claim is established with sufficient certainty. The claim may be established by a judgment but for undisputed claims, a demand for payment sent by the creditor is enough.[49] The creditor may, under certain conditions, obtain a preliminary compulsory security right during a pending lawsuit concerning a debt.[50]

3 *Romanic–Mediterranean jurisdictions*

(a) Italy

No. The conflict is resolved according to the general rules on registration. Art. 2944 ICC states that the sale of Blackacre to Victoria would be ineffective if it is registered after the order charging Blackacre with the debt (*pignoramento*) is registered. The constraint that prevents the sale, resulting from the order charging Blackacre with the debt effective after the notification to Dodgy Dealings Ltd, is not enforceable against

[47] See similarly Peter Mortensen, *Digital tinglysning – rettigheder over fast ejendom*, 4th edn. (Copenhagen: Karnov Group, 2007), p. 281f.

[48] Section 20, Judicial Registration Act.

[49] Section 7-2, Act Relating to Creditors' Right to Satisfaction of Claims, cf. section 7-6.

[50] Sections 33-1 and 33-3, Act Relating to Mediation and Civil Litigation (*lov om mekling og rettergang i sivile saker*, 17 June 2005 No. 90)

Victoria. Since Victoria has registered her purchase before the registration of the order, she will prevail over Z Ltd.[51]

(a) Yes. If Z Ltd can prove that not only did Victoria know about the proceedings, but that she agreed with Dodgy Dealings Ltd to prevent a forced sale of Blackacre, then Z Ltd could act with a revocatory action (art. 2901 ICC), to make the sale to Victoria ineffective and charge Blackacre with the debt directly by Victoria.

(b) No.

(b) Spain

(a) As we saw in the answers to questions 2 and 3, the transfer of ownership of Blackacre requires, in addition to a valid legal act conveying ownership, that Dodgy Dealings Ltd place Victoria in possession of the property. This is normally executed by the physical handover of possession of the property (Dodgy Dealings Ltd consents that Victoria behave as owner) or by the execution of a notarial act.

If, at the time the charge was ordered on Blackacre, Dodgy Dealings Ltd hadn't yet placed Victoria in possession of the property and a notarial act hadn't yet been executed – and even though it might be done later – Victoria cannot avoid enforcement of the order. At the time the charge was ordered, Victoria was still not the owner; when she acquires ownership, she does so with the charge in place and could, thus, lose her property.

If, at the time the charge was ordered, Victoria had already taken possession of the property but hadn't yet registered her ownership, her right of ownership cannot be affected by a charge order issued subsequently.[52]

(b) If Victoria acquired ownership after the charge was ordered but before it attained registration in the *Registro de la Propiedad*, Victoria must continue to bear the burden of the charge unless, at the time of acquisition: she didn't know about the charge; she acquired for value; Dodgy Dealings Ltd was the registered owner; or she, likewise, registered her right of ownership.[53] Here, Z Ltd would have no rights in the property.

[51] See Cass. 14.10.2004, No.20292, in *Arch. Locazioni* 2005, p. 430.

[52] *Tribunal Supremo* decisions of 21 February 1975, 7 April 1989 (RJ 1989/2998).

[53] In its decision of 14 June 2007 (RJ 2007/3516), the *Tribunal Supremo* ruled on a *tercería de dominio* (action by a third-party owner) brought by the acquirer of a charged property

(c) Portugal

I will assume that, on 1 September, Dodgy Dealings Ltd sells Blackacre to Victoria and, therefore, the transfer of property has occurred (art. 408 CC). Victoria has not registered her acquisition, so her right is not enforceable against third parties. The problem arises because land was seized on 1 October in the execution proceeding against Dodgy Dealings Ltd, brought to court by Z Ltd.[54]

Art. 5 (3) LRegC dictates that rights become enforceable against third parties only upon registration. However, Art 5 (4) LRegC defines 'third parties' as acquirers of totally or partially conflicting rights from the same seller. Victoria's right is incompatible with Z Ltd's right. However, they are not to be considered 'third parties', according to the LRegC, since they did not acquire rights from the same seller. Victoria has acquired a right from Dodgy Dealings Ltd, but the seizure of the land is the result of an act from a judicial authority. Therefore, the conflict between Victoria and Z Ltd is not to be resolved under Registration law, but according to the rules of the CC. Hence, transfer of property to Victoria prevails (*prior in tempore, potior in iure*). As a result, Z Ltd cannot enforce its debt against the land because it already belongs to Victoria and is not available to Dodgy Dealings Ltd's creditors.

This solution, however, remains very controversial in doctrine and case law.[55] Despite the reading of art. 5 (4) LRegC, it is claimed that the creditor, Z Ltd, and Victoria should be considered 'third parties' for the purpose of Registration law.[56] Hence, the question of whether or not

lacking pre-emptive registration of the charge. The third party had registered the acquisition after the registration of the charge. The court refused to lift the charge, because the third party was not a mortgaged third party.

54 It should be noted that after the seizure of the land, Z Ltd could not dispose of it, and therefore an eventual sale to Victoria would not be effective (arts. 817 and 819 CC).

55 See Carlos Ferreira de Almeida, *Publicidade e Teoria dos Registos* (Coimbra: Almedina, 1966), p. 268; Isabel Pereira Mendes, *Código do Registo Predial – Anotado*, 17th edn. (Coimbra: Almedina, 2009), p. 167; Miguel F. Teixeira de Sousa, 'Conceito de Terceiros para Efeitos de Registo', **59** *ROA* (1999), pp. 29ff.; Antuno Varela and Henrique Mesquita, 'Anotação ao Ac. 3 de Junho de 1992', *Revista de Legislação e Jurisprudência*, Ano 126°, pp. 19ff.; Mónica Jardim, 'Efeitos do Registo da Penhora Convertido em Definitivo nos Termos do Artigo 119 do Código do Registo Predial', **9** *Cadernos de Direito Privado* (2005), pp. 23–42; Quirino Duarte Soares, 'O Conceito de Terceiros para Efeitos de Registo Predial', **9** *Cadernos Direito Privado* (2005), pp. 3ff.

56 The Portuguese case law reflects this debate. See, e.g., the Decisions of the Supreme Court of 7 July 1999 and 16 October 2008.

the enforcement by Z Ltd will be effective in relation to Victoria will depend upon the priority rule, applied to the moment of the registration:

(1) If the seizure of Blackacre had been registered before registration of the sales agreement, Z Ltd would prevail and it would be entitled to enforce the debt against the land. A non-registered sales agreement, with regard to an immovable, is considered ineffective in relation to the enforcing creditor (art. 5 (4) LRegC).
(2) If the registration of the sales agreement had been made prior to the registration of the seizure of Blackacre, Victoria's right over the land would prevail. The registration of the seizure would not be possible, as it would involve the seizure of an asset that does not belong to Dodgy Dealings Ltd any more and is no longer available to its creditors.

(a) As a principle, it would make no difference. Knowledge and bad faith are irrelevant in a competition between a voluntary transferee (such as Victoria) and an attaching creditor (such as Z Ltd): see question 1.

(b) No, Z Ltd has no other rights than to seize the immovable according to the rules provided by the Civil Procedure Code, on the condition that it has registered its measure prior to the transfer to Victoria.

(d) Greece

If Z Ltd's claim succeeds against Dodgy Dealings Ltd, a court order will be obtained obligating the latter to pay its debts. If Dodgy Dealings Ltd doesn't pay Z Ltd voluntarily, the latter may enforce the court order by compulsory execution[57] and seizure[58] of Blackacre. According to law,[59] seizures must be registered in a special book kept in the Transcription Registry. According to the priority rule, the party who first acquires a right or a claim on a property prevails over any subsequent third party claiming the same (*prior tempore potior jure*).

Furthermore, the seizure of the property dictates that Dodgy Dealings Ltd is no longer allowed to alienate the land and if a transfer is made despite the prohibition, it is relatively ineffective towards Z Ltd.[60] The transfer to Victoria would be ineffective towards Z Ltd if the latter invokes the ineffectiveness of the sale.

The conflict in our case is resolved by the general principles of registration and precedence. Had Z Ltd registered the enforcement measure

[57] Arts. 904 and 992 GCCP. [58] Art. 992 GCCP.
[59] Arts. 993 and 995 GCCP and art. 11 King's decree 533/1963. [60] Art. 997 GCCP.

before registration of the sale and transfer agreement and, thus, before the transfer of the ownership, Z Ltd would be able to enforce its debt against Blackacre and the registration of transfer of ownership to Victoria would be of no importance to Z Ltd. Victoria would have acquired ownership charged with the debt. However, Victoria has registered the purchase and transfer title before Z Ltd and has, therefore, become the legitimate owner of Blackacre without Z Ltd's encumbrance. This leads to the conclusion that Z Ltd couldn't possibly enforce its debt against the land.

(a) Victoria's knowledge is of no significance.

(b) Following a court order, Z Ltd has the right to register a compulsory mortgage[61] in the Transcript Registry in order to obtain a real security for its claims, which can be later enforced by means of a compulsory auction. The mortgage, as a real right, does not arise until it is registered.[62] The same priority and precedence principles shall apply for this mortgage as well.

4 *France and related jurisdictions*

(a) France

Blackacre became, in principle, the property of Victoria from 1 October. But as long as the alienation was not published, Z Ltd can carry out a seizure provided that it is the first one published in the real estate file.[63] The seizure confers, however, no right of preference against the other possible creditors. If Z Ltd prefers to firstly register its judicial mortgage, it has to make it again before the publication of the alienation, after which the mortgages granted by the seller cannot be usefully registered again[64]: the conflict between a mortgage creditor and a buyer is ruled by the land publicity. If the mortgage or the seizure was registered before the alienation, Victoria can purge the real estate only by depositing the price for the benefit of Z Ltd and other possible creditors.

(a) Yes, because Z Ltd can then envisage a Pauliana action that would make the alienation inoperative against the creditor, so Z Ltd would be allowed to register the mortgage and to execute it. It is necessary for the action to demonstrate that this sale causes a damage to the creditor (where the price is lower than the normal value or paid in cash, which is easy to hide), that the debtor was conscious of causing damage to his

[61] Arts. 1261 and 1263 GCC. [62] Art. 1260 GCC.
[63] Art L. 321-5 du Code des procédures civiles d'exécution. [64] Art. 2427 C. civ.

creditor (which can result from conditions of the sale) and that the buyer was conscious himself of this damage, which can be more difficult to prove.

(b) No, in principle, unless Z Ltd has besides a preference, which makes then useless a judicial mortgage. A common, and very effective, preference in practice is the 'preference of the moneylender' granted by the law to the establishment, which finances the purchase of the real estate.[65] The special preferences must, as the mortgages, be registered at the land registry.[66]

(b) Belgium

The seizure of an immovable has to be registered in the Hypothec Register.

The question of whether the enforcement by Z Ltd will be effective, in relation to Victoria, depends upon the priority rule applied at the moment of the registration:

(1) If Z Ltd registers the enforcement measure before the authentic sales deed is registered in the Hypothec Register, Z Ltd will prevail. Victoria will, in that case, acquire the immovable subject to the seizure and pursuant enforced sale. A non-registered sales agreement, with regard to an immovable, is not effective in relation to the enforcing creditor (art. 1577 Judicial Code). Victoria will, in this case, have a contractual claim against Dodgy Dealings Ltd. However, as the latter lacks assets, this claim will probably be unsuccessful.

(2) If the registration of the sales agreement intervenes before the registration of the seizure by the creditor, Victoria will prevail. The registration of the seizure will probably be refused, as it would involve the seizure of an asset that does not belong to the debtor any more in a way that is opposable to creditors.

For the sake of clarity, we add that Z Ltd cannot request, on the basis of the seizure, repossession of the immovable. He can only claim that the immovable is sold after judicial authorisation and with the intervention of a public notary. A contractual clause stating that the creditor will be able to gain repossession or become the owner of the immovable if the debtor is at stake to comply with his obligations, will be held void (art. 1626 Belgian Judicial Code).

(a) Victoria's bad faith would make a difference in one hypothesis, e.g. if the mutual consent intervenes between the seizure proceedings

[65] 'In French, Privilège du prêteur de deniers': art. 2374, 2° C. civ. [66] Art. 2377 C. civ.

and the registration thereof. Victoria, in that case, cannot argue that the seizure did not have any effect towards her lack of registration because the lack of registration can only be argued by third parties in good faith.[67]

(b) No, Z Ltd has no other rights other than to seize the immovable, according to the rules provided by the Judicial Code, on the condition that he has registered his measure prior to Victoria.

5 *England and related jurisdictions*

(a) England

Z Ltd's charging order will have been granted under the Charging Orders Act 1979 with the result that Z Ltd will occupy the position of an equitable chargee of the property from 1 October.[68] Assuming Dodgy Dealings Ltd's land was registered (which appears to be the case), Z Ltd should have protected the priority of its charging order by entering a notice of it in the Register (in particular, in the Charges Register) for Dodgy Dealings Ltd's land. If it failed to apply for such a notice to be entered before Victoria applied for registration of her interest in the property, the charging order will not bind Victoria when she is registered as freehold proprietor of the land.[69] If the charging order does not bind Victoria, Z Ltd cannot enforce its debt against the land.

(If Dodgy Dealings Ltd's land was not registered at the time the charging order was granted, Z Ltd should have entered the charging order in a different register, the Land Charges Register, as a Class C (iii) land charge. If they did not do so, the charge will be void against Victoria when she purchases the land.[70])

Also note, that if the sale from Dodgy Dealings Ltd to Victoria was conducted at an undervalue in order to defeat the claims of Z Ltd against the land, then Z Ltd could apply to the court for an order restoring the position to what it would have been if the sale to Victoria had not taken place.[71] This would then allow Z Ltd to take steps to ensure that its charging order would be enforceable against any subsequent disponees of the land.

(a) This would not affect the preceding analysis.

67 Art. 1 Hypothec Act of 16 December 1851, *Belgian Official Gazette*, 22 December 1851.
68 Section 3 (4), Charging Orders Act 1979. 69 Section 29, LRA 2002.
70 Sections 4 (5) and 2 (4), LCA 1972. 71 Under section 423, Insolvency Act 1986.

(b) Technically, Z Ltd's charging order remains in force and is merely postponed to Victoria's interest in the land.[72] In practical terms, however, the charging order is of no use as Victoria's priority entitles her to ignore the order and dispose of the property to third parties, free of the charging order. Z Ltd has no other rights against the land.

(b) Scotland

Ownership is not acquired by Victoria until the registration of her deed of transfer ('disposition') in the Land Register. Equally, the order does not attach the land until it is registered. Thus, there is a race to the Register between Victoria and Z Ltd. If Victoria had been first to register, the land would have ceased to belong to Dodgy Dealings Ltd and could not be attached by its creditors (such as Z Ltd). As it stands, however, Z Ltd registered first, which means that the order attached the land before it could be transferred to Victoria. Thus, although Victoria became owner when she registered on 1 November, Z Ltd can, ultimately, sell the land in order to recover the debt.

One qualification must be mentioned. It would have been an option, for Victoria, to register an advance notice around the time she made the contract with Dodgy Dealings Ltd. Assuming that she did so, this would create a thirty-five-day priority period during which any disposition registered by her would be unaffected by any rival deed or court decree registered during the same period.[73] So if both the charging order and the disposition were registered during the priority period, the disposition would take preference over the order, even if it was registered second.

(a) It would make no difference. Knowledge and bad faith are irrelevant in a competition between a voluntary transferee (such as Victoria) and an attaching creditor (such as Z Ltd).

Of course, if Victoria knew of the proceedings, she would be unlikely to pay the purchase price unless she was satisfied that no order affected the land.

(b) Z Ltd has no other rights against the land.

[72] Section 29 (1), LRA 2002.

[73] Sections 56–59, Land Registration etc. (Scotland) Act 2012.

(c) Ireland

Z Ltd will not be in a position to enforce its debt against the land as the judgment mortgage will no longer affect Blackacre once Victoria's purchase is completed by registration.

The procedure for charging the land of a debtor with a debt is set out in section 116, Land and Conveyancing Law Reform Act 2009.[74] It requires a creditor, who has obtained a judgment against a debtor, to apply to the Property Registration Authority to register a judgment mortgage against the debtor's estate or interest in land. Once a judgment mortgage is registered in the Land Registry or the Registry of Deeds, the debtor's interest in land becomes charged with payment of the creditor's judgment debt.[75] At that point, the creditor becomes entitled to apply to the court for an order for the sale of the debtor's estate or interest in the land and the distribution of the proceeds of sale,[76] so as to allow recovery of the debt.

The difficulty for Z Ltd lies in the fact that a judgment mortgage takes effect subject to any registered or unregistered right or incumbrance affecting Blackacre at the time of its registration.[77] The judgment mortgage came into effect on 1 October but on 1 September Dodgy Dealings Ltd agreed to sell Blackacre to Victoria. If Victoria entered into an enforceable contract for sale on that date, she would have become the beneficial owner[78] and Dodgy Dealings Ltd would have become a constructive trustee. Therefore, the judgment mortgage would only have attached to Dodgy Dealings Ltd's legal interest in Blackacre, which would have disappeared on 1 November when Victoria's purchase was completed by the registration of her deed of transfer in the Land Registry.

[74] This section replaces the technical and archaic procedure set out in sections 6–8, Judgment Mortgage (Ireland) Acts 1850–88, see Law Reform Commission, *Consultation Paper on Judgment Mortgages* (LRC 30-2004).

[75] Section 117 (1), Land and Conveyancing Law Reform Act 2009.

[76] Section 117 (2), Land and Conveyancing Law Reform Act 2009.

[77] Section 117 (3), Land and Conveyancing Law Reform Act 2009.

[78] Section 52 (1), Land and Conveyancing Law Reform Act 2009. This provision reverses the effect of the controversial decision in *Tempany* v. *Hynes* [1976] IR 101. In that case, the majority of the Supreme Court held that when a purchaser enters into a contract relating to land the beneficial interest passes only to the extent that the purchase money has been paid. Usually, only a 10 per cent deposit will have been paid at this point which means that a judgment mortgage registered during the period between contract and completion could attach to the 90 per cent beneficial interest retained by the vendor. This approach gives rise to numerous difficulties and was subjected to widespread criticism, see Law Reform Commission, *Interests of Vendor and Purchaser in Land During the Period Between Contract and Completion* (LRC 49-1995).

In such circumstances, the judgment mortgage is rendered ineffective and Victoria will be able to apply to the Property Registration Authority for its cancellation. However, if Victoria's agreement was not enforceable,[79] she would not have acquired an interest in the land on 1 September and Z Ltd's judgment mortgage would have priority over her subsequent registered transfer. In such circumstances, Z Ltd would be in a position to enforce its debt against the land.

(a) As Victoria is a purchaser, it will not make any difference if she knew about the proceedings or judgment against Dodgy Dealings Ltd when she entered into the contract to purchase Blackacre. However, if she received Blackacre before the judgment mortgage was registered, and the transaction was made with the intention of defrauding Z Ltd, the disposition is voidable and Z Ltd may apply to have it set aside.[80]

(b) Z Ltd has no other rights against the land.

[79] See the response to case 3 for the requirements which need to be satisfied to create an enforceable contract for sale of land.

[80] See section 117 (5), Land and Conveyancing Act 2009.

Case 13

Hans bought a house. Helda has made a significant contribution to the purchase price.

(a) Hans is selling the house to Chris. Helda finds out and wants to prevent the sale. Will she succeed?
(b) Hans has mortgaged the house to the Bank and has failed to pay. The Bank seeks possession of the property. Can the Bank remove Helda?
(c) Would your answer to (a) or (b) differ if Hans and Helda were married?

(A) Foundational Concepts for Understanding Case 13

This question is addressed to determine if, according to the different legal systems, the mere fact of contributing to the purchase price of an immovable confers some right on this person.

In a majority of the European legal systems, the mere fact that a person contributed to the purchase price does not result in this person becoming a co-owner of the house (Austria, Belgium, Denmark, France, Germany, Greece, Italy, Netherlands, Portugal, Scotland, Spain, Sweden, Turkey and the Nordic countries). For this result to be achieved, the requirements of the transfer should concur. If it is not the case, the one who contributed to the purchase price cannot prevent the owner from selling the immovable. In consequence, the owner would only have to repay the contribution or be liable in damages.

Also, the one who contributes might be removed from the house by the Bank or third acquirer, if this person hadn't any right of possession (Austria, Belgium, Denmark, Finland, France, Germany, Greece, Italy, Netherlands, Norway, Portugal, Turkey, Scotland, Spain and the Nordic countries).

In Austria, Germany and the Netherlands, if both of them conclude a partnership agreement, the house is held in joint ownership which means that neither of them can dispose of the property without the consent of the other. In Denmark, there is a special rule from case law that courts can declare that the contributor is, in fact, a co-owner of the house as long as the other has not yet registered his right in the Land Register. This rule would be applicable to partners who live together, friends, family, etc., who share accommodation. In Norway, Finland and Sweden, the spouse or unmarried co-habitant that contributes significantly to the purchase of a house, is presumed (rebuttable) to be the co-owner.

This question is principally addressed to show the differences that exist in civil and common law systems. Thus, in England, as a general rule when legal title documents to the house are only in one person's name, this person is the sole legal owner of the property. However, the fact that the other person made a (significant) contribution to the purchase price will normally be sufficient evidence that this other person has an equitable (i.e. beneficial ownership) interest in the property. The degree to which he has an equitable interest in the house depends on the degree to which the court considers that both parties intended to co-own the beneficial interest in the house. This is particularly the case if both are co-habitees (e.g. boyfriend and girlfriend), as opposed to some form of commercial arrangement. Nevertheless, the co-habitant that contributed to the purchase price has no power to prevent the owner from transferring his own beneficial interest in the property to a third party.

The answer to whether the Bank can remove the person who contributed to the purchase price depends on certain circumstances, according to the English legal system. Thus, if the mortgage had been granted by the owner after the property was acquired, and without consent (either actual or imputed) from the person who contributed to the purchase price, then the Bank will be bound by this late person's interest in the property if he was in actual occupation. In this case, he cannot be removed. This situation is similar in Ireland where the interest of the contributor will bind the formal owner as an overriding interest if the house is registered in the Land Registry or under the doctrine of notice if the house is unregistered. In most jurisdictions, it makes a difference if both of them were married and the resolution changes depending on the economical regime of the marriage (see case 14).

(B) The Jurisdictions (Presented by Related Jurisdictions)

1 *Germany and related jurisdictions*

(a) Germany

(a) The mere fact that Helda contributed to the purchase price does not result in her becoming a co-owner of the house. Like any other type of ownership of land, co-ownership can only be acquired by notarised agreement and registration of the shares in the Land Register.[1]

Assuming that Hans and Helda are co-owners by fractional shares,[2] Hans can sell his share of the house without Helda's consent.[3] But if he wants to sell the entire house, Helda can prevent the sale because part owners may only jointly dispose of the joint item as a whole.[4]

If Hans is the sole owner of the house, Helda cannot effectively prevent the sale. Even if she has entered into an agreement with Hans that prohibits him from selling the house, this contract would not have effect *in rem*.[5] Hans would only be liable in damages. The most effective method to prevent the sale would be to have Hans and Helda agree on an obligation to re-transfer the house upon the condition that it is sold and to secure the obligation to re-transfer by registering a priority notice (*Vormerkung*).[6]

Hans and Helda could also have concluded a partnership agreement. In this case, the house is held in joint ownership with the result that Hans cannot dispose of the property without Helda's consent.[7]

(b) The Bank cannot take possession of the property. The mortgage only gives it the right to realise the property by compulsory execution (*Zwangsvollstreckung*).[8] This can be done by compulsory auction (*Zwangsversteigerung*) or by enforced administration (*Zwangsverwaltung*) of the property (the latter being inadequate in the present case).[9] After the compulsory auction, the acquirer is entitled to remove everybody who is in possession of the house if the possessor does not have any right to possess (which did not expire as a result of the compulsory auction[10]).

Assuming that Hans and Helda are co-owners by fractional shares of the house, Hans can only mortgage his share of the house without

[1] §§ 873, para. 1, 925; para. 1, BGB, § 47 GBO. [2] §§ 1008–1011, 741ff. BGB.
[3] See § 747 sentence 1 BGB. [4] § 747 sentence 2 BGB. [5] See § 137 BGB.
[6] See BGH, NJW 1997, 861. [7] See §§ 718, 719 BGB. [8] § 1147 BGB.
[9] §§ 866, 869 ZPO, §§ 15ff., 146ff. ZVG. [10] § 93 ZVG, § 885 ZPO.

Helda's consent.[11] If this had been done, compulsory execution is possible in relation to his share.[12] In this case, the acquirer of the auctioned share of the house cannot remove Helda but only claim joint possession.[13]

With Helda's consent, both shares of the house can be mortgaged.[14] In this case, the Bank can realise the house by compulsory execution and the acquirer of the auctioned house is entitled to remove both Hans and Helda.[15]

If Hans is the sole owner of the house, he can mortgage the house without any restriction and the Bank can realise the house by compulsory execution. When Helda lived with Hans, she had a right of co-possession (*Mitbesitz*) only, which does not survive compulsory auction.[16]

If Hans and Helda have concluded a partnership agreement, the house is part of the partnership assets and Hans cannot mortgage the house without Helda's consent.[17]

(c) The answer depends on the matrimonial property regime under which Hans and Helda are living.

If Hans and Helda are living under the statutory property regime of community of accrued gains (*Zugewinngemeinschaft*), the marriage does not affect the ownership of the house and the power of the spouse to dispose of it.[18] But if the house (or, in the case of co-ownership, the share of the house) forms nearly all of Hans' property (85–90 per cent) he may only, with Helda's (previous or subsequent) consent, bind himself to transfer the ownership of the house or charge the house to such an extent that the value is nearly exhausted.[19] Otherwise, the transfer or charge of the house is not effective.[20]

This limitation of disposition is absolute,[21] with the statutory consequence that even an acquisition in good faith of the ownership or

[11] §§ 747, 1008, 1114 BGB. [12] See § 864, para. 2 ZPO.

[13] See Anton Steiner and Dieter Eickmann, *Zwangsversteigerung und Zwangsverwaltung, 1* (Munich: C.H. Beck Verlag, 1984), § 93, note 17.

[14] See §§ 747 sentence 2, 1008, 1114, 1132 BGB and BGHZ, vol. 40, pp. 115ff. (120); BGH, NJW 1989, 831; Sebastian Herrler in Otto Palandt, *Bürgerliches Gesetzbuch*, 76th edn. (Munich: C.H. Beck Verlag, 2017), § 1114, note 1, § 1132, note 5.

[15] § 93 ZVG, § 885 ZPO.

[16] See Roland Böttcher, *ZVG*, 4th edn. (Munich: C.H. Beck Verlag, 2005), § 93, note 5.

[17] See §§ 718, 719 BGB. [18] Compare §§ 1363, para. 2, 1364 BGB.

[19] See § 1365, para. 1 BGB; BGH, NJW 1991, 1739; 1990, 112. [20] § 1366, para. 4 BGB.

[21] BGHZ vol. 40, pp. 218ff.

mortgage would not be possible.[22] But the Federal Court of Justice (*Bundesgerichtshof*, BGH) decided that the limitation of disposition affected third parties only if the acquirer at the time of the obligatory contract knew that the house formed nearly the whole of the vendor's property or that the encumbrance almost exhausted the value of the house, respectively.[23] If Chris and the Bank did not have this knowledge, the transfer and the mortgage are effective.

If the disposition of the house is ineffective, for lack of Helda's necessary approval, she is entitled to assert the ineffectiveness of the dispositions.[24]

If Hans has effectively mortgaged the house, Helda cannot take action against the compulsory execution of the property because the aforementioned limitation of disposition does not apply to a compulsory execution.[25]

If Hans and Helda, by marriage contract, agreed on community of property (*Gütergemeinschaft*), the house would become, by act of law, the joint property of both spouses (marital property; *Gesamtgut*).[26] The house is jointly owned (*Gesamthandseigentum*), meaning that Hans cannot dispose of his share of the house as part of the marital property.[27] His power to dispose of the entire house depends on the marriage contract. If Hans and Helda did not make any provision about the management of the marital property, they can only manage and dispose of the marital property together.[28] If Hans, alone, has the right to manage the marital property he may only, with Helda's consent, dispose of a plot of land that is part of the marital property or bind himself to such a disposition.[29] Without Helda's consent, the transfer and mortgaging of the house are not effective.[30] Although the limitation of disposition is absolute, and Hans is only joint owner of the house, an acquisition in good faith by Chris or the Bank is possible if Hans is registered as sole owner of the house (i.e. the marriage

22 §§ 135, para. 2, 892, para. 1 sentence 2 BGB are only applicable to relative limitations of disposition.

23 BGHZ, vol. 43, pp. 174ff. (177); vol. 106, pp. 253ff.; BGH, NJW-RR 1990, 1154, NJW 1993, 2441.

24 See § 1368 BGB; Otto Palandt and Gerd Brudermüller, *Bürgerliches Gesetzbuch*, 68th edn. (Munich: C.H. Beck Verlag, 2009), § 1368, note 3.

25 Böttcher, *ZVG*, §§ 15, 16, note 72; Steiner and Eickmann, *Zwangsversteigerung und Zwangsverwaltung*, 1, §§ 15, 16, note 163.

26 §§ 1415, 1416 BGB. 27 See § 1419 BGB. 28 §§ 1421, 1450ff. BGB.

29 See § 1424 BGB. 30 §§ 1427, para. 1, 1453, para. 1; 1366, para. 4 BGB.

contract is not entered in the Land Register)[31] and they don't know of the community of property.[32]

If the mortgage is effective against the marital property, the Bank can realise the house by compulsory execution.[33]

If Hans and Helda chose, by marriage contract, to live under the matrimonial property regime of separation of property (*Gütertrennung*),[34] the answer does not differ from the answers in (a) and (b).

(b) Austria

(a) Even though Helda has made a significant contribution to the purchase price, she will not automatically become a co-owner of the house. That can only be achieved by notarised agreement and registration of the particular shares in the Land Register (§§ 361, 825ff ABGB).

Assuming that Hans and Helda became co-owners by fractional shares (based on a contract, by operation of law or due to testamentary dispositions), Hans can sell his individual share of the house without Helda's consent as long as he doesn't harm her rights (§ 829 ABGB). But if he wants to sell the house in its entirety, Helda can prevent the transfer of ownership by not giving her consent to the sale. Both may only jointly dispose of the joint item as a whole.

If Hans is the sole owner of the house, Helda cannot effectively prevent the sale to Chris. Even if she has entered into an agreement with Hans which prohibits him to sell the house, that contract would not have any effect *in rem*. Hans would only be liable in damages.

Hans and Helda could also have concluded a partnership agreement. In this case, the house is held in joint ownership with the result being that Hans cannot dispose of the property without Helda's consent (see above).

(b) The Bank won't try to seek possession of the house but will apply for compulsory auction (*Zwangsversteigerung*), expecting proceeds as high as possible. Needless to say, there is also the possibility to apply for forced administration (*Zwangsverwaltung*). However, in our case, that will not be an appropriate approach.

[31] For registration see § 1416, para. 3 BGB, § 47 GBO.

[32] For predominant opinion see, e.g., Gerd Brudermüller in Palandt, *Bürgerliches Gesetzbuch*, § 1422, note 5 thus until 74th edn., 2015 – opinion changed against predominant opinion: see now 76th edn., 2017; Karl-Heinz Gursky, in *J. von Staudingers Kommentar zum Bürgerlichen Gesetzbuch*, 13th adaption (Berlin: de Gruyters, 2002), § 892, note 249 with further references.

[33] See § 740 ZPO. [34] § 1414 BGB.

Helda can be removed from the house if Hans was the sole owner of it. Her right to live in the house does not stand the compulsory auction. If Hans and Helda are co-owners by fractional shares, Hans is only able to mortgage his share of the house. Execution is possible with respect to his share. The new acquirer can claim joint possession only and cannot arbitrarily remove Helda. The same is true if there is a partnership agreement.

(c) The answer depends on the matrimonial property scheme (*ehelicher Güterstand*) under which Hans and Helda are living. A general distinction is made between the property scheme by law (which has its origins in the marriage) and the regime by contract (which can be constituted as far as provisions of the law are optional).[35]

In Austria, there is a separation of property (*Gütertrennung*) system, which means that marriage neither influences the proprietary situation of the husband nor his wife (§§ 1233, 1237 ABGB). In other words, each spouse keeps his/her present belongings as long as the marriage continues and no prenuptial agreements (*Ehevertrag*) have been made. One significant exception to that rule is laid down in § 97 ABGB. The provision aims to protect the spouse who is not registered in the Land Register, but yet contributed to the preservation or designing of the marital home. It grants him/her a right to keep on residing in the home, provided that a necessity of accommodation (*dringendes Wohnbedürfnis*) has been proven. It is, furthermore, assumed that no other appropriate flat is available or that moving is unacceptable *a priori*. § 97 ABGB is applicable to flats but also to a single-family house that had been used for living purposes.[36] The claim is excluded if losing the house is enforced 'due to the circumstances' (§ 97 sentence 2 ABGB). That is always the case when the registered party is not actually, or legally, able to prevent the disposal. In our case, Hans does not arbitrarily sell the house but the sale is enforced due to circumstances of non-payment.[37] So, the executive auction and removal is supposed to be lawful; Hans will not be in a position to prevent the sale.

To sum up, I can say that the result does not differ from the answer in (a) and (b).

35 Monika Hinteregger, *Familienrecht*, 4th edn. (Vienna: Österreich Verlag, 2009), pp. 82, 86.

36 Herbert Schimetschek, 'Die besonderen Rechtsprobleme der "Ehewohnung"', *ImmZ* 1979, 35 (36); OGH 17.11.1987, 4 Ob 523/87, SZ 60/246 = JBl 1988, 237 = EFSlg 53.081.

37 Susanne Ferrari and Michael Schwimann, in Michael Schwimann (ed.), *Praxiskommentar zum ABGB*, I, 3rd edn. (Vienna: LexisNexis, 2005), § 97 mn 5.

Note: In the primary stages, Hans would have had the chance to avoid the executive auction and Helda would have been able to prevent the selling of the house. If Hans had constituted a prohibition of encumbrance and sale (*Belastungs- und Veräußerungsverbot*) and additionally applied for a note in the Land Register (§ 364c ABGB) early enough, a sale or executive auction would have been impossible. Such an agreement can only be reached between a husband and his wife, or between parents and their children (or their spouses). If the prohibition has been registered, it not only has an effect under the law of obligations, but one *in rem*. Therefore, it prevents executive auction and sales by making any disposals void.[38]

(c) The Netherlands

(a) Let us suppose that the house has been transferred to Hans in sole ownership and not to Hans and Helda in co-ownership. Helda cannot prevent the sale and transfer of the house, even if she lived in it. The mere fact that she contributed to the purchase price does not give her co-ownership of the house.

(b) Upon a forced sale in execution, the Bank will be able to have Helda removed unless she leases from Hans and the lease is *older* than the mortgage. It makes no difference whether or not there is any family relation between Hans and Helda. If Helda leased the house from Hans *after* the creation of the mortgage, the mortgagee and, hence, the buyer in the forced sale of the house are bound to her lease contract (art. 7:226 BW). However, in practice, most mortgage deeds contain a lease clause forbidding the mortgagor to enter into a lease contract. If the mortgagor infringes this clause and enters into a lease contract, the mortgagee, or the buyer in the forced sale, is able to have the lessee removed from the house (art. 3:264 BW).

(c) If, however, Hans and Helda are married or have a registered partnership (art. 1:80b BW), Helda would be able to annul the sales contract if she lived in the house at the time of the sale. She must approve the sale of the house (art. 1:88 BW). As a result, the transfer of ownership is also annulled retroactively (arts. 3:88 and 3:89 BW), so that the sale and transfer are deemed never to have happened. After all, every transfer of ownership should be based on a valid legal

[38] Helmut Koziol and Rudolf Welser, *Bürgerliches Recht*, I, 13th edn. (Vienna: MANZ Verlag, 2006), p. 291

ground such as a contract of sale (art. 3:84 BW).[39] The same rule (art. 1:88 BW) also applies to Hans' contract obliging to charge the property with a mortgage. If Helda did not approve, she can annul this contract and, thus, annul the right of mortgage.

This rule of art. 1:88 BW applies, irrespective of the matrimonial property regime (community of property or separation of property) that applies between the spouses. If the partners made no special arrangements, their individual patrimoniums, in principle, merge upon marriage. In such a case, not only the sale would require Helda's approval but the transfer would also be impossible without her cooperation because she co-owns the property (art. 1:94 BW).

(d) Turkey

(a) Normally, Helda cannot prevent the sale. However, if the selling of the house by Hans to Chris is a fraudulent conveyance, Helda can sue for an interim injunction. Consequently, Hans cannot sell the house[40] and Helda can sue for her share. Although the judge accepts her request, if Hans does not obey this verdict, Helda can demand that the house be seized. When the foreclosure sale of the house takes place, she can get her money back.

(b) The Bank has a real right on the house. The owner of a real right may claim his right from everyone involved. The Bank has a priority on the money as a result of the foreclosure sale of the house. If this money satisfies the Bank, and there is money left over, then that amount will be paid to Helda if she demands a sequestration on the house, which comes after the mortgage of the Bank.

(c) If they are married, the answer for (a) will not differ unless the house is their conjugal home. If the house is the conjugal home of the spouses, Hans cannot sell it without the explicit consent of Helda.

If they are married, the answer for (b) will not differ unless the house is their conjugal home. If the house is the conjugal home of the spouses, Hans cannot mortgage it without the explicit consent of Helda.[41]

[39] Lars P.W. van Vliet, *Transfer of Movables in German, French, English and Dutch Law* (Nijmegen: Ars Aequi Libri, 2000), pp. 24–5.

[40] See Baki Kuru, Ramazan Arslan, and Ejder Yılmaz, *Medenî Usul Hukuku, Değiştirilmiş 18. Baskı* (Ankara: Yetkin, 2004), p. 701.

[41] See art. 194 TCC; Ivy Williams, Siegfried Wyler and Barbara Wyler, *The Swiss Civil Code, I* (Zürich, 1987), art. 169; Oğuzman, M.K., Seliçi, Ö and Oktay-Özdemir, S., *Eşya Hukuku Gözden Geçirilmiş 11. Bası* (Istanbul, 2006), pp. 214–15.

2 *Scandinavian jurisdictions*

(a) Finland

(a) A money contribution, as such, to a purchaser of a piece of real estate or a conventional lease house who is, at the same time, a possible vendor of the same object does not normally establish any proprietary right (*right in rem*). Even if it is granted that the receiver owes the sum of contribution to the contributor, there is merely a personal obligation without any securities or privileges to the house. If this is the case, Helda is in the same position as any of Hans' general claimants. The relationship between Hans and Helda does not make any difference. The trust, or any other similar equitable institution, is not recognised in Finnish law, within the frames of the continental legal systems.

Helda can demand restoration of her contribution. As a general claimant, Helda can bring an action against Hans. In addition, Helda can apply for precautionary measures (*turvaamistoimi* in Finnish) if Hans is still the owner of the house (no valid conveyance to Chris has taken place). The court may order the attachment (*takavarikko* in Finnish) of the house, or another of Hans' properties, to an amount securing the debt as a precautionary measure. The decision can be made a month before the beginning of the trial. In addition, the court may, at the request of the applicant, give an interim order on precautionary measures without reserving the opposing party an opportunity to be heard.[42] The enforcement of the interim order can take place without delay.[43]

The attachment order is possible if Helda can demonstrate that she holds a debt that may be rendered payable and there is the danger that Hans hides, destroys, or conveys his or her property or takes other action endangering the payment of the debt of the applicant.[44]

The bailiff will enforce the attachment.[45] After enforcement, Hans cannot sell the house in a valid way.[46] The notice of attachment will be entered into the Title and Mortgage Register.[47] On the other hand, a purchaser (in this case, Chris) can enjoy the protection of good faith (see the answer to case 12, question (b)).

Neverthless, it is possible that the circumstances of the relationship between Hans and Helda are different. It can be judged that a

[42] 7:5.2 Code of Judicial Procedure.
[43] 8:5 Enforcement Code.
[44] 7:1 Code of Judicial Procedure.
[45] 8:1 Enforcement Code.
[46] 8.8.1 and 4:37 Enforcement Code.
[47] 8:7.1 and 4:33.1/1 Enforcement Code.

co-ownership has taken place. The preconditions of such a judgment are given below in answer (c).

(b) The Bank, having a mortgage, is a privileged creditor. The Bank can charge the house, owing to Hans' default. The position of a mortgage creditor does not, however, entitle one to possess the house or to claim possession on the grounds of the debtor's default. The Bank can merely charge the house by one of the official procedures described above (see the answer to case 12). Hans keeps the house in his possession until the possible enforced sale of the house. Helda is not entitled to possess the house on the grounds of her contribution as a general creditor. As a co-owner, her position is, naturally, different. In such a case, her position is similar to Hans'.

On the other hand, the Bank's privileged position means that Helda's general claim gives way to the Bank's claim. According to the creditors' order, a mortgage creditor always has a better position than a general creditor.[48] The Bank's good faith is not presumed. If Helda is a creditor, she can charge the house after the full payment to the Bank. It means that the Bank can remove Helda.

(c) As a married spouse, Helda can prevent the voluntary sale of the house if the house is a joint home for her and Hans. Accordingly, their apartment is treated as a matrimonial home and she enjoys the occupation right of a non-owner spouse.[49] In this case, Chris' possible acquisition is not valid and no registration will be granted without Helda's consent. On the other hand, the voidable acquisition of Chris can be improved (for details, see the answer to the next question).

The marriage shall be official and registered in the Finnish Personal Register. The same rules are applied to a registered partnership (partnership of two persons of the same sex).[50] Instead, a position as a girlfriend or as an unmarried spouse, or another close relation, does

48 5:47 Enforcement Code.

49 38:1 Marriage Act (1929), www.finlex.fi/en/laki/kaannokset/1929/en19290234.pdf. In addition, the occupation right of a spouse appears as the possession right of the surviving spouse in the case of death of the other spouse. According to 3:1a Code of Inheritance, the surviving spouse has possession right of the common home of the spouses. See www.finlex.fi/fi/laki/kaannokset/1965/en19650040.pdf.

50 8:1 Act on Registered Partnerships (2001). See www.finlex.fi/fi/laki/kaannokset/2001/en20010950.pdf.

not create the protection of a matrimonial home or an occupation right. On the other hand, a marriage does not create co-ownership.

As a rule, a marriage between a creditor and a debtor does not change their positions. Helda's position as a creditor, according to the creditors' order and in relation to the Bank and other creditors, is the same as described above. Helda's matrimonial right does not prevent creditors from charging the house or an enforced and public sale of it. In other words, the Bank can remove Helda even in this situation.

In certain cases and on certain conditions, it is possible that the acquisition of the house is treated as an acquisition for both Hans and Helda. In this case, a co-ownership has been established. It is possible, even if Hans is the only owner according to the documents; that is, he has merely signed the contract (the deed) as a purchaser and has alone registered the acquisition of the house (i.e. as part of a piece of real estate or of a lease). Normally, it is the case of a married or unmarried couple and the house is acquired as their joint home.[51] The judgment is possible, nevertheless, even in other cases. The joint ownership of Hans and Helda is justified by the intention of the acquisition and in the form of interpretation of the contract. Instead of marriage, the intention of the contract is the deciding factor in this situation. Helda's position is called a secret owner (a special kind of *fiducia*).[52]

The secret ownership is valid and effective between the parties (Hans and Helda) but, as a rule, it does not enjoy protection against other persons; that is, against the rest of the world.[53] Chris, as a purchaser, can trust Hans' registration or his deed. Chris has no obligation to find out Helda's secret ownership.

The joint ownership and shares of the owners (as a rule, half for each of them), can be confirmed by a judgment of a local court. After that, the co-ownership will be registered in the Title and Mortgage Register by the announcement of the court.[54] In other words, the secret ownership can be published by the claim of the secret owner. Even precautionary measures can be directed by the court before the trial. Naturally, Hans is not entitled to sell or mortgage Helda's share of the house after the confirmation of her ownership.

[51] KKO 1985 II 167, KKO 1986 II 103, KKO 1989:37 and KKO 2016:37. The Act on the Dissolution of the Household of Cohabiting Partners (26/2011) does not change these rules (in English: www.finlex.fi/fi/laki/kaannokset/2011/en20110026.pdf).

[52] However, the trust as a legal institution is not recognised in the Finnish legal system.

[53] KKO 2003:82 and KKO 1992:168.

[54] 11:7.3 Code of Real Estate.

As a registered owner of the house, Hans can mortgage the whole house to the Bank. In this case, the consent of Helda as a married spouse is not required. In addition, the Bank is protected against Helda's secret ownership, as described above, until it has been published. The mortgage will remain even if the joint ownership is confirmed later.

The same rules apply to leased houses and similar rules to residential apartments.[55]

The crucial matter, in this case, is that Hans has bought the house. The situation would be different if Hans had first purchased or acquired, in another way, a site or a parcel and he and Helda had built the house together on that land. It could be judged that the land had been bought together and there was a secret co-ownership of both the land and the house. In this case, however, as far as the house is concerned, Helda will enjoy protection against third persons, at least in relation to creditors.[56] Hence, in this situation, the position of the land and the house will be different, as far as relations with third persons are concerned.

(b) Sweden

(a) For the acquisition of real estate rights, there are formal requirements. The contract of conveyance must, for example, be in writing, contain an expression of the conveyor's will to assign the property and identify the property and the parties.[57] A contribution to the purchase price from someone not stated as the buyer in the contract of assignment will, as a rule, not give the contributor any right to the property.

However, in situations concerning the partition of an estate in divorce proceedings or after the separation of co-habitees, where some property is to be left out of the jointly dividable estate and to be allotted to the buyer alone (see under case 14), the other partner may, according to well-established case law, acquire 'hidden co-ownership'[58] which, *inter alia,* is to be taken into account within the process of partition of the estate.[59]

[55] 38:1 and 39 Marriage Act (1929). The lack of Helda's consent prevents Chris' registration. It is, however, possible that the marriage of Hans and Helda is not discovered in the registration examination. See 12:1.1 Code of Real Estate.

[56] KKO 2003:82. [57] 4:1 Land Code. [58] Swedish: '*dold samäganderätt*'.

[59] The first Supreme Court cases concerning real property were *NJA* 1980, 705, *NJA* 1981, 693 and *NJA* 1982, 589.

Hidden co-ownership may be founded on express or tacit agreement.[60] The property must have been acquired for the owner's and the co-owner's joint use. If the real property was acquired during their relationship, and is used as their common dwelling, no other evidence is required to prove the intent of joint use.[61] Where the alleged co-owner has made a capital contribution, accepted responsibility for debts at the time of purchase or contributed to the household economically, there may be hidden co-ownership.

It has also been accepted in case law that hidden co-ownership may also arise outside of dissolution of marriage and co-habitation. In one case, the Supreme Court stated that the fact that hidden co-ownership, so far, had only been dealt with in such cases did not mean that such ownership necessarily should be restricted to those situations. A son-in-law had assigned, to a third person, his (possible) right to hidden ownership or his (possible) hidden co-ownership with his wife in the real property formally owned by the father-in-law. The Supreme Court found that the deficiency in the formal requirements should not withhold the right of the son-in-law to assign his (possible) hidden ownership.[62] In another case, the Supreme Court found, with reference to legal scholarship,[63] that hidden co-ownership may arise between siblings, between friends engaged in a non-registered company, or in situations of a family-oriented nature.[64]

[60] Anders Agell and Margareta Brattström, *Äktenskap: Samboende. Partnerskap*, 4th edn. (Uppsala: Iustus Förlag, 2011), p. 76.

[61] Agell and Brattström, *Äktenskap. Samboende. Partnerskap*, p. 77f. Gösta Walin, *Samäganderätt* (Stockholm: Norstedts Juridik, 2000), p. 61, goes so far as to claim that no evidence is needed on the intent of co-ownership. Cf. Supreme Court judgment *NJA* 2002, 3 for a case on open co-ownership, where one of the spouses argued that the property was in fact his. However, Torkel Gregow, *Samägd egendom* (Stockholm: Norstedts Juridik, 2016), p. 112 is of opposite opinion. Cf. Supreme Court concluded that co-ownership is assumed when spouses or co-habitees acquire real property or a housing co-operative apartment for joint use. The fact that the whole or a major part of the price was paid by one of the spouses was not enough to set the assumption aside.

[62] Supreme Court judgment *NJA* 1993, 324. Cf. Gösta Walin, *Samäganderätt* (Uppsala: Norstedts Juridik, 2000), p. 61 and Gregow, *Samägd egendom*, p. 118. *See* also *NJA* 1983, 550, where the Supreme Court rejected the objection that the deficiency in the formal requirements made it impossible to acquire hidden co-ownership.

[63] Håkan Nial, *Om handelsbolag och enkla bolag*, 3rd edn. (Stockholm: Norstedts Juridik, 1992), p. 382f. (now *see* Håkan Nial and Carl Hemström, *Om handelsbolag och enkla bolag*, 4th edn., Stockholm: Norstedts Juridik, 2008, p. 385f.) and Walin, *Samäganderätt*, pp. 58 and 98.

[64] Supreme Court judgment *NJA* 2002, 142. The case concerned whether a legal person may acquire hidden co-ownership, which was answered negatively.

Hidden co-ownership does not directly give rise to a right to have the ownership registered. A promise to sell real property is not binding, unless the formal requirements are fulfilled.[65] This also applies to spouses.[66] For such a right, it is required that the hidden co-ownership is transformed into a regular one, either by formal conveyance or judgment.[67] It may also be transferred through partition of the estate.[68] This might be possible, even by a decision of a partition officer appointed by a court, when the partners disagree on the existence of co-ownership.[69] Hidden co-ownership is of an obligatory nature only and, accordingly, does not affect the rights of creditors[70] or prevent the owner from assigning the property.[71] However, the consent of spouses, registered partners of the same sex and cohabitees is needed for dispositions concerning real property (see under case 14).

Helda might, in this case, prevent the sale of her dividend if she, by judgment, is declared to be a co-owner and succeeds in registering title before Chris. Or, alternately, she could preclude the sale altogether by not giving her consent, if she is married or co-habitates with Hans. If Chris only succeeds in purchasing Hans' dividend, he may avoid the contract due to material breach.[72]

(b) A creditor may apply for an executory sale of a mortgaged property if the debtor is in default. Helda will not be able to prevent this. If Helda does not move voluntarily, she may be evicted by the enforcement authority after an executory sale[73] of the house[74] or on application of the buyer.[75]

65 Cf. Supreme Court judgments *NJA* 1992, 66 and *NJA* 1994, 130, where the Supreme Court concluded that purchase options and offers of first refusal are binding as to the sale of housing co-operative apartments, if the contract otherwise fulfils the formal requirements, and Justice Håstad in *NJA* 1998, 610, who in *obiter dictum* found that this must apply also for real property (for a maximum period of two years, 4:4 Land Code)

66 Supreme Court judgment *NJA* 1987, 726.

67 Supreme Court judgments *NJA* 1984, 772 and *NJA* 1993, 324. See *NJA* 1989, 114 for an example on conveyance, and *NJA* 1987, 137 for an example on a judgment, satisfying the formal requirements for title registration.

68 Agell and Brattström, *Äktenskap. Samboende. Partnerskap*, p. 80; Walin, *Samäganderätt*, pp. 50ff.

69 Walin, *Samäganderätt*, p. 52.

70 Supreme Court judgments *NJA* 1985, 615 and *NJA* 1993, 324.

71 Supreme Court judgments *NJA* 1984, 772, *NJA* 1985, 97 and *NJA* 1993, 324.

72 4:19 Land Code.

73 Generally by auction, 12:1 Enforcement Code.

74 According to 12:36(3) Enforcement Code, the enforcement authority may grant the owner the right to stay on the property for a maximum period of three months after the sale.

75 § 3 (1) Payment Orders and Enforcement Assistance Act; *lagen (1990:746) om betalningsföreläggande och handräckning*.

(c) As explained under question (a) above, Helda's position is much stronger if she is married to Hans at the time of the purchase.

(c) Denmark

(a) If Helda is not a co-owner of the property, according to the deed, or has no other security or pledge on the property, she may not prevent Hans from selling the property. Helda may try to get a declaratory judgment that she is, in fact, a co-owner of the house. However, when a co-ownership is not agreed upon in advance, the Courts are reluctant. If it is proven that both parties have contributed to the acquisition of the asset, it cannot be ruled out that a co-ownership will be found to exist, despite the fact that formal documents indicate the contrary. If this is the case Helda will be the owner of a share of the property. However, such a right may be extinguished if Chris registers his purchase of the property in the Buildings and Dwellings Register at the Land Register in good faith.[76] In case Helda does not acquire title, the amount will be considered a loan and Helda may demand that Hans repay the sum.

(Conversely, if Helda has only contributed to the payment of the running costs of the house, she will not be considered a co-owner but she might, in rare cases, be able to direct a claim against Hans based on unjustified enrichment.)[77]

These rules apply both to partners who live together and friends/ family, etc. who choose to share accommodation.

(b) If the Court finds that Helda is, indeed, a co-owner of the house, but her right is not registered in the Buildings and Dwellings Register, the Bank's mortgage may, in principle, only rest on Hans' share of the value of the property. However, if the Bank has registered its mortgage on the property as such, in good faith in regards to Helda's co-ownership, it may extinguish Helda's claim and ultimately have her removed from the house. However, if Helda has paid rent,

[76] Sections 1 and 5, LRA.

[77] See the ruling of the Supreme Court in U 1980.480 H. Mr A and Miss B had lived together for four-and-half years. During this period they acquired a property. The down payment was paid with funds raised by Mr A and the deed was in his name. Both parties were working full time and sharing the costs. The parties split up, and Mr A sold the property at a profit. The Supreme Court rejected co-ownership under these conditions, but allowed Miss B a claim based on unjustified enrichment. See also Ingrid Lund-Andersen *et al.*, *Familieret*, 5th edn. (Copenhagen: DJØF, 2003), p. 690, Hans V.G. Pedersen, *Familie- og arveret*, 8th edn. (Copenhagen: Karnov Group, 2013), p. 156.

(and, thus, is a tenant) she will be protected by the rules of the Tenant Act.

On the other hand, if Helda's claim is acknowledged by the Courts (or by Hans) and registered in the Buildings and Dwellings Register at the Land Register before the registration of the mortgage, the Bank must respect Helda's share. In this case, Helda cannot be removed from the property.

(c) If the property serves as the family home and the property is a part of the *joint property* of a married couple, the owner of the property (irrespective of how he or she acquired the property) may not sell the property without the consent of the other spouse.[78] If the owner has done so nonetheless, the other spouse may have the transaction set aside if the buyer knew, or ought to have known, that the sale was prohibited. If the house belonged to the joint property of the spouses, Hans could not have mortgaged the house without Helda's consent and the situation would not have occurred.[79]

However, if the house belonged to Hans' *separate estate,* Helda could not hinder the sale or the Bank's repossession of the house.

Again, one may consider whether co-ownership has occurred. It is assumed that co-ownership may arise between spouses if both parties have made a contribution to the acquisition of the asset and if the running costs of the asset have been paid (reasonably) equally by the spouses.

(d) Norway

(a) A 'significant contribution' to a purchase of a house may be one of several circumstances to consider if it is subsequently claimed that the contributor is a co-owner of the house. The contribution, in itself, is not sufficient to establish co-ownership.

Where a spouse or unmarried cohabitant contributes significantly to the purchase of a house meant for the spouses' or cohabitants' common use ('a common project') there is – according to case law and legal doctrine – a rebuttable presumption of co-ownership, sometimes seen as a rebuttable presumption of a tacit agreement on co-ownership.[80] One spouse's housework is also regarded as a contribution to the acquisition of a common dwelling and ordinary household contents.[81]

[78] Section 18, Consolidation of Acts of 23 December 2015, No. 1814 on the Legal Effects of Marriage (Legal Effects of Marriage Act).

[79] Section 18, Legal Effects of Marriage Act.

[80] Peter Lødrup and Tone Sverdrup, *Familieretten*, 8th edn. (Oslo: 2016), pp. 147–57.

[81] Section 31 (3), Act Relating to Marriage (*lov om ekteskap*, 4 July 1991 No. 47).

Co-ownership is not always registered in the Land Register; it is not unusual that one of the co-owners is registered as a sole owner.

Let us suppose that Hans and Helda are unmarried co-owners and that only Hans is registered as owner in the Land Register. Let us further suppose that the object of the sale is the right as sole owner of the house and not only Hans' right as a co-owner. If Chris registers his right in the Land Register, in good faith regarding Helda's right at the time of registration, he will not have to respect Helda's right.[82] It is a case of good faith acquisition. The situation regarding the security right, in favour of the Bank, is the same.

(b) Under Norwegian law, the Bank will normally not 'seek possession', but have the house sold on the basis of the security right. If the Bank, and then also the buyer at a forced sale, does not have to respect Helda's right (see under (a)), Helda will have to move out.

(c) If Hans and Helda are married Hans, as a rule, cannot sell the house without Helda's written consent, whether Helda made a contribution to the purchase or not.[83] The consent is required before registering the sale in the Land Register.[84] Helda can have a contract avoided by judgment if it is entered into without necessary consent. She must raise this claim within six months of this knowledge and no later than one year from the registration in the Land Register (if the buyer succeeds in registering his right without Helda's consent). As for the Bank, Hans also needs Helda's written consent to create a security right in the property; the same rules apply for a sale. These rules on consent, serving to protect the common home of the spouses, apply even where a third party (in good faith) registers his right in the Land Register.

There is no easy way for the purchaser or the Bank to check whether Hans is married or not. In principle, they may request information from the national registration office, but that is a rather cumbersome procedure entailing a request in writing. In practice, the purchaser or the Bank will rely on information given by Hans himself.

[82] It is held that this follows from the Judicial Registration Act § 27 (see under case 1) by analogy, see Thor Falkanger and Aage Thor Falkanger, *Tingsrett*, 8th edn. (Oslo: Universitetsforlaget, 2016), pp. 683–5; Kåre Lilleholt, *Allmenn formuerett* (Oslo: Universiteitsforlaget, 2012), p. 209, cf. *Norsk Retstidende*, 1991, p. 352.

[83] Section 32, Act Relating to Marriage. This requirement may be deviated from in a marriage agreement, cf. section 37.

[84] Section 13, Judicial Registration Act.

3 *Romanic–Mediterranean jurisdictions*

(a) Italy

(a) In this case, the house is considered to be solely owned by Hans and Helda could, under no circumstances, prevent the sale. However, in the case that Helda and Hans are living together as an unmarried couple in the house, and she can produce evidence of the fact that her contribution is not the fulfilment of the moral and material duties of supporting the family Helda, at the possible termination of the relationship, may request the reimbursement of the money she has given to Hans for the purchase of the house by way of unjust enrichment under art. ICC 2041.[85]

(b) Yes. Hans is the sole owner of the house. The Bank could remove Helda.

(c) Unless otherwise agreed, property acquired by spouses during marriage is considered common property under arts. 159 and 177 ICC. As this is the case, Helda may legitimately oppose the sale because, in order to be effective, the sale also requires her consent under art. 180 c 2 ICC. Art. 180 c 2 ICC needs the consent of both spouses for acts exceeding administration in the ordinary course. Moreover, even if the sale took place and were registered, Helda may take action (action of annulment) to cancel the sale within one year from the registration of art. 184 c 1 and 2 ICC.[86]

While considering the house common property, it can guarantee Hans' debt only if it has been evidently incurred in the interests of the family; that is, for the acquisition of the family home. Conversely, if Hans has bought a holiday home, the Bank may compulsorily sell the house and remove Helda. However, the Bank could only retain half of the value, the half belonging to Hans, who was personally liable for the debt guaranteed with the mortgage on the house.[87]

(b) Spain

(a) If Helda's contribution was reflected in the title to the property (because both Hans and Helda signed the private contract of sale, or both

[85] See Court of Cassation, sez. II, 13.03.2003, No. 3713, in *Giur. It.*, 2004, p. 530 annnotated by Digregorio.

[86] See Court of Cassation 11.06.2010 No. 14093 in *Resp. civ. e prev.* 2010, 11, 2362. Note that in this case the time of prescription is less than the ordinary one, that is, of five years.

[87] Art. 189 ICC.

appear as registered owners), Hans may not sell the house without Helda's consent. It is irrelevant whether Helda is just a friend, Hans' girlfriend, wife, or other family relation.

(b) If Hans has mortgaged the house without needing Helda's consent, this is because the house is registered in his name and they are not married; if they *were* married, Hans would need Helda's consent to mortgage the main home and, if he acted without such consent, the consequences would be the same as in the case seen above.[88] In that case, if Hans defaults, the Bank may apply for Helda to be removed and sell the house at auction to satisfy the debt against the proceeds.

(c) If Helda contributed money, but the house is registered in Hans' name alone, Helda may not oppose the sale (unless she disputes Hans' ownership[89]), except if she is married to Hans and the house is their main home. In this last case, Hans needs Helda's consent to sell. If Helda withholds consent, it is up to a court to decide.[90] If, despite not having Helda's consent or authorisation from a court, Hans sells the house to Chris, Helda may apply for the sale to be voided but cannot recover the house if Chris acted in good faith. If Chris need not have known (no one told him, and the fact that the dwelling was a main home was not on record in the *Registro de la Propiedad*) that the house was Hans and Helda's main home,[91] Helda's only remedy is to claim the damages from Hans, caused to her by sale of the house.

(c) Portugal

(a) Helda's contribution to the purchase price has no effect on ownership of the house. Consequently, if the title to the house on the Land Register is in Hans' name alone, Hans would be the sole owner and Helda would not have any kind of proprietary rights. Helda's rights, insofar as they exist, lie in the law of obligations – for example, for

88 Art. 1320 (1) CC.

89 If Helda and Hans married under the *gananciales* (commonality of estates) form of settlement and Hans bought the house after the constitution of that marriage settlement, the house is presumed to belong to the couple's common estate. Even if Hans does not indicate that he acquires the house for the common estate, the house will be registered in his name but under a presumption that it belongs to the common estate (art. 94 (1) *Reglamento Hipotecario* – mortgage regulations). To destroy the presumption Hans will then have to prove that he paid for the house using his own private money.

90 Art. 1320 (1) CC. If Hans or Helda are civil residents of Catalonia and satisfy the rest of requirements under the Catalan Law 25/2010, of 29 July, Hans will also need Helda's consent to sell or mortgage (arts. 234–3 and 231–9).

91 Art. 1320 (2) CC.

repayment of the loan (if it was a loan) or, in some circumstances, for restitution on the basis of the law of unjust enrichment (e.g. if the money was advanced in contemplation of a marriage which did not take place).[92] Accordingly, no special protection for Helda would arise for any reason other than her financial contribution to the sale.

Helda will not succeed in preventing the sale of the house. As the sole owner of the house, Hans is at liberty to sell. Apart from marriage (which is discussed under (c) below) the answer does not depend upon the relationship between Helda and Hans (e.g. girlfriend and boyfriend; mother and son) or upon the fact that Helda lives in the house.

(b) The fact that Helda lives in the house, and the fact that the house is the family residence, do not grant her any protection. In principle, the Bank can initiate enforcement proceedings that will lead to a judicial sale.

(c) If Hans wants to sell the house to Chris, he might need Helda's consent. In Portugal, the default property regime among spouses, in the absence of ante-nuptial accord, is that of community of acquired assets.[93] Under the system of community of acquired assets, there can be joint property and personal property for each spouse. Whatever someone brings into the marriage or receives individually through gifts or inheritances remains his or hers, but whatever someone earns or acquires during the marriage is co-owned by both spouses, regardless of who earned it or whose name is on the title. Property that is brought to the couple or acquired individually is not communicated; only property acquired after marriage onerously is joint property. This is the general idea that defines the system and basically corresponds to the idea that only that which expresses the collaboration of both spouses in the patrimonial effort of marriage will become joint property. The Portuguese Civil Code (CPC) also typifies a system of general community of assets or a system of separate assets. The system of general community of assets is characterised by the fact that the joint property is constituted by all present and future property of the spouses that is not exempted by law. Under the system of separate assets,[94] there is complete and absolute separation between each spouse's property. Under art. 1735 CC, each owner retains ownership and enjoyment of

[92] Art. 1760 CC.

[93] This follows the terminology used by Guilherme Oliveira, *Family and Succession Law in Portgual* (Alphen aan den Rijn: Kluwer Law International, 2012).

[94] There are two cases in which the law imposes the system of separate assets: marriages celebrated without being preceded by the process of publication of bans, and for anyone who is already sixty years old.

all their present and future property, which they can freely dispose of as they wish. The system of community of assets and the system of separate assets is in force if it is stipulated by the intended spouses in the ante-nuptial deed or in the document drawn up before the Registrar of the civil registry office.

Art. 1682-A (1) CC provides that sale of immovables (either joint or personal property) requires the consent of both spouses, unless the spouses are married in a system of separate assets. Therefore, if Hans and Helda were married, he would not be entitled to sell the house without Helda's consent. If Helda refused to give the consent without genuine motivation, Hans can be empowered by a judge to make the act of disposition on his own (art. 1684 (3) CC).

If Hans has mortgaged the house to the Bank and failed to pay, the proceeding would be quite different. As a general principle, each spouse may legally contract debts without the consent of the other (art. 1690 (1) CC). Debts for which both spouses are liable (art. 1691 CC) are discharged using joint property, or in the absence or insufficiency of this, with the personal property of either spouse. In relation to debts for which one of the spouses is exclusively liable, the general rule is that these debts should be discharged using the personal property of the spouse who is liable, and secondarily, by his or her half of the joint property (art. 1996 CC). I will assume that the debt to the Bank is Hans' exclusive liability. So it should be discharged using his personal property and secondarily his half of the joint property.

The Bank must bring an action against both Hans and Helda (art. 28-A (3) Civil Procedure Code). In order to allow the Bank to seize Hans' half of the joint property, and be sure that her share in the common property is not affected by the proceedings, Helda is entitled to request the division of their common property (art. 825 Civil Procedure Code). If the house becomes Helda's personal property, the Bank cannot seek possession of the property and remove her. On the contrary, if the house becomes Hans' personal property, the Bank will be entitled to ask for the judicial seizure and sale of the house. In that case, Helda has a pre-emption right (*direito de remição*) over the house (art. 912 Civil Procedure Code).

(d) Greece

(a) Helda's contribution to the purchase price does not establish any proprietary right to the house, since ownership (or co-ownership) on an immovable can only be acquired by notarised agreement and registration in the Transcript Registry. Since Hans is the sole owner of the house, he has the right to sell the house and Helda cannot effectively prevent the sale.

Helda may seek the return of the money she contributed on the basis of unjust enrichment[95] or, if she has entered into an agreement with Hans which prohibits him from selling the house (this agreement would not have any effect *in rem*), on the basis of the provisions on restitution by holding Hans liable for damages. Helda would then be in the same position as any creditor having a monetary claim against Hans. Under that capacity Helda could seek for precautionary measures[96] by asking a court to prevent the sale for a limited period of time. But in order for the court to apply precautionary measures, Helda must prove that the payment of the debt is endangered by the sale of the house (e.g. if Hans does not have any other property and would become insolvent if he sold the house).

(b) A mortgage is a right *in rem* constituted on the immovable assets of a debtor in order to secure the privileged satisfaction[97] of the creditor's claim from these assets.[98] It is a right of 'value' and thus the position of a mortgage creditor does not give any right to take possession of the house. The Bank cannot ask for possession from Helda. The Bank's only right is to ask for the compulsory sale of the property in order to recover the debt from the proceeds.[99] The new owner of the house may, of course, remove Helda from the house.

(c) The answer would not differ even if Hans and Helda were married. With regard to the answer to (b), the law provides for protection of the use of a family home, but only between estranged spouses.[100] There is no such protection against the spouses' creditors.

4 *France and related jurisdictions*

(a) France

(a) No because Hans is the exclusive owner of the house, since he alone signed the bill of sale. Helda's contribution to the financing of the purchase is either a donation, if Helda wanted to make a gift, or a loan, which Helda must prove.

[95] Art. 904 GCC. [96] Art. 682 GCCP.

[97] The Bank's privileged position means that Helda's general claim gives way to the Bank's claim.

[98] Art. 1257 GCC. [99] Art. 1292 GCC. [100] Art. 1393 GCC.

(b) Yes. Helda has no right to the house, and it does not matter that she lives there.

(c) Yes. If Hans and Helda are married under a regime of community, the acquisition of the house for consideration by means of partially common capital is an '*acquisitio*',[101] which brings the real estate into the community (the property pool for the marriage) in the shape of joint ownership.[102] Now the common real estate can be neither sold nor mortgaged by a married person without the consent of the other spouse, on pain of nullity.[103]

If Hans and Helda are married under the regime of the separate estate or the participation in 'acquisitions', the real estate belongs exclusively to Hans, and Helda is creditor for the advanced capital. Hans can thus freely sell or mortgage the house. However, if this house is the family's place of domicile, rules on the matrimonial regime stipulate that it cannot be transferred nor mortgaged without Helda's consent.[104]

(b) Belgium

(a) Under the Belgian law, the answer to this question depends on the '*causa*' of Helda's payment. If Helda made this payment by way of a gift, in principle she cannot oppose the sales agreement. A gift must have an irrevocable nature (*donner et retenir ne vaut*). However, it is possible in the Belgian law that the gift was made contractually, subject to the condition that the immovable would not be sold within a certain period after the gift. However, this would require an express contractual stipulation.

According to more recent but uncertain case law, the *causa* should remain after the gift, and the gift could disappear (*ex nunc*) if the *causa* disappears. For instance, this reasoning is applicable in a case where parents gifted their son-in-law a parcel of land, making clear that it was intended to offer a place in which they could found their family house. After the divorce between the daughter and the son-in-law, the parents can argue that the *causa* of the gift has fallen away, which entails the termination of the gift and the restitution of the gifted object '*caducité/verva*').[105]

[101] '*Acquêt*' in French. [102] Art. 1401 C. civ. [103] Arts. 1424 and 1427 C. civ.
[104] Art. 215, alinéa 3 C. civ.
[105] Belgian Supreme Court 16 November 1989, Arresten van het Hof van Cassatie 1989–90, 371, Pasicrisie 1990, I, 331.

However, this case law is subject to extensive scholarly debate. Most legal scholars assume that this ground for termination is only applicable to agreements without consideration. The Supreme Court seems to have made a switch in its own case law, stating that the disappearance of the *causa* after the gift is not a ground to terminate the gift.[106]

If the payment of part of the price was not based upon a *causa*, Helda can claim restitution from Hans for that part of the price. This claim would be based upon arts. 1235 and 1375 *et seq.* BCC, which relate to undue payment. This restitutionary claim is independent of the issue of Hans' sale of the house.

(b) This question starts from the factual background that Helda lives in the house. Helda is not protected by her residence in the house or the fact it is their principal family residence. The protection against the sale of a house by one of the spouses (cf. under (a) above) does not apply to the situation in which the sale of the house is initiated pursuant to execution by a creditor.

(c) The answer would only be different if the house serves as Hans and Helda's principal residence. In that case, each of the spouses would be granted a special form of protection, in the sense that the other spouse cannot sell the principal family residence without the other's prior consent (art. 215 BCC). We refer to this in our answer to case 14.

Art. 215 BCC does not impose any restriction upon spouses' creditors. A Bank would need to instigate a proceeding for execution of the debt against both Hans and Helda. For instance, Helda would need to be notified of the command to pay and the deed relating to the seizure. This is the case independent of the status of the house, e.g. independent of whether it is Hans' exclusive property or part of the community between Hans and Helda.

5 *England and related jurisdictions*

(a) England

(a) The legal title documents to the house appear to be solely in Hans' name. As such, Hans is the sole legal owner of the property, and the starting point is that Helda does not have an ownership interest in the house – 'the onus is on [Helda] to show that [she] has any beneficial interest at all, and if so what that interest is'.[107]

[106] Belgian Supreme Court, 12 December 2008, Pasicrisie 2008, 2934.
[107] *Stack* v. *Dowden* [2007] UKHL 17 at [4], [2007] 2 AC 432; see also [5], [56] and [68].

However, the fact that she made a (significant) contribution to the purchase price will normally be sufficient to show that she has an equitable (i.e. beneficial ownership) interest in the property.[108] The degree to which she has an equitable interest in the house depends on the degree to which the court considers that she and Hans intended to co-own the beneficial interest in the house.[109] This is particularly the case if Hans and Helda are co-habitees (e.g. boyfriend and girlfriend), as opposed to some form of commercial arrangement.

Whatever their precise shares, Hans is the sole legal owner but holds the legal title on trust for himself and Helda as beneficial owners. As a beneficial co-owner, Helda probably has a right to occupy the property,[110] and she is entitled to be consulted by Hans 'so far as practicable'[111] regarding the exercise of his powers over the land. Furthermore, provided she occupies the house, Hans (as a sole trustee) does not have the power on his own to transfer the house to Chris free of Helda's interest.[112] However, Helda has no power to prevent Hans from transferring his own beneficial interest in the property to Chris, and she cannot prevent Hans from applying to the court for an order that the property be sold free of anyone's beneficial interests (including Helda's). Bearing in mind that the property was presumably first bought for the purpose of providing housing for Hans and Helda together, and the fact that this purpose appears no longer to be possible given Hans' desire to move, a court may well order that the property be sold, unless Helda is able to buy Hans' share in the property from him.[113]

Had the title documents been put in the joint names of Hans and Helda, they would co-own the legal title as joint tenants.[114] In such a case, irrespective of their beneficial interests in the house, Hans could not convey legal title to the house without Helda's concurrence, and so she would be able to prevent the sale, unless Hans obtained a court order for sale.[115]

108 See *Stack* v. *Dowden* [2007] UKHL 17 at [61], [2007] 2 AC 432.

109 See, e.g., *Lloyds Bank plc* v. *Rosset* [1991] 1 AC 107 at 132–3 (a 'common intention constructive trust'); *Stack* v. *Dowden* [2007] UKHL 17, [2007] 2 AC 432; *Jones* v. *Kernott* [2011] UKSC 53, [2012] 1 AC 776.

110 Section 12 (1) (a), Trusts of Land and Appointment of Trustees Act 1996 (hereafter, 'TLATA 1996').

111 Section 11 (1) (a), TLATA 1996.

112 *Williams & Glyn's Bank Ltd.* v. *Boland* [1981] AC 487.

113 See section 15 (1) (b), TLATA 1996 and *Jones* v. *Challenger* [1961] 1 QB 176 at 183–4.

114 Legal title to land in England can only be co-owned as joint tenants: sections 1, 34 and 36, LPA 1925.

115 Under section 14, TLATA 1996.

(b) This depends on when the mortgage was granted. If Hans mortgaged the property at the time it was acquired, using the mortgage monies in order to purchase the house, the mortgage will have priority over the interests of both Hans and Helda,[116] with the effect that the Bank is able to remove Helda.

If the mortgage had been granted by Hans some time after the property was acquired and without Helda's consent (either actual or imputed[117]), then the Bank will be bound by Helda's interest in the property if she was in actual occupation and so cannot remove Helda.[118] However, this would not prevent the Bank from seeking an order for the sale of the property with vacant possession.[119]

(c) If Hans and Helda were married, Helda would have a statutory right to occupy the matrimonial home.[120] This 'matrimonial home right' does not arise if Helda has a legal ownership interest in the house, but any interest which she might have under a trust does not count for this purpose,[121] so she will have the matrimonial home right if legal title to the house is in Hans' name alone.

The matrimonial home right operates as a charge on Hans' estate in the house.[122] However, if Hans' legal estate in the house is registered, Helda's statutory right is only capable of being protected against third parties by entry of a notice in the register.[123] If Helda failed to enter such a notice at the time when Chris and the Bank register their respective interests in the property (which is normally the case[124]), her statutory right cannot bind Chris or the Bank.

Beyond this, the fact that Hans and Helda were married does not technically alter the trust law analysis (explained in response to case 13 (a) and (b) above). Although, on a purely practical level, their

116 *Abbey National Building Society* v. *Cann* [1991] 1 AC 56 at 93 and 102.

117 As to which, see, e.g., *Bristol & West Building Society* v. *Henning* [1985] 1 WLR 778 at 782; *Equity & Law Homes Loans Ltd.* v. *Prestidge* [1992] 1 WLR 137 at 143–4; *Skipton Building Society* v. *Clayton* (1993) 77 P & CR 223 at 228–9.

118 *Williams & Glyn's Bank Ltd.* v. *Boland* [1981] AC 487.

119 Under section 14, TLATA 1996. See *Bank of Baroda* v. *Dhillon* [1998] 1 FLR 524 at 528–30; M. Conaglen, 'Mortgagee Powers Rhetoric' (2006) 69 MLR 583 at 592–9.

120 Section 30 (2), Family Law Act 1996 (hereafter, 'FLA 1996'). Such rights can also be asserted by same-sex couples who have entered into a 'civil partnership' by registering that partnership under section 1, Civil Partnership Act 2004.

121 Section 30 (1) and (9), FLA 1996. 122 Section 31 (2), FLA 1996.

123 Section 31 (10), FLA 1996.

124 See Kevin Gray and Susan F. Gray, *Elements of Land Law*, 4th edn. (Oxford University Press, 2005), para. 12.94.

marriage may make it easier for Helda to argue that there was a common intention to co-own the property equally.[125]

(b) Scotland

As a preliminary matter, it should be noted that Helda's contribution to the purchase price has no effect on ownership of the house or the rights in it. So, if the title to the house on the Land Register is in Hans' name alone, as the question seems to imply, Hans would be the sole owner and Helda would not have any kind of proprietary rights. Helda's rights, insofar as they exist, lie in the law of obligations – for example, for repayment of the loan (if it was a loan) or, in some circumstances, for repayment on the basis of the law of unjustified enrichment (e.g. if the money was advanced in contemplation of a marriage which is no longer taking place).[126] Accordingly, in the answers that follow, any special protection for Helda arises for a reason other than her financial contribution.

(a) Helda will not succeed. As the sole owner of the house, Hans is fully at liberty to sell. Apart from marriage (which is discussed at (c) below), the answer is unaffected by the relationship between Helda and Hans (e.g. girlfriend and boyfriend, mother and son) or by whether Helda lives in the house.

(b) In principle, the Bank can remove Helda. If, however, Helda is co-habiting with Hans, and the house is her main residence, she can apply to the court to suspend the Bank's right to take possession – and hence its right, as possessor, to remove Helda.[127] Among the factors that the court must take into account in deciding whether to grant a suspension is Helda's ability to secure reasonable alternative accommodation.[128] Even if granted, however, a suspension is likely to be temporary in nature. The effect of marriage is discussed in (c) below.

(c) Marriage has no effect on the ownership of the house as such. But, assuming that the house was a family residence, Helda would have a statutory right to occupy it free of charge.[129] Although unregistered, this occupancy right binds third parties such as Chris or the Bank, and

[125] *Stack* v. *Dowden* [2007] UKHL 17 at [40] and [103].

[126] The leading case is *Shilliday* v. *Smith* 1998 SC 725. This is the *condictio causa data causa non secuta*.

[127] Sections 24B (1), 24C (1) (d), Conveyancing and Feudal Reform (Scotland) Act 1970.

[128] Sections 24 (7) (e), 24B (2), Conveyancing and Feudal Reform (Scotland) Act 1970.

[129] Sections 1, 22 (definition of 'matrimonial home'), Matrimonial Homes (Family Protection) (Scotland) Act 1981.

prevents Hans from conferring an entitlement to occupy on either.[130] So, while the sale to Chris could not be prevented, Chris would not be able to make use of the house. Similarly, the Bank could neither take possession nor remove Helda. The occupancy right is lost if Helda gave her written consent to Hans' original grant of the mortgage, or if she gives her consent now to the sale to Chris.[131]

(c) Ireland

(a) Although Hans is the legal owner, Helda's contribution, unless she intended it as a gift to Hans, will have generated a proportionate equitable interest in her favour under the purchase money resulting trust.[132] If Helda is in occupation of the house, Chris is required to make enquiries to establish if she has an interest in the property. Typically, his solicitor will request this information from the solicitor acting for Hans. If the purchase is completed without making such enquiries, Helda's interest will bind Chris as an overriding interest if the house is registered in the Land Registry[133] or under the doctrine of notice if the house is unregistered.[134] Until recently, the legislature was considering reducing the onus on purchasers to make such enquiries by introducing a statutory provision setting out that a conveyance to a purchaser of a legal estate would overreach such an equitable interest[135] unless it had been protected by registration in the Land Registry/Registry of Deeds.[136] This proposed reform provoked a negative reaction[137] and section 21, Land and Conveyancing Act

130 Section 6 (1), Matrimonial Homes (Family Protection) (Scotland) Act 1981.

131 Sections 6 (3) (a), 8 (1), (2A), Matrimonial Homes (Family Protection) (Scotland) Act 1981.

132 A direct financial contribution, such as paying the deposit or contributing to mortgage repayments, generates an equitable interest under the purchase money resulting trust. See *C* v. *C* [1976] IR 254. Indirect contributions, such as paying household expenses while the legal owner is repaying the mortgage, will also generate an equitable interest. See McC v. *McC* [1986] ILRM 1.

133 Section 72 (1) (j) Registration of Title Act 1964. An overriding interest is one that will bind a newly registered purchaser of registered land regardless of whether the interest appears on the Land Registry.

134 *Northern Bank Ltd* v. *Henry* [1981] IR 1.

135 Overreaching converts an equitable interest in land into an interest in the proceeds of sale generated by the transaction. This means that the purchaser acquires the land free from the equitable interest.

136 See section 21, Land and Conveyancing Law Reform Bill 2006 (as passed by Seanad Eireann).

137 See John Mee, 'The Land and Conveyancing Law Reform Bill 2006: Observations on the Law Reform Process and a Critique of Selected Provisions – Part 1', 11(3) *Conveyancing and Property Law Journal* (2006), p. 67 at pp. 69–72.

2009 maintains the status quo, so that the equitable interest of a person in actual occupation will not be overreached on a sale to a purchaser. If Helda's interest is revealed before the completion of the transaction, the solicitor acting for Chris should insist that Helda join in the conveyance to Chris. If she refuses, Hans will be forced to apply to the court for an order for sale and the division of the proceeds pursuant to section 31, Land and Conveyancing Law Reform Act 2009. No legislative guidelines are provided for a court deciding whether or not to make such an order and so it is difficult to predict how this jurisdiction will be exercised. However, the court has traditionally granted an order for sale on an application by a co-owner pursuant to section 3 or 4, Partition Acts 1868 and 1876,[138] which section 31, Land and Conveyancing Law Reform Act 2009 is designed to replace.

(b) It depends on whether Helda's equitable interest arose before or after the house was mortgaged. If Hans mortgaged the house at the time it was acquired, the Bank will not be bound by any subsequent equitable interest[139] that Helda generates through contributions to the mortgage repayments. Even if Helda's equitable interest arose through a contribution to the deposit, the Bank will not be bound by it, as Helda would not have been in occupation of the house before the simultaneous completion of the purchase and the mortgage.[140] The Bank will be able to remove her in such circumstances.

If Hans mortgaged the house some time after the house was purchased and Helda made her contribution, her equitable interest will bind the Bank if she was in occupation of the house when the mortgage was created.[141] This would result in the restriction of the mortgage to Hans' equitable share of the property. A court will not grant the Bank an order for possession of the entire house against Helda, as her interest is not subject to the mortgage, and the appropriate way for a Bank to enforce its security in such circumstances is to seek an order for the sale of the house pursuant to section 31, Land and Conveyancing Law Reform Act 2009.[142]

[138] See Heather Conway, *Co-Ownership of Land – Partition Actions and Remedies*, 2nd edn. (Dublin: Bloomsbury, 2012), Chapter 5.

[139] *Abbey National Building Society* v. *Cann* [1991] 1 AC 56.

[140] *Abbey National Building Society* v. *Cann* [1991] 1 AC 56.

[141] Under the doctrine of notice in the case of unregistered land, see *Northern Bank Ltd* v. *Henry* [1981] IR 1, or as an overriding interest in the case of registered land, see section 72 (1) (j), Registration of Title Act 1964.

[142] Previously, a Bank with a mortgage over a co-owner's interest in unregistered land would have had to apply for an order for sale under the Partition Acts 1868 and 1876 in order to realise its security. However, a Bank with a charge over a co-owner's interest in

The court will order Hans and Helda to deliver up possession of the property and to join in any conveyance of it. The proceeds of sale will be divided among the parties in proportion to their equitable interests, although Hans' share will be paid to the Bank to discharge the mortgage debt.[143]

(c) Section 3, Family Home Protection Act 1976 requires the prior written consent of the non-owning spouse for any sale or mortgage of the family home by the owner. Although the legislation is designed to protect a spouse with no legal or beneficial interest, it could provide additional protection to Helda if the house is their family home.

(i) If Helda refuses to join in the conveyance to Chris and Hans applies for an order for the sale of the co-owned property pursuant to section 31, Land and Conveyancing Law Reform Act 2009, the court will refuse such an order unless it would be reasonable to dispense with Helda's consent pursuant to section 4, Family Home Protection Act 1976.[144] Section 31, Land and Conveyancing Law Reform Act 2009 is designed to replace the Partition Acts and, in considering a married co-owner's application for an order for the sale of the family home pursuant to the Partition Acts, the courts recognised that to ignore the implications of the Family Home Protection Act 1976 would result in a ludicrous situation where a spouse with no interest in the family home has more power to prevent a sale of that home than a spouse with an interest in the home.[145]

(ii) If Hans mortgaged the house at the time it was acquired it would not qualify as a family home as Helda did not yet ordinarily reside there. Her consent would not have been necessary for the transaction[146] and the Bank would be able to remove her. If Hans mortgaged the house after it became their ordinary residence, her prior voluntary and fully informed consent would have been required[147] and without it the mortgage would be void. If Helda gave her prior written consent to the mortgage she may be estopped from asserting any beneficial interest against the lender so that the Bank will be able to exercise the normal

registered land had no standing to make such an application. See *Northern Bank Ltd* v. *Haggerty* [1995] NI 211 at 217; John Mee, 'Partition and Sale of the Family Home', 15 *DULJ* (1993), p. 78 at pp. 86–7. This lacuna has been filled by section 31, Land and Conveyancing Law Reform Act 2009, which provides that a mortgagee (which is defined as including any person having the benefit of a charge) may apply for an order under that section.

143 See Conway, *Co-Ownership of Land – Partition Actions and Remedies*, para. 8.63.

144 Section 31 (5), 2009 Act provides that nothing in the section affects the jurisdiction of the court under the Family Home Protection Act 1976. See also the response to case 14.

145 See *O'D* v. *O'D* Unreported, High Court, 18 November 1983 at 10–12.

146 *National Irish Bank Ltd* v. *Graham* [1995] 2 IR 244

147 *Bank of Ireland* v. *Smith* [1995] 2 IR 459.

powers of possession and sale in the event of default.[148] However, if Helda is capable of paying off the arrears owed by her husband within a reasonable time and meeting all future periodical payments due under the mortgage, the court may prevent the Bank from realising its security.[149]

[148] *Doherty* v. *Doherty* [1991] 2 IR 458. This approach may not be taken if the court is satisfied that the wife did not, in consenting to the creation of a charge by her husband over the family home, intend it to extend to her beneficial interest, see *Re White (A Bankrupt)* Unreported, High Court, 4 December 1990.

[149] Sections 7 and 8, Family Home Protection Act 1976.

Case 14

Roberto and Susane are married. During the marriage Roberto inherits a house and the couple now lives there. Roberto wants to sell the house to Andrea.

(a) Susane wants to prevent the sale. Will she succeed?
(b) How would your answer differ if Roberto and Susane were living together but not married?

(A) Foundational Concepts for Understanding Case 14

The majority of the European countries with civil law systems have special rules (statutory or case law rules) to confer a special regime to the matrimonial home.[1] This takes place in most cases regardless of which matrimonial property regime the couple has chosen (the most common of which are community of gains or separation of property).

According to this special rule, neither spouse may dispose of the rights that assure the family's housing without the consent of the other. Usually if one of the spouses attempts to transfer such property without the consent of the other, the other has the possibility, under some circumstances, to bring an action to avoid the transfer. In this case it could be understood that the matrimonial home was solely owned by one spouse as it had been acquired by inheritance.

In community systems there are special rules to protect the family home. Furthermore, in the separate property systems, limitations on a spouse's freedom to deal with property are exceptional and tend to be limited to a few special situations, such as the protection of the family home.

[1] Pay attention to the fact that in the questionnaire the spouses are living in the house.

Common law systems have no special rules governing the property relationships of husband and wife. The husband owns and controls his property and a wife owns and controls hers. Nevertheless, the matrimonial home is subject to special treatment. There is no unified regulation of a spouse's right in the family homestead but a melange of statutory provisions have been put together in response of related problems. According to the case law, the non-owner spouse has been reinforced by the courts' willingness to require the owner's spouse's consent to transactions involving the family home.

In conclusion, it can be stated that the family home is a special category of marital property regardless of the features of the system. It is also valid for non-married couples, as in many European legal systems there is special statutory regime applicable to couples living under 'marriage-like' conditions (cf. question (b) below). The analogy to a regime of marital property is heightened by the fact that the couple's home (if acquired together during co-habitation) cannot be sold without the consent of the co-habitee who is not the recorded owner.

(B) The Jurisdictions (Presented by Related Jurisdictions)

1 *Germany and related jurisdictions*

(a) Germany

(a) If Roberto and Susane are living under the statutory property regime (*Zugewinngemeinschaft*) Susane can prevent the sale if the house forms nearly all of Roberto's property and Andrea becomes aware of this fact (see above case 13(c)). She can also prevent the sale if the spouses had concluded a partnership agreement to make the house a partnership asset.[2]

In the case of community of property (*Gütergemeinschaft*), the house is part of the marital property (*Gesamtgut*) unless the testator specified by will that the acquisition is reserved property (*Vorbehaltsgut*).[3] In the former case, Susane can prevent the sale (see above case 13(c)), in the latter Roberto is free to sell the house.

Susane cannot prevent the sale if Roberto and Susane chose the matrimonial property regime of separation of property (*Gütertrennung*).[4]

(b) Susane cannot prevent the sale if they are not married.

2 See §§ 718, 719 BGB and question 13(a) above.
3 §§ 1416, 1418, para. 2 No. 2 BGB.
4 § 1414 BGB.

(b) Austria

(a) According to the Austrian law the marital regime of separation of property prevails.[5] Therefore, property acquired by succession does not belong to the common property of the spouses. Consequently, the house that Roberto inherited is solely his property and he can freely dispose of it. Nevertheless, according to art. 97 the spouse that has a pressing need of accommodation (*dringendes Wohnbedürfnis*) regarding the other spouse's accommodation has an enforceable claim when it comes to retaining the accommodation (*gerichtlich durchsetzbarer Wohnungserhaltungsanspruch*).[6]

If they were getting divorced, the fact that they have been living in the house while married means that it is considered their matrimonial home (*Ehewohnung*). Therefore, Susane has the option of basing a claim on the fact that she depends on staying in the house to secure/ meet her essential needs.[7] The court can – but is not obligated to – order the transfer ownership of, or a right to, the house *in rem* (*Eigentum oder dingliches Recht*) to Susane, or may create a right for Susane *in personam* (*Begründung eines schuldrechtlichen Rechtsverhältnisses zugunsten des Ehegatten*).[8]

(b) If they are not married Susane cannot assert any right over the house and Roberto does not need her consent to dispose of the house.

(c) The Netherlands

(a) The inherited house may or may not belong to both spouses, depending on the matrimonial regime that applies to their marriage *and* on the question whether or not the succession is based on a notarial will. If the couple did not elect any matrimonial regime, the standard regime applies. This involves co-ownership of all property, even property acquired before the marriage and property given to one of the spouses or inherited by one of them (community of property: art. 1:94 BW).

[5] §§ 1233 S 1, 1237 ABGB. See further Helmut Koziol and Rudolf Welser, *Bürgerliches Recht*, I, 13th edn. (Vienna: MANZ Verlag, 2006), p. 478; F. Ferdinand Kerschner, *Familienrecht*, 3rd edn. (Vienna: Springer Verlag, 2008), No. 2/90.

[6] See further Koziol and Welser, *Bürgerliches Recht*, I, p. 475; Kerschner, *Familienrecht*, No. 2/41.

[7] Or if a child they had together has a significant need. § 82 Abs 2 S 1 EheG; see further Koziol and Welser, *Bürgerliches Recht*, I, p. 507; Kerschner, *Familienrecht*, No. 2/147.

[8] § 87 Abs 1 EheG. See further Koziol and Welser, *Bürgerliches Recht*, I, p. 513; Kerschner, *Familienrecht*, No. 2/149.

When Roberto inherits on the basis of a notarial will, the will normally contains a clause (exclusion clause) that property that passes to the heir under the will shall not form part of any possible community of property. This has an effect against third parties, so it binds Susane. Almost all notaries put this exclusion clause as a standard clause in the wills they draft for their clients. It will be taken out only if there is a good reason to do so, which hardly ever happens. The result is that even if the couple is married in community of property, the house will not form part of this community and Roberto will be the sole owner of the house.

However, even if the house only belongs to Roberto, the sale will require Susane's permission under art. 1:88 BW. If the sale takes place without her permission, she can avoid the contract of sale (art. 1:89 BW). As a result, the passing of ownership will be prevented, or reversed in a case where it has already occurred.

(b) Arts 1:88 and 1:89 BW do not apply if the parties are not married and do not have a registered partnership, which has the same effect on property as a marriage (art. 1:80b BW).

(d) Turkey

(a) This home is considered the centre of the life of spouses and consequently it is a conjugal home.[9] According to the Turkish legal system, the spouse who is the owner of the conjugal home does not have a full right of disposal over it.[10] Thus, the spouse who has the ownership of the conjugal home cannot sell or transfer it without the other spouse's express consent. Consequently, Susane will succeed.

(b) If they are not married, Roberto can realise any legal transaction related to his immovable, since Turkey does not have special legislation for unmarried couples who live together.

2 *Scandinavian jurisdictions*

(a) Finland

(a) Roberto and Susane's joint home enjoys the protection of a matrimonial home described in the previous case, and Susane has an

[9] See Şükran Şıpka, *Aile Konutu ile İlgili İşlemlerde Diğer Eşin Rızası, 2. Bası* (İstanbul: Beta, 2004), pp. 82ff.

[10] See art. 194 TCC; Oğuzman, M.K., Seliçi, Ö. and Oktay-Özdemir, S., *Eşya, Hukuku Gözden Geçirilmiş 11. Bası* (İstanbul, 2006), p. 184; Mustafa Alper Gümüş, *Türk Medeni Kanununun Getirdiği Yeni Şerhler, 1. Baskı* (Ankara: Seçkin, 2003), p. 62; Compare, Ahmet Kılıçoğlu, *Türk Medenî Kanunu'nda Diğer Eşin Rızasına Bağlı Hukuksal İşlemler ve Yasal Alım Hakkı* (Ankara: Turhan Kitabevi, 2002), p. 5.

occupation right (see the answer to case 13, question (c)). As a married spouse, Susane can prevent the sale of the house. The quality of Roberto's acquisition – an inheritance or a purchase – or its date does not make any difference. Hence, Susane can prevent the sale.

Roberto needs Susane's written consent in order to sell the house. Without the consent any possible conveyance is not valid and a written consent needs to be inspected as a part of the registration examination after the conveyance.[11] Nevertheless, Susane's position is not strong. A conveyance entered into by one spouse in violation of the restriction will be declared void if the other spouse brings an action to this effect against the transferee within three months of becoming aware of the transaction. If no action is brought in during that term, the conveyance will be valid. In addition, a conveyance of real property will gain validity if the title of the acquirer has been registered, and the acquirer did not know and should not have known at the time of acquisition that the conveyer was not entitled to convey the property in question. These rules apply to leased houses, and similar rules also apply to residential apartments.[12]

A local court may, upon petition, grant permission for a conveyance if the other spouse has refused consent or if, for some other reason, it has not been possible to obtain the said consent.[13]

(b) The situation is different if Roberto and Susane are living together as an unmarried couple or otherwise. No consent from Susane is required for the sale of the house. In addition, Susane's secret co-ownership is out of the question because Roberto has inherited the house.

Although living together is rather common, there are not many sections of written law applicable to unmarried couples. The Act on the Dissolution of the Household of Cohabiting Partners does not regulate the questions presented by this case.[14] From the point of civil law, on a large scale, unmarried spouses are still treated as strangers to each other. Nevertheless, in legal praxis the special quality of the relation between

[11] See 12:1.1 Code of Real Estate.
[12] 38 and 39 Marriage Act. The lack of Susane's consent prevents Andrea's registration. It is, however, possible that the marriage of Susane and Roberto is not discovered in the registration examination. See 12:1.1 Code of Real Estate.
[13] 40 Marriage Act. [14] Act 2011/26.

unmarried spouses is taken into consideration, for instance, in the form of the rules of secret ownership as stated in the answer to question 13(c). The creation of these rules can be explained by the need to draw parallels between married and unmarried couples.

(b) Sweden

(a) Spouses[15] must give their consent in writing before the married owner can convey (or grant limited interest in) real property.[16] The absence of written consent constitutes a ground for invalidity of a conveyance or mortgage,[17] and an application of transfer of title in the Real Property Register is declared dormant until this requirement has been fulfilled.[18] This applies not only to the spouses' joint dwelling, but to real property in general.[19] However, it only applies to joint property, meaning property which has not been declared to be the individual property of the owner, either by the spouses themselves in a signed and registered nuptial deed, by a giver as a condition of the gift, by a deceased as a condition set out in a will, or by a policy-holder in an insurance beneficiary clause.[20]

The requirement of consent does not apply where the spouse is incapable of giving consent, cannot give consent within a reasonable time, or partition of estate has been effected in marriage.[21] Consent may also be replaced by the permission of a court.[22]

Since Roberto inherited the house, it is possible that the house was inherited under the condition of individual property, which would mean Roberto could sell the house without Susane's consent. On the other hand, if there were no such condition, Susane could prevent the sale. If the sale was completed without her consent, the buyer (Andrea) would not be able to register title of ownership. However, if Andrea by some mistake of the Registry has succeeded to become registered as owner, the inscription would override the invalidity.[23]

[15] The same rules apply for registered partners of the same sex, 3:1 Registration of Partnership Act, *lagen (1994:1117) om registrerade partnerskap*.

[16] 7:5 Marriage Code; *äktenskapsbalken (1987:230)*. [17] 7:9 (1) Marriage Code.

[18] 20:7 Land Code. [19] 7:5 (3) Marriage Code. [20] 7:1 and 7:5 (2) Marriage Code.

[21] 7:7 Marriage Code. [22] 7:8 Marriage Code.

[23] 7:9 (2) Marriage Code. *See* Folke Grauers, *Fastighetsköp* (Lund: Juristförlaget i Lund, 2001), p. 340.

(b) Unmarried persons permanently living as a couple in a joint household are considered to be co-habitees.[24] The joint dwelling acquired by the co-habitees for joint use is generally treated as a joint property.[25] The fact that property was acquired through inheritance does not necessarily rule out the possibility of it being treated as joint property, even if the opposite generally can be presumed.[26] For joint property, the same rules on spouses' consent apply to cohabitees,[27] but a purchaser's application to register title will only be declared dormant if the co-habitees have notified the Registry Office in writing that the property is a joint dwelling. However, if the co-habitees or the deceased has provided that the property should be considered as individual property then it is not joint property.[28]

To summarise, Susane cannot prevent the sale as an unmarried cohabitee, unless the Registry Office has been notified that the house is a joint dwelling, but she might be able to invalidate the sale under circumstances that would be rare in the case of inheritance.

(c) Denmark

(a) The answer depends on whether the property belongs to Roberto's separate estate or is the spouses' joint property. As a starting point, a property belongs to the parties' joint property. If this is the case, Roberto cannot sell the house (being the family home) without Susane's consent.[29]

As mentioned, the house may be a part of Roberto's separate estate. A separate estate is created by a pre-nuptial agreement registered in the Land Register,[30] or by deed in the case of inheritance or gift (e.g. the testator leaving Roberto the house may provide that it should belong only to Roberto).[31] If the house belongs to Roberto's separate estate, he may sell it without Susane's consent.

24 § 1 (1) Cohabitation Act; *sambolagen (2003:376)*. This also applies to persons of the same sex.
25 § 3 Cohabitation Act.
26 Governmental proposal *prop. 2002/03:80, Ny sambolag*, p. 47.
27 §§ 23–25 Cohabitation Act.
28 §§ 4 and 9 Cohabitation Act.
29 Section 18, Legal Effect of Marriage Act.
30 Sections 28, 35 and 37, Legal Effect of Marriage Act.
31 Section 28a, Legal Effect of Marriage Act.

(b) If the couple is not married, the Legal Effect of Marriage Act does not apply and Roberto is at liberty to sell the property as he wishes (under the same conditions as Hans in case 13).

(d) Norway

(a) As Roberto has inherited the house, there is no presumption of co-ownership (see under case 13). The rules on consent to transactions concerning the spouses' common home apply (see under case 13, last paragraph).

(b) For unmarried couples, there are no corresponding rules on consent, and as we have no indications of co-ownership, Susane cannot prevent the sale of Roberto's house.

3 *Romanic–Mediterranean jurisdictions*

(a) Italy

(a) The general principle that governs marital property is that, unless otherwise agreed, property acquired by spouses during marriage is considered common property under arts. 159 and 177 ICC. Property acquired as a result of inheritance, according to the provisions of art. 179 c 1 let. b ICC, is an exception, and does not constitute common property between spouses. Susane, therefore, has no power over the property solely owned by Roberto and therefore cannot prevent the sale, unless she can prove that the sale constitutes an actual breach of the duty of economic and material support of the family which should rest on both spouses, such as in the case in which the family is deprived of any home because of the sale.[32] Only in this case would Susane be able to prevent the sale.[33]

(b) Although there is no specific legislation in Italy governing the relationships between unmarried couples, some of the provisions regarding marriage have been applied in case law by analogy with these cases. Looking at the case law, we can say that the answer would not be different from the above where the unmarried couple had children, arguing on the basis of the duty of parents to economically support children under arts. 147 and 148 ICC.[34] Even without children, however some courts have extended the same duties of economic

[32] See Court of Cassation, 15.04.2002, No. 5420, in *Vita Not.*, 2002, p. 1532.
[33] See Court of Cassation, 07.05.1992, No. 5415, in *Vita Not.*, 1992, p. 1159.
[34] See Court of Cassation, 10102/2004.

and material support of the family to the unmarried couple provided under art. 143 ICC for married couples.[35]

(b) Spain

(a) Assets inherited by a spouse are owned by that spouse exclusively, but, as in this case the house is the couple's main home, Roberto needs Susane's consent to sell, or, failing this, he needs authorisation from a court (see the answer to case 13). Susane may oppose the sale.

(b) If Roberto and Susane were a *pareja de hecho* (co-habiting couple), Roberto wouldn't need Susane's consent, unless the couple were subject to a regional statute on co-habiting couples that applied the same rules as for a married couple (as we saw above, this is the case of the Catalan legislation).[36]

(c) Portugal

(a) In a system of acquired assets, property that spouses bring with them to the marriage, and property that is bequeathed to the spouse as an inheritance or gift, is their personal property. The system of general community of assets is characterised by the fact that the joint property is 'constituted by all present and future property of the spouses that is not exempted by law'. Under the system of separate assets, there is complete and absolute separation between the properties of the spouses. Under art. 1735 CC, each owner retains ownership and enjoyment of all their present and future property, of which they can freely dispose. Therefore, the house would be held in joint property if Roberto and Susane were married under a system of general community assets, and it would be Roberto's personal property if they were married under a system of acquired assets or a system of separate assets.

The performance of acts that imply the total or partial deprivation of the family home requires the consent of both spouses, no matter the proprietary status of the house. Therefore, Roberto would not be entitled to sell the house to Andrea without consent of Susane. Art. 1682-A (2) CC provides that one spouse cannot, without the consent of the other, sell,

[35] See Tribunale Savona, 10.06.2002, in *Nuova giur. civ. commentata* 2003, I, p. 905 Annotated by Maura.

[36] The Galician Law 2/2006, of 14 June, applies the same solution if the co-habiting couple registered the partnership in the Registro de Parejas de Hecho from Galicia (*Disposición adicional tercera*). Almost all the devolved regions of Spain have passed legislation on co-habiting couples, but not all such legislation places co-habiting couples on the same footing as married couples for the purposes of this specific case.

charge, lease, or lend the principal house where the family live. In a word, Susane might prevent the sale of the house to Andrea. The court may, upon petition from Roberto, grant permission for a conveyance if Susane has refused consent or if, for some other reason, it has not been possible to obtain (art. 1684 (3) CC).

(b) In a co-habitation outside marriage (conjugal life under conditions similar to those of spouses), the partners share bed and board (*tori, mensae et habitationis*), as if they are married. If Roberto and Susane were living together without being married, Susane could not assert any right over the house. So Roberto is free to sell, and Susane must leave the house.

Co-habitants have certain financial rights on the termination of co-habitation (whether by separation or on death). Co-habitation may be extinguished either by breakdown of the relationship, through mutual consent, upon the initiative of one of the members, or as a result of the death of one of them. In case of a breakdown of the relationship, art. 4 Law 23/2010, of 30 August,[37] makes art. 1793 CC applicable. Thus, if the family home belongs jointly to both partners, either of them may apply to the court for the right to rent the house, under the conditions provided in that article; similarly, if the house is the property of one of the members of the relationship, the others may make a similar application. Dissolution of co-habitation on the will of one of the partners has to be judicially declared when they intend to exercise rights that are dependent upon it.

If co-habitation ends as a result of the death of one of them, art. 5 Law 7/2001 grants the surviving partner the right of occupation of the family home for a period of five years and the use of the contents, and a pre-emption right in the sale of the house for a period of five years. Finally, the survivor partner has the right to rent the house.

(d) Greece

(a) In accordance with art. 1397 GCC, the marriage does not affect the distinctiveness of the spouses' properties, unless the couple chooses to live under the community of property regime.[38] Since the

[37] Amending Law 7/2011 of 11 May.

[38] Art. 1403 GCC. If they had chosen this regime Susane's consent would be necessary in order for Roberto to sell the house to Andrea. According to art. 1403 § 2 GCC a notarial deed agreement and registration are needed in order to establish a community of property regime. Such agreements are extremely rare in practice.

property belongs exclusively to Roberto, he has the right to sell it and Susane cannot prevent him.

If Susane was estranged from Roberto and the couple had children that would continue living with their mother, Susane could ask from a court to be allowed to make provisional use of the house despite the fact that it belongs to Roberto.[39] However, this wouldn't prevent Roberto from selling the house and the buyer wouldn't be bound by the above court order.

(b) The answer wouldn't differ if Roberto and Susane were living together but not married. Susane would then have not even the provisionary protection regarding the use of the house.

4 *France and related jurisdictions*

(a) France

(a) Yes. Certainly, the properties acquired for free are separate properties even in the statutory regime of the community.[40] But as it was explained above, the accommodation of the family cannot be alienated without the assent of the spouse.

(b) Yes. The protection of the accommodation of the family concerns only the married couples, with the exception of the partners and persons united by a civil partnership.

(b) Belgium

(a) She will succeed in the Belgian law. Roberto has acquired the house through a succession, so the house will be his exclusive property according to the statutory family property law rules. The statutory regime for patrimonial family law is acknowledged with a community of gains: everything that is acquired during the marriage is in common, except for the goods which are acquired through a gift or succession. Only if parties have agreed otherwise will the house be in common between Roberto and Susane.

Independent from the proprietary status of the house, Roberto will not be entitled to sell the house to Andrea without the prior consent of Susane. Art. 215 BCC protects the principal house where spouses live in common: 'One spouse can not, without the consent of the other,

[39] Art. 1393 GCC.

[40] Art. 1405 C. civ. However the property will be common if the couple adopted the conventional regime of the universal community (art. 1526 C. civ.).

dispose of the rights on the principal house where the family resides for free or for consideration and can not grant a mortgage on that principal house where the family lives. Neither can he without this consent dispose for free or for consideration over the furniture in the principal house or grant a pledge on it. If however, one spouse whose consent is necessary, refuses to give the consent without genuine motivation, a judge order could analyse this refusal as abuse of rights. In that case, the other spouse who is the owner of the house can be empowered by a judge to make the act of disposition on his own.'

(b) The rule offering the protection to the principal family residence is inserted in the section of the BCC on marital obligations ('primary family law'). However, this regimen has been expanded to persons living in a 'statutory co-habitation', which is a legally recognised regimen. Case law sometimes extends this regimen towards people who are factually living together without any legal basis, but most legal scholars heavily criticise this case law.

5 *England and related jurisdictions*

(a) England

(a) Since 1882,[41] marriage has had no effect, of itself, on the property ownership of a husband and wife. Given that the house appears to have been inherited by Roberto personally, Susane has made no contribution to the acquisition of the house. As such (unlike the analysis in response to case 13 above), Susane could only assert an interest in the house if there had been an express agreement or arrangement between Roberto and herself indicating that she has ownership rights in the house and if she had acted to her detriment in reliance on that arrangement.[42] If Susane cannot show that, she has no ownership interest in the house, and so she has no standing, under normal trust law or land law principles, to prevent the sale.

However, Susane would have the statutory matrimonial home right to occupy the house, given it is being used as the matrimonial home (as discussed in the response to case 13, question (c)). Susane could protect this right by entering a notice in the Register for the land. Technically, entering a notice in the Register does not prevent the sale,

[41] Married Women's Property Act 1882.

[42] *Lloyds Bank plc* v. *Rosset* [1991] 1 AC 107 at 132–3.

as it simply protects Susane's right to occupy, but it will probably prevent the sale in a practical sense, as it is unlikely that Andrea would want to buy the house subject to Susane's matrimonial home rights to occupation.

Susane's matrimonial home rights are brought to an end if her marriage to Roberto is terminated, but the court has power to make an order to the contrary.[43] Further, if Roberto and Susane are divorced before the sale is carried out, she could potentially even be awarded ownership of the house,[44] which would allow her to prevent the sale (as the new owner of the property).

(b) If Roberto and Susane were living together without being married, Susane could not assert the matrimonial home rights referred to in the previous response. Their non-married status also means they could not divorce and so Susane cannot be awarded ownership of the house following a divorce.

Hence, the question whether Susane could prevent Roberto from selling the house depends solely on whether she can assert any interest in the house under trust law analysis. For the reasons described in (a) above, this is unlikely.

(b) Scotland

(a) The answer is the same as to case 13, question (c) in relation to the sale to Chris. As owner of the house, Roberto is free to sell it and cannot be prevented by Susane. But unless Susane consents to the sale, she retains a statutory right to occupy the house, and Andrea, although owner, would not be able to take possession.[45]

(b) Although co-habitants have certain financial rights on the termination of co-habitation (whether by separation or on death),[46] they have no proprietary rights in the immovable property of each other. Nor, normally, are there statutory occupancy rights of the kind mentioned under (a).[47] So Roberto is free to sell, and Susane must leave the house.

[43] Section 31 (8) (b), FLA 1996. [44] Section 24, Matrimonial Causes Act 1973.

[45] Sections 6 (1), 3 (a), Matrimonial Homes (Family Protection) (Scotland) Act 1981.

[46] Sections 28, 29, Family Law (Scotland) Act 2006.

[47] Although the court can grant occupancy rights for a period of up to six months: see Section 18, Matrimonial Homes (Family Protection) (Scotland) Act 1981. Unlike the position for spouses, however, such occupancy rights do not bind third parties such as Andrea.

(c) Ireland

(a) As the house appears to be their family home, Susane's prior written consent is required before Roberto can sell the house to Andrea,[48] regardless of how he acquired it. If Roberto sells it to Andrea without Susane's consent the conveyance will be void unless Andrea or her solicitor can prove that they had made adequate enquiries to establish that the house was not a family home.[49] If Susane refuses to consent to the sale, Roberto may apply to the court for an order dispensing with her consent.[50] The court will grant such an order if it is satisfied that she is unreasonably withholding consent taking into account all the circumstances, including the respective needs and resources of the spouses and any dependent children and whether she has been offered suitable alternative accommodation.[51]

(b) In such circumstances Roberto would be free to sell the house to Andrea as the Family Home Protection Act 1976 only applies to the family home of married couples or civil partners.[52]

[48] Section 3, Family Home Protection Act 1976. [49] *Somers* v. *Weir* [1979] IR 94.

[50] Section 4, Family Home Protection Act 1976.

[51] An order may also be made if Susane is incapable of giving consent by reason of mental disability.

[52] Part 4, Civil Partnership and Certain Rights and Obligations of Cohabitants Act 2010.

Case 15

Joseph owns a farm but lives in town and has not visited it for many years. Jacob has been living and working there for many years without Joseph's consent.

(a) Joseph sues to recover possession of the farm. Will he succeed?
(b) If Joseph sells the farm to Steven who then sues Jacob to recover possession, will Steven succeed?

(A) Foundational Concepts for Understanding Case 15

The majority of the legal systems that have been analysed recognise the institution of adverse possession. From an economic point of view it is understood that this doctrine has some positive effects such as reducing costs in the sense that by quieting old title claims, the doctrine of adverse possession reduces uncertainty and also it reduces the risks associated with title transfers. Thus a potential purchaser who knows that the current possessor has occupied the property for the requisite statutory period is assured that the title he acquires is good.

In general, for the rule of adverse possession to be applied, some conditions are necessary. The possessor must hold the property actually, exclusively, continuously, in open and notorious manner, and adversely to the owner with a claim of right. With the exception of some variations in time periods and minor differences, the doctrine of adverse possession under common law does not differ much from the doctrine existent in most civil law countries.

One important difference between the rule of adverse possession within civil law and common law countries is the significance of the state of mind of the adverse possessor. Most civil law systems more explicitly distinguish between good and bad faith adverse possessors.

Usually, prescription periods are longer for bad faith possessors than for good faith possessors.

In question (a) it was asked about the effect of adverse possession in the different European legal systems. In Germany prescription does not serve to allow acquisition of ownership by possession alone, it is merely a possibility to cure an incorrect registration by possession. On the other hand in Austria under certain requirements an acquisition by means of thirty years' possession as an owner, continuous possession in good faith regarding the legitimacy of his title makes it possible for the possessor to become proprietor.

In the Netherlands acquisition through prescription is possible after having been in possession for ten years, provided that the possessor is in good faith.

In some countries like Turkey there is no recognition of adverse possession.

According to all of the Nordic legal systems, long-time possession may lead to transfer of ownership. However, the rules differ from state to state, with no state having an identical set of rules as any of the others. In Finland and Sweden, good faith acquisition combined with possession and registered ownership for ten years constitutes ownership. In Norway, the period for good faith acquisition is twenty years, having no requirement of registered title. In Denmark and Sweden an acquisition, even in bad faith, with registration and possession as an owner for twenty years, will extinguish the rightful owner's right. The starting points for the rules in Denmark, Finland and Sweden is the combination of registered title and possession. In Norway, a possession by itself is sufficient.

In Italy there is also recognition of the institution of adverse possession, the requirements are possession as an owner (publicly) and twenty years of possession. In Spain there is also recognition of the institution, under some requirements, as the possession as an owner during the period of time fixed in the law. The situation is similar in Belgium, France, Greece, Ireland and Portugal. In Scotland prescription requires a registered title as well as possession (for a period of ten years), and the title must precede the possession.

In England the situation is different as to whether the land was registered or not. According to LRA 2002, a possessor who can establish adverse possession for the immediately preceding ten-year period is able to apply to be registered as proprietor. This will prompt the Registrar to notify the registered proprietor of the squatter's application. The registered proprietor has a period of time to object and, if there is no objection, the squatter will be registered as the new proprietor. In this manner LRA 2002 has reduced considerably the possibility to acquire title by adverse possession where title to land has been registered.

In question (b) it was asked about the conflict between an adverse possessor and a good faith acquirer. This is more complicated to solve as more interests are involved, such as the protection of the third party who trusts in the accuracy of the Register.

In Germany, due to the high level of protection of the registered proprietor, the acquirer can recover possession from the adverse possessor because the registered proprietor remains the owner and can sell the farm to third parties without regard to Jacob's possession of the farm. In the Netherlands the situation is that if acquisitive prescription was consolidated then the Land Register contains incorrect information. In this case, the person who acquired ownership through prescription should be able to set up his title against all third parties.

In Italy the adverse possessor, once having consolidated his title, can oppose his acquisition against the third party in good faith. In Spain as a general rule the one that trusted in the accuracy of the Register is preferred, but under some requirements the adverse possessor should prevail (when the third acquirer knew about the possession of someone else). In Portugal the rights of adverse possessors are referred to as overriding interests and they bind a purchaser even though they do not appear on the Register.

In France, due to the characteristics of the Land Register, the land publicity does not guarantee the persistence of the published right; the situation is similar in Belgium.

In Scotland, as previously stated, a consequence of the insistence on registration for prescription is that a purchaser cannot be caught unawares by the off-Register acquisition of ownership by a possessor. In Ireland if the land is registered the rights of adverse possessors are referred to as overriding interests and they bind a purchaser even though they do not appear on the Register. On the other hand, in England, according to the new LRA, it is more complicated when this conflict arises.

(B) The Jurisdictions (Presented by Related Jurisdictions)

1 *Germany and related jurisdictions*

(a) Germany

(a) Yes, he will succeed. Jacob cannot permanently impede Joseph from asserting his ownership right. He could become owner by prescription only if he was wrongly registered in the Land Register as the owner of the land with the farm, the registration has existed for thirty years and he has had the plot of land in proprietary possession in this period.[1] In Germany prescription does not serve to allow acquisition of ownership by possession alone. It is merely a possibility to cure an incorrect registration by possession.

(b) Steven can recover possession from Jacob. As seen before Jacob could not acquire ownership by prescription unless he was registered in the Land Register as the owner of the plot of land with the farm during the whole period of prescription. Consequently Joseph remained owner and could sell the farm to Steven without regard to Jacob's possession of the farm.

If it is assumed that Jacob has satisfied the requirements for prescription this would imply that Jacob would have been registered as owner for thirty years. For this reason Joseph could not sell the farm to Steven. As Joseph is not registered as the owner of the plot of land with the farm a declaration of conveyance made between Joseph and Steven will not lead to Steven's registration in the Land Register. A transfer can only be registered if the transferor is registered as owner of the right concerned (so-called *Grundsatz der Voreintragung*).[2] There is no possibility of acquiring the ownership of the farm in good faith from Joseph either, because Joseph is not registered as the proprietor of the farm.

(b) Austria

(a) In the case at hand it depends on whether Jacob's possession derives from a contractual relationship or not. In such a case, Joseph can recover possession according to the rules of contract.

If there is no such contract Joseph (who is then to be considered as owner who is not in possession of the property – *nichtbesitzender Eigentümer* – and Jacob on the other hand as holder of the property – *Inhaber*) can claim transfer over (*Übergabe*) of the property (meaning that Joseph is required to give up possession – *Besitz*) according to § 366 ABGB. This of

[1] § 900 BGB. Joseph's right as the registered owner of the land with the farm may only be excluded by public notice procedure (*Aufgebotsverfahren*) and Jacob could be registered as the new owner if the plot of land has been in the proprietory possession of Jacob for thirty years and if Joseph is dead or missing and a registration in the Land Register that required his approval has not been made for thirty years (§ 927 BGB).

[2] See § 39 GBO.

course can apply only if Jacob has not acquired the property by means of thirty years' possession (adverse possession):

(b) An acquisition by means of thirty years' possession as an owner could be considered under the following preconditions: the person must continuously use the property in his function as possessor (*kontinuierliche Besitzausübung*)[3] for a determined period of a minimum of thirty years.[4] Doing so he must act in good faith regarding the legitimacy of his title (*muss an Rechtmäßigkeit des Titels glauben ... zur Rechtsausübung berechtigt zu sein*) (*redlicher Besitzer*).[5] An acquisition is not possible if the property was secretly taken by Jacob (*heimliche Inbesitznahme*) or with the use of force (*gewaltsame Inbesitznahme*) (requirement of the *echter (Natural-) Besitz*).[6]

In court Jacob would have to prove that the prescription period of thirty years has been completed (*Vollendung der Ersitzungszeit*) and that he was in possession (*Besitz*) at the beginning and the end of the time frame. To win the case Joseph would have to prove the fact that the acquisition period was interrupted (*Unterbrechung der Ersitzung*), that Jacob lost possession within the time frame (*zwischenzeitlicher Besitzverlust*), the lack of Jacob's good faith (*Unredlichkeit des Besitzes*), or that the property was secretly taken by Jacob (*heimliche Inbesitznahme*) or in the use of force (*gewaltsame Inbesitznahme*) (requirement of *echter (Natural-) Besitz*).[7]

(c) The Netherlands

(a) Since Jacob has no real or personal right to use the farm, Jacob should leave the land when Joseph orders him to leave. It is different if Jacob has acquired ownership of the farm as a result of acquisitive prescription (adverse possession). Acquisition through prescription is possible after having been in possession for ten years, provided that the possessor is in good faith (art. 3:99 BW). If he is not in good faith he can still become the owner through prescription in twenty years (art. 3:105 and 3:306 BW). In this concrete case, Jacob is not in good faith.

[3] § 1460 ABGB. Gert M. Iro, *Sachenrecht*, 3rd edn. (Vienna: Österreich Verlag, 2008), Rz 6/87.

[4] Comp §§ 1468, 1470, 1477 ABGB. See further Iro, *Sachenrecht*, Rz 6/91; Helmut Koziol and Rudolf Welser, *Bürgerliches Recht, I*, 13th edn. (Vienna: MANZ Verlag, 2006), p. 340.

[5] § 1477 S 2 ABGB. According to § 1463 good faith is required during the whole required duration. Good faith is not given any more if the person gains knowledge of the lack of entitlement (*positive Kenntniserlangung der mangelnden Berechtigung*) or of circumstances that should lead him to doubt his entitlement. See further Iro, *Sachenrecht*, Rz 6/89.

[6] Compare § 1464 ABGB. Even though if not specifically mentioned as a requirement in § 1477; Iro, *Sachenrecht*, Rz 6/90.

[7] See further Iro, *Sachenrecht*, Rz 6/94.

(b) If Jacob has not yet acquired ownership and Joseph sells and transfers the ownership to Steven, the latter will be able to recover the land from Jacob. Let us say that Jacob has now acquired ownership through acquisitive prescription but that Joseph is still registered as the owner in the Land Register. The Land Register then contains incorrect information. Jacob's acquisition has not been registered. Art. 3:24 BW, that protects against unregistered facts, contains an exception for prescription. The person who acquired ownership through prescription should be able to set up his title against all third parties. As a consequence, it should not be allowed for a third party, such as Steven, to claim third-party protection. In this particular case Steven cannot rely on the Register. Art. 3:26 BW, which also protects against incorrectness of the Register and overlaps with art. 3:24 BW in this case, should be interpreted in the same way.

(d) Turkey

(a) Jacob's behaviour is an unlawful interference with the farm. Joseph is the owner of the farm and has a real right, although he has not visited it for many years, he has the right to take measures to prevent any unlawful interference with it.[8] Briefly, yes, he will succeed.

(b) After being registered in the Land Register, Steven becomes the owner of the farm, that's why he will have the right to take measures to prevent this unlawful interference caused by Steven. Briefly, yes, he will succeed.

2 *Scandinavian jurisdictions*

(a) Finland

(a) There are no general rules of occupation in Finnish law – exclusive of the occupation right of a married spouse described above in the answers to cases 13(c) and 14(a). No one can obtain ownership or another kind of property right to a piece of real estate or land or water areas created merely by *de facto* possession while some other person is recognised as the lawful owner. Adverse possession in the proper sense is not recognised or protected by the Finnish law. In this sense, adverse possession or squatter's or possessory title are not acknowledged by the

[8] See art. 683, para. 2 TCC; Ivy Williams, Siegfried Wyler and Barbara Wyler, *The Swiss Civil Code, Version II* (Zürich, 1987), art. 641, para. 2; Oğuzman, M.K., Seliçi, Ö. and Oktay-Özdemir, S., *Eşya Hukuku Gözden Geçirilmiş 11. Bası* (İstanbul, 2006), p. 232.

Finnish law. Besides, there seem to be neither prerequisites nor room for acquisitive prescription for Jacob.

The so-called original occupation is merely a conceptual or historical explanation of the private ownership of land and water areas at the general level. Today, an ownership of real estate has to be grounded on a contract or another kind of legal acquisition. Actual possession of a piece of real estate as such is not and does not create a legal acquisition according to the Finnish law.

Ancient or immemorial enjoyment is seen as a special kind of acquisition in Finland. It cannot, however, create an acquisition of ownership if another person is recognised as an owner, as Joseph is in this case. The same applies to the rules of registration of a title by public notice.[9] Nevertheless, the Finnish Code of Real Estate contains the rule of so-called protection of enjoyment.[10] This protection requires registration of the title, possession as an owner of a piece of real estate for ten years after the registration and good faith at the time of the acquisition of ownership. In this case, Jacob or his predecessor should fulfil these requirements. No such facts are given in this case. Nevertheless, these three institutions have some common features with the rules of occupation (adverse possession) known, for instance, in England. In any case, more than actual possession is needed.

In this case, Jacob, the possessor, seems to appeal to an acquisition of ownership or another kind of property right created merely by actual possession of the farm. Joseph's ownership during Jacob's possession is a given fact. According to the Finnish law, Jacob is not appealing to any kind of legal acquisition if he appeals merely to actual possession. The case would be different if Jacob appealed to a lost deed or another kind of contract or to acquisition of ownership or another type of property right recognised by the Finnish law.

Jacob is the owner of any new buildings if he has constructed them on the area of the farm during his possession. Joseph will not become their owner, on the basis of law, even if he is treated as the landowner and even if the construction works were unauthorised. On the other hand, Joseph can claim their removal.

As a conclusion, Joseph as the owner, can always claim the possession of his farm if Jacob does not appeal to any kind of legal acquisition

[9] See 12:3 Code of Real Estate.

[10] See 13:10.1 Code of Real Estate. These rules are examined in detail in the answer to question (a) in case 6

but merely to possession. In these cases, there are no limits in time and no differences between the various forms of acquisitions of Joseph.

(b) In this case, Steven will have exactly the same position in relation with Jacob as Joseph did. Because Jacob is not appealing to any kind of legal acquisition recognised by Finnish law there are no prerequisites or room for acquisitive prescription for Jacob or negative prescription for Steven. Hence, no demands for registration, possession, or good faith are made on Steven. Steven as the new owner can always claim the possession of his farm.

(b) Sweden

(a) A ten-year possession of real property as an owner will extinguish the rightful owner's ownership, provided that the possession is combined with registration of ownership, not challenged in court during this period and once acquired in good faith.[11] Even in total absence of good faith, the rightful ownership may be extinguished if the bad faith possessor has had registered and unchallenged possession as an owner for a period of twenty years.[12] The bad faith extinction may even be founded on acquisition directly from the rightful owner, and even in cases of severe types of duress.[13] The possession is not dependent on physical holding, it is enough that the possessor has acted as owner and taken measures that fall on an owner.[14]

Both periods start running from the first registration of ownership by an unlawful possessor. Bad faith extinction of rightful ownership is primarily founded on acquiescence, i.e. the rightful owner's passivity, whereas good faith extinction is founded on a combination of acquiescence and the interest of exchange.[15] Good faith acquisition is only possible if the first possession was based on conveyance, i.e. a contract of sale, exchange, or gift, but later possession might for instance follow from inheritance or partition of an estate. Good faith must exist at the time of the conclusion of the contract, but only then.

[11] 16:1 (2) Land Code. [12] 16:1 (1) Land Code.

[13] Henrik Hessler, *Nya jordabalken. Kap 16 och 18. Hävd och godtrosförvärv* (Stockholm: Juristförlaget, 1979), p. 27. Ulf Jensen, *16 kap. Hävd till fast egendom, Jordabalk (1970:994)*, in the Karnov database, per 1 July 2016, note 925. Anders Victorin and Richard Hager, *Allmän fastighetsrätt*, 7th edn. (Uppsala: Iustus Förlag, 2015), p. 257. Folke Grauers, *Fastighetsköp* (Lund: Juristförlaget i Lund, 2016), p. 329.

[14] Bertil Bengtsson, *Sakrättsliga frågor i fastighetsrätten*, 6th edn. (Uppsala: Iustus Förlag, 1991), p. 15. Victorin and Hager, *Allmän fastighetsrätt*, p. 242, n. 1. Grauers, *Fastighetsköp*, p. 329.

[15] Hessler, *Nya jordabalken. Kap 16 och 18. Hävd och godtrosförvärv*, p. 27.

The good faith norm is an objective one and the period starts running from the first registered good faith acquisition. In fact, consecutive possessors – also the 'good faith' acquirer – may even be in bad faith.[16] Good faith acquisition of real property might especially occur in cases of complicated property relations, forgery, minority and the like.

So, depending on whether Jacob or his predecessor knew, or ought to have known, about the unlawfulness of the possession and the total period of possession, he might acquire ownership and Joseph might not be able to vindicate. This effect only follows if Jacob and his predecessors have possessed the property as owners, not as users.[17]

(b) The rules on good faith and bad faith possession, described above, presuppose that the possessor has a registration of title. If the ownership has passed over to Jacob due to these rules, Steven cannot invoke rules on (ordinary) good faith acquisition, which presupposes that the seller was registered as the owner.[18]

(c) Denmark

(a) As a starting point, even if Jacob lives on and runs the farm, he has no right to it. Two possible modifications to this exist namely; (1) That Jacob is considered to be a tenant, and (2) Jacob might obtain prescriptive title to the property.

As regards a possible tacit tenancy agreement, if Jacob has paid to live on the farm he may claim to be a tenant, in which case he is protected by the mandatory provisions of the Rent Act. If Jacob in fact runs the farm for Joseph, Jacob's labours may constitute payment of rent.[19] However, the question is understood to mean that Jacob is working at the farm on Jacob's account and interest, meaning that a tacit tenancy agreement would be out of the question.

Under the Danish law, prescriptive title to real estate may be obtained if one has had the property in actual possession acted as its proper owner for at least twenty years.[20] Title may be acquired even if Jacob knows that Joseph owns the farm, as long as Jacob presumes that Joseph tolerates Jacob's use. Title may not be acquired if Jacob's possession of

[16] 16:1 (3) Land Code. See Hessler, *Nya jordabalken. Kap 16 och 18. Hävd och godtrosförvärv*, p. 27 and Jensen, *16 kap. Hävd till fast egendom, Jordabalk (1970:994)*, n. 927. Grauers, *Fastighetsköp*, p. 330.

[17] Hessler, *Nya jordabalken. Kap 16 och 18. Hävd och godtrosförvärv*, p. 26.

[18] 18:1 Land Code. [19] Section 1, Rent Act.

[20] Palle B. Madsen *et al.*, *Formueretlige Emner*, 7th edn. (Copenhagen: Jurist- og Økonomforbandet, 2013), p. 401f.

the farm follows from a contract, from statutory rules, or is prohibited by statutory rules, which, however, does not seem to be the case here.

Thus, assuming that Jacob has run the farm for at least twenty years, he might have acquired a prescriptive title to it.

(b) In the following it is presupposed that Jacob has acquired the right to the farm according to the rules of prescriptive title described above.

To protect his right against Joseph's contract partners (such as Steven), Jacob will have to register his right in the Land Register.[21] If Jacob has not done so and Steven buys the property and registers his claim in the Land Register in good faith, Steven will as a starting point extinguish Jacob's claim to the property.[22]

Generally, a contractual partner in good faith need not state his claim within any particular time. However, regarding prescriptive title there is a special rule in section 26, Land Registration Act. According to this provision the transferee, Steven, must invoke his right against Jacob within two years after Steven registers his sales contract on the property. If Steven does not do so, Jacob's prescriptive title will become fully effective also against Steven after the expiry of the two years.[23]

(d) Norway

(a) If a person in good faith uses immovable property as his own for twenty years, he may acquire ownership.[24] Theoretically, this may be the case also for an entire farm, for example in a situation where somebody buys the property trusting a register title based on a forged document (see cases 1 and 6).

(b) If Jacob has acquired ownership under the rules referred to under question (a), his right is protected, without registration, against Joseph's general creditors as well as an acquirer who has in good faith relied on Joseph's registered title.[25]

3 *Romanic–Mediterranean jurisdictions*

(a) Italy

(a) Once he has proven his title, Joseph could recover possession of the farm by evicting Jacob. However, Jacob could argue in defence that he has acquired the ownership by adverse possession, if he can provide

[21] Section 1, LRA. [22] Section 1 (2), LRA.

[23] Section 26 (1), LRA and Madsen *et al.*, *Formueretlige Emner*, p. 409.

[24] Act on Acquisition by Continuous Possession (*lov om hevd*, 9. December 1966 No. 1).

[25] Section 21 (2), Judicial Registration Act.

evidence of the fact he acquired possession in a non-violent manner (peacefully), has lived on the farm as if he were the owner, acknowledged or potentially acknowledged as such by all (publicly) and has retained uninterrupted possession for at least twenty years. Given this, Jacob's claim will prevail over Joseph's.

(b) Assuming that Jacob's possession satisfies the requirements for adverse possession, in no case will Steven prevail over Jacob, even if Steven's purchase has been registered before registration of the court order declaring Jacob owner by adverse possession.[26] As soon as Jacob has obtained a court order recognising him as the owner by adverse possession, he could oppose his acquisition against Steven.

(b) Spain

(a) If Jacob has been living on the farm publicly, peacefully and uninterruptedly for ten years (or twenty years, if Joseph lives abroad), has behaved as owner of the farm and has done so in good faith because he acquired the farm from someone he thought was the owner and was entitled to convey ownership (a third party other than Joseph, obviously), he will have acquired ownership of the farm and Joseph may not claim it back from him.[27] Moreover, if Jacob has registered his right with the *Registro de la Propiedad*, such registration facilitates proof of these requirements.[28]

(b) If Jacob did not acquire the farm by virtue of a valid legal act conveying ownership (for instance, he simply moved into the farm) or, though he did enter into a valid legal act of acquisition with a third party, he did so in bad faith, because he knew the farm did not belong to the person conveying it, then he must possess the farm publicly, peacefully and uninterruptedly for thirty years in order to acquire ownership of it and not be removed by Joseph.[29] Moreover, he could be penalised with a fine of three to six months for occupying the farm without proper authority.[30]

If according to the Land Register, when Joseph sold the farm to Steven he was entitled to do it, Steven bought it in good faith and, in addition, Steven registered his title, then Steven will be able to recover possession of the farm from Jacob. However, Steven will not be successful if Jacob proves that Steven could have known (before the

[26] See Court of Cassation, 03.02.2005, No. 2016 in *Riv. Not.*, 2006, p. 208.

[27] Arts. 1941 and 1957 CC.

[28] Art. 35 Mortgage Act 1946.

[29] Arts. 1941 and 1959 CC.

[30] Art. 245 (2) Penal Code.

purchase) that Jacob was living and working in the farm or if Jacob proves that, after the purchase, Steven allowed him to continue living and working in the farm for at least one year.[31]

(c) Portugal

(a) Ownership in Portugal has a perpetual nature, and does not extinguish by the non-use of the land. However, Joseph's ownership can extinguish due to adverse possession by Jacob. Jacob is in possession of the farm if he has *corpus* (factual control) and *animus* (the factual control exercised by Jacob is an expression of a real right over the farm or a claim of right).[32]

In order to allow adverse possession, Jacob's possession must be public and peaceful (art. 1297 CC). Possession is peaceful, e.g. Jacob has not taken the possession in a violent way;[33] and it is public if it is of such character that would give notice to a reasonable person.[34] Jacob shall not hide his acts of possession towards third parties and especially of Joseph. He must act in such way that Joseph can be aware of the possession when he visits his parcel of land.

In order to benefit from the adverse possession, Jacob should have had possession of the farm during at least twenty years. The Portuguese CC provides for short delays of ten and fifteen years, but these short terms are subject to two additional conditions, e.g. (1) the possession is grounded in a title (that would have transferred ownership if it was valid, or if the transferor would have been the legal owner) which has been subject to registration; and (2) Jacob is in good faith, which means that he did not know and did not ought to know at the moment of the taking of the possession that he was not the owner.[35] It emerges from the *casus* that these two additional requirements have not been met.

[31] Art. 36 *Ley Hipotecaria* (LH).

[32] A claim of right exists if the person believes he has rightful claim to the property, even if that belief is mistaken. A negative example would be a timber thief who sneaks onto a property, cuts timber not visible from the road, and hauls the logs away at night. His actions, though they demonstrate actual possession, also demonstrate knowledge of guilt, as opposed to claim of right.

[33] Art. 1261 CC. [34] Art. 1262 CC.

[35] Art. 1296 CC. See António Santos Justo, *Direitos Reais* (Coimbra: Coimbra Editora, 2012), p. 174; António Menezes Cordeiro, *Tratado de Direitos Reais* (Coimbra: Almedina, 2005), p. 94; José de Oliveira Ascensão, *Reais* (Coimbra: Coimbra Editora, 2012), p, 104; Luís M.T. Menezes Leitão, *Reais* (Coimbra: Almedina, 2015), p. 133.

If Joseph sues Jacob in order to recover possession of the farm, Jacob will counter claim that he has acquired the house by adverse possession.[36] An action for reinstatement of possession (*acção para a restituição da posse*) will not succeed if Jacob can prove that he was in adverse possession of the farm for a continuous period of twenty years.

Since Jacob had successfully obtained title to property by adverse possession, he may (optionally) bring an action in court to 'quiet title' of record in his name. He might ask the Court to recognise that he is the owner of the house, and then have the judicial decision inscribed in the Land Registry. Arts. 89ff. of the Notary Code provide a formal procedure – called *Escritura de Justificação Notarial* – that would allow Jacob to have his acquisition settled in the Land Registry. It is a complex and public proceeding, in charge of a Notary, which will provide Jacob a deed to register in the Land Registry Office (art. 116ff. LRegC).[37] However, if his right were challenged in Court by someone, Jacob would not benefit from the presumption of art. 7 LRegC (that he is the owner), and no reversal of proof would exist.[38] Therefore, Jacob would have to prove before the Court that he had acquired ownership of the house through adverse possession.

(b) If Jacob did not acquire the farm by virtue of a valid legal act conveying ownership (for instance, he simply moved into the farm), or, though he did enter into a valid legal act of acquisition with a third party, he did so in bad faith, because he knew the farm did not belong to the person conveying it, then he must possess the farm publicly, peacefully and uninterruptedly for twenty years in order to acquire ownership of it and not be removed by Joseph.

The rights of adverse possessors are referred to as overriding interests and they bind a purchaser even though they do not appear on the Register. If Jacob can prove that he was in adverse possession for twenty years before Steven purchased the farm, Steven will not be able to recover possession of the farm and Jacob will be entitled to be registered as owner. If Jacob had not accrued twenty years' adverse possession when the transaction occurred, time will continue to run in his favour under the doctrine and Steven will need to institute legal proceedings quickly if he wishes to recover possession.

36 José A.R.L. González, *Direitos Reais e Registal Imobiliário* (Lisbon: Quid Juris, 2009), pp. 270–1.

37 José A. Mouteira Guerreiro, *Registos e Notariado* (Coimbra: Almedina, 2010), pp. 100ff.

38 Decision of the Supreme Court (Uniformisation Case Law) 1/2008, in *DR* of 31 March 2008.

In Portugal, acquisitive prescription can be invoked against a transferee for value who relied on the contents of the Register (*usucapio contra tabulas*).

(d) Greece

(a) Art. 1045 GCC regarding 'adverse possession' provides that a person who has had in possession a foreign property for twenty years shall become owner of the property (extraordinary acquisition by possession) without any further preconditions. The acquisitive possession is interrupted by the commencement of a legal action for action claiming ownership against the possessor.[39]

Joseph will therefore succeed to recover possession of the farm only as long as he sues[40] Jacob before the latter completes twenty years in possession of the farm.

(b) Steven's success depends only on how long Jacob has actually stayed in possession of the farm. The moment Jacob completes twenty years in adverse possession of the farm he shall immediately become owner of the farm to the detriment of the up-to-that-time lawful owner, regardless whether this was Joseph or Steven. The sale of the farm from Joseph to Steven doesn't affect in any way Jacob's acquisitive possession.

4 *France and related jurisdictions*

(a) France

(a) Joseph's property right cannot be declared extinguished only because of non-use: the right of property is imprescriptible.[41]

But Joseph's action will fail all the same if Jacob succeeded in acquiring a new right of property by acquisitive prescription, which requires a continuous, peaceful, public and not ambiguous possession,[42] during a sufficient delay. Since the reform of the prescription by the law of 17 June 2008, the delay is reduced to ten years if the owner is *bona fide* and leans on a just title, that is an act that would have made him an owner if the assignor had been himself an owner.[43] If one of these two conditions is not performed, the delay is as before, thirty years.

[39] Art. 1049 GCC. [40] Art. 1094 GCC. [41] Art. 2227 C. civ. [42] Art. 2261 C. civ.
[43] Art. 2272 C. civ.

(b) The same answer. The solution depends only on the behaviour of Jacob. It doesn't much matter that Joseph still appeared in the real estate file as owner: the land publicity does not guarantee the persistence of the published right.

(b) Belgium

(a) As a starting point, it is to be noted that ownership in the Belgian law has a perpetual nature. This means that the ownership of Joseph does not extinguish by the non-use of it, even not after more than thirty years.

This does not mean that the ownership of Joseph cannot extinguish due to acquisitive prescription by Jacob. Jacob can argue that he has become owner of the farm if the following conditions have been met:

(1) Joseph has had the possession of the farm during at least thirty years. The BCC code provides for short delays of ten or twenty years but these short terms are subject to two additional conditions, e.g. (1) the possession is grounded in a lawful title, this is a title which would have transferred ownership if the transferor has been the legal owner and (2) Jacob is in good faith, which means that he did not know and did not ought to know at the moment of the taking of the possession that he was not the owner (art. 2265 BCC). It emerges from the facts submitted that these two additional requirements have not been met.

(2) Joseph has had a possession which is said to be 'sound', meaning that it has four characteristics:
- the possession is peaceful, e.g. Jacob has not come taken the possession in a violent way and that he has reacted in a normal way against violent actions undertaken towards the farm by third parties.
- the possession is public, e.g. Jacob does not hide his acts of possession towards third parties and especially of Joseph in such way that Joseph can be aware of the possession when he visits his parcel of land.
- the possession is continuous, e.g. Jacob has exercised factual control in a regular manner. If there are unusual interruptions in the factual control exercised by Jacob, his possession could become unsound.
- the possession is unambiguous, e.g. the factual control exercised by Jacob can only be interpreted by third parties as the expression of the possession over the farm.

(b) The answer does not differ from the answer under question (a). If Joseph sells the farm to Steven, the acquisitive prescription will, from that moment on, continue to work against him.

5 *England and related jurisdictions*

(a) England

(a) Jacob has been a trespasser on the farm and Joseph has a *prima facie* right to recover possession from him. However, Joseph will not be able to do so if Jacob has been in adverse possession of the farm for a sufficient period of time. Jacob will be in adverse possession if he has possession of the land and if that possession is adverse to Joseph's interests.[44] As Joseph has not consented to the possession, the possession is adverse to Joseph's interests, even if it is not inconsistent with Joseph's use or intended use of the land.[45] The key question, therefore, is whether Jacob is in possession of the farm: 'there are two elements necessary for legal possession: (1) a sufficient degree of physical custody and control ("factual possession"); (2) an intention to exercise such custody and control on one's own behalf and for one's own benefit ("intention to possess") … without the requisite intention, in law there can be no possession.'[46] It seems likely on the facts that Jacob was in possession of the farm, given he was living and working there for many years. It is unnecessary for Jacob to intend to own the farm; it suffices that he intended to possess it.[47]

If the farm was not registered at any time, then after twelve years of adverse possession Joseph is unable to sue Jacob to recover possession and Joseph's title to the land is extinguished.[48]

If title to the farm was registered, then Jacob's rights depend on when his adverse possession began. If he completed twelve years in adverse possession of the farm prior to 13 October 2003, then Joseph would hold the farm on trust for Jacob, and Jacob would be entitled to apply to be registered as proprietor of the farm.[49] In such a case, Joseph could not evict Jacob.

[44] *J.A. Pye (Oxford) Ltd.* v. *Graham* [2002] UKHL 30, [2003] 1 AC 419 at [35] and [69].

[45] *Buckinghamshire County Council* v. *Moran* [1990] 1 Ch. 623 at 639; *J.A. Pye (Oxford) Ltd.* v. *Graham* [2002] UKHL 30, [2003] 1 AC 419 at [45].

[46] *J.A. Pye (Oxford) Ltd.* v. *Graham* [2002] UKHL 30, [2003] 1 AC 419 at [40].

[47] *J.A. Pye (Oxford) Ltd.* v. *Graham* [2002] UKHL 30, [2003] 1 A.C 419 at [42] and [71].

[48] Sections 15 (1) & 17, Limitation Act 1980.

[49] Section 75, LRA 1925. In this scenario, Jacob's right to be registered as proprietor came into being before 13 October 2003, with the effect that the right to be registered continues to be effective and Jacob will continue to have a defence to eviction proceedings, notwithstanding the coming into force of the LRA 2002: Sch. 12, para. 18 (1) and (2), LRA 2002.

If the farm is registered but Jacob was not in adverse possession of it for a period of twelve years before 13 October 2003, then he can only avoid being evicted by Joseph if he is able to be registered as the proprietor of the farm. In other words, in contrast to the position prior to 13 October 2003, mere effluxion of time does not render Jacob immune from eviction proceedings: until he is registered as the owner, Jacob is liable to be evicted by Joseph. Jacob is entitled to apply to be registered as proprietor of the farm after he has been in adverse possession of it for ten years. However, such an application will be rejected if Joseph objects (which seems likely). Joseph then has two years in which to remove Jacob from the farm. If Joseph fails to do so within that two-year period, Jacob is entitled to apply once again to be registered as proprietor of the farm, and his application will be accepted by the Registrar.[50]

(b) (This response is written on the assumption that Jacob's possession satisfied the requirements for adverse possession.)

If title to the farm was not registered when it was in Joseph's name, the sale to Steven triggers an obligation to register the title.[51] Once Steven's title to the farm is registered, his ability to recover possession from Jacob depends again on how long Jacob has been in adverse possession of the farm. If Jacob was in adverse possession for twelve years before the sale to Steven, his right to the farm would bind Steven if Jacob was in actual occupation of the farm at the time Steven bought it,[52] or if Steven had notice of Jacob's interest.[53] Given that Steven wants to sue to recover possession from Jacob, it seems likely that Jacob was in actual occupation at the relevant time. On the other hand, if Jacob had not been in actual occupation for twelve years before the sale to Steven, Steven will be able to evict Jacob once Steven has been registered as the legal proprietor of the farm.

If title to the farm was registered and Jacob had completed twelve years of adverse possession prior to 13 October 2003, Joseph would hold the farm on trust for Jacob and Jacob could apply to be registered as proprietor.[54] Although Jacob appears not to have become registered as proprietor (or Joseph could not sell to Steven), he appears to have been in occupation of the property at the time Steven bought it, and so Steven would be bound by Jacob's interest unless either (a) Jacob's occupation would not have been obvious on a reasonably careful inspection of the

[50] Sch. 6, LRA 2002. [51] Sections 4 (1) (a) (i) and 4 (2) (b) and 6 (1), LRA 2002.
[52] Section 11 (4) (b) and Sch. 1, para. 2, LRA 2002. [53] Section 11 (4) (c), LRA 2002.
[54] See n. 49 above.

farm and was not known to Steven; or (b) Jacob was asked about his interest in the property prior to the disposition to Steven but he did not disclose his interest in the property.[55] It seems likely that Jacob's occupation would have been obvious on a reasonably careful inspection, which means Steven cannot recover possession of the farm from Jacob.

If title to the farm was registered but Jacob had not been in adverse possession of it for twelve years before 13 October 2003, then he could only avoid being evicted by Joseph if he had been registered as the proprietor.[56] If Jacob had not applied to be registered as owner of the farm before Joseph sold it to Steven, his right to apply would continue to exist but any such application will be rejected if Steven objects. After that, Steven has two years to evict Jacob; if he fails to do so, Jacob can apply again to be registered as proprietor of the farm, and his application will be accepted by the Registrar.[57] In other words, under this scenario, Steven can successfully recover possession from Jacob until Jacob has succeeded in being registered as proprietor.

(b) Scotland

(a) Joseph will be able to recover possession; for Jacob cannot acquire ownership by possession alone, while Joseph cannot lose ownership by neglect alone.[58]

In theory, Jacob might have acquired ownership by acquisitive ('positive') prescription. But prescription in Scotland requires a registered title as well as possession (for a period of ten years), and the title must precede the possession.[59] As the idea is that the title is validated by the possession, it follows that the title will not initially be valid. Thus a disposition signed by anyone at all is a sufficient title for prescription provided that it purports to convey the land in question: the law imposes no requirement of good faith. But the deed must then be registered in the Land Register or, as the case may be, the Register of Sasines,[60] and in practice the Registrar (the 'Keeper') will not accept such a deed for registration if an apparently 'live' title (such as Joseph's)

[55] Sch. 3, para. 2, LRA 2002. [56] See text accompanying n. 50 above.

[57] Sch. 6, LRA 2002.

[58] Extinctive ('negative') prescription does not apply to the ownership of land: see Sch. 3, para. (a), Prescription and Limitation (Scotland) Act 1973.

[59] Section 1, Prescription and Limitation Act (Scotland) 1973.

[60] For the difference between the two Registers, see the answer to case 1.

is already on the Register or, in the case of the Land Register, without first notifying the owner, who is then likely to take immediate steps to assert his title.[61] This limits prescription to the unusual case of land the ownership of which is unknown or uncertain. As the ownership of Joseph's farm is both known and certain, it follows that prescriptive acquisition would not have been available to Jacob.

(b) The position would be the same as before. Acquisitive prescription requires a registered title as well as possession, and in practice Jacob would not be able to register his title. Thus Steven, like Joseph, can recover possession from Jacob.

(c) Ireland

(a) Joseph's action to recover possession will not succeed if Jacob can prove that he was in adverse possession of the farm for a continuous period of twelve years.[62] The limitation period for actions to recover land is twelve years and on the expiry of the limitation period, Joseph's title to the land will be extinguished[63] and Jacob will be entitled to apply to be registered as the owner of the land.[64] To qualify as adverse possession, the possession must be without the owner's consent, which is the case here.[65] The person claiming adverse possession must be able to satisfy the physical and mental requirements of the doctrine. Jacob's possession of the farm must be exclusive and sporadic acts of possession by Joseph down through the years will prevent the limitation period from running.[66] Jacob must have engaged in strong and obvious acts of possession;[67] living and working on the farm would probably be deemed sufficient possession.[68] He must also have the requisite intention to possess the land and to exclude the true owner and all others from the land.[69] If Jacob mistakenly believed that he was the true owner of the farm he will be deemed to have the requisite

[61] Notification is a prerequisite for registration, and no registration can take place if the owner objects within sixty days. See section 45, Land Registration etc. (Scotland) Act 2012.

[62] Section 13, Statute of Limitations 1957.

[63] Section 24, Statute of Limitations 1957.

[64] Section 49, Registration of Title Act 1964.

[65] Or any lease or licence must have expired, see *Bellew* v. *Bellew* [1982] IR 447.

[66] *Feehan* v. *Leamy* [2000] 1 IEHC 118; *Mulhern* v. *Brady* [2001] IEHC 23; *Dunne* v. *Irish Rail* [2007] IEHC 314; *Dooley* v. *Flaherty* [2014] IEHC 528.

[67] *Doyle* v. *O'Neill*, Unreported, High Court, 13 January 1995.

[68] Note that grazing cattle on the land without other acts of possession would not be sufficient to maintain an action for adverse possession, see *Brown* v. *Fahy*, Unreported, High Court, Kenny J, 25 October 1975.

[69] Known as '*animus possidendi*'.

intention.[70] In recent times, the fairness of the doctrine has been called into question[71] and the law on adverse possession may be given further consideration in a future Law Reform Commission publication.

(b) As the land is agricultural, it can be assumed that it has been registered in the Land Registry.[72] Therefore, section 72 (1) (p), Registration of Title Act 1964 applies, which provides that a purchaser will take the land subject to the rights of persons acquired or in the course of being acquired under the Statute of Limitations by way of adverse possession. The rights of adverse possessors are referred to as overriding interests and they bind a purchaser even though they do not appear on the register. If Jacob can prove that he was in adverse possession for twelve years before Steven purchased the farm, Steven will not be able to recover possession of the farm, and Jacob will be entitled to be registered as owner. If Jacob had not accrued twelve years' adverse possession when the transaction occurred, time will continue to run in his favour under the doctrine and Steven will need to institute legal proceedings quickly if he wishes to recover possession.[73]

[70] *Murphy* v. *Murphy* [1980] IR 183. Note that although Clark J suggested in *Kelleher* v. *Botany Weaving Mills Ltd* [2008] IEHC 417 that *animus possidendi* cannot co-exist with a belief in ownership, this authority is unlikely to be followed.

[71] It seems unlikely that the reforms proposed in the *Report on Reform and Modernisation of Land Law and Conveyancing Law* (LRC 74, 2005), pp. 322–39 will be adopted. For a discussion of the reaction to these proposals, see Woods, 'The Position of the Owner under the Irish Law on Adverse Possession', 30 *DULJ* (2008), p. 298. Recently, in *Dunne* v. *Irish Rail* [2016] IESC 47, para. 23, Laffoy J commented that the doctrine of adverse possession remains controversial and stated: 'There would seem to be a need for a review of the recommendations made by the Law Reform Commission in 1989, 2002 and 2005 with a view to bringing clarity to the law in this area.'

[72] See case 11, n. 66 above.

[73] Note that sending a solicitor's letter to Jacob demanding possession will be insufficient to stop time running for the purposes of the Statute of Limitations 1957, see *Mount Carmel Investments Ltd* v. *Peter Thurlow Ltd* [1988] 3 All ER 129. Also, a letter sent by the owner to the adverse possessor asserting ownership will not stop time running against him; see *Mahon* v. *O'Reilly* [2010] IEHC 103.

Index

Books in THE COMMON CORE OF EUROPEAN PRIVATE LAW series

Transfer of Immovables in European Private Law
Edited by Luz Martínez Velencoso, Saki Bailey and Andrea Pradi

Protection of Immovables in European Legal Systems
Edited by Sonia Martin Santisteban and Peter Sparkes

The Rise of Moral Damages in European Contract Law
Edited by Vernon Valentine Palmer

European Condominium Law
Edited by Cornelius Van Der Merwe

Time Limited Interests in Land
Edited by Cornelius Van Der Merwe and Alain-Laurent Verbeke

Unexpected Circumstances in European Contract Law
Edited by Ewoud Hondius and Christoph Grigoleit

Personality Rights in European Tort Law
Edited by Gert Brüggemeier, Aurelia Colombi Ciacchi and Patrick O'Callaghan

Precontractual Liability
Edited by John Cartwright and Martijn Hesselink

Environmental Liability and Ecological Damage in European Law
Edited by Monika Hinteregger

The Enforcement of Competition Law in Europe
Edited by Thomas M. J. Möllers and Andreas Heinemann

Commercial Trusts in European Private Law
Edited by Michele Graziadei, Ugo Mattei and Lionel Smith

Mistake, Fraud and Duties to Inform in European Contract Law
Edited by Ruth Sefton-Green

Security Rights in Movable Property in European Private Law
Edited by Eva-Maria Kieninger

Pure Economic Loss in Europe
Edited by Mauro Bussani and Vernon Valentine Palmer

The Enforceability of Promises in European Contract Law
Edited by James Gordley

Good Faith in European Contract Law
Edited by Reinhard Zimmermann and Simon Whittaker

Lightning Source UK Ltd.
Milton Keynes UK
UKOW06n2036090617
302958UK00011B/189/P

9 781107 187092